HISTORY

MANKIND
AND HIS STORY

NEW EDUCATIONAL LIBRARY

ADVISORY EDITOR

LORD GORELL, C.B.E., M.C., M.A.

Pictographs of North American Indians; the earliest form of writing.

Early Egyptian hieroglyphs carved in stone; used from about 3400 B.C.

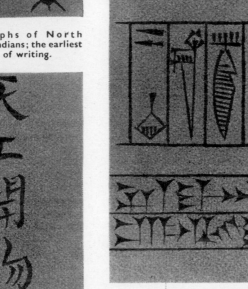

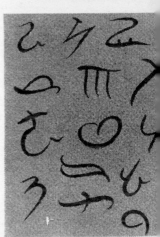

(Above left.) Modern Chinese writing; the symbols represent ideas, as do hieroglyphs of ancient Egypt. (Centre top.) Early Sumerian picture signs, forerunners of Assyrian cuneiform, of which two examples of c. 2700 B.C. and 650 B.C. are shown beneath it. (Right.) Later Egyptian symbols used in writing on papyrus. (Below left.) Letters of the Greek alphabet in use 600 - 300 B.C., and (right), Latin alphabet dating from about 600 B.C.

DEVELOPMENT OF WRITING
Modern alphabets are a development from the pictograph. In the Western World they show mainly Greek and Latin influence.

HISTORY

MANKIND
AND HIS STORY

ADVISORY EDITOR

MAX BELOFF, B.Litt., M.A.
Reader in the Comparative Study of Institutions in
the University of Oxford

CONTRIBUTORS

Olwen Brogan, M.A.   *Prof. G. R. Potter, M.A., Ph.D.*
Edward Crankshaw   *Sir John Pratt, K.B.E., C.M.G.*
Norman Dees, B.A.   *Prof. G. J. Renier, Ph.D.*
T. Fish, Ph.D.   *Prof. J. Simmons, M.A.*
E. H. U. de Groot, M.A.   *W. E. Styler, M.A.*
H. V. Livermore, M.A.   *C. V. Wedgwood, M.A.*
Prof. C. M. MacInnes, M.A. *P. D. Whitting, B.A.*

ODHAMS PRESS LTD · LONG ACRE · LONDON

Made and printed in Great Britain by Odhams (Watford) Ltd., Watford
S.557.9R.R.

CONTENTS

HISTORY AND SOCIAL LIFE

This leaf from a calendar of a Book of Hours by Simon Benninck (1485-1561), now in the Victoria and Albert Museum, is one of a series depicting the labours of each month—in this case August harvesting. Contemporary work of this kind, where it exists, is a valuable aid to accurate reconstruction of past conditions.

CHAPTER I

APPROACH TO HISTORY

EVER since men began to write history they have speculated and argued as to its intellectual and practical significance. There are few motives that have not served as an incentive to historical inquiry and to historical writing. Ancestral piety, religious enthusiasm, political animus, patriotic exhilaration and the pure curiosity of the scholar or gossip—any one of these may serve to turn the mind from the contemplation of the here and now and the endless demands of day-to-day life, towards an exploration of the past. Experience does not allow one to say with assurance that any one of these motives is more likely to produce better history than another, whether our criterion be fidelity to verifiable fact or artistic competence.

Sometimes it is the subject which grips the mind of the historian and impels him towards that study and no other, as Machiavelli was driven by the weakness and divisions of his Italy toward the study of the vicissitudes of the great Roman Republic. At other times the urge to historical study may be a personal one and it is the student who seeks for a subject as a painter or sculptor might seek for a model upon which to let his creative imagination work. Such, we know, was the case with Edward Gibbon.

Varieties of Treatment

One historian will write of the history of his own country and of his own times like Thucydides or Clarendon; others will find their historical imagination kindled by the remote in space or time, Prescott following in the wake of the Conquistadores or Maitland tracing the social pattern of pre-Conquest England. Some will be content to treat of some narrowly defined period or subject in the minutest detail, while others feel confined unless they can bring the whole human story into a connected narrative as H. G. Wells attempted in his *Outline of History*. Others may begin with projects of great scope and find themselves so gripped by the intricacies of a small part of their story that they die before they are in sight of their achievement. Thus Macaulay's great *History of England*, intended as an account of the origins and development of the society of his own age, is the story of only a single decade.

History—Science or Art?

Because historical writing is a branch of creative intellectual activity, because it is inseparable from the life of civilized communities, and because such communities are capable of infinite variety in their spiritual and mental outlook, it is futile to attempt to define its province, or to lay down precise boundaries between what is and what is not history. Much of the writing about history has been concerned with problems which the practice of the great historians shows to have been unreal. So it is, for instance, with the once much-debated question as to whether history is a science or an art. If it were not a science, that is to say an organized form of knowledge about objective reality, and a method of adding to such knowledge, it could not have captured the attention of successive generations of serious and practical men. If it were not an art how could it have attracted and held so many readers in every age? Philosophers—and particularly political philosophers—have argued as to whether one learns from history, whether it is a practical as well as theoretical study. But here again, if history does not instruct as well as inspire, how is one to understand the persistent preoccupation with historical studies, of great statesmen in every era?

The philosophy of history has, of course, a legitimate and necessary role. It may, as in a work like Professor A. J. Toynbee's *Study of History*, render history itself more meaningful by clarifying our minds as to the nature of the possible fields of historical study and as to their interrelation, as well as by endowing us with new mental concepts with the help of which we may elucidate phenomena which might otherwise seem chaotic and without shape. Alternatively, the approach may be through historical technique. By applying his practical experience as an archæologist and historian of Roman Britain, R. G. Collingwood contrived in his philosophical writings such as his *Autobiography* and *The Idea of History*, to explain the mental processes involved in discovering a new piece of historical knowledge, or in tackling a specific historical problem. In so doing, he contributed to the discussion of the nature of history, the valuable and valid point that because history is the story of man's conscious activity, the historian's task is incomplete unless what he relates has been assimilated into his own consciousness and has become part of his own mental experience. By a parallel, though not identical, process of reasoning the Italian philosopher-historian Croce has arrived at his doctrine, that all history is "contemporary history," in other words that we can have no understanding of periods or struggles whose issues and outcome are meaningless for us in our own time. We do not merely reconstruct history; we relive it.

Specialization

It should not therefore be necessary, in introducing the present volume, to rehearse the arguments in favour of historical studies generally. It is not generally disputed that they are of pressing relevance and of immediate utility, whether by providing explanations of the political problems which confront us as citizens, or by helping us to understand the world and country in which we live as individuals, by heightening our awareness and hence our enjoyment. If the case needs arguing, this has been done with great eloquence in A. L. Rowse's *The Use of History*.

It is rather the scope and form of this volume which requires some explanation and perhaps some justification. The last half-century has seen profound changes in the general approach to history, as it has in other branches of intellectual activity. As with workers in other fields, the historian has been confronted by a sudden over-whelming increase in the amount of material at his disposal in the shape of observed and classified evidence—in his case documentary and archæological. For this reason, the study of history has tended to become more and more subdivided by period and subject, and the organization of the profession has tended to encourage intensive specialization. The disappearance of a leisured or semi-leisured class has largely confined historical writing to those whose profession is the study and teaching of history. Of the contributors to this volume, all, with the exception of four, are whole-time teachers of the subject in universities, schools or in the adult education movement.

History and Education

It is significant that the diversion of public interest from constitutional and military matters—in spite of political crises and the greatest of wars—has tended to thrust forward what is called economic and social history into a more important position, relatively speaking, than it has ever occupied before. This has again increased the number of separate techniques required by anyone who wishes to write general history and has diminished the number of those bold enough to do so. Professional prestige has increasingly accrued to the specialist, and the younger historians have acted accordingly.

But in history, as in other fields, a reaction has set in against the over-intensive subdividing of knowledge. As the importance to the individual and the community of general education is increasingly perceived, the historian is asked to play his part, to provide a rational and coherent account of the past which will enable the ordinary intelligent and conscientious layman to orientate himself in the modern world, to increase his critical awareness and to enable him to distinguish between the fruits of honest and disciplined inquiry and the mere repetition of convenient half-truths. Whether disguised as "education for citizenship" or as "current affairs" it is history which has provided the backbone of the curriculum in recent educational experiments in the Forces, and among adult civilians, as well as among school children.

No one book can meet a demand of this kind. What has been tried in the present work, is to provide a tentative synthesis of up-to-date scholarship on those periods and problems of history which are most likely to attract the attention of the present generation and to direct the further reading of those whose appetites may be stimulated by what we have to offer.

We have not tried to write a universal history. The English-speaking reader is born into a particular complex of institutions and ideas which, for convenience, we call Western Civilization. It is the development of that civilization from its origins on the eastern and northern shores of the Mediterranean that we have tried to trace in these pages. During the last few centuries, the mechanical abilities which this civilization has developed have brought it into contact, and often violent contact, with other civilizations of very different origins and with widely different outlooks. Sometimes these civilizations have been annihilated and their influence largely dissipated. Such, for instance, has been the case with the New World civilizations uprooted by the Spanish conquest in the sixteenth century.

Western Tradition

In other cases, although such civilizations have been profoundly influenced by the West, their vitality has not been extinguished and their contacts with the West remain one of the outstanding phenomena of the present age. This is true of India, of China and of the Moslem world. In such cases we have been content to describe the impact of the West upon these civilizations, without going back to tell their own independent and self-contained earlier history. In one case—that of Russia—historians argue as to whether it belongs in essence to the Western World or whether its Byzantine and Asiatic heritage, as against the West's predominantly Roman roots, make of it a separate civilization. In this case it has been felt that the important role which Russia has played for three centuries and more, as a part of the Western states'

A MONK AT HIS DESK

Compiled and illuminated by Eadwine, a monk of Christ Church, Canterbury, about the middle of the twelfth century, the Canterbury Psalter is particularly interesting for its illustrations of contemporary life. This self-portrait shows the monk sitting in a handsome chair writing with a quill pen, holding in his left hand a knife used to trim the nib. The manuscript is now in the library of Trinity College, Cambridge.

system and the interaction today between Russian and Western social and political ideals would have made its exclusion pedantic.

Since what we were concerned with is the historical background of Western society as a whole, it is clear that the effort had to be made to reunite the separate strands of political, religious, economic, social, military and intellectual history. For we have learned in our time that the outcome of great historical struggles is dependent upon unpredictable combinations of all these factors. Furthermore,

EIGHTEENTH-CENTURY COTTON PRINTING

Founded in 1759 by Christophe Oberkampf, the Jouy cotton factory near Versailles was granted the title of "Manufacture Royale" by Louis XVI. In honour of this event, several cottons (of which the above is an example) were printed in the Chinese style, illustrating the various operations carried out at the factory.

since we are concerned with the present, we have found little to commend it, in the normal straightforward division of the past into chronological slabs, labelled according to the centuries. Historical development, even within a single civilization, is uneven in pace, both as between one century and another and as between one country or group of countries and another. Nor is it unnatural to demand greater detail concerning the near at hand, than the remote.

These remarks may help to explain the admittedly rather unusual and at first sight complicated arrangement of the separate chapters of this book. In spite of the fact that the arrangement is not the customary one, and of the abruptness of the transitions where one historian hands over the narrative to another—a device for which we hope the greater liveliness of the specialist on his own field is adequate compensation—it should not be difficult for the reader to find his way about. The visual reminders of place and period—

maps, illustrations and time charts—should be regarded as aids in this direction and as an integral part of the book, not mere decoration. To recreate the past, we must first visualize it with the contemporary eye.

The arrangement of the chapters is, then, dictated mainly by the logic of the subject-matter. We begin with the pre-classical civilizations of the Near and Middle East, to which, as the author shows, we owe many of our fundamental concepts about Man, God and Society. It enables us also to come into contact with events which are not the less "historical" because our evidence about them is so largely a matter of material relics as contrasted with written and oral tradition. The chapter which follows, on "The Ancient World," treats of that period and those countries from which spring in the last resort our religions, our philosophies, our science and our most enduring political and social institutions and concepts. The Middle Ages and the Renaissance are grouped together as being the two historical concepts used to describe the centuries during which this classical heritage was remoulded to serve new peoples in a new geographical setting. It is the period of the making of Europe, and with its end, by general consent, begins the modern world. Finally it marks Europe's first contact with an alien civilization.

Of the modern world, the two enduring features have been the division of Europe between different and often warring branches of the Christian religion and a system of independent sovereign states, impelled towards competition and strife by dynastic, national and economic forces. The birth of this states-system and its early results are the essential themes of the fifth chapter.

European States System

The establishment of this European system of warring states and creeds was contemporaneous with the first great movement of discovery and expansion. One result of this was the creation in the southern part of the western hemispheres of a new branch of Western Civilization. The account of the Spanish and Portuguese conquests thus merges into an account of the history of modern Latin America.

Between the middle of the seventeenth century and the French Revolution, we have the classical age of warring states, when the pattern of modern international relations was set, and when political, economic and administrative institutions were shaped to meet the needs of commerce, war and empire. Such is the subject-matter of "Balance of European Power in the Mercantile Age." By contrast with the previous period, we have in this, as an active element in the general European scene, the great power of Russia—a country which had lived a life remote from the West ever since her earlier civilization based on Kiev had succumbed to the Tartar invasions. The halting contacts of the sixteenth and seventeenth centuries were replaced by a conscious effort at territorial expansion towards the West and the assimilation of Western techniques, while at the same time rapid strides extended Russian authority in Asia. It is thus a suitable point at which to chronicle the "Advent of Russia," and the story begun here is made to include the all-important Russian Revolution of our own times.

Much of the rivalry of the great Powers in the mercantile age was fought out over imperial issues. It was the eighteenth century which saw the battle for North America fought and decided and the predominance of British over French and Spanish influences assured, just as the previous century had seen Dutch competition eliminated. But the establishment of this British pre-eminence was only the prelude to a struggle of still wider import, out of which emerged the two great North American nations, the United States and Canada, whose interrelated development is treated in the chapter on "The Rise of North America."

With the end of the eighteenth century, we reach the second great turning-point in modern history. On the one hand, the new technical developments collectively known as the Industrial Revolution profoundly altered the distribution of economic and military strength, and so made radical changes in the pattern of world politics. On the other hand the French Revolution and the subsequent development of new political movements in many parts of the world released powerful new energies and provided a ferment of ideas which permanently coloured the outlook of important new social groupings, whose advent was part of the Industrial Revolution itself.

From Individualism to Collectivism

It therefore seemed inappropriate to try to divide the period between the French Revolution and the outbreak of the First World War at any fixed point. Instead, two chapters (X and XI) have been devoted to a review of the whole period. In the first of these, attention is concentrated on the French Revolution itself and on the shifting of revolutionary thought in the nineteenth century under the impact of industrial development from mainly individualist to mainly collectivist foundations. In the second, attention is concentrated upon the changes in international relations and the effect upon them of the new ideas of nationalism, in some cases enhancing the consciousness of existing states or establishing new nation-states, and elsewhere acting as a solvent of historic empires.

The tensions created by this double process are analysed, and an examination of the effect upon war potential of the industrial changes of the century serves as a prelude to an examination of the relations between the European states on the eve of the First World War.

Contemporary History

The nineteenth century was, to an even greater extent than the eighteenth, a century of overseas expansion and of imperial growth. With the coming of the twentieth century the period of European expansion merged into a new era of which the keynote was the spread of nationalist movements to the Asiatic and African continents and the consequent assertion of claims for self-government or independence. In the chapter on the British Empire and Commonwealth, the interaction of imperial and national ideas is worked out in its most complex setting. After the loss of the original American colonies, there set in another period of growth and development in the course of which were evolved those principles alluded to in the earlier chapter dealing with Canada, which have resulted in the modern association of self-governing nations in the British Commonwealth.

The challenge of modern thought to the whole colonial idea, and new responses, such as the idea of trusteeship, have had to be confronted by Great Britain in the many lands at very different stages of development, which make up the Colonial Empire of today. Finally, there is the unique case of India, where the unity created by British rule has failed to stand the painful transition to unaccustomed self-government. In the subsequent chapter, the horizon is broadened to include the differing colonial practices and doctrines of other imperial powers in Africa, Asia and Indonesia—in particular France and Holland. The question of the European impact upon the Moslem world of the Middle East, after the collapse of the Ottoman

Empire, and the intensive rivalries induced by the strategic importance of this area, for long the meeting-place of British and Russian as well as of other European influences and ambitions, falls into place in this general picture.

In a sense, the chapter dealing with the Far East links on in subject directly to the two preceding ones. For although neither China nor Japan with their ancient and independent civilizations has been the scene of colonizing activity in the ordinary meaning of the term, the impact upon them of the European Powers was a product of the same movement of expansion as affected other parts of the globe. In the twentieth century, the Far East has come to rival the Middle East as a potential danger spot and as a nodal point of imperial rivalries. Furthermore, the proximity of the Soviet Union and of its own vast and rapidly changing Asiatic domains has added to the impact of modern nationalism that of the equally challenging and dynamic force of communism. The importance which issues fought out in China have assumed for the rest of the world, is perhaps the best indication of how the study of Western Civilization and its fate broadens of necessity into a study of the contemporary world as a whole.

Lack of Evidence

The last two chapters of this book endeavour to do for the first half of the present century what two earlier chapters did for its predecessor. Clearly the task is a more difficult and complicated one. It can indeed be argued that the story of events so recent, and the analysis of forces to which we are ourselves subjected, forms no part of the proper task of the historian. Clearly it is harder to achieve the same measure of perspective and detachment with regard to the achievements and conflicts of our own age. From the point of view of his materials, the historian, particularly of diplomatic history and of political history in the narrower sense, is hampered not, as in the case of the nineteenth century, by the very abundance of materials, but by their scarcity. Where the evidence of archives and personal testimony is lacking, the temptation to rely upon rumour or guess-work is a powerful one. To stop at some arbitrary point in the past would, however, have been to diminish the potential value of the book as a guide to the interpretation of the contemporary world and the narrative has for this reason been brought down substantially to the end of the Second World War in 1945 or, in certain instances, even later.

Historical Imagination

Clearly, only a selection of the most important aspects of the period could be even touched upon. In the first of the two chapters concerned we trace some of the results of the new demands for economic and social security and of the new preoccupation with social welfare—demands arising from the experience of industrial society and from its impact upon agrarian communities—upon the structure and purposes of the State. Whatever form it has taken, communist, fascist, social-democratic or even reformist-liberal, the modern State accepts duties and arrogates rights far greater than those claimed by the most despotic of monarchies in historic times. The increase of functions has been accompanied by increasing claims for doctrinal allegiance, and just as the sixteenth-century world was split asunder by rival religious creeds so the twentieth-century world is best pictured as the scene of conflicting secular religions.

In the final chapter we are confronted with the effect of these changes upon international relations and the gradual emergence of the belief that current technological changes have made it impossible for human civilization to survive in a world of warring states. The story of the League of Nations, the first effort to apply these lessons to the practical tasks of international organization, is told here, and its failure analysed. The book concludes with an analysis of the causes, nature and probable effects of the Second World War, in whose uneasy and painful aftermath it has been written.

It is obvious that a work of such ambitious scope, covering so wide a range of subject-matter and dealing with so great a segment of the world's history must make some sacrifices. The greatest of these is that in the interests of brevity it demands from the authors a constant effort at abstraction and generalization. History takes on the aspect of a vast panorama of impersonal forces working out towards predestined ends. It is too easy to forget that history is the sum total of individual lives and that its major issues have often been determined by personal decisions. To eliminate the personal factor, to discard the biographical for the statistical approach is not merely to deaden the colouring. In a very real sense, it is to risk distorting the truth.

The value of historical studies varies in strict proportion to the extent to which they enable the student to attune his mind in imaginative sympathy to the mind of some figure of a past age, to see his problems as he saw them and to feel the appeal of the same ideals. Only in this way can historical studies enlarge one's awareness of human potentialities and contribute to one's understanding of contemporary events. For this reason, the reader of a book such as this would do well to regard it not as history in itself but as a guide to history.

Documentary Evidence

The periods and subjects dealt with are those that have seemed to the authors of most significance and most worthy of study and reflection. Different readers will feel attracted to different sections of the narrative and when they find that period or that strand of inquiry which seems to them the most relevant or the most fascinating they would be well advised to concentrate upon it. The books mentioned in connexion with each chapter are, of course, no more than a mere selection of the works in the English language which are available on the subject. But they have been carefully chosen, both for their intrinsic merits and because through them the student may find readier access to the whole literature of the subject and gain some insight into the original sources—documentary and others—back to which, in the last resort, all historical inquiry must inevitably lead.

CHAPTER II

ARCHÆOLOGY AND THE HISTORY OF THE ANCIENT NEAR EAST

WE know very little of the million years of Man's history. Museums with their collections of bones, flints, tools etc., show the stuff which has prompted guesses as to his development during the greater part of that time before he emerged as hunter, sower, reaper, writer, with city-going ways in settled habitations, at first in the valleys of the Nile, the Euphrates, the Tigris, and the Yellow River.

This chapter is concerned with the early recorded history of a limited area, i.e. south-west Asia, the basin of the eastern Mediterranean and those territories behind it which alone concern us here: Palestine, Syria, Eastern Asia Minor, Armenia, Mesopotamia and Persia; not Egypt. The choice of this area and the exclusion of Egypt are not arbitrary, but dictated by the high quality and age of man's achievements here, and especially by the significance of the civilization and culture of this area for the later story of Western man.

The sources of information for such a study up to little more than a hundred years ago were the Bible, the Greek and Roman classics, local traditions and the reports of travellers. Today there is much less dependence on traditions, native or foreign, because more and more contemporary sources, written and unwritten, are available. But traditions are not thereby done away with or despised; the modern mood is one of respect for tradition.

The result of accumulation of archæological evidence has been not only to fill in what was long known of the later history of the ancient Near East, but also to make possible provisional reconstructions of its earliest history. Egypt was first described early in the nineteenth century, and its ancient language was interpreted by 1822. That was much. But now we have evidence of prehistoric settlements at sites about forty miles north-west of Cairo, on the north-eastern banks of Lake Karoun, and about two hundred and forty-five miles south of Cairo. All three are neolithic settlements. From 3000 B.C. onwards to Christian times, new material, literary and non-literary, is such that any portion of it will provide a life's work for one man.

Mesopotamia was opened up archæologically little more than a hundred years ago, and the beginnings of the decipherment of its script came about twenty years earlier. Diggings between the two wars, in Upper and Lower Mesopotamia, put us right at the beginnings of the historic civilizations there in the fourth millennium, and even, in Upper Mesopotamia, as far back as neolithic or primitive times.

In Persia, too, prehistoric material has been dug up, at Susa; but for most of the historic times before Christ, we depend on non-native material, especially Mesopotamian written evidence, for our reconstruction of such of its history as we know.

The aim of modern archæology is, briefly but inexactly, to dig out what lies buried beneath the debris of centuries. But there is not merely the digging; there is also the digger, and his intentions. Thus, St. Helena, in the fourth century A.D., organized excavations near the site where, according to tradition, the grave and the cross of Jesus were, in order to recover that cross. For a long time in Europe and the United States of America expeditions to Palestine were organized, or at least canvassed, in the hope that light would be thrown on the biblical narrative, and, maybe, prove that the Bible is true.

But the digger of today has a purer intention. He is not out to unearth proofs or gold or silver, or what we may describe as showpieces for museums. He welcomes literally any old thing, even the smallest and poorest witness to man's presence,

14

crafts and beliefs. He may find gold and silver (as in Egypt and Mesopotamia), mosaics (as at Ghassul in Transjordania), a new script (as at Ras Shamra in Syria). But his scale of values is not that of the gold-digger or the curio hunter. To the excavator of today the seemingly worthless piece of broken pottery may be worth more than a ton of gold; for what he really seeks is a complete picture of the site, its history and culture. Nothing less will satisfy him.

This explains, for example, the bulky reports of excavations which alone are acceptable to the modern archæologist. There you will find almost everything relating to things found on the site: location, absolute and relative, size, shape, colour, with photographs or sketches of the typical and unusual, and, possibly, a chemical analysis of some material as an aid to the reconstruction of the story of its making. Consequently, the published report will tell the discerning reader almost as much

as if he himself had been on the expedition.

The technique in use today in the Near East is open to fierce criticism, but it seems to achieve the excavators' purpose in a manner which was impossible with earlier methods. To illustrate, let us take the method of getting at the mound (often named the *tel*) and into it. In the very early days of excavation, a perpendicular shaft was put down, and off it passages, long or short, were cut. This method suggests coalmining. It is still used for special local purposes, e.g. by Woolley at Atchana, behind Syrian Antioch, in 1938, to trace the drainage system. But it is expensive and there is always the problem of disposal of the debris and of the control of the workers down out of sight. The results are poor: the method gives no accurate picture even of the portion worked.

Later, the trench method was used and it still is, on occasion; for example, Garstang used it at Jericho to discover the

REMAINS OF THE CITADEL AT JERICHO

Excavations at Tel-es-Sultan in 1907-09 found the site of Jericho, the first Canaanite city to be attacked by the Israelites. It was probably destroyed in the fourteenth century B.C. In this photograph there are remains of houses and of the inner wall of the citadel standing to a height of three or four feet.

EXCAVATION AT TEL GHASSUL

The Pontifical Biblical Institute sent an expedition to the lower Jordan Valley, north of the Dead Sea, and unearthed a city dating from the early Bronze Age which in that region was approximately between 2500 and 1900 B.C. It was one of the so-called "cities of the plain" mentioned in the Old Testament.

ages of the seven city walls. But this method is otherwise rarely used now, because it gives doubtful results, and is quite inadequate in respect of the total end in view. Finally, came the method of treating a mound as one treats an onion: peeling it, one layer, or part of a layer, at a time. This is not so easy as might appear, but where it can be done effectively, the levels of the ancient city or town are peeled off in the reverse order of formation: that is, the topmost, or last in date, first, and the bottommost, or first in date, last.

But which layer lies on top of, or below which? In Palestine, for example, buildings of different epochs lie on the same level. How is it possible to arrive at the correct differentiation of level, and of date? The answer is, by the science of stratigraphy, of which the foundations were laid by Sir Flinders Petrie who worked out a sequence

chronology based on types of pottery.

Petrie worked first in Egypt. There he noticed that pots, pans, decorated vessels, provision jars and the like varied in form in the various periods of the Pharaohs whose dates were known from other sources. This, as yet a mere theory, he tested and confirmed at Tel-el-Hesi, in Palestine, in 1890. He cut vertical walls on the edge of the mound, collected the potsherds which he found there, making careful note of the exact position where each was found, and compared form, decoration and colour of level with level. Without any written documents to guide him he found that the site was occupied for about one thousand years, from long before Solomon until the time of the Greeks in Palestine.

His deductions were proved correct by his American pupil, Bliss, who continued work on the site after Petrie left it. Bliss discovered written material on the site, and by this was able to establish the chronology of the stratum in which the document was found (*c.* fourteenth century B.C.) and, with this as starting point, went on to establish the chronology of the entire sixty-feet-high pile of debris.

Clearly, where there are no direct aids to dating, such as written, datable material (as in Palestine where dated material is rare and ancient pottery abundant, and where other indirect aids, such as architecture, are confusing) finds of pottery are a godsend, and unlock many doors into the past which otherwise would have remained closed. But it should be noted that some archæologists, in opposition to others, hold that pottery is valuable as a key to chronology but *not* to culture.

Culture

At this point we may ask what is meant by culture. Briefly this: all that men have made of their environment by putting their bodies and minds into it. Culture, therefore, will include not only pots and pans, houses, crafts, industries, but also, and chiefly, the contemporary interpretation of the world and of man's place in it. This last is as much the concern of the archæologist as is any other element of culture, whether economic, social or artistic.

As to differentiations of culture, "headings," such as Stone, Bronze and Iron are familiar. They serve also for the ancient Near East. To use Palestine as an illustration, almost all archæologists are content to retain the divisions Stone, Bronze and Iron. But some prefer to talk of "native, Canaanite, Israelitish and Jewish-Hellenistic." Here the principle of division is ethnological. And, where Stone, Bronze and Iron are retained, there is debate as to the date of the end of the Iron Age. For instance, the distinguished Finnish archæologist, Saarisalo, would end the Iron Age at 300 B.C., and not, as do many others, at about 50 B.C.

In ancient Mesopotamia divisions of the culture beginning with the earliest, in time sequence to about 3000 B.C., are: Sakjegözu, Halaf-Samarra, Ubaid, Uruk, Jemdet Nasr. These names are not names of materials, as are stone, bronze, iron, but of places. The first two are sites in Upper, and the last three in Lower Mesopotamia. At each place some distinctive material element of culture, e.g. pottery, was found proper to that place. But not there only, though first there. Hence the use of what is primarily a place name for cultures found not only on the site which bears that name but on the other sites perhaps far away and called by other names. For example, at Ubaid, a site in Lower Mesopotamia, was found a special type of painted pottery which has been taken as the characteristic stuff of the place. Similar pottery has been found in Upper Mesopotamia and in the Indus Valley. That suggests that the culture first noted at Ubaid cannot be limited to Ubaid, and that we can properly speak of an Ubaid culture outside Ubaid. This applies to other similar descriptions. Such cultures are in fact composite. More, the types overlap. And this is true of the better-known differentiations, the Stone, Bronze and Iron.

Some are inclined to judge that without written, contemporary evidence, all that the archæologist builds up from non-literary remains, such as flints, pots, bones, walls, is merely guess-work. But by now the guesses are well controlled by tested criteria, such as stratigraphy. It is, however, true that for the dating of a stratum and its contents, the presence alongside it of authentic and datable written material of which, luckily, there is an abundance, is decisive, and yearned for by the digger.

Building Up History

Of the ancient scripts, we can say that Egyptian, Sumerian and Akkadian have been mastered. Of the rest, Hittite yields to recent labours, but Urartian and Hurrian studies are as yet in only the first stages. Material for the writing of the history of the ancient Near East thus exists, in abundance for some places and periods, in short supply for others. By authoritative interpretations of literary and non-literary finds, the historian builds up what he can. Whatever the problems and the gaps in evidence which still tease the detectives of the local human story, archæological dis-

EARLY SUMERIAN WRITING
This memorial tablet now in the British Museum records that both Eannatum and his father Akurgal were governors of Shirpula (Lagash), modern Telloh.

coveries do not usually destroy the old pre-exploration knowledge. Rather they put content into traditional words of cult, law, commerce, peoples, familiar from the Hebrew and classical writings. They help us to say when and where, and hazardously, why, new groups emerge and old groups disappear; what has been their stock, their contribution to local culture and civilization, and to political change. Further, and some think most important, the finds recover not only the means but the ways of old communications between areas and groups, those paths of diffusion, peaceful, as by trade, hostile, as by war, which make some unity out of the pell-mell of peoples, the babel of languages, the bazaar of deities, the chain-store of goods, and the varieties of artistic forms in pottery, architecture and the plastic arts. Such are the Mesopotamian-type cylinder seals found in the Indus Valley, the cuneiform tablets of Egyptian Amarna, the ivory plaques found

at Samaria, Cretan pottery of Palestine and Syria, Ashtarte figurines found all over the Semitic Near East. By such discoveries does the archæologist make, so to say, one world of what, without them, would be areas in isolation.

The question: who gave what to whom? is to be decided by the objects found on the sites. The ancient Near East had, by and large, all the food needed for man and beast on the local farms and fields. It had, too, all the metal it needed, but that was much more localized, especially, though not only, in eastern Asia Minor. It remained for caravans, sailing vessels and commercial travellers to push the stuff around, or, as frequently for victorious armies, such as the Assyrian pre-eminently, to carry it off as booty or have it paid annually as tribute. Clearly Egypt and Mesopotamia, especially Lower Mesopotamia, in virtue of their geographical position, developed and maintained an individuality of civilization and culture not possible in Syria which could not but be a corridor for caravans and armies *en route* back and forth between Egypt, Asia Minor and Mesopotamia. Hence, for the archæologist, the finds in Syria, for example at Atchana, fifteen miles north-east of Antioch, of a tablet dated Hammurabi I, and of Cretan motifs on pottery, always raise the question: what foreign influences show themselves here, what traces are there of immigrants and imports from other lands and from across the sea? This is true of Palestine also, miserably poor as the finds have proved.

It is more important to note that it was *men* who were on the move with goods or with weapons, mixing their languages and ideas. Or they may have been stationary, as garrisons in subject lands. All were devotees of their homeland deities, and the furniture of their minds had been made far away in Babylonia, Egypt, Crete or eastern Asia Minor. Here again, this was particularly so in Syria and in Palestine where foreigners traded, invaded, settled or were settled, and even toured with the annual regularity of the early and latter rains.

Discoveries in the decade before the Second World War on the Euphrates and in Syria, the growing mastery of Hittite,

Ugaritic and Hurrian languages, and the intensive, concentrated archæological research in Palestine have put an end to vague talk of the second millennium B.C. as a millennium of migrations and have made it possible to name some of the migrants, read their speech, follow their traces, and estimate their place in the general mosaic of large and small states, and also to analyse the shower of cultural influences which rained down on the contemporary Semitic field.

This may be illustrated by the Hurrians, the biblical Horites. The little we know of them is much compared with what we knew only fifteen years ago. They came, it is likely, from the region south of the Caucasus, with the head of a modern Armenian

SUMERIAN TROOPS IN BATTLE ORDER

This funeral stele of the third millennium B.C., now in the Louvre, Paris, portrays foot soldiers, led by Eannatum of Lagash, in an attack over dead bodies. The soldiers' bodies are protected by broad shields, two men behind each shield. The lower portion shows soldiers on the march bearing lances; in front a protective buckler is carried.

and the speech of Urartians (first millennium inhabitants of what is now Armenia) or akin thereto. They have been traced from the Zagros hill country, east of middle Tigris, about 2400 B.C., and later, nearer in to the Tigris region and in southern Mesopotamia, on the evidence of personal names on documents of the third and second millennium B.C., and in Syria-Palestine, about the fifteenth century, on evidence, especially of Ras Shamra documents. It may be that when evidence increases and is better known, we shall have an answer to the question whether these Hurrians were carriers of Mesopotamian culture, especially myths. It is odd that the Hurrian version of the flood story is the only one known to us that has a hero whose name approximates to the name of Noah of the Bible. But here we are in a field where there is more fog than daylight.

It is, indeed, most proper that we should remember that, thanks to the archæological discoveries, we know a lot about what a man carried on his back as he moved about the world or stayed at home, but we know considerably less about what he carried in his head, his thoughts, and in his heart, his loves. This is especially true of the third millennium B.C., in that area of Lower Mesopotamia called Sumer. The number of documents found on sites there of that age is beyond counting. But they are almost all what are known as temple records, or administration chits and dockets.

Hymns and Myths

It is not until, at earliest, the end of that millennium, and possibly only early in the next millennium, the second, that we get what can properly be called religious texts, such as hymns and myths. All the signs are that the Sumerians who used writing extensively for purposes of daily economic life and, less so, for recording the civic works undertaken by kings, did not write down the kind of thing which would help us to reconstruct the essentials of their religious beliefs. We know they had gods, feasts, sacrifices, prayers, for the texts mention them, together with various religious functionaries. But such meagre information does not lead us far into the heart of

things concerning the religion of the day.

From the second millennium onwards, in Mesopotamia, we are much better supplied with relevant material, some of which tells us of contemporary notions as to how things came to be as they are, what is the will of the gods for men, and how that will can be, and was, allegedly, discovered.

Place of Religion

In respect of Palestine it should be noted that archæological discoveries throw no light upon the orthodox Hebrew cult of Yahweh (Jehovah). Efforts have been made to interpret the Lachish letters said to be of the time of Jeremiah, in a manner to enlighten our darkness. But the first enthusiastic conjectures have not stood the test of later scrutiny. Outside Palestine, the papyri found at Elephantine, in Egypt, show that the religion of Jewish exiles there was far from orthodox by Old Testament standards. To mention one, and a crucial point, the chief god had a spouse, and perhaps, more than one! The texts date from the fifth century B.C. though the community had been at Elephantine, near Assouan on the Nile, early in the sixth century. These texts, together with non-literary material found in Palestine by archæologists, help to fill in the picture which horrified the prophets, the enemies of the popular religion.

Two points may be mentioned which help to understand something of the place of religion, at least in the Semitic world. The first is, that the Semitic groups, large and small, all thought of themselves as "chosen" of their local or national deity. The Mesopotamian tradition, for example, is firm that the gods in council chose dwellings of their heart's content, and people to serve their needs and purposes. Hence, passing over the compelling relevant evidence from the third millennium when for most of the time the land was dotted with small-town kingdoms, the later Babylonians were the people of Marduk, and Assyrians of Assur. The biblical story of the divine choice of Israel is more dramatic and is set within a historical framework. But the essential idea is the same in every place. An Assyrian would not have questioned the Hebrew claim to be chosen of Yahweh. He would only have asserted the greater power of the god who had chosen himself.

The second point is that they all had a ready explanation of the public evils which beset their lands with all their consequences: the local god was angry: Yahweh in the Old Testament; in Babylonia, the great god Enlil. Did the enemy profane, pillage, destroy the temples? Enlil had willed it or had permitted it. All went back to the "word" of Enlil. And a whole class of religious functionaries, the *kalu*, were occupied in bewailing the dread effects of Enlil's anger, and in efforts to turn away his wrath. As to private evils, these were considered the results of this man's sin or of his father's, or of some other family relative. On the other hand, extant literature shows that some people took the line that there was no accounting for these things or for the actions of the gods and the principles on which they fixed men's fate.

Everywhere the gods reigned and nowhere was there any effort to abandon them. In Egypt, Ikhnaten is considered to have tried, in the fourteenth century B.C., to impose the Sun as the god of the land. In Palestine, according to the mind of those who gave us the Old Testament as we now have it, the Hebrews had, really, only one god, however easily popular practice may have followed many gods. In Mesopotamia, even though there were not so many gods as there are names of gods, there is no evidence of anything approaching monotheism at any period before Christ. But in all these lands religion, in belief and in cult, mattered greatly.

It is customary to describe the Lower Mesopotamian towns as either *city-states* or *temple-states*. The former recalls the Greek sort, characterized by an enclosing wall and an autonomous political life. Ancient cities in the Near East were girt by great walls—for defence, no doubt. This feature may be more important for an understanding of the economy than the temple towers and the royal palace which the walls enclosed. In any case, the use of the term *temple-state* does bring out one essential of all the cities known to us,

namely, it is alleged that the temple was the hub of the place, the focus of civic life. By temple in this context is meant a whole complex of which the chief parts were the ancient equivalents of our own Westminster Abbey, Buckingham Palace and the apartments of the functionaries who served them: priests, scribes, judges, royal servants and archivists.

From the Sumerian period (third millennium B.C.), there is material sufficient for a description of contemporary society within the walls. There is no recognizable, essential change during almost a thousand years of Sumerian history about which we are well informed.

If we choose to describe that society as a

PRINCE OF SUMER
This statue of Gudea, Prince of Shirpula (Lagash), now in the Louvre, shows a typical Sumerian face of about 2300 B.C.

theocracy, there is evidence for the description. Not only is there the tradition that the gods made man to build cities and temples and to labour in the fields and the ditches for the table of the gods. There is also the evidence of the town names, e.g. Ur written out as "the abode of Nanna" (the moon god), Larsa (place of the sun's abode), and the impressive documented fact that treaties as to boundaries between states were said to be made not by local king with local king, but by local god with local god. And the spade has revealed the *temenos*, the sacred enclosure taken up by the temple(s) and the palace. (At Ur, excavation has shown that the *temenos* measured four hundred by two hundred yards.)

Contemporary society was primarily agricultural. This economy was imposed by the very nature of the physical environment (alluvial plain and marsh land). Given organized labour, that environment supplied the primary physical needs of man: food, clothing and shelter. For illustration, consider what early third millennium archaic texts from Ur reveal: barley meal,

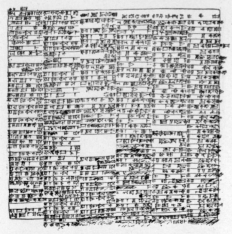

SUMERIAN WAGE LIST OF 2300 B.C.
Workers of different categories—freeborn, slaves, women slaves, and children—are listed by name, against which is set the payment in grain made to each over a period of thirteen months, and finally summarized. The list is recorded on a clay tablet.

wheat, corn, fish, poultry, sheep, oxen, oil, malt, reeds, timber, skins, ropes, threads, baskets and beer. By means of texts one can follow the great increase in vegetable produce. And there was always to hand the clay which the natives early learned to use not only for an excellent quality of brick for building but also for writing.

The key men are, as we should expect, the farmer, the shepherd, the weaver, the clothier, on whose continuous labour, on the spot, the life of the communities depended. Thus, the men who dug and cleared canals, cut and bound reeds, sheared the sheep, brewed the beer, and the scribe are those who made it possible for us to recover the small but essential features of the town's business.

Can we speak of that society as a peasantry? It had, indeed, two of the features which scholars note as typical of a peasantry: permanent occupation and yearly cultivation of land, and the co-operation of women. There was also the mark of feudalism: a hierarchy of ownership with like duties to the group unit.

Was there private ownership? Yes! but ownership of what? Note that private ownership of land, so characteristic of a peasantry such as we know in modern Europe, cannot be proved for the period of the Third Dynasty of Ur, of which we have most evidence under this head, and, perhaps, not for any period in the Sumerian Age. The weightiest evidence on this point is the class of text called *di-til-la*, which are, in effect, judgments of court on matters in dispute amongst the townsfolk. We read of sales of children, slaves, houses, gardens, but never of the sale of fields. This evidence is not conclusive but it does square with the appearances that all cultivable land was the property of the temple-state which farmed out land to temple officials and to soldiers, both officers and men.

The service which these two classes rendered was, throughout ancient history in the Near East, estimated higher than any other in value to the community. But tenancy of land, under the state, and ownership of oxen, sheep, boats, houses, of which we have evidence in the records, sum up the substance of what we know for the earlier period, under the head of private property. The fact that we have so much documentation of temple fields may be because they were not private, and that records would serve as a check on private ambitions.

The documents show very clearly that labour was thoroughly organized. Of course, some measure of organization was imposed by local conditions. Thus, the entire flat land of Lower Mesopotamia is under water twice yearly: in the spring, owing to the downflow of the waters of the melting snows of the mountains in which the Euphrates and Tigris have their source, and in the rainy season. The land cannot be tilled effectively if the two rivers are not dammed and their waters used for irrigation. This is impossible without the co-ordination of the labour of the whole population of the city or kingdom. Egypt had the same problem with the Nile, and tackled it communally also. Either dam the waters and divert them by canals, or perish, is, even today, a law of local life.

The scope and degree of organization of temple-state economy is illustrated, in respect of ancient Mesopotamia (Lower), by the masses of clay tablets found on local sites. Take one point only, that of the system of "book-keeping." The raw material is the day-to-day accounts of imports, sales, contracts and expenditure of temple property. Each account is dated with day of the month (they had twelve lunar months with, at intervals, an intercalary month) and the year of the reigning king (dated either by the number of his reign-year, or by some important local or national event). At intervals these daily entries were entered summarily in accounts covering periods of months, even of years. A last stage was the entering of the records in "files," in special clay cases, around which was run a cord which passed through a hole made in a clay docket on which was written a summary heading of the nature and time-range of the contents. The Sumerians were even the pioneers of the wage sheet; on clay, of course!

Unfortunately we cannot describe the economy of cities and kingdoms in other parts of the ancient Near East with the fullness which contemporary records have

SEAL OF ATANAHILI OF TAANACH
Illustrating foreign relations in Palestine in the second millennium, the seal shows: (left) an inscription in Mesopotamian script and language—"Atanahili, son of Habshi, servant of Nergal" (the latter being the Mesopotamian Lord of the Underworld): (centre) Egyptian symbols, and (right) a scene common on Mesopotamian seals.

made possible for ancient Sumer. Egyptian mural paintings tell us much of the small tasks of the people, but for the organization of the working life of peoples we have nowhere such rich material as is extant from ancient Lower Mesopotamia. Here is the home of, or at any rate, the highest known expression of, the business ability usually attributed to the Semite. But apparently the first signs of it are amongst a non-Semite-speaking folk, the Sumerians, who did in fact give to their Semitic successors in those parts a heritage in religion, writing, and, probably, mathematics, which, with developments, served Mesopotamia throughout recorded pre-Christian historical times.

Each temple-state, large or small kingdom, had its king. We are best informed about each kingship in Mesopotamia, Egypt, Hatti and Palestine. In the first, the local king was a kind of tenant-farmer of the property of the gods, and he, his wife and his children were the earthly representatives of the god, his spouse, and their children. Naturally, his function was to care for the property of the gods and the well-being of their people according to the will of the gods revealed by dreams, omens and astrology. There is proof that the kings of the late third millennium were in

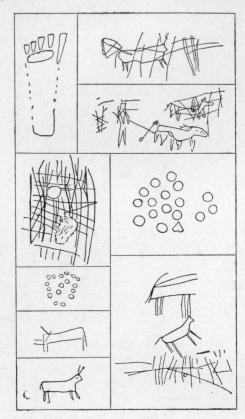

PRIMITIVE ART

Neolithic cave drawings at Gezer showing the cave dweller as hunter and farmer. The punch holes are decorative, or possibly, a form of number-sign.

some sense divine during their lifetime, and, for instance from the Third Dynasty of Ur, that they were honoured with hymns and sacrifices after their death.

In Palestine, according to the Old Testament narrative, a king was given to the Hebrews as a necessary evil. And, according to that same account, many of them were an evil in the land, for they failed to do that which was their primary function: encourage rightness, or righteousness, within the state. But latterly, much has been done to show that the real king was Yahweh. Of course, that is not new. But, for example, it is claimed that references to "the king" in the Psalms are to be inter-

preted as applying, not to the earthly king but to the heavenly king, Yahweh.

We are on safer ground when we ask what was the title to authority. History is familiar with titles based on family connexions, or hereditary succession, on the call to, or seizure of, power by an experienced soldier, and on the principle of adoption. In the ancient Near East, at any rate, the general rule was succession by heredity. Thus, if we take the first millennium, in Assyria: from Adadnirari II (911 B.C.) to Aššurnirari VI (753 B.C.) succession to the throne is kept within one family. A new family succession begins with Sargon II (722 B.C.) and obtains, through sons or brothers, until shortly before the fall of Nineveh (612 B.C.). In Babylonia from during the ninth century B.C. the kings are related. The later so-called neo-Babylonian dynasty (625-539 B.C.) is dynastic. In Israel and Judah, kings are connected by family, though not the same family, during the first millennium down to the fall of Jerusalem (586 B.C.). In Egypt, the same preference for family succession appears; so also, though we are not well informed, in Syria and Phœnicia.

The impression is general that the Semitic kings, at least, were despots and autocrats. That is extremely doubtful. That they ruled, not always justly, can be assumed. But all within a framework of a code, described by the eighth century Sargon: "to maintain justice and regulate right, that the strong may not oppress the poor," and with the consent of at least the elders, and according to the directions of diviners and astrologers. All this left small margin for whim and mood.

The charge of absolutism can be substantiated here and there in the history of the Hebrew monarchy. Saul and David, for example. The latter, on his personal order, is said to have put to death seven of Saul's family to get even in a blood feud.

Some kings of the ancient Near East became what we should call emperors. There were empires in the third millennium B.C. (Agade and Ur III), in the second (Hittite), in the first (Assyrian, Babylonian and Persian). And in each millennium

Egypt made a bid, with more or less success, for an empire, as far as Carchemish on the Euphrates. This means simply that by force of arms a larger or smaller number of neighbouring states and tribes were made dependent upon or allied to the conquerors.

Excavators of sites have found clear traces of empire all over the ancient Near East from the south of Palestine—"Egypt across the border"—to Susa in modern Persia. But we must go to the literary remains to discover the details of the organization of empire. Luckily, the Assyrian records of the first millennium B.C. provide much of what we want to know. Briefly the matter stood thus: in Assyria proper, governors, appointed according to the king's good pleasure, were responsible for order in the provinces over which they were set. They saw to it that the local populations gave military service and, in some cases, forced labour. Under them were prefects, sub-prefects and city mayors. Some cities were exempt from the control of a governor; for example, the old capital city, Assur, and Harran, and, during the Assyrian dominion over Babylonia, the capital Babylon, Borsippa, Nippur and Sippar. Such autonomy was a privilege. It was a favoured-city arrangement. Beyond the provinces of Assyria, the king's representative was described as "he who brings tribute," i.e. tribute due on oath, to the Assyrian king. Finally, in those parts of the empire which, for obvious reasons, were but loosely attached to Assyria, it was enough that they recognized Assyrian sovereignty and paid yearly tribute.

A word about treatment of foreigners, again in Mesopotamia. At one time, it was the fashion to talk about opposition of Sumerian against Semite, and vice versa, in the third millennium. That neat and easy interpretation of current history cannot be held for a moment. And, to pass to the first millennium B.C. within Mesopotamia, documents prove that foreigners were under no disabilities. They were free to enter and even to occupy land. But they thereby undertook such forms of national service as were demanded of natives. And in contract documents, personal names show that Egyptians, Elamites, Jews, Aramæans and any others were as free to make contract as were the natives. Only in the Jewish land was there a blood test (after the return from exile). For a time, however, the Egyptians put a bar on foreigners settling in the Delta.

Slaves who were an important element in Near Eastern society were recruited from foreign lands whence they were brought as part of the loot of war, and in the homeland where a man might give himself and his family as a human tool in payment of a debt. In Mesopotamia, if the code of Hammurabi is our guide, the slave was a thing. But in the Hittite and Old Testament law the slave was treated more like a human being with full human rights to which he could appeal. And in Sumerian wage lists, the distinction between hired labour and slave labour appears in the amounts given for work done.

A recent discovery in the Arabah, the

SYRIAN GODS
Terracotta figurines of deities, possibly gods of fertility, used in cult, in Syria. These examples are now in the collection of the Ashmolean Museum, Oxford.

KING NAR-MER AND HIS VIZIER.
EGYPTIAN SLATE PALETTE, c. 3000 B.C.

KING AS A BULL. EGYPTIAN SLATE RELIEF, c. 3200 B.C.

TIME

5000–

	ASIA MINOR AND SYRIA		GREECE AND ROME
B.C.		B.C.	
3000	Settlements at Ugarit, Byblos (Syria), Jericho, Megiddo (Palestine), Mersin (Cilicia).		
2000	Hittites establish kingdom.		
1900	Egypt supreme beyond Beirut.		
1600	Hittites spread into Syria and to Babylon.	1700	Pelasgi hold Peloponnesus.
circa			
1500	Alphabetic writing in Syria.	1550	Hellenes hold Peloponnesus
1400	Late Bronze Age. Hittite power at greatest. Amarna Age.	1400	Knossus destroyed.
1350	Palestine and Phœnicia reconquered by Egypt.	1313	Cadmus, a Phœnician, introduces letters into Greece.
1250	Exodus of Hebrews from Egypt (date uncertain).		
1200	Iron Age. Fall of Hittites. Philistines, Phœnicians begin trade with Mediterranean coast lands and islands.	1183	Siege of Troy.
1100	Henceforward Syria a battle ground (Assyria versus the small states, singly or in leagues).	1100	Mycenean art flourishes Greece.
		1050	Invasion of Greek islands Dorians.
933	Northern tribes of Israel secede.	950	Internal dissension in Sparta.
		900	Colonization by Greek state Etruscans settle north of Tibe
		880	Lycurgus codifies Spartan law
		800	Rise of Sparta.
760	Beginning of period o. Hebrew prophetic activity (Amos, Hosea. Isaiah, Micah).	753	Foundation of the city of Rom
		747	Rome taken by the Sabines.
		736	First Messenian War.
722	Fall of Samaria; end of Northern Kingdom (Israel).	734	Greeks found Syracuse.
		680	Coinage introduced in Greec
		650	Second Messenian War.
		600	Foundation of city of Ma seilles.

ASSYRIAN PRIEST, c. 880 B.C.

ASSYRIAN HUNTING SCENE, c. 720 B.C.

DECORATED BRONZE BELT FROM PERSIA, c. 1500 B.C.

CHART

B.C.

	EGYPT	B.C.	MESOPOTAMIA
		5000	Settlements at Tepe Gawra and Nineveh.
00	Settlements in Nile Delta.	4000	Settlements at Kish, Uruk, etc.
		2800	Contemporary literature for temple-states of Sumeria.
50	Phœnicians invade Lower Egypt.	2000	End of Sumerian rule.
		1900	Ashur trades with Cappadocia.
00	Hyksos rule Delta.	1800	Ascendancy of Babylon. Mari trade with Cyprus and Crete.
8	Rameses II conquers Arabia, Persia.	1600	Babylon overthrown by Hittites. Mathematical texts Hurrians from east (Caucasus?) reach Mediterranean
		1500	Domination by Hurrians.
0	El-Amarna letters (diplomatic) relating to Syria.	1400	Kassites rule in Babylonia.
0	Haremhab reorganizes the country.		
0	Rameses II fights Hittites for restoration of Asiatic Empire.		
8	Rameses III defeated by combined forces from Libya and Aegean islands.	1200	Assyria free to expand.
00	Egyptian authority in Asia becomes purely nominal.	1100	Assyria gains control of main trade routes between Tigris and Mediterranean.
00	Egyptian Wen Amon reaches Byblos with stock of papyrus rolls.		
00	Age of anarchy and civil wars.	900	Era of many wars between Babylonia and Assyria which lead to disaster for Babylon.
2	Egypt conquered by Ethiopia.	738	Assyrians capture Damascus.
		722	Sargon II takes Samaria.
5	Reign of twelve contemporary kings.	711	Assyrians lose empire.
		689	Assyrians sack Babylon.
1	Ashurbanipal attacks Thebes.	612	Assyria divided between Babylon and Media.
5	Final overthrow of Egyptian power in Syria.	604	Nebuchadnezzar founds Neo-Babylonian Empire.

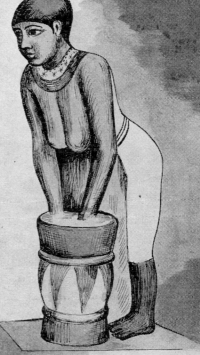

WOMAN BREWING BEER.
EGYPTIAN LIMESTONE STATUE,
c. 2500 B.C.

RY PLATE FROM SAMARIA, c. 800 B.C.

CHEEK PLAQUE OF ORNAMENTAL BIT; PERSIA 2000 B.C.

vast depression stretching from the Sea of Galilee to the Gulf of Aqaba, is said to establish that in Palestine, there were not only domestic and temple slaves, but also, as elsewhere, state slaves. It is maintained the practice of state slavery obtained down to the time of Ezra and Nehemiah.

At the other end of the scale we have for Palestine hints in the Old Testament, pointing to luxury furnishings, e.g. beds of ivory in the houses of the wealthy, especially in the northern kingdom. But perhaps we do better to use housing as a guide to status rather than to material wealth.

Poverty there was, undoubtedly. But poverty is a relative term. The Egyptian Sinuhe who escaped from Egypt into Palestine, told, on his return, of the wealth of the sheiks, in cattle, bread and wine. But, by Egyptian standards, he thought them poor, living in sand, lacking beds and baths!

What is more interesting is the contemporary attitude to those who were poor, especially so poor that they had to sell themselves for livelihood. In general we may say that the local kings, certainly of Mesopotamia, sought to keep their peoples in employment—and on a pay-roll of cereals, wool and metals. And we have, for example, in the reform texts of the Sumerian Urukagina, c. 2600 B.C., measures against exploitation by the managerial class, who overcharged for their services. But in the code of Hammurabi the assumption is that all classes—freemen, plebeians, and slaves—will be able to pay the state-fixed prices for professional services, e.g. of a doctor.

Wherever humans settled, they practised the arts and crafts. The spade has made us familiar with their tools and the finished articles. But it is from the literary texts that we have come to know something of contemporary science. The Babylonians were in this field, as in some others, easily first, and it is they who have most influenced the West in mathematics and in astronomy.

Babylonian mathematics began with the Sumerians. They are the outcome of local economic needs, such as field measurements in a land of highly developed agriculture. Their astronomy was born of a belief that the stars were the divine will writ large.

Authorities on Babylonian mathematics have established that by the time of Hammurabi of Babylon (eighteenth century B.C.) arithmetic and geometry had reached a high stage of development. The theorem of the later Greek Pythagoras concerning the square on the hypotenuse was already applied, and, later, they were able to compute the volume of a pyramid, which the Egyptians could not. But it must not be forgotten that the Babylonians did not reach their conclusions by rational demonstration, which is the essence of science. That was the achievement of the Greeks.

Unfortunately we do not know the names of the individual pioneers or of those who developed the local scientific heritage, in Babylonia. Indeed, it is only in the Hebrew Old Testament that attention and interest is focused on personalities other than the warrior kings.

If, and in so far as, the area of our study became a cultural unity, we must, it would seem, seek the roots of it in ancient Sumer. Invaders and successors in Mesopotamia accepted the highly developed social structure created by the Sumerians during the thousand years in which they dominated southern, and at times, northern Mesopotamia and parts of Syria. And why not? These later and smaller men had nothing better of their own to put in the place of that which the Sumerians had made to meet local needs. And as for the peoples in Palestine and Syria, they were, culturally, always a mosaic, and given their position in the ancient Near East and the ceaseless press of armies and traders, could not be other than a mosaic. And that mosaic as the archæologist pieces it together, is, in not a few details, Mesopotamian.

What was needed in order that the culture of the ancient Near East be passed on to Europe was a pipe-line. Semitic colonists, such as the Phœnicians, traders from the Mediterranean isles, exiles, such as the Jews who migrated increasingly westward after the loss of political independence, and, almost, of living space, travellers such as the Greek Herodotus—these amongst others, were agents of diffusion of Near Eastern culture in towns and cities of Europe. But it was Alex-

POTTERS' CRAFT IN ANCIENT EGYPT

Highly developed in ancient Egypt was the craft of the potter—the oldest art in the world. In this wall painting in the tomb of Amenhotep, in the Valley of the Kings at Thebes, the potters of about 1400 B.C. are seen at work modelling and firing their pots.

ander of Macedon, and, later, the generals of Rome, who, by making one world of at first part and then the whole of the Mediterranean, established the pipe-line which carried living waters to the West: the waters of science and of religion, in particular the religion of the Jews. And so out of that ancient world which the archæologist rediscovers, have come, on his showing, ideas which are still vitally alive in our time and land; and not only ideas, but also the alphabet by means of which some of the discoveries of the archæologist are communicated in this chapter.

Test Yourself

1. Which period after 3000 B.C. was the most vital for later European civilization and culture? Give reasons for your choice.
2. Is there anything in the physical nature of Syria which made political and cultural unity almost impossible?
3. If Assyria, in the first millennium, was so powerful, how do you account for its sudden and final overthrow?
4. How do you explain the fact that in spite of much digging so little written material and works of art have been found in Palestine?
5. What things were used as mediums of exchange? When was money first introduced into the Near East?
6. Which countries first used iron? What advantages did iron bring?

Answers will be found at the end of the book.

RECONSTRUCTION OF

Basing his drawing on archæological researches, the artist has given his impressions of the completed palace of King Minos in Crete. Built about the year 2000 B.C., on the site of a former palace and added to in succeeding centuries, until it was finally destroyed by fire about 1200 B.C., the palace was one of the finest buildings of that age. A curious feature of the design is to be seen in the fine pillars which taper towards the base. The great staircase, flanked with wall paintings, as shown in the picture, leads to the Hall of Colonnades and the

PALACE AT KNOSSOS

queen's reception rooms. In front of the palace people are seen carrying on their normal business; there are the wine and water carriers, soldiers and serving maids, and a visitor to the queen being carried away in a chair accompanied by servants bearing gifts. The jars in the foreground on the right give an idea of the abilities of the Minoans in the manufacture of pottery; they were used for storing water, wine and grain. The costumes depicted by the artist are based on the reproductions to be found on contemporary decorated pottery.

CHAPTER III

THE ANCIENT WORLD

A NCIENT history has for its primary setting the Mediterranean Sea and the lands around it, and as the two thousand years between the legendary lawgiver, Minos, and Justinian, the codifier of Roman law, roll by, all the major peoples of the European continent, Greeks, Romans, Celts, Germans and Slavs come for the first time upon the stage of history.

Classical Greece, or Hellas, has long acted as a magnet upon the affections of civilized man, but earlier folks had sailed these waters long before the coming of the Greeks. In the Bronze Age there grew up on the islands and coasts of the Aegean a culture which later ages were to remember in the tales of Minos of Crete and his labyrinth at Knossos. This civilization, called Minoan by archæologists, which reached its climax between 2000 and 1000 B.C., was in close cultural relationship with Egypt, but had its own marked characteristics. Its people belonged to that short, dark-haired human type commonly called the Mediterranean race, which has long been indigenous from Spain to the Levant and which seems always capable in the long run of absorbing newcomers to the region. These Minoans were sailors, traders and artists, and their rulers dwelt in vast palaces, among whose frescoed halls court ladies walked in narrow-waisted, flounced dresses so different from anything we find in classical Greece or in Egypt.

Indo-Europeans

Shortly before 2000 B.C. mankind was on the move beyond those imposing northern mountains, the Balkans and the Alps, which have never been able to prevent determined invaders from descending upon the Mediterranean world. The Indo-Europeans now, for better or worse, come upon the scene. Some of them, whom we shall meet later, entered Italy, others, ancestors of the Greeks, made their way into Greece, bringing with them new types

of pottery, new types of houses and new gods. They settled as a warrior caste among the earlier inhabitants, and absorbed the higher civilization of the Aegean world. By 1600 B.C. their culture, which we call Mycenæan, was akin to that of Crete, with which they became closely associated, but when in about 1400 B.C. Knossos fell, perhaps through Mycenæan action, Mycenæ in the Peloponnesus became the leading power of the Aegean and its influence spread even wider afield than had that of the Minoan sea-kings.

Dorian Invaders

As the thirteenth century B.C. nears its close there is evidence of growing insecurity. At what point the rulers of Mycenæ should be called Achæans is not clear, but fresh warrior clans moving southward may have displaced earlier dynasties. By 1223 B.C. Achæans appear among a host of sea-rovers attacking Egypt; the overlords of the Greece of the Homeric poems are the Achæan kings of Mycenæ and the historic kernel, whatever it may be, of that great Achæan adventure, the siege of Troy, must belong to about the same time.

About 1000 B.C. there befell the cataclysm remembered in Greek history as the coming of the Dorians. The Dorians were barbarous kinsmen of the Achæans, who had remained in the country north of Greece. Now they set out for the south and the usual tale of such migrations follows, men being slain, women enslaved, cities sacked. This is the dark age of ancient Greece, when the fine arts of the earlier civilization disappear and new arts and crafts have to be built up, slowly and painfully, from the ruins of the old. One of the greatest of all technical revolutions was slowly taking place, iron weapons and tools displacing those of bronze. The Dorians settled more thickly in certain areas than in others; they picked the best sites of the Peloponnesus, and in Sparta they reduced the previous inhabitants, henceforth called the Helots, to serfdom; elsewhere, notably in Attica, the earlier population, the Ionians, prevailed. Many Achæans and Ionians fled across to the east coasts of the Aegean and here the lore of the old days was not allowed entirely to fade out; here the nobles would gather in their halls and listen to bards singing of the past, and the memories preserved in their songs were later collected by Homer and woven into the great epics, the *Iliad* and *Odyssey*.

Greek City-States

By the ninth and eighth centuries the Greek world was settling down and there was emerging its most characteristic feature, the *polis* or city-state, from whose name and the life therein derives so much of the pattern of our western communities. Greece is singularly well adapted for the development of numerous small, independent cities. Much of Greece is mountain, incapable of cultivation, though in those days not so denuded of vegetation as now. Between the mountain ribs are, however, many small pockets of cultivable land. A tribal group would take possession of such an area, choosing a convenient hill for its stronghold. Sometimes newcomers took over a citadel which had belonged to their predecessors. The clan chiefs gravitated to the strongholds and aristocratic communities grew up in which the primitive kings who at first had been the leaders were squeezed out, except in a few backward states like Sparta. To the Greek, or Hellene as he called himself, his city was all. Aristotle has summed up the Greek view of the city-state when he says that men came together in cities so that they might live and remained there so that they might live the good life. The civilized man was the dweller in a city. With the development of the cities, law and order came into being, dispensed by the elders of the clans and encouraged by religion, especially by Apollo through his oracle at Delphi.

The more peaceful conditions enabled commerce to develop and population to grow; in time it became necessary to find some way of providing for superfluous mouths. So there began the age of colonization which spread the Greeks far and wide about the Mediterranean coasts and which went far towards creating a unity out of the Mediterranean world. Many of the most famous cities of history originated in this period, Syracuse on its headland, Marseilles (Massalia) with its ideal landlocked Greek harbour, Byzantium, the forerunner of Constantinople. The constitutions of these colonies were like those of the homeland, but with few exceptions they were independent of their home cities save for ties of sentiment.

About 700 B.C. there came an important economic innovation, the invention of coinage, which seems to have taken place in the kingdom of Lydia, bordering the Greek colonies of the Asia Minor coast. The new medium of exchange was seized upon by a quick, commercially minded people like the Greeks and the resultant changes in the distribution of wealth aggravated the discontents now manifest in many of their little states. Ambitious individuals rose up in many cities, generally with popular support, and set up one-man rule, an illegal kingship to which the Greeks gave the name of tyranny. In all cases the tyrannies were comparatively short-lived and either a conservative aristocracy reasserted itself, or a real popular government was established.

Athenian Democracy

The latter was the case in Athens where a democratic constitution was promulgated when the tyrant was cast out in 510 B.C. The word democracy had a simple and clear meaning to the Greek. *Demos* was the ordinary citizen; *democratia* was rule by him, a rule more real than that of our democracy governing through elected representatives, for the governing body was not an elective one, but the assembly of the whole body of citizens. Such a system was made possible only by the smallness of the city-states whose citizens could all be assembled in some open space, or perhaps the town theatre, and listen to and debate speeches.

But before Athenian democracy attained its fullest development, Greece had passed through one of the great testing-times of

RELIEF FROM THE PALACE OF PERSEPOLIS; PERSIA 5th. CENTURY B.C.

WINGED IBEX.
PERSIAN SILVER,
5th. CENTURY B.C.

TIMI
600-

	ASIA		AFRICA
B.C.		B.C.	
586	Jews taken into captivity by Nebuchadnezzar.	569	Egypt invaded by Nebuch nezzar.
539	Cyrus, King of Median Empire, takes Babylon, and founds Persian Empire.	525	Egypt becomes a Persian vince.
536	Jews return to Jerusalem.	500	Carthaginians make voyage discovery down west coas Africa.
521	Persian Empire extends from N.W. India to Dardanelles.		
485	Xerxes becomes King of Persia.	480	Hamilcar invades Sicily bu defeated.
		460	Egypt revolts from Per domination.
333	Battle of Issus: Alexander overthrows Persian Empire.	332	Alexander conquers Egyp
327	Alexander invades India.	323	Ptolemy becomes ruler Egypt.
323	Death of Alexander and partition of his empire.	320 circa	Ptolemy carries off 100 Jews to Egypt.
		290	Alexandrian Library founde
		273	Grain trade develops betw Egypt and Rome.
		228	Carthagena in Spain foun
		206	Carthaginians driven out Spain.
198	Palestine under Syrian rule.	146	Destruction of Carthage.
192	Syria at war with Rome.		
167	Syria attempts to exterminate Jewish religion—Revolt of Judas Maccabeus.		
133	Pergamum bequeathed to Rome.	41	Mark Antony adminis Roman affairs in East f Alexandria.
88	War with Mithridates.		
64	Syria conquered by Pompey.		
63	Pompey captures Jerusalem.	30	Mark Antony and Cleop commit suicide. Egypt comes a Roman provinc
40 circa	Herod becomes King of the Jews.		
4	Birth of Jesus Christ.		

EARTHENWARE ORNAMENT
FROM AN EGYPTIAN COFFER,
400 B.C.

THE GOD BES.
EGYPTIAN LIMESTONE
STATUE, 350 B.C.

HERCULES AND BUSIRIS.
GREEK VASE PAINTING, 6th. CENTURY B.C.

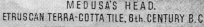

MEDUSA'S HEAD.
ETRUSCAN TERRA-COTTA TILE, 6th. CENTURY B.C.

CHART

B.C.

GREECE	B.C.	ROME
4 Solon reforms Athenian constitution.	510	Establishment of the Republic.
6 Cyrus of Persia captures Sardis in Lydia.		
0 Establishment of democracy in Greece.		
0 Beginning of historical writing in Greece.	*circa*	
6 Persia conquers Thrace and Macedonia.	480	War with Volsci (Coriolanus).
0 Persians defeated at Marathon.	449	Plebeians given constitutional rights.
0 Athens burnt by Xerxes. Persian fleet destroyed at Salamis.	442	First Colony (Ardea).
8 Athens rebuilt.		
Parthenon begun. Great age of poets and philosophers.		
Peloponnesian War (ends 404).		
9 Philip becomes King in Macedonia and (338) master of Greece.	367	Plebeians eligible for Consulship.
	343	First Samnite War.
	312	Via Appia and first Roman aqueduct begun.
9 Gauls invade Greece defeated at Delphi.	266	All Italy subject to Rome.
8 Roman ambassadors first appear at Athens and Corinth.	264	First Punic War.
War between Macedonia and Rome.	241	Carthaginians driven from Sicily.
	218	Second Punic War. Hannibal defeats Romans in Italy.
Macedonia and Greece become Roman Province.	202	Hannibal defeated at Zama.
5 Libraries of Athens sent to Rome.	149	Third Punic War.
	133	Attempted reforms by Gracchus.
	102	Marius destroys Teutoni.
	101	Marius destroys Cimbri.
	81	Sulla Dictator.
	60	First Triumvirate.
	58	Cæsar in Gaul.
	55	Cæsar in Britain.
	48	Cæsar becomes Dictator.
	44	Cæsar assassinated.
	43	Second Triumvirate.
	31	Octavian (now Augustus) master of the Roman world. End of Republic.

ROMAN CUTLER'S SHOP.
RELIEF FROM A TOMBSTONE, c.1st. CENTURY A.D.

GIRL WITH PIGEONS.
RELIEF FROM A
GREEK TOMBSTONE,
4th. CENTURY B.C.

ACHILLES BANDAGES
PATROCLUS. GREEK VASE
PAINTING, 510 B.C.

GREEK WARRIOR

Dressed in a close-fitting singlet and a short leather skirt this Greek warrior is protected by a domed shield and conical helmet. In his right hand is poised a long spear while at his left side is a short sword in its scabbard.

world history. Cyrus the Persian, and his successors, had mightily increased the Persian realm and had advanced through Asia Minor. The Greeks on its western fringe for a time acquiesced in Persian rule, but soon they quarrelled with the conqueror and implored their fellow-Greeks across the Aegean to help them, a call to which Athens and Eretria responded. But their help was of no avail and in 490 B.C. Darius, the Persian king, sent a punitive expedition across the sea which landed at the Bay of Marathon, twenty-two miles north-east of Athens. The citizen levy marched out to meet it and, to everyone's astonishment, signally defeated the Persian force. This victory, due to the heavy armour of the Greek foot soldier, who bore down the lightly armed Persians with a weight that made up for his lesser numbers, electrified the Greek world; but the excitement soon died down and few Greeks paid any attention to the inevitable Persian re-

turn. One of those few was Themistocles, who realized that the key to the conflict would be sea-power and persuaded the Athenians to build two hundred ships of war.

Happily for Greece the invasion was delayed, but as the year 480 B.C. approached, a mighty host assembled at the Dardanelles. Xerxes, the successor to Darius, was now ready for the great combined operation in which his army would march along the coast to Greece, while a fleet would keep pace with it. As Xerxes approached. disaster followed disaster; Leonidas and his heroic Spartans fell at Thermopylæ and many states of northern Greece made terms with the invader. The women and children of Athens were sent across to the island of Salamis and her menfolk went aboard ship. In the narrow waters between the island and the mainland Themistocles made his stand and the great fleet of the invader sailed in to its destruction under the eye of its king. This brilliant naval victory was followed by a great land battle the following year, when the Spartan Pausanias led the Greeks to victory over the Persian army at Platæa.

For a time the two chief victors, Sparta and Athens, worked in amity, but isolationist Sparta withdrew into her shell. She could not do otherwise; her whole economy was based on Helot labour, and the small army of Spartan citizens was needed to keep the Helots down. The Spartan training had grown out of this paramount necessity, and the Spartan constitution, with its two kings, its council of old men and its powerful, elected magistrates whose chief duty was to maintain the Spartan discipline, was too rigid to be modified. Athens was left the responsibility and glory of freeing the Asiatic Greeks from Persian control and of maintaining that freedom when won. This Athens did by means of a league of cities, the Delian League. The success of her league brought her great rewards, in opportunities of dominating the trade of the east and north-east just at a time when she was able to make full use of them, being now at the zenith of her artistic craftsmanship. Athenian goods penetrated everywhere, not merely because Athens was powerful and her traders enterprising, but because her goods were, in fact, the best to be had. The poor soil of Attica could not feed the growing city, so Athens became increasingly dependent on her foreign trade to pay for the corn that came to her from the south Russian wheatlands. Having thus established herself as a leader in a crusade of liberation she was, as time went on, compelled to maintain this dominant position in order to live.

At home the triumphs of war were to be surpassed by those of peace. The Persians in 480 B.C. left the Acropolis, the citadel of Athens, in ruins; this disaster gave the opportunity for a new epoch in the adornment of the city which was taken when Pericles became the leading figure in the state. Then the great new Parthenon, the temple of Athena, was built (448-438 B.C.) and a colossal statue of the goddess was set up outside it. Athens was also enriched by her poets who wrote the plays performed at the festivals of Dionysus.

In 431 B.C. a war broke out, engendered by commercial rivalry in western waters between Athens and Corinth. This fetched in Sparta's Peloponnesian League against Athens and involved all Greece. It is a petty war when we consider the size of the states engaged, but its results, the hopeless division of the Greeks and their ultimate ruin, were grave. Sparta could not win until she could find a fleet, and this she could not do until Persian gold was obtained to pay for it. For the Persian Empire still lived on and kept a watchful eye on Greek affairs, and immediately the Athenian Empire, as the Delian League may now be more correctly called, became weak, the Persians got the chance for which they had been waiting.

Where Athens failed was in not granting political privileges to her allies to compensate for their diminished sovereignty. When the Peloponnesian War was at its height Sparta and her allies came to be regarded as the liberators of Greece; but they could not take Athens' place as a unifying factor, so the history of the early fourth century B.C. is of increasing Greek disunity and, what is worse, of increasing factional strife within the city-states themselves. This in later years made the way easy for Macedonian and then Roman domination.

Greek philosophy had already arisen before the fifth century B.C in the cities of Ionia in western Asia Minor. In the fifth century Periclean Athens drew to herself the best contemporary men of letters. With the enrichment of life on all sides, the increased knowledge of the world, and the development of literature, there grew up a demand for what we call the higher education, and teachers arose to expound rhetoric, mathematics, grammar and philosophy, to fit young men to play their part in political and social life. Conservatives,

SPORT IN ANCIENT GREECE

This large bronze statue represents a Greek fighter resting, and is a reminder that Greek pugilists fought naked and used leather gauntlet-like thongs (the caestus) to bind the hands to make the blows more effective.

like the dramatist Aristophanes, felt that the intellectual, sceptical spirit of the day was undermining the solid virtues of the older Athens and they attacked the teachers of the new wisdom and of artful argument who "make the worse appear the better cause." Those attacked included Socrates though he, more than any other thinker, was interested in goodness and truth.

Socrates criticized the extreme democracy of his day and let his view be known that the wise should govern, which did not always happen in Athens where, at that time, all magistrates, except generals, who, in those days came in that category, were chosen by lot, not election. His pupil Plato (427-347 B.C.) carried on his work and developed a system of moral philosophy. He felt that political good could only be achieved if the rulers were philosophers and understood the nature of the good. So he set up his famous school, the Academy, in the groves of Academus, and left many treatises, the most famous of all being the *Republic*, in which an ideal system of government is laid down.

Plato's most distinguished pupil was Aristotle (384-322 B.C.), who established a school of his own, the Lyceum. Where Plato was mystical and a poet, Aristotle was a scientist and, besides his vast range of philosophical speculation, he studied nature and wrote works on biology.

Rise of Macedon

Meanwhile, a certain Philip, who became King of Macedon in 358 B.C. had been in his youth a hostage in Thebes, then the chief military power in Greece, and made good use of his captivity by studying the army of his captors. When he returned home he copied and then improved on Theban methods. It took him twenty years to dominate Greece. The only sustained resistance was put up by Thebes and by Athens, under the desperate leadership of Demosthenes, who strove mightily to preserve the independence of the Greeks. When in 338 B.C. Macedonian supremacy was conclusively asserted, Philip announced that he would lead the Greeks against Persia, an adventure which his assassination in 336 B.C. prevented. This desire of Philip's to be a leader of all the Greeks is a sign of the times. He was the most powerful of a number of rulers just outside Greece proper who had come within the sphere of Greek culture and who sincerely desired to share it. The Macedonians were racially akin to the Greeks and despite a lingering barbarism were not unfitted to be vehicles for the spread of Greek civilization.

Alexander's Conquests

Alexander, Philip's son, one of the greatest military geniuses of all time, now strides through history and, in thirteen years, turns the world upside down. He was a romantic and his head was filled with the tales of the heroic age. The notion of invading the crumbling Persian Empire was in the air in his childhood, but what to Philip was a useful expedient for keeping his subjects quiet and interested, with a good chance of loot and some territorial gains into the bargain, was a divine enterprise to Alexander, who entered into it with all the ardour of a crusader.

In 334 B.C. he crossed the Dardanelles and after a pilgrimage to Troy began his march eastward. A year later he met and defeated Darius III at Issus, and the western part of the empire was his for the taking. After that nothing could stop him, nothing seemed to satisfy him. He besieged and took Tyre. He conquered Egypt, and was acknowledged as Pharaoh by the powerful Egyptian priesthood. He then turned against the heart of the empire and his victory at Gaugamela in Mesopotamia laid Babylon and Persia at his feet. He was now the ruler of the Persian Empire, but there were its eastern provinces to secure and he set out on his long march into Afghanistan and Turkestan where he took Samarkand and founded a colony beyond it, which he called Alexandreschate, "the farthest Alexandria" (now Chodjend). Finally he entered India and conquered the Punjab. But beyond the Indus his troops would not march and he had to return to Babylon where he was carried off by a fever when about to start on a new expedition round Arabia (323 B.C.)

Alexander had little time for administration and left the empire of Darius much as

GREEK WORLD IN THE FIFTH CENTURY B.C.

Greek settlement was widespread around the coasts of the Mediterranean, and the colonial movement of the eighth and seventh centuries B.C. resulted in the foundation of cities on the Black Sea, in North Africa and in the western Mediterranean (including the south of France and eastern Spain). The chief cities of the Delian League—a confederation of Greek states with its headquarters at Delos—dominated by Athens, are indicated.

he found it. But his new cities, of which Alexandria in Egypt was the greatest, initiated a new phase in the spread of Greek civilization. Twenty-five of them are known and they were generally chosen with an eye to their commercial possibilities. His successors were to continue this great new phase of planned colonization. An old device in a new guise was thought up to reconcile the unwilling Greeks to participation in the world-empire which their genius was expected to adorn. The gods of Hellas had never been very widely separated from the human race, and the habit had grown up of paying divine honours to outstanding individuals, like founders of colonies, after their death. It was not a far cry from this to acknowledge the super-

human achievements of Alexander by according him divine honours in his life-time, and in 324 B.C. the Greeks were commanded to do so. Thus the new world we are entering is one of deified monarchs, whose divine character enabled them, in theory at any rate, to transcend the old national and city-state barriers.

The death of Alexander threw the world into confusion. After a generation of struggles between his generals a more or less stable system emerged which was to last until Rome fell heir to it, with three major dynasties of Macedonian origin reigning in the eastern Mediterranean lands, the Ptolemies in Egypt, the Seleucids in Syria and Asia Minor (their initial holdings east of the Euphrates soon fell away

CHIEFTAIN'S HOUSE IN HOMERIC TIMES: HOW

The residence of the head of a Greek community of about 900 B.C., provided shelter for the people in time of war and was generally the centre of cultural and domestic activities. The house was constructed of wood framing fitted with rough stonework covered, except at the base, with plaster. The scene shown by the artist is typical of the period. An important

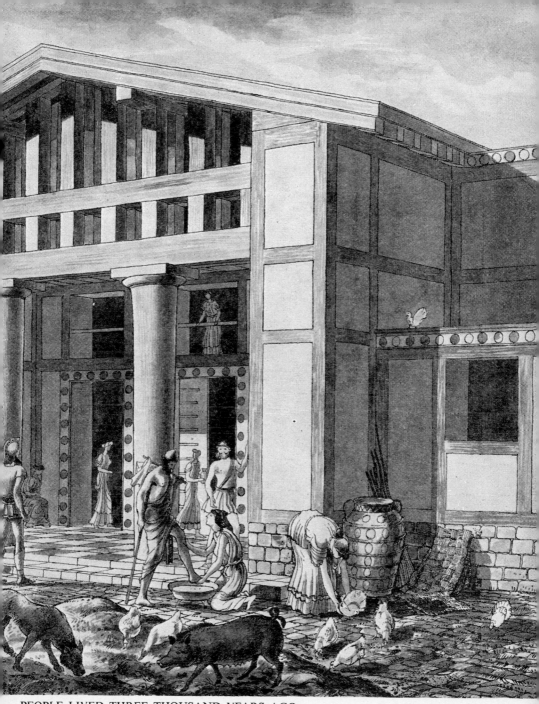

PEOPLE LIVED THREE THOUSAND YEARS AGO

traveller arrives on horseback and is greeted by a servant with refreshment, a more humble visitor is having his feet washed prior to entering the hall, warriors and water carriers are going about their daily tasks. Animals feed on the rubbish littering the courtyard. In the pens under the colonnade on the left are cattle which are reserved for sacrifice to the gods.

ROMAN CITY IN AFRICA

Built about A.D. 100 by the Emperor Trajan, Timgad, the ruins of which are near Constantine, Algeria, was designed as a place of settlement for retired veterans of the Roman legions. It is built on the traditional Roman pattern.

from them) and the Antigonids in Macedon. As make-weights in the diplomatic picture of the age a group of smaller states should be noted. Greece always remained liable to Macedonian interference so her small cities banded themselves into two leagues, the Achæan and Aetolian; Athens and Sparta maintained a precarious and decadent independence. The glories of the independent city-state found a last home in Rhodes, ruled by an enterprising oligarchy. Rhodes took up the mantle of Athens as a naval and commercial power, keeping the seas clear of pirates. Lastly, there was Pergamum in western Asia Minor.

These three centuries from the death of Alexander (323 B.C.) to the death of Cleopatra (31 B.C.) are known as the Hellenistic period. It was the period when Rome came of age and began to absorb Greek culture, and the culture handed on to her was that preserved and extended by the Hellenistic Greeks. Greek civilization, though diluted in the process, became very much more widespread, being carried far inland into areas untouched by the expansion of the earlier colonial period. Greek became the common language of commerce and of culture, that is, of the cities, throughout the dominions of the Hellenistic kings.

Economically, the Hellenistic Age is full of interest. The period starts with the impulse given to every sort of activity by the enormous hoards of Persian gold captured by Alexander and put into circulation in such ways as the payment of great armies, the payment for the building and adorning of the new cities and royal palaces. The new monarchs vied with one another in magnificence and their courts were centres for the expenditure of wealth. Alexandria rapidly became the wealthiest city on the Mediterranean and her traders not only sent their goods all over its waters but also made their way to India.

For the first time men became conscious of a single civilized world—the world of all those, whoever they might be, who understood Greek and could appreciate its literature, art, music and athletics. So literature and the arts flourished. Great libraries, notably those of Alexandria and Pergamum, were collected and scholars preserved and wrote commentaries on the works of the past. The Hellenistic world appreciated its heritage and did its utmost to hand it on. Its scientists were adepts at exact observation and patient collection of facts. Great strides were made in mathematics, astronomy and geography; but the stumbling-block was the failure to develop scientific instruments. Archimedes, with his pulleys and levers, his "screw" for hoisting water and his experiments with specific gravity.

was in a class by himself. A water-organ, an air-gun and a simple steam-engine were later to be evolved by Alexandrian scientists, but these were toys and their practical possibilities were neglected. The unlimited supply of cheap labour available in the slave-markets meant that the ancient world lacked one of the most powerful stimuli to practical inventiveness.

Rome

Rome lies at the first good crossing of the Tiber, fifteen miles from the sea, at a point where a cluster of low hills, in particular the easily fortified Palatine, comes close to the river on the south. Primitive villages grew up on these hills before 1000 B.C. and their inhabitants in time banded together for common action. And so, very gradually, Rome of the kings emerges, about which a later age was to weave the foundation-legend of Romulus and Remus, the divine twins, preserved from the flood and suckled by a she-wolf.

The young town on the Tiber had many perils in its early days, which were shared by the other Latin towns of the lowland. All around, a few hours' march across the Campagna, was hilly country inhabited by tribes who were always ready to supplement their own scanty subsistence by raiding the fatter lands below. Across the Tiber to north and north-west were other hills, where dwelt enemies of still more formidable character, the Etruscans. This people had, according to the Greek historian, Herodotus, migrated from Asia Minor to Italy during the dark ages of the invasions. They established themselves as a ruling caste, controlling the iron mines of Elba and engaging in active trade with the Greeks, of whose civilization they were apt pupils, developing a high degree of skill in metal work and terracotta statuary.

During the seventh and sixth centuries B.C., they succeeded in dominating some of the country south of the Tiber, including Rome. The Etruscan kings have a bad name in Roman legend, but Rome owed her first contacts with civilization to them. They brought their architecture, art and commerce with them; they also brought their discipline and the emblems of authority which the Romans retained after their expulsion, including the fasces (rods and axes), and the cloak worn by generals.

Towards the end of the sixth century B.C. Rome got rid of both Etruscans and kings. The supreme executive and military power (imperium) formerly wielded by the kings, with all that it implied where there was a citizen army, was henceforth vested in the supreme magistrates, the consuls. There were two consuls, equal in power, but holding office for only a year, elected by the comitia, the assembly of the people. The checks upon their power were that they could veto one another's acts, and their short term of office. Other magistrates, all elective, were instituted as the work of government expanded, until finally a regular ladder of promotion developed. These magistrates, during and after their year of office, had a seat in the senate, so the senate, once the old tribal council of fathers, is the centre of the constitutional edifice of the republic, the repository of the collective wisdom of the Roman body politic. When exceptional peril demanded the temporary expedient of a single strong ruler, a dictator was nominated by the consuls, but when the emergency was over he was required to lay down his powers. Throughout the republican constitution we find a sense of order and discipline combined with flexibility fostered by the perils which surrounded Rome and which the Greeks, in their more isolated communities, failed to develop.

Latin Allies

In the early days of the republic, Rome concluded an alliance with the Latins around her and took the lead in their ultimately successful struggles with the hill tribes. Rome's title to the mastery of Italy is to be found in her readiness to assume responsibility. Rome also very early developed a major instrument of conquest, her military colonies, which were planted at strategic points linked by military roads. The Latin Allies were generally allowed to share in the colonies, which were a valuable outlet for hungry mouths.

The Etruscans did not give up the country south of the Tiber without a struggle but towards the end of the fifth century they were assailed from a new quarter as Celtic tribes began to cross the Alps. The Celts or Gauls became marked off from other peoples of Indo-European stock during the second millennium, in the land about the upper Rhine. As they multiplied they spread far afield. Successive waves penetrated into what is now France and across the Channel into Britain; others pushed to the northern edge of the German highland zone; others marched east to Bohemia; and yet others set out on that path to the south which has lured so many northern wanderers. Some entered the Valley of the Po and harried the Etruscans.

City of Rome Sacked

In 390, Gauls poured across the Apennines bringing fire and sword into the heart of Etruria and finally defeating the Roman citizen army and sacking the city of Rome itself, a disaster to the republic's prestige which it took half a century to restore. By 340, however, Rome's territory marched with the fertile lands of Campania, behind which lie hundreds of square miles of difficult, mountainous country. Here Rome once more became involved in wars between mountaineers and the more civilized valley-dwellers on whom they sought to prey and who sought Roman protection.

The conquest of Italy was a long and arduous business. Rome always insisted that her allies should provide contingents of fighting men to her armies, thus, as her confederation grew so did the forces at her disposal, and in times of adversity she was able to maintain several armies in the field at once, a great feat for an ancient state. By 268 all Italy south of Lombardy was within Rome's ingenious system of alliances. Rome had even entered into alliance with the Greek colonies of the south, and it is therefore not surprising that she soon found herself at odds with Carthage, the hereditary enemy of the Greeks of Sicily.

Carthage was the offspring of the Phœnician city of Tyre, and had been founded about 800 B.C. near modern Tunis, on the richest part of the North African coast. The Carthaginians were daring seamen and to them goes the credit for some of the most exciting voyages of antiquity. They explored the west coast of Africa as far as Sierra Leone; their trade with the "tin islands"—Cornwall—is attested by the Greeks. Their greatest enemies were the Greeks, equally daring merchant adventurers and far better craftsmen. The Carthaginians tried many times to secure control of Sicily in order to drive these opponents from the western Mediterranean.

The first war between Rome and Carthage (the First Punic War) lasted from 264 to 241. Now for the first time, Rome became involved outside her own peninsula. The Romans, always unwilling mariners, were forced to take to the sea. The dogged Romans were not to be turned from their objective and they finally beat the enemy on his own element and thereby took possession of their first province, all the island of Sicily with the exception of the territory round Syracuse.

Rome now had command of the seas and during the next decades her power in the western Mediterranean increased, while Carthage declined. When Hannibal, Carthaginian governor of Spain, prepared for his war of revenge he decided that he must take his army to Italy, for only there could Rome be defeated, and to get there he must go by land.

Hannibal's Army

The Second Punic War (218-202) shows Rome at her grandest. Hannibal, marching through Italy after his spectacular crossing of the Alps, met army after army and anni-hilated them, but the Roman senate and people did not flinch. They had sent an army to the south of France to try to intercept him in 218 and, when it failed to do this, ordered it to invade Spain. The fact that this army was never recalled, illustrates the spirit of the senate, on which the direction of the war fell. The rock on which Hannibal foundered, however, was the loyalty of the Italian confederation. He had counted on being received in Italy as the liberator of its cities from the tyrant power of Rome, but few of them deserted to him. His chances of being welcomed by the Italians were materially reduced by his arrival with Gaulish allies in his train; the

ROMAN MOSAIC FROM THE TEMPLE AT PALESTRINA

Flooding of the Nile is the subject of this Roman mosaic and it is shown with startling realism and detail. The scene is Roman in treatment, but Egyptian plants (including the lotus), animals, birds and canoes are faithfully reproduced.

Gaulish raids were too vividly remembered by the Italians. In the latter part of the war Scipio, a Roman general of genius, persuaded the senate to make the logical answer to Hannibal by invading Africa. Hannibal was recalled and in 202 was defeated at Zama.

The Romans who marched to world power were more than the inhabitants of the city on the Tiber. The armies that crossed the seas contained an increasing proportion of Italians, and these soldiers shared the glory and the booty; the ships that carried them were provided by Greek and Italian seaports; the growing commerce of Italy was handled by Italians as well as Romans. The full Roman citizenship extended over a wide belt in the centre of the peninsula, and into scattered colonies throughout its length; from these towns Rome recruited officers and minor officials and, as years went by, some famous Romans, including Cicero and Marius.

Before Hannibal's elephants had made their fruitless charge at Zama the stage was set for Rome's entry into the Greek world.

In 204 a boy king ascended the throne of the Ptolemies and Philip V of Macedon and the Seleucid king of the day, Antiochus, evolved a scheme to despoil him of his outlying dominions, including certain Aegean territory. The vigilant island of Rhodes and the kingdom of Pergamum looked round for a means of stopping the aggressors, and soon a stream of Hellenistic embassies visited Rome and used all their persuasive skill and flattery on the ready ear of the senate. Rome agreed to intervene and Philip was roundly defeated in 197. The Romans then withdrew from Greece, but four years later they were called back to drive out Antiochus who had attempted another invasion. Henceforth Rome was involved permanently in Greek affairs.

Greek culture had begun to penetrate Roman social life in the third century. Well-to-do Romans adopted the custom of keeping Greek slaves or freedmen to teach their children, and new generations were growing up with a knowledge of literature and the world undreamed of by their

ROMAN SHIPS, A.D. 100

Merchant ships in an Italian harbour. Though small, they were stoutly built with a single mast, square-rigged sail and a high poop and cabin. They were steered by a large sweep, like an oar, on one side. Note the lighthouse behind the larger ship, the dinghies on left and right, and the wine jars being carried ashore from the ship on the right.

elders, and also with a fluent command of Greek. The process was accelerated when victorious soldiers began bringing home Greek works of art, books and prisoners.

Unhappily, the corrupting effect of un-limited power began to tell upon the Romans. No Hellenistic army could with-stand the legions and vast quantities of more lucrative booty than libraries fell into the hands of the campaigners from pro-consuls downwards. The wealth of the east seemed there for the taking and greedy hands were outstretched to clutch it.

Tribute-Paying Provinces

The year 146 saw the end of the last shadow of Greek independence, and also the destruction of Carthage. The province of Africa, corresponding roughly to modern Tunisia, and of enormous value to the growing city of Rome because of its corn exports, was then created. In 133 Rome acquired her first possession east of the Aegean by a new and surprising method, for Attalus, the last king of Pergamum, bequeathed her his kingdom, which now became the province of Asia. The posses-sion of Spain led to increased Roman interest in the land between Spain and Italy, and the country south of the Ceven-nes and up the Rhône valley as far as Vienne was made into the province of Narbonese Gaul (122).

Conquered territories were organized as tribute-paying provinces, governed by Roman magistrates sent out at the end of their year of office. The chief provinces went to proconsuls, the others to pro-prætors, and it is to be noted that whereas in Rome the power of the supreme magis-trate, the consul, was curbed by his col-league, he was allowed to exercise absolute authority, military as well as civil, un-checked in his province.

The Roman constitution was able to adapt itself to the changing needs of over three hundred years and Romans managed to dwell together without any serious internal strife developing. There were crises, but these were weathered by the sound good sense of the average citizen. In the early days of the republic there had been a long contest between the patricians, the old noble clans and their dependants, and the plebeians, persons outside this charmed circle, the poorer citizens and later comers to Rome, who were not allowed to become magistrates or to have any voice in the government of the city. The plebeians threatened to secede from Rome, and formed their own assembly which elected its own magistrates, the tribunes. At this point the patricians gave way and the plebeians were gradually admitted to all public offices, while the tribunes became part of the constitution, being granted, as "protectors of the plebs," a roving right of veto over the acts of any other magistrate. In the new nobility of office that grew up, there were notable plebeian families as wealthy and haughty as the patricians. Another issue, the hunger of the really poor for land, was solved in the course of Rome's wars as land for coloniza-tion was always obtainable from a victim.

Post-war Italy

After the Hannibalic war the senate was the master of Rome. The assembly, it is true, had to vote in favour of a declaration of war, but the conduct of that war, and the peace negotiations which followed, were left to the senate. For a time there was no unrest among the attenuated population, for there was land near Rome to be had for the asking. Vast tracts in central and southern Italy were untilled after the depredations of the war, and the senate leased it to anybody willing to take it over. The rich investor could acquire broad lands and turn them into profitable cattle or sheep ranches, run by the plentiful slave labour. This process continued unchecked for two generations and more, until the population of Rome had recovered from the setbacks of the great war and an un-employment problem arose among the city proletariat.

The dangers of the situation were per-ceived by those who were not solely given over to feathering their own nests, and various reformers, too hesitant, or too headstrong, tried to better the conditions of the state. The noblest of these were the two brothers, Tiberius and Gaius Gracchus, tribunes respectively in 133 and 123, who

COSTUME IN THE
ANCIENT WORLD

EGYPTIAN, 3000 B.C

CRETAN FASHIONS BEFORE THE
DESTRUCTION OF KNOSSOS,
ABOUT 1500 B.C.

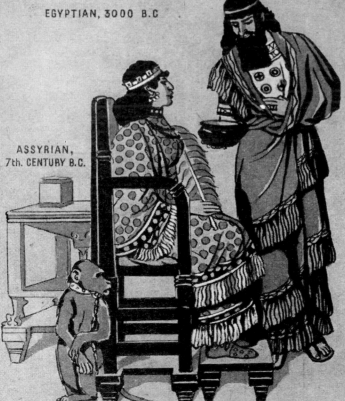

ASSYRIAN,
7th. CENTURY B.C.

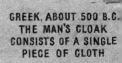

GREEK, ABOUT 500 B.C.
THE MAN'S CLOAK
CONSISTS OF A SINGLE
PIECE OF CLOTH

EGYPTIAN, 1450 B.C.

BRONZE AGE IN WESTERN EUROPE

ROMAN, 1st. CENTURY B.C.

tackled the land question, seeking to recover public land which had been absorbed into private estates, and to distribute it among landless men. They achieved a considerable measure of reform despite senatorial opposition. Gaius introduced the famous state issue of cheap corn to all Roman citizens who cared to apply for it, an early example of social security which, in spite of drawbacks in its operation, must have prevented much misery.

State and Ex-Soldier

The lively but melancholy last century of the republic is, however, dominated not by rival policies but by rival generals. The landless civilian was quite happy in Rome with its excitements and its cheap corn; it was now the landless ex-soldier who clamoured for grants and who knew that his only chance of getting them was through his old commander to whom, therefore, he gave his unwavering support. The old constitution had not envisaged a professional army, so no provision had been made by the state for the ex-soldier. The problem of the military man with the army at his back might not have assumed such proportions had not the next two generations seen several major wars which revealed military leaders of genius.

In the first of these wars Germanic tribes move into the orbit of the Mediterranean. For many years the Germans, inhabitants of the north European plain, had been pressing against the Celts in the hill country to the south of them. Towards the end of the second century certain tribal groups, the Cimbri and Teutoni, migrated in search of new homes. They entered Gaul and marched through the land burning and ravishing, invading the Roman province where they destroyed the armies sent to meet them. The Roman people, thoroughly alarmed, called for their most distinguished general, Marius, who had been in Africa fighting a Berber chieftain. He hastened home, raised and trained an army, and in the successive years, 102 and 101, annihilated the Germans at Aix-en-Provence and north-west of Milan.

The next war (91-89 B.C.) was a bitter internal struggle between Rome and her Italian allies who had attempted to secede. The war was brought to an end only by the granting of Roman citizenship to the allies which might earlier have prevented war. The political arena in Rome was given over to the feud between the aristocratic Sulla and Marius the people's favourite. Finally, Sulla, returning home from a series of brilliant victories in Asia Minor over Mithridates of Pontus, used his troops to drive the Marians from Rome. He then purged the city of his enemies by his notorious proscriptions, in which lists of obnoxious persons were posted up and their murderers rewarded. Then, as dictator (81-80) he promulgated a series of laws designed to strengthen the senate and to prevent another military man from following his own example, laws destined very soon to be flouted.

Pompey, a lieutenant of Sulla, had won distinction in Spain and had then dealt with the dangerous slave rebellion of Spartacus, another symbol of the unrest of the times. In 67 he was called upon to meet the menace of the pirates who now infested every corner of the Mediterranean, a campaign necessary because Rome, though mistress of the seas, had not carried out the responsibility that entailed of preserving a navy adequate to police them. The extraconstitutional command given to Pompey was followed by another when he was called upon to campaign against Mithridates who was now making a second attempt to drive the Romans from Asia Minor.

First Triumvirate

Pompey enjoyed his expected success, annexed several more provinces, including Syria, and thus made an end of the Seleucid kingdom. He then returned to Italy and, to everybody's astonishment, disbanded his army, as the law ordained. The foolish senate began to quibble about ratifying his eastern settlement and giving his veterans their well-earned land grants. This sent Pompey into the arms of another scheming and far more subtle politician, Caius Julius Cæsar, and his ally, the great financier, Crassus. The three of them formed an unofficial alliance, the First Triumvirate, which enabled them to sweep the political

STREET OF ABUNDANCE, POMPEII

Eruption of Vesuvius in A.D. 79 buried Herculaneum and Pompeii under a thick stratum of lava and ashes. Excavation has revealed the features of these towns and this view of a street in Pompeii shows clearly the type of dwelling house with blank wall to the street (light and air being admitted by an inner courtyard), a wayside fountain, paved sidewalks and narrow paved roadway with ruts made by chariot wheels.

board. Cæsar's popularity, Crassus's money, Pompey's military reputation and his needy veterans, ensured their success.

Cæsar became consul for the year 59 and in 58 proceeded to his chosen sphere, the provinces of Cisalpine and Narbonese Gaul, whence he got his momentous chance of intervening in the affairs of the Gaul of the free Celts. He was first invited to check an attempted migration of the Helvetii of north-west Switzerland, and then to drive out a German invasion. His brief visits to Britain were by-products of his main activities. At the end of his ten-year command Gaul was part of the Roman Empire and the birth of modern France was assured.

His partner, Crassus, had meanwhile met his death while fighting the Parthians across the Euphrates. The Parthians were a warlike people from the Caspian region which had moved into Persia and Mesopotamia, where they inherited some of the assets of the old Persian tradition and some

ROMAN EMPIRE
in the second century A.D.

ILLYRIA

ETRURIA

MARE ADRIATICUM

MARE TYRRHENUM

CORSICA

ROMA

SAMNITES

SARDINIA

Foundations of the Roman Empire

0 20 40 60 80 100 120 140 160

ROME 509 B.C.   ROME 338 B.C.

MAGNA GRAECIA

MARE CASPIUM

DACIA

PONTUS EUXINUS

REGNUM PARTHORUM

ESIA

THRACIA

ippopolis

Sinope

Trapezus

A R M E N I A

Byzantium

GALATIA

Held from 114-117 A.D.

Smyrna

ASIA

CAPPADOCIA

Caesarea Mazaca

Athenae

M E S O P O T A M I A

CRETA

CYPRUS

Antiochia

SYRIA

Ctesiphon

NUM

PHOENICIA

SINUS PERSICUS

Tyrus

Caesarea

Alexandria

A R A B I A

AEGYPTUS

CA

Arab Trade Caravans carrying jewels, silk, peppers and spices from the East

SINUS ARABICUS

C W B

of the civilization of the eastern Seleucid provinces. Cæsar returned from Gaul to find the senate, which now had the support of Pompey, preparing to oppose him by force of arms. Instead of disbanding his army at the River Rubicon, the frontier of metropolitan Italy across which no general might take his army, he marched on towards Rome. Pompey retired across the Adriatic to build up his strength. Cæsar followed and defeated him at Pharsalus in Thessaly (48).

End of the Republic

Egypt still enjoyed a specious independence, the last of the old Hellenistic states to remain outside the grasp of Rome. Cæsar, in pursuit of Pompey, came to Alexandria and, while trying to sort out the dynastic quarrels of the Ptolemies, met Cleopatra, to whom he left her crown. He returned to Rome as dictator and endeavoured to bring some order into the Roman state, while at the same time preparing a great expedition against Parthia. But republican feeling was still sufficiently strong in the Roman aristocracy to engender the conspiracy which brought about his assassination in 44.

Brutus and the "liberators" met with scant applause and soon had to flee. After sundry political manœuvres a Second Triumvirate emerged: Antony, consul at the time of Cæsar's death; Octavian, Cæsar's great-nephew and heir; and the make-weight, Lepidus. This new coalition entered Rome with its troops in 43 and new proscriptions ensued in which, to his lasting disgrace, Octavian yielded up the elderly orator and politician, Cicero, to the vengeance of his personal enemy, Antony. They then divided the world between them and Antony sailed east to meet Cleopatra and to break with and be defeated by Octavian in 31. The Roman Empire of which Egypt now became part, after the death of Antony and Cleopatra, was very differently run from the decaying republic. Cleopatra had saved Egypt from republican tax-gatherers even if Octavian was fated to have its treasure.

The somewhat disreputable Triumvirate now gave place to Octavian as Augustus.

Old feuds of the republic had eaten each other up. After years of conflict the world was at his feet and content to stay there provided that he did not too openly flout its prejudices. He could now set to work to organize the empire. On the constitutional side he made a great play of restoring the republic, and permitted the senate and magistrates to function outwardly as before, but he took care to safeguard and legalize his own position. He was vested with the tribunician power by virtue of which he could summon the senate and control the magistrates; he had overriding powers *(maius imperium)* over all provincial governors; he reserved to himself the management through his own legates of all the provinces on the frontiers where it was imperative to maintain strong garrisons. He built up a fund for the proper upkeep of a standing army and for the provision of land and gratuities for ex-soldiers. He devised a system of frontier defence and, through his generals—for he himself was no soldier—waged a long series of frontier wars to ensure the security of the empire. The disappearance of the republic was an unmixed blessing for the empire at large, which now enters upon a long period of development as the largest stable unit into which Europe has ever been united.

Municipal Government

The peaceful development of the empire and the general contentment of its people were fostered by its system of municipal government. The emperor might be far away and an autocrat, but each little community or *municipium* could develop a life of its own in which it took considerable pride and every town with any pretensions had its official temples, its forum, its baths, theatre and amphitheatre. The communities tended to be dominated by their richer men, but the rich man, to be elected to the municipal council, had to be willing to spend liberally on his city and his fellow-citizens.

Great armies were stationed along the frontiers and became centres of Romanization. The non-citizen troops, the auxiliaries, were rewarded with citizenship on retirement so there was a progressive increase in the scope of the Roman citizenship, until in A.D. 212 it was extended to all free inhabitants of the empire.

The luxury and magnificence of Rome are only one side of the picture. In trying to understand the problems of the empire and the causes of its decline we must remember that the imperial state lived on a very narrow margin, and that its economy was not altogether sound. Even the great armies that are so imposing were difficult to maintain and were kept down to numbers barely sufficient for the needs of defence. The Mediterranean world on which the empire was based is not and was not a region of vast natural wealth. Rome and the Hellenistic kingdoms before her seem to have been unable to maintain a stable balance of trade, even in their most prosperous periods, and to have depended on windfalls, like Alexander's haul of treasure, or Octavian's confiscation of the Ptolemaic hoards. The great public works which are a feature of the Roman Empire seem to flag during the second century, as if there were no more capital to invest in new ones; towns adorned with fine monumental walls in the first century too often never grew sufficiently to fill the space within them. The Romans themselves commented on the adverse balance of trade with India, which helped to drain the empire of its specie.

Within the empire, we can watch the spread of industries from province to province. The cultivation of Mediterranean plants also spread outwards. Wine had long been one of the principal exports to the Celts; now the cultivation of the vine, as of other fruits, spread far afield. The great vine-growing districts of France and the Rhineland began to achieve fame.

In every phase of ancient history we come up against the institution of slavery.

ROMAN AQUEDUCT

Colossal aqueducts brought fresh water from the hills to Roman cities. The best preserved is that known as the Pont du Gard, near Nîmes, France. This series of superimposed arches rising to 160 feet above ground was built in the time of Augustus.

Slaves were used on the land; the most intractable captives, or condemned criminals, were sent to the living death of the mines; slaves from the east, with their skill and ingratiating manners, were chosen for household and commercial tasks, and it was they who stood the best chance of gaining their freedom as a reward for good service or through saving up their small wages and purchasing it. There was thus an element of hope in the life of a slave and once he was free he was admitted to Roman citizenship. By the end of the republic there was a large number of these freedmen in the body politic, and many came to hold positions of great trust in the imperial offices.

Slaves also played a part in the gladiatorial shows, which originally arose as funeral games. The bravest, most promising fighters captured in the wars would often be reserved for the gladiatorial schools, in which their life was exciting and dangerous but from which they might, if they were lucky, retire with their freedom. Not only were there the regular fights between armed men, but there were all sorts of extra shows, exhibitions of strange wild beasts and fights between them and men variously armed.

The old Roman population had long been in danger of being swamped by the cosmopolitan influx which a great capital attracts. But the vigour of the Roman people and the discipline of their language and traditions were such that Rome and Italy could absorb much alien stock and latinize it, just as modern America absorbs the most diverse immigrants. The empire did, however, become increasingly orientalized, though the old Roman spirit periodically reappeared in its pristine grandeur.

The religious picture of the later years of antiquity is vastly different from the days of the Olympian gods of Hellas, or of the early Roman Jupiter. The old gods of the city-state had done very well for these small communities and provided men played the game according to the rules the gods might be relied on to behave on their side. The most active minds before the fourth century B.C. were more concerned with the life of the *polis* than with religious speculation, and later on there were the various philosophical schools to occupy them. There was also scope for the more religious temperaments in the mystery cults, which offered an after-life more attractive than that of the shady underworld commonly postulated.

Into the Hellenistic and Roman worlds many new divinities were to make their way: but the empire had a formal cult of its own. Its eastern provinces had long been used to deified saviour-kings, and the

PORK BUTCHER'S SHOP IN ANCIENT ROME

This carved relief of an ancient shop shows a butcher chining a rib on the chopping block. Behind him are his scales, and in front a wooden rack from which joints are suspended. To the left is the proprietor with tablets of accounts open on his knee. Such shops were usually managed by slaves who were often able to purchase their freedom by saving up their small share of the profits from the business.

CHARIOT RACING

The Greeks introduced chariot racing to the Romans, with whom it became as popular as gladiatorial shows, surviving into the Byzantine Empire after the Christian emperors had suppressed the gladiators. The four-horse chariot shown above is about to make the dangerous turn round the post at one end of the circus.

Roman emperors were admitted to divine honours with alacrity.

Christianity arose in the obscurity of Palestine. It made headway in the first place among the Jewish communities which had spread far and wide among the Hellenistic cities. At first it received little attention from the authorities, who were used to the Jews and had come to an arrangement allowing them to offer prayers for the emperor instead of sacrificing to his image.

Christians were first persecuted as scapegoats for the accidental burning of Rome in A.D. 64, and the earliest mention of them is Tacitus's account of this persecution by the Emperor Nero. The earliest extant portions of the Christian Scriptures are papyrus fragments of the first half of the second century A.D. found in Egyptian rubbish-heaps. Christianity made its way for a time with comparatively little persecution, enjoying the great advantages of the remarkable organizing ability of its earliest leaders, and the universality of its appeal, which made no distinction between persons and which, unlike its chief rival, Mithraism, so popular in the army, welcomed women to its cult. The real conflict with the state largely developed over emperor-worship.

The empire in general throve until the middle of the second century. The first grave external peril had to be met in the reign of Marcus Aurelius (161-180). German tribes were on the move again and the impact of one uneasy group upon another disturbed the Marcomanni north of the middle Danube, who, pushed from behind, burst through the Roman frontier and shook the empire to its core. It required heroic efforts to cast them out and few conquerors deserve our sympathy more than the quiet philosopher-emperor who had to leave his studies to lead his armies in most arduous campaigns. The resources of the empire were severely strained by these thirteen years of war and by fresh civil wars which broke out in 192 after the assassination of Commodus, unworthy son of Marcus. Henceforth the emperors who managed to make themselves secure for any length of time, tended to increase the despotic character of their office, so that the formally constitutional system of Augustus disappears and is replaced by autocracy.

The third century is one of the blackest in European history. To continual internal

STREET SCENE IN ROMAN ITALY

In a Roman street of about the first century A.D., the people are seen at their normal activities—purchasing goods in the shops, slaves fetching water from the public fountain, and distributing wine from the wine cart to a shop. On the right is a biga, or small chariot, used by the more wealthy people. The streets are just wide enough to allow for its passage, and

IN THE FIRST CENTURY A.D.

the wheel ruts may be seen as well as the stepping stones on which people crossed to avoid the refuse which often littered the streets. Houses are large and spacious, and blocks of flats three or four storeys high were features of the residential quarters. Owners of shops, as may be seen, usually lived on their own premises as is frequently the case today.

warfare we must add the onslaught of new and ever more dangerous barbarians, the Goths across the Danube, the Alamanni, Franks and Saxons across the Rhine and along the coasts, while in the east a new Persian dynasty brought a new period of Iranian aggression. Plagues took their toll of life, bandits appeared on the highroads, pirates on the seas. Communications were disrupted, the treasury was empty, trade diminished and the currency was debased.

Despite its tribulations and despite temporary breakaways in a few provinces, the empire held together. Many of the short-lived emperors showed extraordinary vigour and military prowess and managed time and again to drive off the barbarians. At last a man arose strong enough and fortunate enough to secure undisputed control. This was Diocletian (284-305),

ROMAN BATH

In Roman villas, such as that at Chedworth, in Gloucestershire, which dates from the second century A.D., the baths consisted of a series of rooms of varying degrees of heat, somewhat similar to the modern Turkish baths. Hot air from the furnace flowed not only under the mosaic floor, but also up through ducts in the walls.

an administrator rather than a soldier, who, like Augustus, could choose good generals to serve him.

Having secured his frontiers, Diocletian undertook a comprehensive reorganization of the empire, increasing the efficiency of the army, but decreasing the power of individual military commanders who might scheme for the imperial purple. He took the momentous step of dividing the empire into eastern and western halves under two collegiate emperors, to ensure its more efficient government and protection. The re-establishment of peace helped the recovery of economic life. Diocletian undertook the reform of the coinage, which was carried on by Constantine. This fundamental reform and the care with which the standard, once established, was maintained in the Eastern Empire, powerfully aided its longevity. The taxation system was over-hauled and efforts were made to make the burden fall more equally, but the maintenance of the army and the increased bureaucracy continued to be a heavy strain.

Constantine and "New Rome"

To strengthen his own position Diocletian adopted the outward appurtenances of oriental, particularly Persian, despotism. The emperor was now, in fact, a god, and exacted worship as such. This policy, however, brought the problem of the Christians to a head. They were now a large and powerful community and he could not permit a state within a state to add to his troubles, so it was decided to try to stamp out Christianity, and large-scale persecution was tried which failed signally and had to be allowed to die down. Constantine was to reverse the system and take the Church into partnership in maintaining the unity of an increasingly Christian empire.

The Christians had supported him in his struggles with political rivals and he legalized Christianity by the Edict of Milan (313) and gradually adopted the faith himself.

Like Diocletian, Constantine chose to reside in the eastern part of the empire, though he did not tolerate a colleague in the west. His new era was to have a new capital and he built "New Rome which is Constantinople," on the site of the old Greek colony of Byzantium. The most gravely threatened frontiers of the day were those of the Danube and the Euphrates, and the shores of the Bosphorus midway between them was the best point for the headquarters of defence. Byzantium had a fine natural harbour and an easily fortifiable site; it could obtain supplies with equal ease from the Black Sea or the Mediterranean areas. It also lay at the crossing of great commercial east-west and northsouth routes.

New Dynasties

Constantine succeeded in establishing a dynasty, which mitigated the succession difficulty. There were still bitter conflicts for the purple, but these became less frequent in the Byzantine world. New Rome, like the oldest Rome, lived in the midst of perils, and to survive, had to be united. The supreme authority, the *imperium*, once held by the consuls, and maintained by Augustus, was vested in the emperor, but the emperor was the servant of the state. Few Byzantine emperors failed in their duty to put the state before personal interests.

The dynasty succeeding the Constantinian house was that established by Valentinian in 364. Under him the division of the empire into eastern and western halves was re-established and endured, save for a few brief months under Theodosius the Great (394). The empire in the west was rapidly disintegrating. It was not strong enough to resist the cumulative effects of continual barbarian onslaughts, nor had it the vitality to absorb the numerous German mercenaries enlisted in its weakening fighting forces or the German colonists settled on the lands that their brethren had ravaged. The west had no Constantinople. Consequently Old Rome, cut off from the sea and starved out and deprived of any help or control since the movement of the government eastwards, became an easy prey to barbarian assaults and was sacked by Alaric, the Visigoth, in 410, and again in 455 by the Vandals, a Germanic tribe operating from North Africa where it had taken Carthage and set up a kingdom. In the east, Goths might

GATHERING OLIVES IN GREECE
An Attic figured vase of the fifth century B.C., now in the British Museum, bears a graphic representation of the gathering of the olive harvest. Olive oil formed an important part of the diet of the people of the lands bordering the Mediterranean

ravage the Balkans and trample the ruins of Athens; Vandals might sail up the Hellespont; but they could not subdue the city of Constantine.

Byzantine civilization is not a creative civilization, except in art and architecture, and there to only a limited extent. Its mission was to preserve and protect. Its greatest single work of preservation was the codification of the Roman Law, undertaken by the orders of Justinian (526-565), who was also the builder of St. Sophia, the greatest architectural triumph of his world. The law which had built the republic and sustained the empire had grown slowly in the practice of the Roman courts, from the decisions of the prætors and the edicts of the emperors. Now a digest was made of this great body of material and the transmission of Rome's most characteristic creation was ensured.

Byzantium also preserved the Greek tongue and the knowledge of the ancient

Greek learning, gradually handing them on to the west. It played the major part in the Christianization of the Slav peoples, who began to bear down upon the shrinking Balkan provinces in the sixth century. The greatest danger to Christendom, however, was to come from another direction, when Islam arose in Arabia in the seventh century. The eastern provinces of the empire, Syria and Egypt, were lost, but heroic efforts managed to keep the Saracens east of Taurus and thus to preserve the highlands of Asia Minor, the main reservoir for recruits for the hard-worked imperial army.

Constantinople now assumed her historic role of the shield of Europe and for centuries she was to hold out against Islam and thus give the west time to outgrow its dark ages. The reasons for her success may be briefly summed up; the geographical advantages of Constantinople; the strong Roman conception of duty to the state; sound finances based on a reliable coinage, which enabled Constantinople to become the mart of Europe and the East and thus to build up wealth to maintain her indispensable army and navy; the careful diplomacy which became traditional at the Byzantine court; the strong but superstitious Christianity of the inhabitants which bound them together with the strength to resist that other fanatical religion, Islam.

It is one of the ironies of history that the great city was to fall in 1204 to its co-religionists and bitter enemies, the crusaders of the west, but even they could not rob it of its secular task and after their ejection in 1261 it managed, though greatly weakened, to maintain itself against the Turks until 1453. The story of the Byzantine Empire is the story of a long rearguard action bravely and loyally fought.

Test Yourself

1. How did the Greeks come to be the most widespread people of the Mediterranean seaboard?
2. What did the term "democracy" mean to a Greek, and what do you know of the rise and decline of Athenian democracy?
3. How did Rome achieve and maintain the mastery of Italy?
4. What factors brought about the downfall of the Roman Republic?
5. Give some account of the organization and government of the Roman Empire about A.D. 120.

Answers will be found at the end of the book.

PALACE OF CTESIPHON ON THE TIGRIS

Ctesiphon, the once splendid capital of the Persian kings, was utterly destroyed by the Saracens in A.D. 637. All that remains is the ruin of the Palace of Chosroes I, standing alone in the wilderness with its gigantic arched roof 95 feet high, and having a span of 83 feet; a remarkable achievement of early engineering (sixth century, A.D.).

CHAPTER IV

THE MIDDLE AGES AND THE RENAISSANCE

THE Middle Ages comprise more than a thousand years of human history, from about A.D. 300 to about A.D. 1500. This is a longer period than from the time of the discovery of America to the present day, and any generalizations about these years must necessarily be inadequate. One great fact had had its effects from the outset—the life and teaching of Jesus Christ and His followers had meant that Europe was slowly becoming a Christian community. Christianity, embodied in the institution of the Church, and feudalism, the attachment of all duties to the possession of land and their accompaniment by a class-conscious order of society based on mutual obligations, provide essential features of these years of vital and purposeful development.

New Western Civilization

When the Emperor Constantine I decided in the fourth century to live on the Bosphorus in the city that was to be named after him, he was consciously taking up a position on the frontier and leaving Rome, Italy and Western Europe to their fate. East and West slowly drifted apart and, equally slowly, the only world society of civilized men (outside China) ceased to be Mediterranean and became one of Western Europe. The creation of this western European civilization was the work of the Middle Ages, and the vigour and the vitality of that achievement have not yet been exhausted. Something of this vitality was imparted to the West by the movement of many peoples during the fifth and sixth centuries when Ostrogoths and Visigoths, Franks, Vandals and Lombards contributed fresh blood and ideas to the heritage of the ancient world.

That the newcomers destroyed a good deal that was of value to the world as they advanced cannot be denied; for theatres, temples, villas, even cities and libraries,

they had little respect, even if the extent of their depredations was very much exaggerated later. Yet, in a strangely respectful fashion, most of them at first sought to become Roman citizens, and, as allies, shared in the fortunes of the tottering empire. Their leaders were willing to accept titles and decorations from a distant emperor as well as marriage alliances.

It was towards wealthy Italy that the footsteps of many peoples turned and there the pressure reached cracking-point in A.D. 410. Rome fell before the onslaught of Alaric and his Goths, an event which led St. Augustine to write his famous and influential book, *The City of God*, and caused St. Jerome in Bethlehem to record the dismay and lamentations of the East. From Italy some of the Visigoths moved to southern France and Spain, while Burgundians from eastern Germany crossed the Rhine and Franks settled near Cologne, gazing in greedy anticipation westward to the Roman Gaul that was soon to be their inheritance.

In North Africa

From yet another wild tribe of Eastern Europe, the Vandals made their predatory way to Spain and thence, under their great leader Gaiseric, in 429 moved to North Africa. There they settled all along the Barbary Coast, and from Tunisia (the site of ancient Carthage), they could threaten Rome. Never, until the unpredictable changes caused by transfers of populations and the restless shifting of displaced persons in the twentieth century, were so many peoples on the move together. Cutting through their former neighbours, in the middle of the fifth century, came the mounted Mongols known as Huns. They were led by a genius for cavalry warfare, Attila, whose ferocious followers crossed the Rhine in 451, but were repulsed in

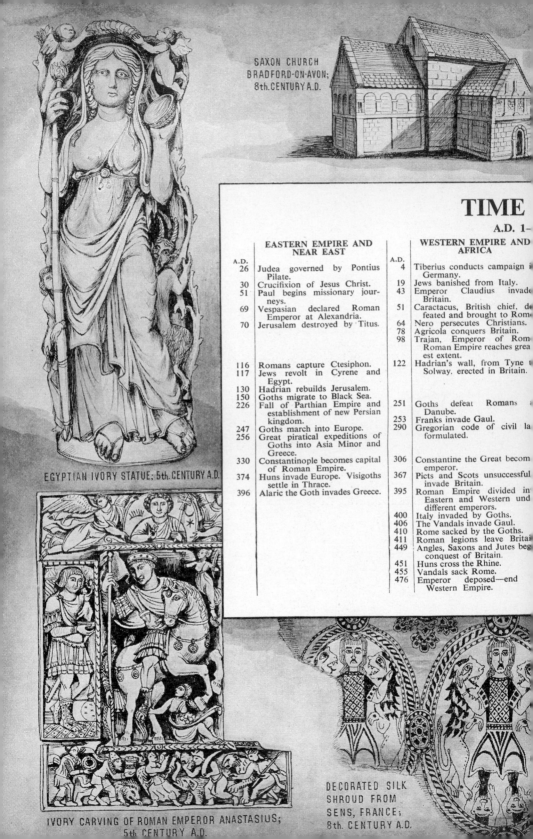

SAXON CHURCH
BRADFORD-ON-AVON;
8th. CENTURY A.D.

TIME

A.D. 1–

EASTERN EMPIRE AND NEAR EAST

A.D.	
26	Judea governed by Pontius Pilate.
30	Crucifixion of Jesus Christ.
51	Paul begins missionary journeys.
69	Vespasian declared Roman Emperor at Alexandria.
70	Jerusalem destroyed by Titus.
116	Romans capture Ctesiphon.
117	Jews revolt in Cyrene and Egypt.
130	Hadrian rebuilds Jerusalem.
150	Goths migrate to Black Sea.
226	Fall of Parthian Empire and establishment of new Persian kingdom.
247	Goths march into Europe.
256	Great piratical expeditions of Goths into Asia Minor and Greece.
330	Constantinople becomes capital of Roman Empire.
374	Huns invade Europe. Visigoths settle in Thrace.
396	Alaric the Goth invades Greece.

WESTERN EMPIRE AND AFRICA

A.D.	
4	Tiberius conducts campaign i Germany.
19	Jews banished from Italy.
43	Emperor Claudius invade Britain.
51	Caractacus, British chief, de feated and brought to Rom
64	Nero persecutes Christians.
78	Agricola conquers Britain.
98	Trajan, Emperor of Rom Roman Empire reaches grea est extent.
122	Hadrian's wall, from Tyne t Solway. erected in Britain.
251	Goths defeat Romans Danube.
253	Franks invade Gaul.
290	Gregorian code of civil la formulated.
306	Constantine the Great becom emperor.
367	Picts and Scots unsuccessful invade Britain.
395	Roman Empire divided in Eastern and Western und different emperors.
400	Italy invaded by Goths.
406	The Vandals invade Gaul.
410	Rome sacked by the Goths.
411	Roman legions leave Britai
449	Angles, Saxons and Jutes beg conquest of Britain.
451	Huns cross the Rhine.
455	Vandals sack Rome.
476	Emperor deposed—end Western Empire.

EGYPTIAN IVORY STATUE; 5th. CENTURY A.D.

IVORY CARVING OF ROMAN EMPEROR ANASTASIUS;
5th CENTURY A.D.

DECORATED SILK
SHROUD FROM
SENS, FRANCE;
8th. CENTURY A.D.

ROMAN SHIP;
2nd. CENTURY A.D.

MOSAIC FROM
RAVENNA, ITALY;
6th. CENTURY A.D.

CHART

EASTERN EMPIRE AND NEAR EAST	A.D.	WESTERN EUROPE AND AFRICA
	477	First Saxon settlement in Britain.
	481	Clovis I founds kingdom of Franks.
	496	Clovis converted to Christianity.
Beginning of great period of Byzantine Empire.	529	Benedictine order of monks instituted.
Justinian becomes emperor: Roman laws codified.	540	Byzantine power established in Italy.
Persians defeated by Belisarius.	568	Italy conquered by Lombards.
Vandals overthrown in Africa.	597	St. Augustine introduces Christianity into Britain.
Birth of Mohammed.	600	England wholly under Saxons.
Persians conquer Egypt.	617	Beginning of Northumbrian supremacy in England.
Persians overrun Asia Minor.		
Mohammedan religion founded.	673	Anarchy in France.
Egypt conquered by Arabs.	688	Wessex becomes ruling power in England.
North Africa completely subdued by Arabs.	711	Moslems invade Spain.
	720	Moslems invade France.
Invasion of Empire by Haroun-al-Raschid.	732	Franks gain victory over Saracens.
	787	Danes' first invasion of Britain.
Empire at war with Bulgarians and Saracens.	800	Charlemagne founds Holy Roman Empire.
	814	Death of Charlemagne.
	829	Egbert assumes title of King of England.
	837	War between Wessex and the Danes.
	871	Accession of Alfred as King of Wessex.
	887	Final separation of France and Germany.
Rise of Fatimite dynasty in North Africa.	900	England divided into counties and shires. Establishment of county courts.
Conquest of Crete by Byzantines.	911	Northmen settle in Normandy.
Fatimites become masters of Egypt.	994	Norwegians and Danes invade England.

IVORY CARVING FROM
CONSTANTINOPLE; 5th. CENTURY A.D.

CHURCH OF ST. APOLLINARE, RAVENNA; 6th. CENTURY A.D.

France near Troyes, Attila himself dying in 453 after a visit to Italy where he was persuaded by Pope Leo I not to sack Rome.

After Attila's death, a second wave of Goths (Ostrogoths) moved from the Balkans into Italy. Their ruler, Theodoric, believed himself to be the agent of the Emperor Zeno, in whose name he overthrew the Teutonic war lord, Odoacer. In the first quarter of the sixth century Theodoric and his Arian (non-Catholic) followers controlled the destinies of Italy from Ravenna. But in spite of a rule that was strong and enlightened, that brought peace, justice and a measure of prosperity, the Ostrogothic dominion had not the elements of permanency, for it had insufficient numbers behind it and Catholics in Italy disliked its unorthodox teaching.

In France, as we may begin to call the Gaul of Julius Cæsar, the opposite was the case. There the infiltrating Salian Franks, at first humble allies of the Gallo-Roman rulers, found in the ranks of their aristocracy a leader who combined the virtues of the statesman and the warrior—Clovis. This brutal young leader routed Syagrius, at Soissons, in 486, and made himself master of much of eastern France and, more wonderfully, dictator of the destinies of his freedom-loving followers. The pious legends recorded in strange Latin by Gregory of Tours, tell of his marriage with the Catholic Burgundian princess Clotilda, of further victory in battle and, in 496, of submission to the Christian God of battles. The price paid was the long and sometimes disastrous connexion of the Catholic kings of France with Rome, but the reward, after Clovis's death in 511, was the effective allegiance of most of France to the Merovingian dynasty.

Institutional Christianity had undergone a hardening process since the assembled bishops at Nicæa, the city of victory, had formulated in 325 the creed of the West rather than of the East and made the Trinity in Unity the unassailable tenet of orthodoxy. For more than a thousand years after that date, politics and religion were inextricably intertwined. In the Eastern Roman Empire the intelligent and literate inhabitants of its great cities followed the course of religious controversy and the personalities of religious leaders with an enthusiasm such as the modern world evinces for the football or baseball team, the film star and the prize fighter. Jerusalem was still almost literally the centre of the Christian faith, while in Egypt groups of militant recluses were living lonely lives of an asceticism possible only in such a climate, but providing also the originals of the monasteries which were later to be so different and so powerful in the West.

Although the successors of Constantine (Arcadius, Marcian, Leo and Zeno) were, with the exception of the great Theodosius, men of insignificant calibre, Constantinople remained a great and wealthy capital. The centre of world trade and high finance, with a ceremonial court unequalled in the world for its impressive splendour, with paved streets where rich and poor, Greeks and barbarians, priests and devotees moved in a colourful never-ending stream, its rulers in the sixth century determined to regain what had been lost to the strangers who had poured in from beyond the Rhine and Danube. In 527 Justinian, son of a Macedonian peasant, succeeded his uncle Justin as emperor. A fussy busybody, always at work, confident in his own mediocre abilities, he united the Mediterranean world for the last time in human history, and left great monuments of stone and marble and still more enduring ones in the Codes of Roman Law upon which much of the jurisprudence of the civilized world is based. How much he owed to the peerless courtesan whom he raised as his consort to the imperial throne will never be known, while his partisanship in the howling riots of Greens against Blues in the arena, or his senile devotion to strange details of seemingly meaningless theological controversy, make him a somewhat strange figure to us.

With a notable gift for choosing servants of ability and capacity, he appointed generals who regained for the last time the Mediterranean coasts for the emperor. An "endless peace" with the Persians, the overthrow of the Vandal power in a wonderful march from Sfax to the north of Tunisia, and the invasion of Sicily, led to the regaining of Syracuse, Messina, Reggio, Naples and finally Rome, from the Ostrogoths. Not all this could be held, and the successful general Belisarius received little recognition of his skill and efforts, but Italy was again Roman until the Goths made way for the less civilized Lombards.

Bishops of Rome

Twenty-one Lombard kings ruled in Italy in the two hundred years between the death of Alboin (572) and of Desiderius (774), a long stretch in the history of a people. The last of the barbarians, the Lombards, like the Ostrogoths, were Arians and at variance with the religion of the peoples over whom they ruled. "Unspeakable" was the favourite epithet for popes to apply to these heretics who lived for the most part as conquerors aloof and apart from the population of the northern plain in which they settled most thickly and to which they gave their name. With the death of Justinian the imperial armies returned from Italy to Asia Minor to repel the recurring threat from the side of Persia. Old Rome was thus able to regain something of its former pre-eminence in the peninsula, for its bishop had by now obtained an authority and power hitherto unknown. It was by now universally believed in the West that St. Peter had been the first Bishop of Rome and that his bones, with those of St. Paul, could and did work miracles on behalf of their custodian. The bishops of Rome, although at first scarcely regarded even as equals by the proud prelates of Jerusalem, Constantinople and Alexandria, could not fail, from the very name and traditions of their city, to rise to a special and admitted position of superiority. The coming of the Lombards corresponded with the election by acclamation of the wealthy Roman patrician, Gregory, as pope in 590.

The first of the great medieval popes was a monk of the order of St. Benedict. The Roman-minded Benedict of Nursia had, in 529, given order, constitutional government, stability and purpose to those who sought in the West to imitate the asceticism and the communal piety of the religious communities of Egypt and Asia. St.

Benedict taught the lesson that the ordered life of simplicity and moderation is more acceptable to the Almighty than the record-breaking prodigies of the enthusiast, and that men can achieve in physical association and in regulated community of purpose a life far more God-like than that of the isolated enthusiast. The three-fold vows, terrible in their implications, of chastity, obedience and poverty, were to be observed for life, inside the grounds of an institution, by a society of males determined to secure eternal salvation by devoting themselves to the service of God.

Together they lived, worked, prayed and ruled; with a reasonably varied rationed diet, with due provision for sleep, exercise and intellectual recreation, the coarse, home-spun Benedictine garment, worn night and day, became a symbol of a new order in which the churchman might replace the noble and the soldier. When, in a great prelate, such as Gregory, these virtues were allied to inherited influence and capacity to command, the papacy controlled men, lands and wealth in Italy, equal to those which were at the disposal of a barbarian monarch or the representative of an absentee emperor. "Woe is me, if I preach not the Gospel"—by his teaching and by his example the pope expounded to the plague-stricken, despondent and disillusioned Roman people the Christian way of life as he knew it.

Rivals to Christianity

Gregory had travelled much during his early manhood, knew Constantinople well, administered great estates in Sicily and did not fail to remember the wild and virile tribes who lived in the outer darkness of pagan ignorance north of the Alps. He sternly ordered the rather stupid Italian monk who was to become the first Archbishop of Canterbury to carry the true faith to Britain, and by the time of his death in 604, Kent and much of southern England had adopted the Christian Faith. Two generations passed before it became certain that an English, British or Irish variant of Roman orthodoxy was not to prevail, but in the end the pope's decisive action proved to be of immense significance

DEVELOPMENT OF THE MEDIEVAL CASTLE

This drawing shows how the castle developed between the eleventh and the fourteenth centuries. The earliest form consisted merely of a wooden palisade built on a piece of high ground surrounded by a dry ditch with steep sides. This moated mound was known as the motte (6) and constituted the main defensive position. Abutting on to the motte was a lower part of the fortress, known as the bailey (9), and the whole area of the defences was surrounded by a wooden palisade. Later, on the motte was raised a wooden tower which in turn gave way to a small stone one. At the end of the eleventh century this was replaced by a larger building known as the keep (7). As stone building developed and the need for greater protection arose, stone walls (3) replaced the old wooden palisades. Later, wall towers (4) were erected, battlemented and projecting from the face of the wall to give shooting positions against attempts to scale or mine the walls. A moat (1) was dug around the whole castle and filled with water as an additional defence. Towers developed from the square type shown on the right in the picture to the round and semi-circular varieties on the left. These towers had staircases (11) inside to allow access to the battlements (10) or to the top of the tower itself from a small turret (5) the doorway to which can be seen. The roofs (12) were of wooden tiles or stone shingle. Access to the castle was by the drawbridge (15) to the main gate (13) over which was suspended the portcullis (14). This was a grille which could be lowered to prevent raiders from entering, but permitted the defenders to shoot through it. Above the portcullis is the wall barbican (16), another emplacement from which the main gate could be defended. The great hall (2) was originally in the keep, but about the end of the thirteenth century was moved to the position shown. To show its great size and the manner in which it was supported by huge pillars from the kitchens beneath, the artist has cut away the wall. The chapel (8) shown here is one such as a wealthy castellan would have, though in a smaller castle it might be incorporated in the main building. The building of castles for practical purposes ceased in the fifteenth century; structures bearing resemblance in form dating from 1450 were, in the main, castellated manor houses designed primarily not as defence works but for residential use. Existing castles continued to have military value until after the Civil War when Cromwell ordered them to be slighted and the vast majority were dismantled and otherwise rendered unfit for military purposes.

for Europe and for the world, for it linked Britain permanently with Western Europe.

While Augustine, Mellitus, Paulinus and Felix were preaching successfully from one Saxon village to another, Mediterranean civilization came to an end, and a religion, rivalling Christianity in popular appeal, came to unite the nomads of the desert.

Much obscurity attends the life of the prophet Mohammed who, in 622, at the age of fifty, was able to lead a party of pilgrim fathers from Mecca to Medina. To this illiterate Arab trader were vouchsafed the divine revelations which enthusiastic followers wrote down for all time in the Koran. The religion which he founded was one of the purest monotheism, with any image or representation of the diety fiercely proscribed, with fixed prayers and fasts, observances and marriage regulations, with alcohol eschewed, and rules of conduct with punishments for disobedience carefully and explicitly defined.

Resignation to the will of God was the essence of Islam, but it was combined in the seventh century with an intense conviction that it was the divine will that a united Arab civilization should confront the Eastern Roman Empire and its former dependencies. The Caliphate, which embodied these expansionist longings and which enabled Medina to become for Arabia what Geneva was for Europe in the days of Calvin, was powerful enough— it would have been even more powerful had Islam not developed deep religious divisions soon after the prophet's death.

Jerusalem fell in 638, and became a third holy city for the Arabs. By 647, the inhabitants of Palestine, Syria, the Lebanon, Persia, Iraq, Egypt and the Sudan had been compelled to adopt the new religion. Even Constantinople was in danger, but the Byzantines were tougher than their reputation suggested and the enemy turned elsewhere. The whole northern coast of Africa, formerly so valuable to the empire, became a Mohammedan preserve. From Morocco the passage into Spain in 711 was easy. The Visigothic rule there was neither

EXTENT OF MOHAMMEDAN CONQUEST AT THE TIME OF THE FIRST CRUSADE A.D. 1096

popular nor competent and in an astonishingly short five years the Saracens or Moors (as they began to be known) were ready to move round the Pyrenees. Thus Europe was in serious danger of being forced into submission, through events in Spain, to an alien religion and Asiatic peoples. Narbonne, Montpellier, the Mediterranean coast as far as the Rhône, was occupied; Burgundy and Aquitaine were threatened.

The successors of Clovis had allowed themselves to become phantom kings with the trappings of sovereignty but none of the reality. In their veins ran sacred royal blood, their hair must never be cut, they must come forth in a wagon yoked to oxen, they exuded a kind of magic charm. Youthful degenerates, dying one after another in their early twenties, their authority was wielded for them by their bailiffs, known somewhat curiously as Mayors of the Palace. This office, like all others, soon became hereditary. The head of this family of officials later known as the Carolingians, in 732 was the terrible Charles the Hammer. It was he who turned back the Saracen tide in that year at Poitiers, becoming once more master of most of Gaul, keeping the power of his bishops within bounds while helping forward the missionary efforts of Englishmen like Boniface to bring a little sweetness and light across the Rhine. Charles's son, Pepin, after some dark intrigues and curious adventures, persuaded the pope to approve his assumption of the title and attributes of king of the Franks. He was elected by the people at Soissons, crowned and anointed later, being raised on a shield before the host in arms, while the last Merovingian lost his sacred long hair and disappeared into a monastery.

This was the apotheosis of common

TWELFTH-CENTURY ORGAN

In the Canterbury Psalter, now in the library of Trinity College, Cambridge, is this impression by a twelfth-century monk, Aedwine, of a small pipe organ, the forerunner of the great instruments now installed in churches and cathedrals. This particular organ is played by two men, who are seen giving instructions to the four blowers operating the bellows beneath.

MEDIEVAL DISPENSARY

Drawing from a manuscript Medica, of the early thirteenth century, belonging to Trinity College, Cambridge, showing three stages in the dispensing of medicine—the weighing of the ingredients (shown in the circle)—pounding the mixture with a pestle and mortar—and concocting the "brew" over a fire. On shelves, are dried herbs and pots of simples.

sense; it was also a revolution. The price demanded and paid was the deliverance of the pope out of the hands of the Lombards and the fullest restoration of the estates of the Church in Italy. That Franks should fight Lombards on behalf of St. Peter was something new, and few of Pepin's followers agreed with any enthusiasm, but the thing was done. The independent Vatican City of the twentieth century with its postage stamps, coins, radio transmitter and peculiarly dressed guards is the visible result of Pepin's action.

Teutonic custom demanded the equal sharing of the property of the father by his sons. Pepin's inheritance was therefore shared on his death in 742 by his two sons Charles and Carloman. But throughout the ages the obvious equity of dividing property equally among children has conflicted with the equally obvious desirability of keeping great estates together. Circumstances, therefore, almost forced brothers to quarrel over their inheritance. A serious civil war would have occurred in France had not Carloman opportunely died in 771, leaving his brother (soon to be called "Great" and to be familiar to later generations as Charlemagne) alone and unchallenged. This great and legendary hero, served by men like the equally legendary

and heroic Roland, was, in truth, an enormous giant of a man, six feet four in height and broad in proportion, towering over his subjects, and filled with a restless energy that took him hither and thither, always bent on movement and conquest. Unsuccessful across the Pyrenees, he was more successful beyond the Alps and most successful over the Rhine. Marriage with a daughter of the Lombard King and an appeal from Rome brought him to Italy in 773 where, next year, he became King of the Lombards. More visits to Italy followed, culminating on Christmas Day, 800, in Charlemagne's coronation as Roman Emperor by the pope in the Basilica of St. Peter.

At a time when a woman, Irene, usurped the seat of the Cæsars at Constantinople, this coronation of Charles as "Emperor and Augustus" even if engineered by ecclesiastics and unwillingly acquiesced in by the monarch, was an event of profound significance.

It was a token, as it were, of a new-found unity of western civilization, based no longer on the Mediterranean but upon Italy, France and western Germany. The peoples of the West were now united in allegiance to one overlord; the Church registered and blessed an accomplished

FIFTEENTH-CENTURY FRIAR PREACHING

Reproduced from the manuscript of the Golden Legend now in the Fitzwilliam Museum, Cambridge, this picture shows a mendicant friar preaching before the door of a church. These preachers played an important part throughout the Middle Ages, since, unlike the diocesan clergy, they were free to go where their services were most needed.

fact. With a frontier pushed to the Elbe and beyond, German heathens tamed and superficially Christianized, laws made for all subjects of the emperor, travelling agents sent round to see to their enforcement, scholars and schoolmasters encouraged, Charlemagne left a memory of successful achievement, restless energy and effective administration. What he was, Barbarossa, Charles V, Louis XIV, Napoleon and Hitler sought to become. With his death in 814 the darkness of a changing, feudalized world settled on Europe for more than a century.

Disruptive Forces

The unity of western Christendom had no sooner been exhibited in the person of Charlemagne than it was disrupted from without as well as failing to cohere from within. Louis the Pious has been accused of allowing the Church to become too rich and powerful, and of then dividing his dominions, Teutonic fashion, among his sons. But far more serious were the disruptive forces which formed the second flood of barbarians in Europe, Mongols, Saracens and Vikings. Scandinavia in the ninth century had been neither Romanized nor Christianized: the Northmen were the finest shipbuilders and navigators in the world, a large population in a poor country, fierce, warlike and predatory. The British Isles, Iceland, Greenland, Flanders, France felt the weight of their mighty outward thrust; any river that was navigable from the sea provided an inlet; the Strait of Gibraltar was passed, North Africa, southern France, even Italian cities such as Pisa were attacked.

In England, to which the invaders, chiefly Danes, devoted much attention, the influence of the Scandinavians in the east was long and profoundly felt; in France, Rollo, leader of the Northmen, made himself master of Rouen, so that by 911 the province of Normandy was on the way to substantial independence of Charles the

Simple and a new and great breeding ground of future colonizers, to be known as Normans, had come into existence. Wherever they went they showed amazing adaptability, and equally amazing capacity for organization. After some preliminary looting of Church property, the Scandinavian settlers were willing not only to embrace Christianity but soon to propagate it. To traditions of equality they added a rare willingness to obey when obedience was necessary for success; disciplined subordination without servile submission to any overlord carried these unique warriors as conquerors to England, southern Italy, Sicily and Palestine.

Power of the Church

Before the magic year A.D. 1000, the organized Christian Church of the West had become an international society much more advanced and with far greater powers of resiliency and recovery than had been the case when Gregory I had struggled to assert the prerogatives of the Roman Pontiff against the Eastern Patriarchs, or when Leo III had begged and secured the protection of the ruler of the Franks against the Lombards. It was another Leo who, about 850, secured Rome against the Saracens and fortified against all intruders what came to be known as the Leonine City. Physically secure, Pope Nicholas I (858-867), could make use of the strange semi-forgery known as the Pseudo-Isidorian Decretals, a collection of decrees of early popes, supposed to have been miraculously discovered in Spain but actually invented for local purposes in the province of Reims and sent to Rome, to exalt the power of the pope at the expense of the metropolitans, to make excommunication a powerful weapon and largely to free the papacy from dependence on the Empire.

No sooner had this taken place than the popes themselves fell into the power of the Roman nobility. Just as archbishops, bishops and abbots everywhere, needing, in an age of violence, the protection which only the expensively equipped mailed horseman could give, became dependent upon the great landowners who were their neighbours, so, too, the Bishop of Rome became the nominee of Roman factions and Italian adventurers. Contemporaries told the darkest stories of the tenth-century papacy; and because the greater ecclesiastical offices were at the disposal of the nobility and for the nobility, the territorial organization of the Church into provinces, bishoprics and parishes, was retained and even improved, while the clergy continued to provide the literate class alone capable of drafting charters and documents, of comprehending and expounding the scriptures and of reading the classics. The highest and the basest motives, repentance for sin or fear of the hereafter, combined with a comfortable feeling that it was always possible to arrange for Church property to be kept "in the family" secured the physical possessions of the Catholic Church.

In addition, the great experiment in co-operation initiated by St. Benedict had resulted in the establishment of many Benedictine houses in the West. Alone and isolated, dependent upon the desires and capacity of the abbot, the monasteries of Merovingian and Carolingian times fell into disrepute and decadence. From this they were rescued to some extent by St. Chrodegang of Metz and St. Benedict of Aniane, but decisively by the great Burgundian monastery founded in 910 by William of Aquitaine at Cluny.

Growth of Feudalism

Partly by a new idea—i.e. making new houses dependent upon Cluny for guidance, inspection and control, but mainly by finding the right men, among them Odo, Maieul, Hugh, an incomparable succession of great abbots—the Cluniac movement became a source of reform and missionary activity, and a model for others to copy. At Cluny, efficiency was combined with goodness, and with growing security in France, its influence spread.

Soon men came to realize that the growth of feudalism was attended by two natural consequences where the possessions of the Church were concerned. A spiritual office, that of bishop or abbot in particular, carried with it power and wealth. In the tenth and eleventh centuries, therefore, men were paying a cash premium for high

H.E.L.—C*

BUSY HARVEST SCENE IN A

In a village of the fourteenth century, the artist has shown villagers gathering corn which they will store in the great barn, seen in the centre, and later will grind, to provide food for the winter, at the watermill on the right. A second field is being ploughed ready for next season's crops while the third on the left remains fallow and is used for cattle and pigs to feed on the weeds. These three fields, in which each peasant had his own strip, were used

VILLAGE OF FEUDAL TIMES

in rotation. The houses were of mud and wattle, and each had its own plot of ground much in the same way as houses do today, and one villager keeps bees besides the usual pigs and oxen, honey then being the only known method of sweetening. The manor house, beyond which is the common grazing ground, has a courtyard for sheltering animals in time of war. On the left in the picture is the church and in the distance a castle, surrounded by forest.

Church offices which they then hoped to make hereditary. To any such tendencies, however, Church policy had long been opposed. Character, piety, suitability, merit, the wishes of clergy and people must be decisive in the election of the higher clergy—purchase was condemned as simony. It had further come to be accepted that no priest might marry and found a family. The monastic reformers were particularly opposed to clerical concubinage and against these two evils, simony and concubinage, Cluny waged war. Little help came from Rome before the year 1000, but in the eleventh century the popes were released from bondage to the local nobles by imperial intervention, and it became possible for reformers to be freely chosen as popes and to resume their earlier influence and power.

Of these reformers at Rome the best known, and rightly, is Hildebrand, Pope Gregory VII. Nephew of the Abbot of St. Mary of the Aventine, with quite possibly some Jewish blood in his veins, Hildebrand, because of his character, abilities and opportunities, was created a cardinal by Leo IX and became a leading figure at the Roman *Curia*. Just then the Holy Roman Empire suffered the rare but disastrous occurrence of a minority. Henry III died in 1056, leaving a six-year-old son, Henry IV. For ten years the imperial authority suffered from attacks by factious nobles and ambitious prelates almost unresisted by an intriguing and incompetent female regent. The common man, whose leading interest was that there should be peace among the great ones, found instead that life in the fields became less secure as quarrels were fought out around him. Lands and rights that had belonged to the emperor passed to nobles and bishops, and over the wide territories of the Church as well as over the

EARLY SIEGE GUNS IN ACTION

French armies in 1390 assaulting the fortified town of Africa, on the Barbary coast; an illumination from a manuscript copy of Froissart's Chronicles of the late fifteenth century, now in the Harleian Collection at the British Museum.

appointment of the hierarchy, the reformed papacy was quick to claim a favourable position. In particular, Gregory VII believed, and fought all his life to secure, that the symbols of ecclesiastical power, such as the bishop's crozier, should not be passed on by lay hands (i.e. of king or emperor). Men understood the concrete far better than the abstract, and round the investiture contest, simony and clerical marriage, great issues were fought out.

The pope had the better case, better put by his propaganda services; he was able to sow dissension among the vassals of Henry IV, while (although not without difficulty) uniting the ecclesiastics of Western Europe in defence of his ideals. Henry IV submitted in 1077 at Canossa, just in time to save his crown and, by a personal humiliation, regained much of his former position. Political disaster followed, however, and, later, Pope Gregory had to appeal to the Normans in southern Italy for help. He died at Salerno in 1085, in gloom and depression. None the less he had succeeded in re-establishing what the coronation of Charlemagne by the pope had suggested, that the spiritual power was superior to the temporal and that the disposal of royal crowns lay with Rome. What was sauce for the emperor was also sauce for the kings; Philip I of France relatively easily bent to the papal will, while even the masterful William the Conqueror gained his position in England partly because he steadfastly upheld the Hildebrandine ideals.

After the eleventh century, Rome in many respects provided the Christian world with a working international organization. Advised by the College of Cardinals, princes of the Church drawn from every country, served by the *Curia*, the most efficient and most highly organized body of civil servants in the world, the popes steadily became more influential. What had formerly been a variegated mosaic of biblical precepts, conciliar decrees, papal opinions and advice, was gathered together about 1140 into a textbook, the *Decretum*, that became, later, the first part of the codified Canon Law. For much that concerned human welfare—questions of conduct, perjury, wills, marriages, tithes, as well as clerical litigation proper—the pope's court provided an international tribunal, the validity of whose decisions was everywhere accepted, even if sometimes accompanied by complaints about expense or allegations of corruption. Ordinary men knew more of Church law than they did of State law; the pardoner and the archdeacon were more familiar figures than the itinerant justices, the peasant was more likely to hear the contents of a papal bull or brief expounded than to know of royal assizes, writs and parliamentary statutes.

All Western and Central Europe was divided into provinces (archbishoprics), dioceses (bishoprics) and parishes. The parish church was the only large and substantial building that most men and women ever saw, and its minister was often the only man for some miles around who could, though sometimes with difficulty, read and write.

In addition to the considerable number of secular clergy, there was a large force of Regulars—monks and friars. From the days of St. Benedict to those of Innocent III the services of the monasteries to Europe were immense; they were havens of piety and scholarship, their members respectable and influential. After the Benedictines and the Cluniacs came the Cistercians, severe puritanical reformers owing their original inspiration to the work of Stephen Harding, the Englishman (abbot in 1110), but achieving permanence and popularity because of the deserved reputation for holiness and eloquence of that great missionary and leader of men, St. Bernard of Clairvaux (c. 1090-1153). Fewer in numbers were the severe Carthusians (the monks to whom Wesley often alluded in his sermons), living terribly ascetic lonely lives, representatives of an order that could boast that it had never been reformed because it had never needed any reform. At the end of the Middle Ages when Sir Thomas More seriously contemplated, and equally seriously rejected, the monastic life, it was with the Carthusians that he had proposed to associate himself. Almost equally few in numbers, but very different in the character of their discipline, were the canons regular, the Premonstratensians, who were almost beneficed clergy living by a Rule and in community, and the Augustinians, more explicitly monastic and later to attract young Martin Luther.

The power of the medieval papacy reached its highest point at the opening of the thirteenth century. Innocent III (1198-1216) was strong enough to secure the submission, for interested reasons it is true, of Philip Augustus, the most powerful monarch that France had known since Charlemagne, and John of England. Innocent III likewise decided the fate of the empire by his support of the claims of Frederick of Hohenstaufen. He also interfered across the Pyrenees and in Scandinavia, as well as in Italy. In 1215, Magna Carta year, he presided over the œcumenical council of the Lateran which defined doctrine in such essential matters as transubstantiation, encouraged yet another crusade, anathematized heretics, and secured the abolition, long overdue, of trial by ordeal, which was based on the belief that guilt or innocence could be detected by dropping the accused in water or requiring him to carry a red-hot iron for a prescribed distance.

Underground Activity

Heresy, ranging from simple denial of the elements of the Christian Faith to the assertion of the need for better lives of clergy and laity alike, based upon an open Bible, had recently made its appearance on a large scale. There was some discontent in Rome itself but this subsided; the real focus of heresy was in the south of France. The Languedoc was independent of the King of France, the most powerful local magnate being the Count of Toulouse, Raymond VI. His dominions were affected by a spontaneous semi-communist movement in the neighbourhood of ever-turbulent Milan, that of the Humiliati; and by the Poor Men of Lyons, severe psalm-singing, puritanical opponents of the clergy who were known as Waldensians, after their leader, and whose organization showed remarkable powers of persistence and underground activity.

The sharp-witted passionate citizens and nobles of the south had a philosophy as well as practical grievances based on a desire to read the Bible in the mother-tongue or to listen to popular sermons. The superficial but attractive notions of Dualism, implicit in much of St. Augustine's writings (as later, in those of Calvin) were developed around the episcopal city of Albi, and their adherents became known as Albigenses. The leaders were the Perfect, who taught that matter was sinful and who practised extremes of abstinence both in food and in living. They had a sacrament of supreme reconciliation with God Who alone was good, the *consolamentum*. Their followers, who accepted this teaching but lived ordinary country or civic lives, received the sacrament only when dying.

Henry Suppressed by Force

Such an intellectual movement could scarcely have obtained a large number of followers, even in Provence, without greater inducements than a simple creed of renunciation. Support came to them because the secular clergy were peculiarly lax in their habits and neglectful of their parochial duties, while the southern nobles looked with greedy eyes on the wide Church lands and supported those who advocated a clergy freed from the ties of property.

Argument was ineffective and the movement grew until much of the country of Toulouse seemed lost to Mother Church. Threats, therefore, followed on pleading; a special papal legate was sent to talk to the count who submitted to the application of sanctions in the form of interdict and personal excommunication. The legate, however, was murdered in 1208 by an over-zealous vassal, an act as fatal as the murder of Becket had been a generation previously. For it enabled Innocent III to bring in armed force; the archers and cavalry of Philip Augustus and then of Louis VIII came south, burning and massacring on behalf of orthodoxy. Brute force was successful and in twenty years all signs of public disbelief had been eliminated, Catholics sometimes dying alongside heretics, as at Béziers, when wild bodies of armed northerners, bent on conquest and loot, cared little to differentiate between the birds who flocked together. And thus the

ASSAULT ON A TOWN BY AN ENGLISH ARMY

The storming of a coastal town by a landing party armed with bows and arrows, primitive guns and culverins is the subject of this illustration from the "Chronique d'Angleterre," by Jean de Wavrin, a manuscript in the British Museum.

CHIEF MEDIEVAL TRADE ROUTES

MILES

0   125   250   375   500

Chief Trade Routes   Arrows show main direction of   Fairs
Trade in Product Superimposed

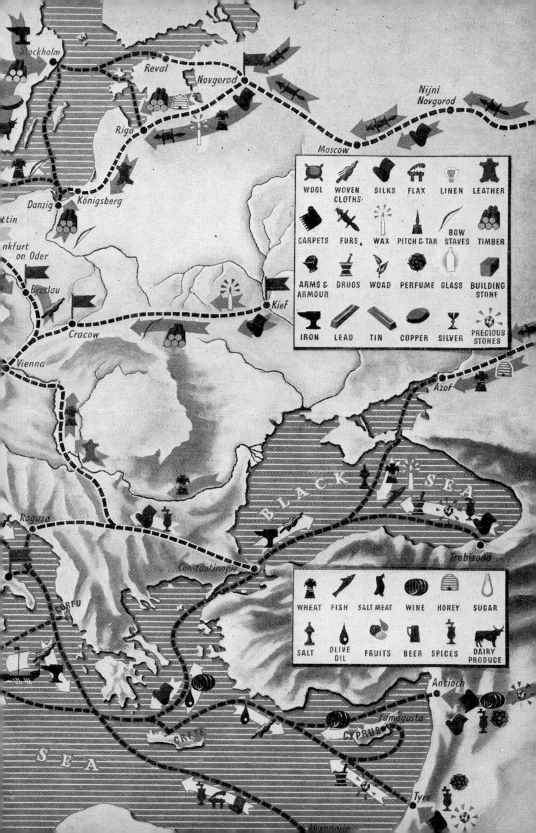

SCHOOLMASTER AND PUPILS IN THE FIFTEENTH CENTURY

This miniature from a manuscript of 1492, in the British Museum, shows a medieval school-master seated in a high-backed Gothic chair with open book before him and four pupils seated on stools. Pupils were few in those days and schools often met in the church porch or the gatehouse of monasteries. Above is a hanging shelf on which are two ink-horns and dredgers of sand used to dry the ink before the days of blotting paper.

authority of Paris was extended to the Mediterranean while at the same time papal supremacy was reasserted in the lands between the Rhône and the Loire.

Security against a recrudescence of the Albigensian heresy was found in a medieval institution as characteristic of the age as either parliament or university—the Inqui-sition. At first the "ordinary" (the diocesan bishop), then special papal legates, and finally a systematized organization of spies and detectives used spiritual weapons, added to imprisonment, third degree and torture, to ensure that all went to Mass and did not venture to criticize the established religion. The medieval Inquisition, stimu-lated by authorizations to require temporal support where necessary and by a proce-dure which rendered condemnation (usually accompanied by confiscation of property although relatively seldom by the extreme penalty of death at the stake) easy, was effective enough. Only when, as in Bohemia in the fifteenth century, supported by an army were heretics able to survive.

Weight of learning as well as weight of numbers was used to eliminate opposition to the teaching of the Church. The noble-born Castilian, Dominic of Guzman, was sent as a kind of missionary to Toulouse. By his example, for he was as ascetic as any of the Perfect, by his preaching, and by his powers of argument, he converted many. He also attracted some like-minded priests and obtained the support of some rich laymen; soon the little group formed itself into an Order and obtained papal recogni-tion. They were to be the preachers *par excellence*, the trained disputants of the Church as well as the exponents of the faith. Learning was of the first consequence for such men and Dominican friars were among the most zealous students.

The Dominicans were an order of students and preachers, but that they were friars at all, pledged to individual and corporate poverty, and undertaking constant intercourse with the world (as opposed to the monks who were theoretically confined within the bounds of their house and pledged only to personal poverty), was due to the life work of St. Francis of Assisi (1182-1226), the founder of the other great order of friars.

As a young man, illness, and a single-minded reliance upon certain gospel precepts, decided him to embrace a life of poverty and service. There were plenty of destitute men in the thirteenth century, but it was new for them to be told to delight in their poverty and that salvation could be had through complete renunciation of all private goods. Added to this was the duty of leading others to God by example, advice and exhortation; above all, perfect humility. The man made the order. However impracticable St. Francis was in an imperfect world, his determination that his followers should combine personal renunciation with care for the spiritual welfare of others, was decisive. The attractiveness of the new teaching and the new teacher soon

KNIGHTS JOUSTING

Two knights armed cap-à-pie in combat before the king, René d'Anjou and ladies of the court. The king points with an arrow to the victor who has pierced the hand of his adversary. The illustration is from the fifteenth-century manuscript "Petit Jehan de Saintré," by Antoine de la Salle, now preserved in the British Museum.

brought followers. The "lesser brethren" obtained the indispensable support of the pope, while organization and regimentation, neither very acceptable to St. Francis himself, followed. Although Lady Poverty became in the end a titular rather than a reigning queen, the ideal of service in the world, among the poor and for the poor, was not lost.

From Italy the Grey Friars carried their teachings of simplicity and service to France, Spain, Germany and the British Isles. Originality they combined with unquestioned orthodoxy; they were soon, also, to prove as acceptable students and teachers at Paris and Oxford as the Dominicans who borrowed the notion of corporate poverty from them. Pope Innocent III once dreamt that his palace, the Lateran, was about to collapse but was prevented from doing so by a friar who held up its walls. The dream came true in the sense that but for St. Francis and St. Dominic, national Churches out of communion with Rome might have made their appearance before the sixteenth century. The devout England of Henry III, engaged in putting on an incomparable "white robe of churches," shows a high esteem for the Grey Friars and, in modern times, more has been done in Britain than in any country to preserve and interpret the records of their medieval achievement.

St. Francis and Evangelization

Among the unfulfilled desires of St. Francis had been the evangelization of the Saracens to whom he paid a brief visit. Since the end of the tenth century, when Italy itself was threatened with an Islamic incursion, a mighty change in the religious and political balance of power had been wrought by the Crusades.

The First Crusade, led by Godfrey of Bouillon, Baldwin of Flanders and Bohemund of Otranto, moved spontaneously eastwards in 1096. The appeal of the Eastern Emperor, the willing eloquence of Pope Urban II and some religious enthusiasts, the restless and irresistible energy of the Norman-French knights, promises of eternal salvation, hopes of loot or of profitable foreign investment (a fief in a new country), combined with the ever lively fear of Islam to initiate a movement, characteristically medieval and largely unsuccessful. No permanent western state, under international guidance, could be established on the shores of the eastern Mediterranean, but freedom of access to Bethlehem and the Holy Sepulchre was secured and the main onslaught of the East on the West postponed for more than two centuries, by which time not even the genius of Mohammed II and Suleiman the Magnificent could make it successful.

King of Jerusalem

Jerusalem was entered by the crusaders on July 15, 1099, Godfrey of Bouillon becoming Advocate of the Holy Sepulchre, a title which pleased his own piety and modesty and emphasized the essentially ecclesiastical character of the whole business. He was really, however, what his successors became, feudal King of Jerusalem and feudal overlord of a new state. Thus, in the eyes of many, the war was over. In fact, however, it had only begun and it had been so far successful only because the Mohammedans were disunited as never before and were so preoccupied with civil strife as to be willing to neglect, momentarily, the most sacred of all military obligations, that of constant war against the enemies of Allah. When the great Saladin had secured co-operation between Syria and Egypt and had reduced the independent emirs, like Usama, to obedience, the continued authority and even residence of Europeans in the Holy Land became increasingly precarious. The Westerners had great advantages; sea-power gave them an incomparable base and secured the continued supplies of men and equipment so long as these were available. They had better weapons, better discipline, more money, and the incredible genius for conquest and organization shown by Normans everywhere. The whole weight of the papacy was behind them.

Fifty years after the first knights had set out, another great wave of religious enthusiasm was set in motion by St. Bernard, who preached Conrad III into the second crusade and induced Louis VII of

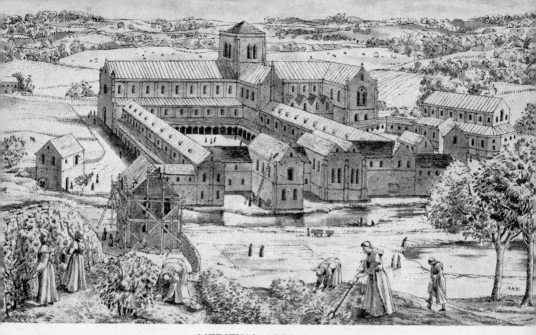

MEDIEVAL ABBEY

In the fifteenth century the abbey was ideally a hive of industry and the centre of what cultural life existed in its neighbourhood. It was a self-supporting community and the artist here shows the monks and lay brothers busy about their varied tasks in a Cistercian abbey. The abbey church is in the middle distance, the cloistered quadrangle branching from it into the foreground enclosed on the left by the living quarters of the lay brothers and servants. The monks lived in the building enclosing the quadrangle on the right. The buildings at the end of the cloister and parallel to the stream are the kitchens and refectory (or dining-room) of the monks. The large building on the right in the picture is the monk's infirmary, the lay brothers having their own separate infirmary and refectory. The house in the left foreground being roofed is the guest house reserved for visitors and travellers.

France to join him in an ill-conceived and unsuccessful enterprise. It was worse than a failure, for it provoked successful retaliation; in 1187 Jerusalem was regained for Islam, but the title of King of Jerusalem long remained to adorn various European monarchs. In sight of the walls of captured Jerusalem, but not inside them, came Richard I of England, conqueror of Cyprus and Acre. Individualist to the core, he was the embodiment of a difference of national outlook between English and French knights, now for the first time apparent. On the same crusade, the most popular of emperors since Charlemagne, Frederick Barbarossa, had perished *en route*.

There were other crusades to follow, three more at least, one of which led to the fall of Constantinople and to the temporary formation of an unwelcome and incompetent Latin empire in the Balkan peninsula; another which the greatest of medieval French kings, St. Louis, led to Egypt; and a third which attracted the future Edward I of England—but none achieved its purpose. When Acre fell in 1291 two centuries of Western effort had to be written off. Yet men had learnt much about the Orient, the Italian cities had grown rich on the proceeds of transport and the exchange of commodities, kings had profited by the absence of noble rivals and the popes had obtained the credit for the initiation and general direction of the whole enterprise.

Conditions of trade, of course, varied enormously with the centuries and with the countries concerned. It is, however, possible to generalize in that, throughout the Middle Ages, transport was slow and laborious. The Roman roads were used

BUSY FIFTEENTH-CENTURY PORT

St. Maurice d'Agaune, on the River Rhône, a town and port which flourished in the fifteenth century, is illustrated in the "Commentaries of Cæsar," a contemporary manuscript now preserved in the British Museum.

when available and so long as they were usable, but few long stretches of road were safe for travellers or passable for wagons. Goods went by mule or pack-horse and men travelled in company for protection. Pilgrim routes and trade routes were for this reason often identical for much of the way. The alternative mode of transport was by water, by coastwise ships and by boats along the rivers. These latter, although often impeded by many tolls, were invaluable links in the commercial chain.

The Mediterranean was necessarily the centre of most of the luxury trades. Intercourse with the Middle East had never entirely ceased since Roman times, and Alexandria rivalled Constantinople as the

permanent depot and emporium where gems, silks, ivory, carpets, muslin, spices and sugar sweetmeats might be obtained. The crusades heightened the demand for these and similar commodities, while more orderly conditions in the West enabled the rich to pay for them. Bezants from the Eastern Empire, augustals from Sicily, gold florins from Florence formed a kind of standard international coinage, while bills of exchange, if introduced by the Jews, were soon adopted by Christian traders.

Venice and Genoa, most obviously, controlled the Levant trade, Venice constantly expanding the republican empire of St. Mark to secure a monopoly of this trade and finding itself obliged to embark upon expansion by land, westwards to the River

Mincio and eastwards to the River Isonzo in order to secure the northward passage over the Brenner to the Rhine and Elbe or north-east to the Danube. From Genoa, similarly, the road was clear to Basle and to the Rhône. Exotic luxuries joined with homely necessities to find distribution centres in the great fairs, particularly in Champagne, whither merchants from all parts resorted and where the international code of merchant law was applied in specially constituted courts. Into the countryside the goods found their way on the mule and even on the back of the transient pedlar.

The wine trade, originating principally from southern France, was concentrated on the Garonne and Dordogne, with Bordeaux as the chief distributing centre for England and the northern countries. From England there came in exchange wool, wool-fells and leather, English wool being renowned as the finest in the world. It was made up into fine cloth in Flanders and in Tuscany, and by the fourteenth century, really elaborate methods of collection, credit and payment were operative. Schemes of insurance were not unknown, and through them, as also by other methods, the law of the Church forbidding usury might be evaded without difficulty. Kings encouraged and protected trade in bulk, for it provided a welcome addition to their declining rents and feudal revenues. When, as in north Germany, there was no effective monarch to act as guardian, the cities themselves leagued together to secure common protection. The northern trade in furs, skins, hemp and herrings was largely controlled by the Hanseatic League with its depots (known as Steelyards in England) in various cities and arrangements for debt-collecting and dealing with defaulters.

An Industrialized Land

It is a little curious, although explicable by internal conditions, that the German cities, even such notable ones as Cologne, Frankfurt, Nuremberg, Augsburg or Ratisbon, never achieved an importance comparable with that of the cities of the Low Countries or of Italy. The turbulent democracy of Bruges, Ghent, Brussels and Liége was the offspring of a relatively industrialized land where weaving, fulling, dyeing and all the operations of clothmaking kept a busy proletariat in steady employment. There, too, outcrop coalmining, armour-plate manufacture, metal-working of all kinds, combined with a carrying trade and exchange facilities to form a real nucleus of energetic enterprise. When the dukes of Burgundy by inheritance, marriage, purchase and violence entered into possession of these cities they were able to draw from them wealth in abundance provided they interfered neither with their trade nor with their liberties. When Charles the Bold did both, he was lost.

Political Activity

With the Italian cities the case was different. After the death of Frederick II (1250) Naples failed to advance and became the ineffective capital of a ramshackle, feudal state, while Rome, in spite of republican idealism, associated with Cola di Rienzo (1312-54), was necessarily subordinate to its bishop who was also pope. It was in north Italy that the communes asserted their independence of emperor, pope and nobles alike. Imperial invasions had caused the rise of the Guelf and Ghibelline parties, nominally supporters of papacy and empire respectively, but actually adherence to either was often as meaningless as the allegiance of the Cockney schoolboy to Oxford or Cambridge. The nobles, alone in Europe, were largely, as a class, excluded from political power, unless they were prepared to become citizens and live within the city walls. This did not, moreover, mean mob-rule, democracy, or even popular government, but it led to feverish political activity soon degenerating into faction fights, to struggles for power and the spoils of office and, too frequently, to a characteristically Italian submission to a dictatorship, avowed or disguised. In some cities the *podesta*, the supposedly neutral "foreigner" who could moderate disputes, became the governor of the town and one after another the Lombard cities which had leagued against Barbarossa, lost unity and liberty.

Mighty Milan fell to a tyranny, under the first Visconti and then the Sforza families. In Florence the magnates lost ground to the commons, and these in turn were riven by quarrels between merchants and artisans. The richer element won and their victory was clinched by a proletarian revolt in 1378, within the same decade as the Peasants' Revolt in England.

The rising failed, and the Medici banking firm used the situation with great adroitness to the advantage of the family. In the fifteenth century the artistic and cultural achievement of Florence was largely due to this fact.

Venetian Empire

Venice remained unique. There the doge (dux, duce) became a kind of lord mayor or constitutional monarch and the affairs of the great overseas power were managed by a cabinet, known as the Council of Ten, and limited to a governing class of a known number of families. Partly because geography made the foreign policy of Venice clearly outside the scope of party politics, partly because the city grew wealthy and renowned under its constitution, and partly because jealous and greedy enemies constantly threatened, the city long remained powerful and wise but had to struggle hard against Genoa for supremacy in the Mediterranean. A long war weakened both cities but left Venice in the end victorious and exhausted. When in the fifteenth century the Turk attacked again, the Venetian Empire offered, as before, notable resistance, but this time it was on the defensive and, ultimately, mainly unsuccessful. Even so, at the end of the Middle Ages, Venice was rightly regarded with wonder, admiration and jealousy as one of the great powers of the world.

If medieval civilization reached a peak of perfection in its few notable great cities, the achievement in this sphere must not be allowed to detract from less spectacular but in some ways more permanent efforts made elsewhere. Civilized Europe, at the beginning of the Middle Ages, was the Europe of the Roman Empire, the lands west of the Rhine and south of the Danube. By the end of the Middle Ages the Christian religion, the authority of the pope and of the secular prince, the essentials of law and order, had been brought as far as Poland and the great belt of the eastern marshes. Charlemagne had settled the area between the Rhine and the Elbe; the work of his successors was to assert their authority and religion in the more difficult land between the Elbe and the Oder and even beyond.

The steady pressure eastwards of this colonizing process continued relentlessly. The stem-duchies of Germany were nothing if not aggressive; Albert the Bear, who established himself in Brandenburg in 1135, and Henry the Lion, who founded Lübeck in 1158, were, with some justice, claimed by Nazi writers as early examples of Hitler. The frontier, as in nineteenth-century America, was a moving one. In the thirteenth century the Teutonic Knights came from the Holy Land and from Hungary to Christianize Prussia, Courland and Livonia. Men from the Low Countries and even from England joined in the work. Towns were built, marshes drained, forests cleared. The monasteries proved themselves invaluable allies of the early settlers and frontier blockhouses like Berlin and Marienburg provided bases from which Wends, Poles and Czechs could be forced into submission. A Poland converted to the Catholic faith and allied with Lithuania, however, proved not only unsubmissive but at Tannenburg (1410) secured an independence of the Teutonic warriors which marked the beginning of the modern Polish state.

Landowners

The fact that knights of all nations joined in the crusades against the Eastern heathens and that people from many parts of Europe came to populate (somewhat thinly) the German lands, provides evidence of a certain community of outlook and accepted ordering of society which characterized the medieval world. Land was the necessary and practically the only basis of life, and therefore of society. Landowners and land cultivators, knights and peasants, were the two classes to be found in every country. Kings were but the largest landowners and the clergy, too, owned, corporately, large estates. The soil was cultivated in primitive fashion along traditional lines, the village community working in co-operation to provide subsistence for itself and a surplus for its owner. The great open fields ploughed by oxen could provide food in no other way. Life was hard and living conditions were often wretched for the serf, but he was conscious that most others were like him and that he fared as his father had done.

The knight was a monopolist to whom many customary payments were due (e.g. for the use of his oven or mill) but he was often far away and his bailiff or agent was usually a peasant himself. If the landowner was a cleric there would be tithe to pay as well as personal service, but tithe paid in kind at least meant that the fortunes of priests and bishops depended largely upon the weather and the state of the crops—they shared the life of their parishioners and tenants to the full. Only the knight, who was expected to protect his serfs from attack, could afford a few rough luxuries. He had horses and armour, he lived in a defensible stone house or castle with a number of attendants, he knew something of the world outside. His lady might dress in dyed cloth and experience some of the pleasures and difficulties of entertainment. The castle was the school for future knights, who, as boys, learnt riding, jousting, hawking and the rough martial sports that prepared for the tournament and battlefield. Troubadours recited the valiant deeds of legendary heroes and the chaplain provided most of the learning that was necessary for an illiterate society. All over Europe a common code of conduct—chivalry—assured acceptable intercourse between the members of the ruling class of every country.

The townsman was not easily fitted into this framework, although the town was usually, like the monastery, under a corporate landowner exacting services and dues. The towns were the natural allies of the kings, who maintained order, and the homes, for the most part, of free artisans. "City air makes a man free," they said, and the serf who resided within city walls for over a year was no longer subject to his former owner. In the towns, coins were made and circulated; the greater landowner had his town house and was often cordially disliked by the artisans. The numerous popular insurrections of the fourteenth century were as much town affairs as country affairs, as the English

FARMERS' YEAR SHOWN IN TAPESTRY

Seasonable occupations on the farm are depicted in this long tapestry frieze now in the Victoria and Albert Museum. It dates from the fifteenth century and is of German workmanship. This section shows corn being reaped in August, followed in September by harrowing.

Peasants' Revolt (1381) amply illustrates. Town life was more varied than that of the countryside, but often less healthy. Houses were small and crowded together, fires were frequent and disastrous, while epidemics, of which the Black Death is the most familiar, took a terrible toll of human life wherever men congregated in numbers.

Knight, bishop and corporate town alike owed military service to the supreme landlord, king or emperor. Churchmen and townsmen paid money rather than personal service and this in itself strengthened the power of the Crown. It also helped to bring about the rise of the professional soldier, who, as retainer or mercenary, found a permanent occupation which at least avoided the painful monotony of perpetual field labour. No medieval force could stand up to an efficiently conducted cavalry charge by armoured knights, but efficiency was often lacking and peasant armies under royal leadership and armed with a new weapon such as the English long-bow could do much execution. The Hundred Years War between England and France illustrates from its length and its conduct much of what was best and worst in medieval society. The disciplined forces that followed Edward III and Henry V to notable victories were recruited in part by conscription possible only in an efficiently administered country, and some who learnt from these campaigns the tactics and organization necessary for success, passed on to Italy to sell their services to the city-states.

Medieval society is sometimes regarded as static. In so far as this was so, it can be accounted for by the warlike habits of the nobility and the celibacy of the clergy. The best elements in society were constantly removed by the violence of almost perpetual warfare, including the mimic warfare of the tournament, and by the refusal of the educated class to assume family responsibilities. Not without reason are castles and cathedrals the principal monuments of medieval achievement, for they embody the

FIELD OF THE CLOTH OF GOLD, 1520

Incidents in the meeting of Henry VIII of England and Francis I of France are reproduced in great detail in this engraving from a contemporary painting now at Hampton Court. The meeting near Ardres in north-east France, was arranged by Francis, who was seeking England's aid in a dispute with the Emperor Charles V, and was staged in the most magnificent and impressive manner. The English cavalcade is seen approaching from the left escorting King Henry, who is preceded by the Marquis of Dorset carrying the Sword of State.

needs, the resources and the aspirations of the leading men of their age.

The Hundred Years War, an important agent in the disintegration of medieval society, was fought on the soil of France. In that land, too, evidence of another kind —that men's ideas were undergoing a steady change—had already become apparent to all. The pope who made the most extravagant claims for the supremacy of the Holy See over all kings was Boniface VIII (1294-1303), the inaugurator of the Papal Jubilee of 1300 which was so successful and so widely imitated later. He it was who came into collision with a determined French king, Philip the Fair, the employer of astute and crafty agents and the relentless champion of power politics and secular supremacy. A powerful French king was not prepared to forego the right to tax French clergy and was not willing to accept a papal claim to ultimate world sovereignty. Picking a quarrel over some words let drop by a bibulous bishop, Philip sent his agent, Guillaume de Nogaret, to accuse the pope of vice and heresy. Nogaret stormed the papal palace and so shocked the aged pope that he died soon after.

Administrative Reform

Popes were never so powerful later. The authority of the secular prince was upheld by Dante and, more explicitly, the supremacy of the lay state by Marsilius of Padua, the champion of the emperor, Lewis the Bavarian. Two years after the death of Boniface VIII, a French pope, Clement V (1305-14), decided to live at Avignon, where his palace was separated by only the Rhône from the French dominions. Men believed that the Avignon popes, seven in all, were now the agents of the kings of France, an impression heightened by the violent suppression of the Templars. Actually a great work of centralization and administrative reform came from Avignon, but the greater efficiency meant more financial pressure on the clergy, and those outside France, particularly in England, protested noisily. Litigants spoke more of the expense of the Roman *curia* than of its impartial justice, and, influenced as much by his observations

of fourteenth-century papalism in England as by scholastic speculation, Wyclif gave a radical twist to current dissatisfaction.

As he was writing, the appeal of St. Catharine of Siena and the pressure of Christian opinion induced Gregory XI (1370-78) to take his cardinals and administration back to Rome, but with alarming results. Two popes were elected in 1378 in circumstances that made it easy for those who had political and economic reasons to adhere to one or the other.

Restoring Unity

This great schism lasted from 1378 to 1415 and forced men to think hard about the purpose and meaning of the Christian Church and about the nature of international obligations. For a generation, men wrangled about the best way to restore unity to western Christendom and at last succeeded in doing so at a meeting of the united Catholic nations at Constance in Agincourt year, 1415. Although an emperor, Sigismund, took the lead in getting the assembly summoned, it was the now consciously national prelates, especially those of England, who secured the election of Martin V in 1417. Reform was discussed, too, but nothing was done.

It had been hoped by some of the wisest Church leaders that General Councils might meet at regular intervals and introduce some element of democratic, or at least of episcopal and national, control into what had become an autocracy. Two such councils, Siena and Basle, followed Constance but they failed to bring peace to the Czech Hussites, to join forces with the Greek Christians or to secure either moral reform or improved administration. An anti-pope was elected in 1439, but men had had enough of double-popes and the conciliar movement ended in failure. The modern state, national and omnicompetent, was on its way.

To Constance in 1415 had come a figure little noted at the time, but in fact the harbinger of a new European outlook upon life, Poggio Bracciolini. This man was a priest and a papal secretary, but his life was devoted neither to religion nor to administration. He had learnt some Greek from Chrysoloras at Florence—for Greek was being studied in Italy half a century before Constantinople fell to Mohammed the Conqueror in 1453—and he could write Latin most elegantly. With a passionate fervour he hunted out classical manuscripts from every corner of Western Europe, including England. Never was there so blatant a self-advertiser, and the indefatigable devotee of Roman letters and archæology exhibited his Latin style to the world in publications of strange indecency. The craze for elegant Latinity was started by Petrarch (1304-74) and it lasted beyond the Middle Ages, slowly merging into the creative study of the civilization of Greece and Rome which is still refreshingly active.

From the classical revival, which is part of the Renaissance, sprang a real emancipation of the human intellect which resulted both in devastating (and in some cases unanswerable) criticism of medieval Christianity, and in a revived interest in religion and in the Bible, of which Erasmus was the apostle and the Protestant Reformation a consequence. The Italian city-state was the forcing ground of this strange and prolific movement; the wealthy citizens or the millionaire tyrants were the patrons, and the desire for fame which they shared with the artists whom they employed left monuments which the invaders of Italy from 1494 to 1943 spared when they might have destroyed. The works with brush and chisel of Botticelli and Michelangelo do not stale with time nor with frequent reproduction, nor does fuller knowledge of all that Leonardo da Vinci did and attempted make his genius any the less wonderful.

Gothic architecture had never been happy in the strong sunlight and clear backgrounds of Italy, while the great mass and graciousness of the Cathedral of Florence or of St. Peter's, Rome, were specially well suited to the homeland of the Latins who borrowed so much from Greece by reflex action. The architecture of the Italian Renaissance soon found admirers and imitators far north of the Alps. So, too, did the other sides of the Renaissance, its conscious cult of courtesy, its vast interest in politics and in the springs of power, its wonderful emancipation of women, limited though this latter was. Education, too, was for the first time studied experimentally by Vittorino da Feltre and his few followers in the northeast of Italy. So, also, was it in the Netherlands where the Brethren of the Common Life linked scholarship with piety.

When Charles VIII of France, against the advice of his best counsellors, accompanied a well-equipped force across the Alps, he changed the face of the Italian peninsula, justified the testimony of Savonarola at Florence, renewed French and Spanish interest in Naples and forced Venice to revise its claim to be a first-class power. The event is often thought of as marking the end of the Middle Ages. Symptomatic it was, but it was neither king nor pope nor humanist who wrought the transformation that makes the later sixteenth century so essentially different from the world of 1500. It was the invention of printing obscurely in the Rhineland, and the discovery in 1492 of the West Indies by a Genoese sailor in the service of Spain that opened up the prospects of a new world, both of the mind and of physical geography, and so made possible the civilization of the modern world.

Test Yourself

1. What were the causes of the fall of the Roman Empire?
2. State what, in your opinion, were the significant factors attending the coronation of Charlemagne.
3. What were the reasons for the Crusades and what did they achieve?
4. What do you know of the life of St. Francis and of his followers?
5. Describe the main characteristics of the medieval city-state.
6. What do you understand by the Italian renaissance? What were its chief characteristics?

Answers will be found at the end of the book.

CHAPTER V

THE REFORMATION AND THE BIRTH OF MODERN EUROPE

THE dates with which it is customary to mark off separate epochs in European history are little more than convenient punctuation marks. The political period which begins with the invasion of Italy by Charles VIII of France in 1494, and ends with the Treaty of Westphalia in 1648 marks the transition from the medieval to the modern world. It is the great formative period of European history.

The previous chapter closed with the appearance of the printed book. In the ensuing century books, which had before been reckoned at most in thousands, were to be reckoned in millions. They ceased to be the possessions only of the learned and wealthy and became a general means of instruction, amusement and propaganda.

Use of Printed Literature

A printed vernacular literature sprang up with astonishing speed and greatly encouraged growth of conscious national feelings. Political and religious propaganda by means of the pamphlet or the broadsheet was well developed within two generations of the discovery of printing. Before the close of this epoch regular weekly newspapers were appearing in most of the countries of Western Europe. In 1631, France was the first to publish a government-controlled weekly, *La Gazette de France*. In England, thirteen years later, Milton issued his great pamphlet *Areopagitica* (1644) defending a free Press.

There was thus created a far more vocal public opinion than earlier ages had known. Intellectual influences could now work on larger and more widespread groups than ever before. This is the most important factor to be taken into account in considering the rapid change and development of political and religious opinions in this epoch—a period marked by experiment and discovery in almost all realms of thought.

Before the end of the fifteenth century Leonardo da Vinci was striving vainly to master for mankind the secret of flying. The great anatomist, Vesalius (1514-64), published his pioneer investigations in the structure of the human body; the French surgeon, Ambroise Paré (1509-90), revolutionized the technique of surgery: the Englishman William Harvey (1578-1657) discovered the circulation of the blood. Copernicus (1473-1543), Kepler (1571-1630) and Galileo (1564-1642) discovered the working of the planetary system and the motion of the world. In the realm of philosophy Francis Bacon (1561-1626) in his *Novum Organum* laid down the rules of scientific investigation by experiment and experience, and just before the close of this period René Descartes (1596-1650), the father of modern philosophy, traced out the methods of logical abstract thought in his *Discours de la Méthode*.

The economic background to this mental activity was the gradual shifting of society in Western Europe from a land to a money basis. This process had been going on for generations but was to be completed during the sixteenth century. It must not be thought that the landowner ceased to be a person of importance, but his importance grew to be strictly relative to the money income which he could also command. The demand for greater comfort in everyday life accentuated this trend.

Growth of Merchant Class

A class of financiers had grown up early in urban Italy with great banking dynasties like the Medici in Florence. Such dynasties appeared next in Germany, where the greatest name is that of the house of Fugger. The money markets of Europe shifted thence, at about mid-century, to Antwerp and the Netherlands. Antwerp's importance in this regard depended largely

TIME CHART
A.D. 1000—1500

EASTERN EUROPE AND ASIA	WESTERN EUROPE AND AFRICA

EASTERN EUROPE AND ASIA

A.D.
- 1004 — Arabs sack Pisa. Rule of Samanides overthrown in Persia.
- 1006 — Mohammedans settle in N.W. India.
- 1012 — First persecution of heretics in Germany.
- 1054 — Split between Roman and Greek Churches.
- 1065 — Seljuks invade Asia Minor.
- 1071 — Seljuks take Jerusalem.
- 1083 — Henry IV occupies Rome and is crowned there.
- 1095 — Byzantine Empire calls on rest of Europe for aid against Turks.
- 1096 — First Crusade to the Holy Land.
- 1099 — Jerusalem captured by Crusaders.

- 1100 — Latin kingdom of Jerusalem organized as feudal state.
- 1147 — Second Crusade.
- 1169 — Saladin, preaches Holy War against Christians.
- 1187 — Saladin takes Jerusalem.
- 1190 — Third Crusade led by Richard I of England.
- 1202 — Fourth Crusade: Constantinople captured and Latin empire established.
- 1222 — Mongol incursions into S. Europe.
- 1228 — Sixth Crusade.
- 1241 — Great Mongol invasion in S.E. Europe.
- 1244 — Saracens retake Jerusalem.
- 1261 — Constantinople recaptured by Eastern Empire.
- 1271 — Marco Polo travels in Asia and China.
- 1273 — House of Habsburg founded.
- 1288 — Othman lays foundation of Turkish power in Asia Minor.
- 1291 — End of European states in Asia Minor.
- 1310 — Knights of St. John of Jerusalem established at Rhodes.
- 1353 — Beginning of Turkish invasion of Europe.
- 1363 — Rise of Tamerlane who conquers Persia and Syria.
- 1373 — Treaty of Peace with Ottomans; Eastern Emperor becomes vassal of Turks.
- 1390 — Byzantines lose last possessions in Asia Minor to Turks.
- 1398 — Tamerlane invades India.

- 1415 — Civil war follows martyrdom of John Huss for preaching heresy at Prague.
- 1422 — Turks lay siege to Constantinople.
- 1424 — Turks conquer Smyrna.
- 1453 — Turks capture Constantinople; end of Eastern Empire. Ottoman Empire founded.
- 1456 — Turks conquer Athens.
- 1459 — Turks conquer Serbia.
- 1480 — Turks invade Italy.
- 1498 — Venice superseded by Lisbon as main trade port. Vasco da Gama reaches India via Cape of Good Hope.

WESTERN EUROPE AND AFRICA

A.D.
- 1001 — Romans rebel against Emperor and Pope.
- 1002 — Massacre of Danes in England.
- 1003 — Beginning of frequent invasions of England by Danes.
- 1015 — First system of municipal government at Benevento, Italy.
- 1017 — Canute becomes King of England, Denmark and Norway.
- 1049 — Council of Reims to regulate election of bishops and abbots.
- 1066 — William of Normandy invades England and is crowned King.
- 1071 — Norman conquest of England completed.
- 1073 — Reorganization of the English Church.
- 1074 — Norman barons revolt against William.
- 1084 — Rome sacked by Normans.
- 1086 — Mohammedan rule revived in Spain. Carthusian order of monks founded. Compilation of Domesday Book in England.
- 1106 — Henry I of England secures Normandy.
- 1154 — Nicholas Breakspear, an Englishman, becomes Pope.
- 1167 — Oxford made a university.
- 1170 — Murder of Thomas à Becket.
- 1171 — Henry II acknowledged Lord of Ireland.
- 1208 — Foundation of Franciscan order of friars by St. Francis of Assisi.
- 1215 — King John accepts Magna Carta.
- 1241 — Founding of League of Hansa towns.
- 1259 — Henry III renounces all French possessions except Gascony.
- 1265 — First English Parliament called.
- 1282 — Wales conquered by Edward I.
- 1290 — Jews expelled from England.
- 1294 — England at war with France over Gascony.
- 1295 — Beginning of Franco-Scottish alliance.
- 1296 — Edward I subdues Scotland.
- 1302 — States-General set up in France.
- 1303 — Pope imprisoned by the French.
- 1306 — Robert Bruce, King of Scotland.
- 1314 — Bruce defeats Edward II at Bannockburn.
- 1315 — Foundation of Swiss independence.
- 1317 — Adoption of Salic Law in France.
- 1328 — Independence of Scotland acknowledged.
- 1331 — Flemish weavers settle in England.
- 1332 — First division of Parliament into Upper and Lower Houses.
- 1338 — Commencement of Hundred Years War.
- 1340 — Edward III assumes title of King of France.
- 1346 — Edward defeats French at Crécy. First use of gunpowder.
- 1347 — Calais captured by English.
- 1348 — Black Death devastates Europe.
- 1367 — War of Hanseatic League against Norway and Denmark.
- 1381 — Peasants' Revolt in England led by Wat Tyler.
- 1382 — Wyclif translates the Bible.
- 1388 — Persecution of Lollards in England.
- 1393 — Statute of Præmunire limits power of Pope in England.
- 1401 — Rise of the Medici in Florence.
- 1407 — Charter to Merchant Adventurers granted by Henry V.
- 1415 — Henry V defeats French at Agincourt.
- 1420 — Henry V crowned King of France. Portuguese explorations of Africa organized by Henry the Navigator.
- 1429 — Joan of Arc raises siege of Orleans; Charles VII crowned at Reims.
- 1431 — Joan of Arc burnt at Rouen by English.
- 1440 — Gutenberg invents printing by movable type.
- 1441 — Portuguese round Cape Blanco.
- 1444 — France establishes first standing army.
- 1445 — Cape Verde discovered by Dias.
- 1453 — End of Hundred Years War.
- 1455 — Beginning of Wars of the Roses.
- 1475 — Edward IV invades France.
- 1476 — Caxton establishes printing press in London.
- 1485 — End of Wars of the Roses and beginning of Tudor dynasty.
- 1492 — Ferdinand drives Moors from Spain.
- 1494 — French invasion of Italy.

upon the fact that it was the main distributing centre for the wealth of the Spanish and Portuguese overseas empires. The mineral wealth of South America, which the Spanish monarchy vainly endeavoured to keep in Spain itself, caused a general fall in the value of money which lasted throughout the period with which we are dealing, and was the source of a profit inflation which worked strongly in favour of sections of the new merchant and industrial classes and against those elements in society such as the lesser French nobility whose revenues took the form of fixed rents. The poorer classes of society were also variously affected by the change; thus in England and other parts of Europe the period marks a complete disappearance of serfdom while in Spain and elsewhere its burdens became more firmly riveted.

Because of developments in military technique, actual cash was more than ever the root of power, and the success of a king or ruler depended largely on his ability to lay his hands on it. Kings were thus driven to rely on, and therefore to consider more and more carefully, the merchants and middle classes. The privileges which these had secured in the Middle Ages on the question of controlling taxation thus became of the first importance, and we find a sharp dividing of the political ways between countries, such as France and Spain, where the Crown avoided or crushed these privileges and thus achieved despotism, and countries like England and the northern Netherlands where the middle classes successfully defended their privileges and laid the foundations of modern parliamentary democracy.

Political thought reflected the changing values. Machiavelli in his *Prince* (1513) clearly set down the practical ideal of the successful ruler—ruthless, unscrupulous, governed only by considerations of what would contribute to his power. He was describing with frankness methods which were in common use, but this, the earliest handbook on power politics, was not well received. A decent reticence, it was felt,

BUILDING IN THE EARLY SIXTEENTH CENTURY

From the pages of Polydore Vergil much may be learnt about craftsmen and their work. In this contemporary woodcut, from an edition published in 1503, builders are seen at work upon a scaffold under the supervision of the master mason.

GLASSBLOWING IN THE FIFTEENTH CENTURY

Illustrating the process of glassmaking, this drawing now in the London Science Museum shows, in rear, the ovens where the glass was melted; on the left, a man firing coloured wares; and in the foreground, one of the workers blowing a flask into shape.

should be preserved on the methods of practical government and the most popular theory developed to cloak royal despotism was that of the Divine Right of Kings.

The outstanding event of the period was, of course, the Reformation. The religious movement, or rather series of religious movements, which broke once and for all the theoretical unity of Western Christendom, owed their astonishing effect, as has been seen, at least in part to changes in the social and economic structure and perhaps still more to the speed and enthusiasm with which in this immensely fertile period ideas were propagated. They also owed not a little to the growing sense of nationality among the Western European peoples.

Some of the nation-states as we know them today were already recognized: France, Spain, England, Scotland and Denmark. Others, like Poland, were to decline or, like Hungary and Bohemia, be submerged in great empires. Italy and Germany were signally to fail to become united nations, though in each of them

during the latter part of this century a small opportunist principality was to establish itself as the nucleus of a later nation-state.

The young nation-states carried within them survivals from the feudal period. Most of them were saddled with a reigning dynasty; while ill-advised or incompetent monarchs occasionally lost their crowns (as Charles I lost both Scotland and England, and Philip II of Spain lost the Netherlands), a clever king (or minister) could harness the new force of national consciousness to make a more powerful support for the royal government and the dynasty than any hitherto known. France is the most striking example of this with the reign of Henry IV, and the administration of Richelieu, leading to the despotism of Louis XIV, but Gustavus Adolphus of Sweden and Christian IV of Denmark did much the same thing; so in rather different degrees did Philip II in Spain, and the Tudors in England. Strong monarchies often meant strong despotisms, but we must remember that except in a few unusual cases the alternative might well be the total disruption of the state. The catastrophic decline of Poland, where no king in this period fully swayed or inspired the nation, and during which it declined heavily in territory and power, is evidence of this, and the total failure of Charles V to impose himself as a national leader on Germany is perhaps one of the keys to the modern German problem.

Dynastic Rivalry

Thus the great issues of religious and political faith were often fought out within the terms of outmoded dynastic and personal quarrels. The dominating motif of this century and a half is the antagonism between the dynasties of Spain and France. The Habsburgs, originally Austrian dukes, and occasionally Holy Roman emperors, by the luck of clever marriages and unexpected deaths acquired in the person of the Emperor Charles V, the hereditary title to the Netherlands, Spain, and a large part of Italy, in addition to their Austrian domains. The kings of France vainly contested the Habsburgs' Italian domination, but after a hundred and fifty years of struggle did succeed in exhausting their resources in Spain and curbing their power in Germany. This quarrel which fits best into the old and simple idea of dynastic rivalry may also be seen in more modern terms as a struggle for the balance of power in Europe.

A by-product of this long dynastic struggle was the preservation and solidification of the Protestant states of Europe. Both combatants—France and Spain— were Roman Catholic powers, but each was willing to support Protestant rebels against the other. With the French government this, indeed, became a guiding principle of policy. Thus the chief political and religious fissures ran in transverse directions and the existence of the one led to the perpetuation of the other.

The first or Italian period of the Franco-Spanish rivalry lasted from the invasion of Italy by Charles VIII of France in 1494, in pursuit of shadowy dynastic claims to land and vague ideas of glory and plunder, to the Treaty of Câteau Cambrésis in 1559.

The details of the futile Italian campaigns of successive French kings are not important.

The most spectacular of the monarchs who engaged in this wasteful strife was Francis I (1515-47). This cultured egoist was at least a lavish patron of the arts, who left the mark of his brilliant personality on the literature and architecture of his country. As a soldier Francis was successful on his first invasion of Italy at Marignano (1515), but was totally defeated at Pavia (1525).

Charles V, head of the House of Habsburg, Francis's antagonist on the European scene, became King of Spain in 1517 and was elected Holy Roman Emperor in 1520. This hard-working, slow-thinking and uninspired monarch controlled more land than any ruler since the collapse of the Roman Empire. The Habsburg hereditary lands in Austria he settled on a loyal and subservient brother. Evidently he was a menace both to Francis I and to the theoretical balance of European power. But the chief importance in European diplomacy and strategy of his accession to authority in the Netherlands and in Germany was that it transferred the keypoint of the Franco-Spanish rivalry from Italy and the Mediterranean to the Low Countries and the Rhine.

France and Italy

The French were slow to see this. Even after his defeat at Pavia, Francis I continued to struggle for the control of Italy, but could not regain the Duchy of Milan with its valuable control of the Alpine passes. His son Henry II listened to the overtures of the rebel German princeling, Maurice of Saxony, and signed the Treaty of Chambord (1552) which promised him as a reward the Lorraine fortresses of Metz, Toul and Verdun, keys to the western approaches to the Rhine. Even so, Henry did not abandon his father's Italian projects until the Treaty of Câteau Cambrésis seven years later. By this time the long years of war and the shift towards the Atlantic of the main routes of world trade had reduced the value of the Italian prize.

The Treaty of Câteau Cambrésis marked the relative, not the absolute, defeat of the French dynasty in their struggle with the Habsburgs. They retained, for instance, Metz, Toul and Verdun, while renouncing only their Italian claims. The real cause of the temporary settlement between the two rivals was not the weakness of France but the increasing fear of both protagonists of the growth of heresy in their dominions.

The advent of the printed book had brought speculative thought and argument within the reach of the laity throughout Christendom. The development of the nation-state meanwhile encouraged the parallel development of national Churches rather than an international Church. These changes above all gave to the various reformers of the sixteenth century the popular following and the effective political support which enabled them to succeed where earlier reformers had failed. Martin Luther (1483-1546), a German Augustinian monk, is the dominating figure of the early Reformation. At Wittenberg in 1517 he protested in his celebrated theses against the sale of indulgences. This hawking of the right to eternal bliss for money was the most generally evident of the many corruptions of the sixteenth-century Church. Its other evident weakness was the worldly character of many of its priests, not least the pope himself, while the position of the papacy as an Italian principality was profoundly embarrassing to the supposedly international character of the Holy Father.

Naturally enough there were movements towards reform within the Church itself; there were loyal Catholic lay critics, like the great scholar Erasmus, whose best-selling volume *In Praise of Folly* attacked the vices of the Church but was never intended to attack the Church as an institution. But such scandals and such attacks were of far greater consequence in the more literate, more active, more speculative sixteenth century than at any earlier period. Moreover, the changing structure of society postulated a new organization in place of a Church whose overriding claims irritated national susceptibilities and whose right to contributions in money exasperated the growing middle class.

The career of Luther shows the new forces at work. There was nothing heretical in Luther's theses, but the pope—mistakenly as it turned out—took them seriously. He sent a bull ordering Luther to recant. Luther, a very popular preacher, a brave, stubborn man, and a vigorously self-conscious German, saw no reason why he should give in to a foreign secular prince, which was, after all, what the Holy Father had become. He burnt the bull. He also burnt the volume of Canon Law. In the interests of papal authority this could hardly be allowed to pass. The pope urged the new young emperor, Charles V, to call Luther to order before a Diet.

The Diet met at Worms and Luther was summoned to appear. By this time his preaching and pamphleteering had rallied most of literate and a great part of illiterate Germany to his side. His progress to Worms was triumphal. In the imperial presence he refused to recant. "Here stand I, I can no other, so help me God!" he is supposed to have said. The emperor put him to the ban of the empire, but the Elector Frederick the Wise of Saxony carried him off to safe hiding at the Wartburg, where he made his famous translation of the Bible. This action of Frederick the Wise marks the first step in the alliance of the young Lutheran Church with the State.

Luther's teaching meanwhile, a strange blend of national anti-papalism and early Christian love for the humble and meek, had far-reaching effects. The oppressed peasants of Germany surged into revolt. The revolt threatened to overturn the property rights in which a man of Luther's substantial yeoman background could hardly fail to believe. He accordingly denounced it in no measured terms. His defection—for so the peasants felt it—undoubtedly dealt their cause a serious moral blow, though it is questionable whether, whatever Luther's action, their revolt could have succeeded. It was in fact stamped out with indescribable barbarity.

From this time onward the young Lutheran Church, in the shadow of the Saxon State, preached in politics a doctrine of passive obedience in all matters where the individual conscience was not involved. This was a very comfortable doctrine for the new national rulers and it is not sur-

EXECUTION OF SAVONAROLA

*Savonarola, monk and reformer and at one time virtual dictator of Florence, was tortured
and burnt in 1498, after preaching contrary to the commands of the pope. The scene of his
execution with two companions is vividly depicted by an unknown Florentine artist.
The authority of the Church is indicated by the figure of the bishop seated in front of the
Palazzo Publico seen in the background on the right.*

TYPEFOUNDING AND PRINTING

Above, a sixteenth-century typefounder makes movable types by hand, and below, Gutenberg, generally held to be the inventor of printing, shown producing his first book.

prising that Lutheranism was encouraged in other German principalities while it assisted the growth of powerful nation-states in Sweden and Denmark.

In the Holy Roman Empire, however, it had the very opposite effect on national solidarity. The emperor, abandoning the hopeless struggle to eradicate heresy, conceded at Augsburg in 1555 the right of each individual prince to impose his own religion within his own lands. This principle (*cujus regio ejus religio* as it was called) went far to complete the fatal division of Germany.

While Luther's reform was sweeping over Germany another doughty fighter had appeared in Switzerland. At Zurich, Ulrich Zwingli aroused the strong feelings of local patriotism and independence of the stubborn, industrious Swiss. Attempts to bring him and Luther into line with each other failed; both were too ardent theologians and too tepid statesmen to modify their differing views of the sacrament. The movement thus remained separate and the rapid progress of Zwinglianism in the Swiss cantons was cut short with the life of Zwingli, himself killed at Cappel fighting the forces of the Roman Catholic cantons in 1531. Yet the same Alpine region was to bring forth—though not in Zwingli's person—the Reformed religion which was most seriously to alter the face of Europe.

In 1536, John Calvin (1509-64), a French theologian, was asked to make his home in Geneva as teacher and preacher. Here he founded his theocracy. Calvin elevated the doctrine of grace and predestination as the basis of his creed; but its real significance lay in its attitude to government. No passive obedience to the secular authority here! The Calvinist Church *was* the state. It was organized on a democratic basis, each church being governed by an elected body of lay elders and deacons. But it enforced discipline among its members and it was utterly intolerant. At Geneva there was a true theocracy. In other countries, whither this remarkable faith spread, the perfect fusion was never quite reached.

As a dominating influence in the state, Calvinism, with its intolerance and its discipline, showed an ugly side. But enthusiastic missionaries carried it to many countries where it could not hope to dominate and where it produced instead a closely organized and often persecuted minority in society. The refusal of the Calvinists to accept compromise made them indigestible elements in the body of the state, while their admirable organization and their single-minded fanaticism enabled them to survive persecution more effectively than any other Protestant sect. They were in due course to enforce the first real edict of toleration from the French government; they were to make the backbone of the national resistance to Spanish authority in the Netherlands; and—a fact often overlooked—it was their intransigence in Scotland which precipitated the Civil Wars in Great Britain and led to the collapse of the Stuart experiment in absolutism.

Almost coeval with this great division in the Church a reforming movement of real power had at last begun within the fabric of the Roman Catholic Church. In 1540 the Basque soldier, Ignatius Loyola, founded the Society of Jesus. In a sense the Jesuits may be called the last and greatest of the military orders. Members of the society were not, of course, soldiers in the ordinary sense; they were priests, highly trained in discipline and highly organized under their general for educational and missionary work the world over. They carried the Gospel to China and the Indies. But above all they set themselves to win back relapsed Europe.

But their greatest weapon was education; as educationists they must rank among the most enlightened in the world, and the excellent teaching and the efficient but moderate discipline of their schools won them pupils from all classes of society. They took special pains to attract the sons of reigning princes who, as they grew up, would carry Jesuit ideals into every walk of public life. One of their greatest teachers, Peter Canisius, won back Austria for the Church. In Poland they established and confirmed that hold of the Catholic Faith over the country which has made of Poland the eldest child of the Roman Catholic Church and very largely cut her off in

PAPERMAKING AND BOOKBINDING
Interior of a sixteenth-century paper mill (above) showing pulping machine and press; (below), fifteenth-century bookbinders sewing sheets and pressing the bound book.

MEDIEVAL AND RENAISSANCE
COSTUME IN EUROPE

BYZANTINE: 6th. CENTURY

ANGLO-SAXON: 11th. CENTURY

16th. CENTURY: EARLY TUDOR

14th. CENTURY;
FRENCH INFLUENCE
GENERAL

15th. CENTURY: MIXTURE OF "CUT"
AND DRAPERY POPULAR

DUTCH, MID 17th. CENTURY;
LACE EXTENSIVELY USED

EARLY JACOBEAN, 1610; FARTHINGALES
COMMONLY WORN BY LADIES

culture and feeling from most other Slav peoples. Their work in Bohemia was only more superficial because it came in the wake of a foreign and conquering Austrian army, but it was extensive even there and has left its marks.

Too late to prevent the Reformation, but in time to stem it, Pope Paul III had called a Council at Trent. It sat intermittently between 1545 and 1563. Its president was the Jesuit Lainez and it was under his influence that the Roman Catholic Church reformed its doctrine and clarified its position. The work of this Council still forms the basis of Roman Catholic doctrine.

Other phenomena marked the regeneration of the Church. The foundation of the Capuchins, the reformed order of Franciscans, provided the counter-reformation with yet another army of missionaries and zealots, while St. Theresa reformed the Carmelite Order. After a long night it was a great awakening.

The counter-reformation, however, could not hope to regain all Europe to the old religion once more, for the Reformation had been accompanied by the wholesale seizure of Church property. This process by which the secular ruler took over and often resold ecclesiastical lands had the effect, naturally, of entrenching the new-formed religions among the middle classes who profited most largely by the despoilment of the Church. It not only created a vested interest in Protestantism but also completed the shifting of the centre of social gravity towards the higher and wealthier sections of the middle class. While the economic motive undoubtedly played an important part in establishing the new religions it is a mistake to overestimate it, more especially in individual cases. The persecutions which in the course of the next century were launched by both sides in the religious conflict met with stubborn and often heroic resistance from countless men and women who were not dying for vested interests but for religious beliefs.

While the progress of the Reformation and the development of nation-states was

SIXTEENTH-CENTURY POTTERS

One of the many interesting drawings in the original manuscript of "The Three Books of the Potter's Art," by Cavalière Cipriano Piccolpasso (1524-79), now in the library of the Victoria and Albert Museum. It shows the primitive potter's wheel, turned by a thrust from the foot as the clay is skilfully shaped with the hands.

FURRIER AND ASSISTANTS AT WORK

This woodcut of the late sixteenth century depicts on the left a master furrier and his two assistants making up the furs, which have previously been well beaten in the open air. In the showroom to the right an assistant attends upon a lady and gentleman, who, judging by their fur-trimmed costumes, are good customers.

thus disintegrating the old conception of united Christendom, the threat to its very existence from the Turkish enemy had reached horrifying proportions under two great sultans, Selim and Sulieman. Intent on immediate and selfish ends the Christian rulers of Europe were by no means unwilling to call in the Turks to help them against their rivals. The pope himself had, for instance, encouraged them to molest the Venetian Republic; in 1542 Francis I had sought their alliance against Charles V, and Queen Elizabeth instructed the first English ambassador to Turkey to urge as a principal reason for friendship between the two countries the common dislike felt by the Turks and the English for "idolaters."

Sultan Selim I (1512-20) had concentrated on uniting and solidifying the Moslem East. He thus left to his son Sulieman the Magnificent (1520-66) an empire much strengthened and doubled in extent. Sulieman immediately turned his attention to the squabbling and divided Christian states of Europe. In campaigns by sea and land he took possession one by one of the chief strategic points—the key fortress of Belgrade and the Mediterranean strong-points of Rhodes and Cos. In 1526 he utterly defeated the Hungarian armies under their king, Louis, brother-in-law of the Emperor Charles V, at the Battle of Mohacs. A generation of intermittent warfare failed to liberate Hungary, and by the Treaty of Adrianople (1562) the Christians were left with only a narrow strip of the borderland and even for this they had to pay tribute. During these wars Vienna had been twice seriously menaced and Turkish cavalry had been seen skirmishing in southern Germany as far west as Ratisbon.

At the same time the Turks dominated the Mediterranean. Tripoli and Algiers acknowledged their suzerainty, the Venetian fleet suffered heavy setbacks and the coasts of Italy were constantly raided. When they seized the island of Cyprus three of the Mediterranean powers—the King of Spain, the pope and the Venetian Republic—at length joined forces and the great sea victory of Lepanto (1571) at least checked further Turkish expansion by crippling, if not utterly destroying, the Turkish fleet.

On the mainland, however, the Turks maintained their conquests, although by the end of the sixteenth century the zenith of their power was past. A corrupt state, governed for long periods by harem intrigue and the whims of the palace troops, its long rule over a great part of the European mainland has left an ineradicable mark on those Christian nations—the Greeks, the Serbs, the Bulgars, the Rumanians and in

WINTER SPORTS IN THE SIXTEENTH CENTURY

On a frozen river in Holland, skating and other winter sports are in full swing. A careful study of the picture provides interesting information about the customs, costume and architecture of the period. The engraving was made in 1570 by Hieronymus Cock, master of Pieter Brueghel, the great sixteenth-century painter.

a lesser degree the Hungarians who were only gradually to emerge from its control, many of them not until the nineteenth century. Much that divides the culture of Eastern from that of Western Europe can be traced to this long alien rule.

While this cleavage between Eastern and Western Europe was coming into being, the political institutions of Western Europe itself were going through a period of crisis. The Middle Ages had seen the development of a representative system of government, England and Scotland had their Parliaments, France and the Low Countries their *États Généraux*, the German Empire its *Stände*, the Spanish kingdoms their *Cortes*. These gatherings increased in influence as the ruling princes needed more ready money for their expensive war policies. It was thus a natural development for rulers

to try to break, curb or evade this power in the interests of a more highly centralized and efficient government; and it was not absolutely a chance that the princes were on the whole more successful in the regions where the Roman Catholic Church was strongest (Spain and France) and least successful where the Calvinist doctrine had gained firmest hold.

The keypoint of this struggle in the sixteenth century was the Netherlands, and in the seventeenth century Great Britain. Philip II, who had succeeded his father Charles V as King of Spain and ruler of the Netherlands in 1555, was anxious to establish throughout his dominions the unchallenged authority of the Crown and of the Church. It was particularly important for him to do this in the Netherlands as he derived the most important part of his income from these rich provinces. But the Netherlands nobility and townsfolk alike resented the infringement of their privileges and there was equally widespread irritation at his religious policy in a country which had been strongly infected by Calvinist doctrine. A first abortive revolt (1567) failed and was stamped out with iron-handed severity by the Duke of Alva.

One of the leading Netherlands nobles, however, the Prince of Orange, had escaped to Germany whence—seeking the help of other Protestant princes and of the French Huguenots—he organized a fresh rising in 1572. This rising was successful at least in so far as the northern provinces were concerned. It established, after a war known to the Dutch as the Eighty Years War, the independent Dutch Republic. But the southern provinces, which we know as Belgium, remained for a complex of religious, economic and racial reasons loyal to the Spanish Crown.

The most remarkable feature of the long struggle of the Dutch Republic was that it maintained throughout the war, in spite of interludes of crisis during which the Prince of Orange as commander-in-chief exercised an overriding authority, the principles of representative rule by the estates, the local representative bodies of the provinces and by their estates-general, the parliament of the whole confederation. The preservation of this principle and successful defiance of the greatest authoritarian power in Europe over a long period had an important effect on the political institutions and thought not only of Europe but, later, of the New World.

Protestantism and Commerce

The truce of 1609 which marked the emergence of the northern Netherlands (Holland) as an independent nation was also the prelude to a remarkable period of economic growth. Its major port Amsterdam replaced Antwerp as the financial capital of the world and the Dutch became the acknowledged pioneers in many departments of commercial and financial life, as well as in certain branches of technology such as the new scientific agriculture of the seventeenth century. The fact that Holland was a Protestant and a relatively tolerant country helped towards the popular indentification of Protestantism and toleration with commercial prosperity.

The conflict of the representative against the authoritarian state is seen in even sharper operation in the English Civil Wars (1642-60). Here the first two Stuart kings tried with the best intentions to put Divine Right into practice. James I met with increasing opposition from highly articulate parliaments representing the powerful cross-section of landed gentry and city men who controlled the money of the country. Charles I, equally unable to control his parliaments, made the fatal experiment of trying to do without them. This policy led to the crisis of the Civil War in which he was defeated and finally beheaded (1649)—the first king in Europe to suffer a trial at the hands of his people, or at least of a section of them.

Huguenot Party

The rivalry between France and Spain which had been temporarily stilled at the Peace of Câteau Cambrésis (1559) became active again in the latter half of the century. But the French monarchy, torn by religious dissension and weakened by a series of ineffective kings, was in no position to maintain the balance of European power. Only the sustained revolt of the Netherlands and the English defeat of the Armada (1588) checked the overwhelming ambitions of the Spanish monarchy.

The serious religious fissure was the chief cause of France's weakness. The Calvinists had made great headway in the country where they were called by a name borrowed from one of the city factions of Geneva—the Huguenots. The Huguenot party included an influential section of the nobility, more especially the Bourbon King of Navarre. The extreme Roman Catholic party in time became identified with another group of nobility, the Guise family, who sought to maintain a paramount influence on the Crown. Thus the old pattern of feuds among the nobles is disclosed under the newer one of religious conflict.

In the bitter religious wars which disturbed France for the last forty years of

ELIZABETHAN STREET:

In the centre of the main square of a small town as it would appear in Elizabethan times are seen the town hall where justice was dispensed and the stocks where miscreants were exposed ignominiously to the public gaze. On the right is the inn where a hunter arrives with his kill, while others are taking refreshment outside. On the left is a merchant's house with a

CENTRE OF TRADE

visitor on horseback being greeted on arrival. Goods for sale are arriving at the market which was held beneath and around the hall, and customers are departing with their purchases. The lack of traffic is emphasized by the fact that it was possible to play bowls in the square. In the distance is the church and to the right in the background is the manor house.

the century it was naturally the aim of Spanish policy to intervene. But this intervention, intended to reduce France to the level of a satellite power, recoiled ultimately on its perpetrators. The extreme Roman Catholic party became identified with Spanish intervention and in consequence united the moderates and the Huguenots alike behind the young king Henry of Navarre who, on the murder of the last Valois, Henry III, in 1589, became the lawful King of France.

In order to secure his position with the Roman Catholic majority and more especially in the capital Henry had himself changed his religion. The end of the wars and the withdrawal of Spanish troops from the soil of France (1598) was marked by the promulgation of the Edict of Nantes, justly celebrated as the first official recognition of the fact that two religions might exist under a single sovereign. In this it differed entirely from the earlier imperial settlement at Augsburg. That had secured the coexistence of two religions in the Holy Roman Empire merely by giving each prince the right to impose a faith on his subjects; there was no suggestion that in any individual principality of the empire more than one religion should be practised.

The Edict of Nantes, on the other hand, guaranteed the existence of a minority religion in a state whose ruler belonged to the Roman Catholic Church. It was, however, a bold and practical political agreement, not based on any revolutionary theory, and came simply as the outcome and the settlement of an exhausting civil war. It gave the Huguenots rights of worship in certain places and equal civil rights with the rest of the population, their effective guarantee being the possession of over a hundred fortified and garrisoned towns. What the Edict did was in fact to create a state within a state. It was an anomaly which, with the further developments of the French monarchy, could not last.

Henry IV (1589-1610) was probably the greatest and certainly the most popular king France has ever known. A jovial personality, a brave soldier and a remarkably shrewd statesman, Henry embodied in his person much of the growing national consciousness of France. He not only restored prosperity to a country worn out by wars, but he laid the foundations, by his personal popularity, of popular loyalty to a paternal monarchy which was to play so important a part in the next generations.

As a statesman, however, he did not lose sight of the Spanish problem and his foreign policy was directed, in peace and war, to controlling and curbing this still threatening power, though his murder by a Spanish agent in 1610 postponed for a generation the final settlement between the two great powers.

The monarchy, now firmly established survived the minority of his son, Louis XIII. It was this king's minister, Cardinal Richelieu (1624-42), who reorganized the administration and founded the greatness of the French monarchy. He curbed the power of the nobility in the provinces by placing local government in the hands of Crown-appointed officials—the *intendants* —recruited from the upper strata of the middle class. He checked the separatist tendencies of the Huguenots and, while leaving them religious toleration, removed all vestige of political or military power. He encouraged letters, arts and sciences but made them minister to the Crown; thus he founded the Academy for French literature, and organized the first French newspapers. He strove, on the whole successfully, to raise a French national army independent of hired mercenaries. His chief failure was in finance, which, partly owing to an expensive war policy, he failed to place on a secure basis. Thus, although he laid the foundations of the despotic monarchy in France, he left also the fatal weakness which in the next century undermined the whole structure. His greatest triumph was, however, in the subtle foreign policy which led to the crippling of the Spanish power and the establishment of French domination throughout Western Europe.

The conflict known as the Thirty Years War was the culmination of the wars of religion and of the struggle between France and Spain. It was fought in Germany; that was both Germany's misfortune and her

MAY DAY FESTIVAL—EARLY SIXTEENTH CENTURY

From the calendar of an illuminated Missal in the Victoria and Albert Museum, this miniature by Simon Benninck (1483-1561) illustrates the month of May. May Day is being celebrated by morris dancing in the market place, while a party of horsemen is seen bringing in the may.

fault for the issues at stake had very little to do with Germany.

The war broke out in 1618 with a Protestant revolt in Bohemia against the newly elected Habsburg king who was shortly also to become Holy Roman Emperor as Ferdinand II. The Bohemian rebels, hoping to gain the support of the Protestant princes of Germany and powers of Europe, elected for their new king, Frederick, Elector Palatine of the Rhine, son-in-law of James I of England, nephew of the Prince of Orange and cousin of the King of Denmark. Out of jealousy, caution or temporary embarrassment, all his potential allies failed and the Battle of the White Mountain (1620) drove him out of Bohemia and placed that country under Austria for three centuries. Frederick lost not only Bohemia but the Palatinate which had been occupied by Austria's Spanish allies. They had seized it for the simple reason that it secured them a land route from North Italy (one of their best recruiting grounds) to the Netherlands where the War of Independence still continued.

The Dutch and the French were both menaced by this strategic move and the Dutch immediately offered refuge to Frederick. The French, after some vacillation, subsidized Christian IV of Denmark to intervene. The English, more hesitant, gave qualified help to two able *condottieri* (professional leaders of mercenary troops), Mansfeld and Christian of Brunswick. These latter failed to achieve anything and Christian IV was defeated by Wallenstein, the great imperial general who combined the resources of a financier with the gifts of a commander. His admirers believe he aimed at uniting a new Germany pivoting on the Elbe and including Bohemia, his native land. At any rate he carried the imperial eagles and the Roman Catholic Church back to the shores of the Baltic.

This did not suit Richelieu, whose diplomatic machinations caused the emperor to dismiss Wallenstein and whose offers of

TURKISH FAIRGROUND—EARLY SEVENTEENTH CENTURY
Designed by a native artist, this drawing from the Album Amicorum of W. Leutkauff, 1616, now in the Victoria and Albert Museum, shows a turkish fair with three different types of roundabout, a swinging platform for children, and in the centre a canopied swing. There are also the inevitable musicians and vendors of useful articles and mementoes.

subsidies launched Gustavus Adolphus of Sweden into the war as the new Protestant champion. Gustavus Adolphus defeated Wallenstein at Lützen (1632) but was himself killed. Intrigues at the imperial court and fear of Wallenstein's ambitions led to his murder early in 1634. A strong Spanish army was now sent to help the emperor and the Swedish tide was decisively turned by their defeat at Nördlingen (1634). At this point the emperor made a moderately satisfactory peace at Prague, but Richelieu at this juncture declared war on the emperor's kinsman and ally, the King of Spain. In 1639 with the capture of Breisach, the key fortress on the Rhine, the French cut the Spanish life-line to the Netherlands and in 1643 at Rocroi utterly destroyed the Spanish infantry, a blow from which their armies never recovered.

Meanwhile by sea the Dutch had wrought destruction no less fatal on the Spanish Navy, in 1639 at the Battle of the Downs, and in 1640 off Itamarca, thus driving them, not only out of the narrow seas, but virtually off the coast of their own Spanish America. For four years (1644-48) diplomats of a dozen nations met at Münster and Osnabrück in Westphalia to discuss terms, while the war continued to rage desperately over German soil. The peace which ultimately emerged set the seal on Germany's failure to achieve national unity; it not only perpetuated the division into innumerable states but gave her princes the right to make foreign treaties and war irrespective of the emperor. It also practically attached Alsace to France, a step forward in the French march towards the Rhine frontier initiated in 1552 by Henry II when he acquired Metz, Toul and Verdun. To the credit of this deplorable settlement it must be added that it contained clauses recognizing the independence of the Swiss confederation. That of the Dutch Republic was recognized in a separate treaty.

The general effect of this war, which was the culmination of the conflicts of the past century and a half was, for Germany, disastrous. The social and political degeneration of the empire were apparent long before it broke out; its economic decline, with the shifting of the trade routes away from Central Europe to the seaboard and more especially to the Atlantic seaboard, ante-dated the Thirty Years War by at least a generation. It is incorrect, therefore, to ascribe the degeneration of Germany totally to the war, though it is true that her population dropped by at least a third. The disaster was, however, morally irreparable, for the war put an end to any hope that the Holy Roman Empire would achieve the union of the German states, and left among the Germans themselves an abiding sense of resentment, inferiority and a bitter hatred of the French.

Out of the confusion of dynastic and national strife a new great power had emerged by 1648. The French monarchy, centralized, civilized, intelligent and aggressive, was to dominate the politics and culture of Western Europe for a long time to come. In the realms of thought the revolution from the age of faith to that of reason was all but complete. Descartes, in so many ways the acme of the lucid French genius, had published his great work in 1635, and six years before the Peace of Westphalia, the scientist, Isaac Newton, had been born in a Lincolnshire village.

Test Yourself

1. In what sense may the age of Luther be said to mark the real beginning of the modern world?
2. Explain the importance of northern Italy and the Netherlands in the politics of this period.
3. In what sense is it true to say that the latter part of the sixteenth century and the first part of the seventeenth saw an "industrial revolution"?
4. Why is the Thirty Years War so important in the history of Germany and of Europe as a whole?

Answers will be found at the end of the book.

CHAPTER VI

THE FIRST AGE OF DISCOVERY

To the Western Europeans of the medieval period the world was a stable and unified Christendom bordered by a more or less remote infidel fringe. Their notion of the general disposition of sea and land was vague; and they were possibly clearer about the topography of Heaven and Hell than about that of Africa and Asia. It had not always been so. In ancient times a peak of geographical knowledge was reached in the middle of the second century after Christ with the Egyptian writer, Ptolemy, who had at his disposal accurate information about the whole of the Mediterranean world, as well as reports of expeditions to East and West Africa and the stories of travellers from parts of Eastern Asia. But within three centuries of his death, Ptolemy's treatise on geography was lost to Europe. Thereafter most writers were content with a more or less fanciful conception of the universe derived from a literal reading of the Hebrew scriptures.

Religion and Map Making

If some churchmen admitted that they did not know the shape of the earth, others were ready to affirm that it was a flat disk. Moreover, maps were frequently drawn from a religious rather than a geographical point of view, and preconceived notions and a misplaced desire for symmetry might require the inclusion of the Garden of Eden, or at least the placing of Jerusalem at the centre of things. Nevertheless, there were thinkers who continued to consider the world as a sphere and sketched out their conception of the world on that assumption. The Venerable Bede, for example, described the earth as a globe with cold polar zones, a torrid central zone and intermediate temperate zones: however, he considered the torrid zone too hot to be inhabitable and argued against there being inhabitants of the southern temperate zone.

Nor was there much inquisitiveness about the outside world. The stable and unified Christendom was sufficient to itself. It had its own community of traditions and institutions. It acknowledged the supremacy of Papal Rome as the successor to Imperial Rome, and the Roman Church administered a common religion, accompanied by a general ecclesiastical law, a unified learning, and an international language and literature in Latin. The unity of the West thus tended to be comprehensive and exclusive. It also tended to be static: medieval feudalism was a conception of a stationary society firmly rooted in the soil.

Mohammedan Influence

But if medieval Europe had a limited outlook, it was not a closed continent. Already in the seventh century the new religion of Mohammed had spread from Arabia across North Africa, until in 711 it forced its way into Spain, tumbled down an insecure Christian monarchy, and in the course of a few years overran almost the whole of the Iberian Peninsula. Though the Moslem wave was stopped in southern France, a rift had been opened in the flank of Christendom—a rift that was not closed for more than seven centuries—and it was in the long struggle for reconquest that the nations of the Peninsula were formed. Beginning from a tiny nucleus of resistance in northern Spain, the Christian revival soon resulted in the formation of a number of states, whose internal struggles frequently obscured the larger issue of the reconquest. But as the Moslems were pushed back, the larger or more vigorous Christian states absorbed the others, until finally the two nations of Spain and Portugal emerged. In both of these nations a form of political and religious nationalism had been generated which was to serve as the propelling force for an imperial expansion overseas.

But it was not only as enemies that the Christians of the Iberian Peninsula were influenced by the Moslems. For a long period men of the two religions dwelt side by side, and in the intervals of exchanging knock for knock, they were able to exchange something of their ways of life and thought. Moslem civilization, scarcely less than that of the Christian West, was the heir of Hellenistic culture, and, even more than the West, had claimed the heritage of Greek science. With the contact of the two civilizations in Spain, the knowledge of the ancient geographers which had been preserved by the Moslems flowed back into Europe in the thirteenth century. Roger Bacon and Albertus Magnus, writing in the second half of that century, both showed a much clearer conception of the world than their predecessors: Albertus Magnus, for instance, scouted the popular error that those who might inhabit the southern hemisphere must inevitably fall off the world, and declared that the known climates are repeated in the lower hemisphere; this lower hemisphere he supposed to be largely inhabited, and if there were no intercourse between its inhabitants and the known world, it was simply because of the great seas that lay between.

While the nations of the peninsula were engaged in their struggle, the generality of Western peoples became acutely conscious that the birthplace of their religion lay in infidel hands and sought possession of it in the Crusades.

Development of Trade

The Crusades were not a national struggle in the sense that the Peninsular reconquest was: but, unlike it, they involved travel to distant lands and the organization of sea expeditions. These were not indeed the first large-scale maritime ventures of the medieval period. The Norsemen had long since ranged as far afield as the Mediterranean and North Africa. Nor were the Norsemen merely warriors and raiders. They found their way to Greenland in the tenth century and established colonies which lasted some three hundred and fifty years, and from Greenland they sailed on to discover the land they called Wineland, which may have been the American mainland. But the main body of Europe displayed little interest in the discoveries of the Norsemen, and after about 1410 even the settlements in Greenland were abandoned, apparently owing to difficulties in obtaining supplies.

The relations established by the Crusaders with the eastern Mediterranean, on the other hand, endured. The Crusaders had grown accustomed to the enjoyment of commodities which hitherto were little known in the West—spices, sugar, silks and carpets. Merchants from the seaports of Italy went to seek out these commodities in the Moslem ports of the Levant. This movement coincided with a general expansion of trade in the West, and the feudal conception of a static social order attached to the land yielded to the mobile influence of commerce. Trade between the Moslem and Christian worlds became lucrative and even necessary, especially to the states of Genoa and Venice, whose inhabitants obtained spices in Alexandria, Tripoli and other Moslem ports.

Growth of Tartar Empire

But the Italian merchants saw little of what lay beyond the Levant ports. They had no direct contact with those who produced the commodities they sought, and the East still remained a legendary region, where, according to rumour, dwelt the mighty emperor Prester John, and where was to be found the Earthly Paradise. The story of the existence of the fabulous Prester John dates from the middle of the twelfth century, when a letter purporting to have been written by Prester himself was circulated throughout the West. This letter gave an eloquent and imaginative account of the enormously opulent and mighty emperor, the zealous defender of the Christian Faith, the overlord of many vassal kings, whose realms even included a river flowing out of paradise. This forged letter was widely read. The fabled riches of Prester John drew the attention of Europe to the East, and the illusion of a mighty Christian power in Asia served to widen the narrow conception of a Western European Christendom.

The legend of Prester John therefore stimulated interest in the East. But it was not until nearly a century later that direct contact was made and maintained for roughly a hundred years, from 1250 to 1350. This contact was made possible by the rise of a new power in Asia, following the capture of Pekin by the Tartars in 1214. During the succeeding half-century the Tartars built up the vastest empire that had ever been known, stretching from the Danube to the China Sea, and ruled over by the Great Khan at Pekin. The peoples of the West were at first alarmed by rumours of this great expansion. But their fears were allayed by the tidings that the Tartars were not Moslems, but religious tolerators who were as ready to listen to Christianity as to any other religion. Accordingly in 1245 a Franciscan missionary, John of Pian de Carpine, took a message from the pope to Karakorum in the heart of Mongolia, and in 1251 William of Rubruck visited the same place. Between these two visits, a Tartar emissary came to France.

It was, however, a Venetian merchant family which seized the opportunity afforded by the creation of the tolerant Tartar Empire to make a thorough investigation of the East. Two brothers, Niccolo and Maffeo Polo, who were engaged in trade between Venice, Constantinople and Soldaia on the Black Sea, travelled eastward in 1260 to sell jewellery to the Khan of the Kipchak Tartars, and finding their return cut off by military operations, continued still eastward until they came to Pekin. Here the Great Khan received them and asked for a hundred Christian missionaries to debate with the priests of other religions at his court.

Wealth of the East

The Polos returned to Europe, and departed again for the East, accompanied by Niccolo's son, Marco, who was to spend seventeen years in the service of the Great Khan, and by means of his record, written in prison at Genoa, to enlighten the West about the peoples, towns, commerce and wealth of China, middle Asia, Arabia and East Africa. The *Book of Ser Marco Polo* was at once an adventure story, an exuberant introduction to the ways of the East and a commercial guide. It dazzled the West with accounts of the luxuries and vastness of the Great Khan's Empire—the profusion of desirable commodities, the Grand Canal some five hundred miles long and crowded with shipping, the system of post-horses, the raised and paved highways, scenes of wealth and plenty that were unknown in Europe.

Trade Routes Opened

Already the Italians had taken advantage of Tartar acquiescence to open a route to the East by which they could obtain their silks and spices without paying the high tolls that were levied at the Moslem ports of the eastern Mediterranean. Genoese established themselves at Tabriz in Tartar Persia, whence they could reach India and China overland or by sea. The use of these routes was, of course, conditional on the goodwill of the Tartars in Persia and in China. But already in the beginning of the fourteenth century commercial freedom was threatened when the Persian Tartars were converted to Mohammedanism. In 1368 the Tartar Empire in China was broken by a native rising, and a Chinese dynasty came to power and drove all foreigners out of China. The final bar across the land route to the Orient was set up by a new Moslem power, the Ottoman Turks, who, spreading out from their home in North-eastern Asia Minor, crossed the Hellespont and reduced Constantinople in 1356, and, defeating a crusade of Western knights at Nicopolis in 1396, opened the way for an invasion of South-eastern Europe. Already the Genoese and Venetians had seen their commerce in Eastern Europe threatened, and setting prudence before valour, they made treaties with the Ottomans and paid them tribute. The trade with the East was therefore subject to similar vexations as at the beginning of the thirteenth century. But the immense development of commerce in Europe made the prize for circumventing these difficulties much greater than it had been before.

Only a few years after the Italians had accepted the terms of the Ottomans there was born in Portugal the man who gave the impulse to the series of discoveries which led to the opening up of the whole world to

Original Settlements in the New World of the British French & Dutch & the New World Possessions of Spain & Portugal circa A.D. 1650-1700

BRITISH

IN DISPUTE BETWEEN BRITISH & FRENCH

FRENCH

PORTUGUESE

SPANISH

DUTCH

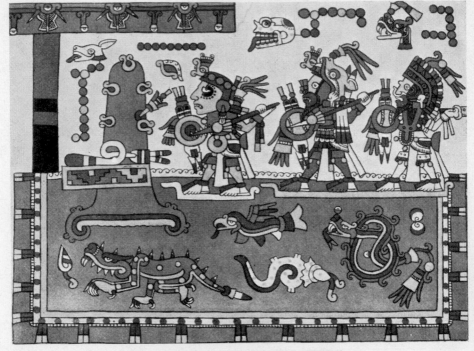

PAGE FROM THE ZOUCHE CODEX

The early Zapotec, or late Maya, manuscript known as the Zouche Codex, is one of the most notable examples of art left by the early inhabitants of Central America. This British Museum photograph shows three noted warriors leading an attack by boats on an island city. The original is painted on deerskin covered with a white pigment.

European knowledge and influence. By its very nature this age of exploration is unique and unrepeatable in the history of Western man. Yet the father of the great discoveries was born, lived and died in the narrow confines of Portugal, and never travelled farther afield than the northern tip of Africa.

The Infante Dom Henrique, rather inaccurately known as Prince Henry the Navigator, was born in 1394. His father, John I of Portugal, had raised himself to the throne at a moment when the growing power of Castile seemed likely to absorb his country, had trounced the Castilians on the field of Aljubarrota in 1383, and established a new dynasty in Portugal. Prince Henry was, therefore, a youth at a time when Portugal's sense of national vocation was running high. At the end of the

eleventh century, the little kingdom had been merely a county. The northern half alone had then been reconquered; from the waist downward Portuguese territory was still in Moslem hands. But the doughty Afonso Henriques (1111?-85) had established Portugal as an independent kingdom, and recovered Lisbon from the infidels; and his successors had rounded out its territory by driving back the Moslems, until in the middle of the thirteenth century Portugal reached the territorial limits it holds today, one of the earliest European states to do so.

Having preceded the rest of the peninsula in ejecting the Moslems, it was perhaps natural the Portuguese should conceive the idea of carrying the reconquest into enemy territory in North Africa. Prince Henry and his brothers certainly desired to emulate the deeds of their ancestors, and King John was persuaded by them to organize an expedition which was completely successful in capturing the Moroccan town of Ceuta in 1415. From the time of this venture Prince Henry kept ships at sea to guard the passage to North Africa, and about the same time he began sending forth ships to feel their way down the west coast of Africa. These first voyages were not entirely original, for a Genoese had visited the Canary Islands in 1270 and Portuguese mariners paid two visits to the same islands before 1341. But those expeditions seem soon to have lapsed, and it was left to Prince Henry to conceive a method of exploration and organize the means to carry it through. "Beyond comparison ambitious of achieving great and lofty deeds," Henry made the discoveries his life's work, and whatever meed of praise must be reserved for the daring captains of the various expeditions there can be no doubt that it was his knowledge and tenacity of purpose that moulded their personal efforts into a national enterprise.

Exploring Africa's Coast

Prince Henry's purposes are summarized under five headings by the historian Azurara. They are scientific, to obtain knowledge of the lands of West Africa; commercial, to establish trade with any Christians who might be there; strategic, to ascertain the strength of Moslem power in Africa; political, to find a Christian king who would join against the Moslems; and religious, to spread the Christian Faith. Attempts have been made to arrange these purposes in some order of priority, and the economic purpose has perhaps attracted undue attention. Henry's ships sought trade; but his ships, his intelligence service, his cartographers, pilots and books had to be paid for. He himself died deeply in debt, a seeker for knowledge, not a merchant prince.

The first success of the Portuguese was the discovery or rediscovery of the Madeira Islands and their subsequent colonization. Generally speaking, the early Portuguese mariners hugged the coast, their ships being too tiny and their equipment inadequate for oceanic sailing. The African shore with its shoals and long rollers was dangerous for coasting and there were places where insidious currents threatened disaster. For years Cape Nun seemed to forbid the passage of seafarers: it was after twelve years of effort that Gil Eanes passed Cape Bojador in 1434. Once this obstacle was overcome the Portuguese ships pressed forward, league by league, year by year. From 1437 to 1440 there was a lull while Prince Henry embarked on an injudicious and disastrous attempt to capture Tangier. But in 1444 and 1445 Senegal and Cape Verde were reached. The African desert lay behind, and the coast could be explored.

Meanwhile, the Portuguese had sailed to the archipelago of the Azores, seven hundred miles west of Lisbon. These and the Madeiras were found uninhabited, were colonized by means of royal concessions, and were soon sending cargoes of sugar to Europe. The establishment of these outposts made Portugal the first Atlantic power. Nevertheless, by the time of Prince Henry's death in 1460, the Portuguese had reached only the region of Sierra Leone, not a very great prize for forty years of effort. Yet in the equal period that followed they were to sweep down the African coast to the mouth of the Congo, round the Cape of Good Hope, up the East African coast to Mombasa, and finally across the intervening sea to India, thus attaining the old ambition to bring spices direct from the East.

Columbus and the Atlantic

The three great explorers who carried through this enterprise were Diogo Cão, who in the years 1482-86 set up inscribed landmarks at the Congo River and beyond; Bartolomeu Dias, who rounded the Cape of Good Hope in 1488 and Vasco da Gama, who covered the final stretch to India in 1498, and who by reason of his place in Camoens's national poem, "The Lusiads," has become the epic hero of the Portuguese discoveries. With the consequent opening of the seaway to India, King Manuel of Portugal became "Lord of the Conquest, Navigation and Commerce of Ethiopia,

Arabia, Persia and India." The fleet which Pedro Alvares Cabral took out in 1500 was completely paid for by the sale of the spices it brought back, notwithstanding the loss of half the vessels by shipwreck. And for good measure, this same expedition discovered the coast of Brazil.

In the century that elapsed between the birth of Prince Henry and the final attainment of India the Portuguese had done great things, and though they had not hesitated to make full use of the knowledge and ability of foreigners in their voyages, they treated the discoveries as a national enterprise. By the middle of the century, however, it was clear that there might be rivalry about the discoveries, especially with Castile. In 1344 a Castilian prince had obtained a royal title to the possession of the Canaries, and the Castilians had accordingly challenged Prince Henry's right to colonize these islands, which in 1480 were at length adjudicated to Castile in return for recognition of Portuguese claims to north-west Africa and to other islands in the Atlantic.

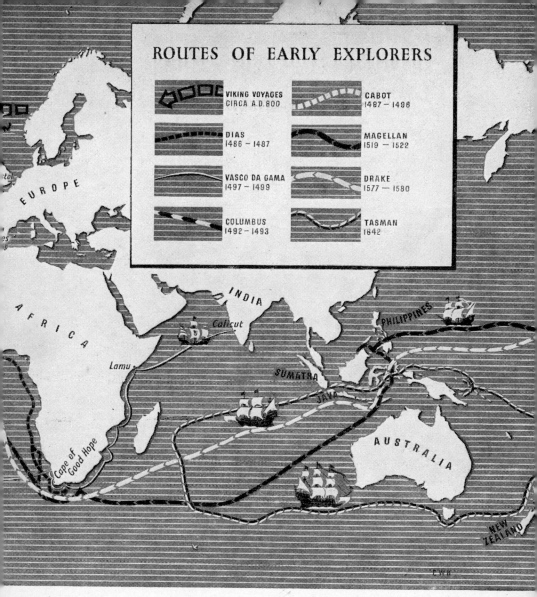

ROUTES OF EARLY EXPLORERS

VIKING VOYAGES CIRCA A.D. 800	CABOT 1497 — 1498
DIAS 1486 — 1487	MAGELLAN 1519 — 1522
VASCO DA GAMA 1497 — 1499	DRAKE 1577 — 1580
COLUMBUS 1492 — 1493	TASMAN 1642

Despite this agreement, Portugal recognized the danger to her monopoly, and enforced a policy of strict secrecy with regard to further discoveries. Soon after the agreement, the King of Portugal issued an order that foreign sailors found cruising in Portuguese African waters should be treated as pirates.

Such was the position when Christopher Columbus began his career. Born in Genoa in 1451, the son of an unsuccessful master weaver, Columbus settled in Portugal in 1479 and married a sister of the governor of the island of Porto Santo in the Madeiras. Of the journeys he made during his sojourn in Portugal little is known. But when he proposed to King John II that he sh.... a voyage of exploration into the ...., perhaps to discover new lands, perhaps to find a new way to Asia, his offer was refused. Certainly the Portuguese had no preconceived ideas against the possibility of land to the West: John may have felt that he had many more experienced pilots than Columbus for such an errand. In 1486 Columbus tried his fortune in Spain, but his plans were rejected by a committee of experts four years later. Despite this setback, Columbus remained unshaken in his purpose and beliefs and at length obtained the royal assent in 1492. There is little doubt that Columbus was an enthusiast much given to inaccurate and visionary discourses. He had probably found the Portuguese too exact and too experienced to listen to him, and also too intent on opening the way to India by the Cape of Good Hope. But the Spaniards in 1492 were on the verge of completing their reconquest by driving the Moslems out of Granada. Spaniards, and especially the monarchs Ferdinand and Isabella, were in the same mood of national and religious exaltation as the Portuguese had been in 1415. Almost certainly Columbus hoped to find a way to eastern Asia, for he took a letter from Ferdinand and Isabella addressed to the Great Khan. He also expected to find new lands. He did not expect to find a new continent.

America Discovered

Leaving the Canaries in September, 1492, Columbus sighted an outlying island of the Bahamas on October 12. The journey of five weeks was a short and auspicious one by the standards of African coastal exploration. He found Cuba, and identified it with the mainland of Asia, and the island now shared by the republics of Haiti and Santo Domingo, which he christened Española (anglicized as Hispaniola) and believed to be Japan. Raising a fort there, he returned to Europe and was blown into Lisbon, where he told his story to John II. The Portuguese King, now assured of reaching India by the Cape of Good Hope, was disturbed: it seemed for a moment that Columbus might have undermined the long-laid Portuguese designs on the sea-route to India.

Ferninand and Isabella, naturally accepted Columbus's account of his venture and awarded him the titles they had promised. Columbus's belief that he had found India accounts for the application of the word Indies, which has remained. Almost at once, the pope, who happened to be a Spaniard, granted the Spaniards a title of possession. The Portuguese lodged a protest in view of their own designs upon the East and their prior rights in African waters, and at length accepted a line of demarcation to run north and south 370 leagues west of the Cape Verde Islands. By limiting the Spaniards to the possession of whatever lay beyond this line, the Portuguese reserved Brazil to themselves.

Death of Columbus

Columbus naturally began his second voyage in 1493, full of hope. In fact, he found nothing that could be identified with what was known of Asia, and compensated for the non-appearance of the wealth of the Orient with a series of theoretical proofs of the rightness of his beliefs, which were both inexact and unconvincing. On his third journey he landed on the coast of Venezuela (1498), and rightly guessed that he had discovered a very great continent. But now his ideas of the distribution of land masses were quite confused, and harking back to the forged letter of Prester John, he supposed that the Orinoco flowed out of the Earthly Paradise. His administration of Hispaniola ended in disorder, and he returned to Spain a prisoner in irons. By order of Isabella he was released, but he had lost the eminence to which the promise of his first voyage had raised him. The news that Vasco da Gama had reached, by the Portuguese route, what was indubitably India, and had brought home valuable spices, must have been a very bitter blow to him: his death in 1506 attracted little attention.

The experiences of other sailors gradually induced the belief that a huge land mass barred the way to the coveted East, and Spanish mariners vainly sought a passage through this barrier. Meanwhile, the Portuguese were enjoying the fruits of Vasco da Gama's pioneering voyage. The second expedition to India, that of Pedro Alvares Cabral in 1500, though profitable, involved the Portuguese in hostilities in the East. This was not a crusade against the Moslems in alliance with Oriental Christians, as they had hoped, but a war which concerned the political rivalries of Indian states. From the moment Portugal upset the balance of

DISCOVERY OF THE MAGELLAN STRAIT

Gottfried's "Historia Antipodium," 1655, contains this engraving which shows the three ships of the explorer, Magellan, passing, in 1520, through the narrow rocky strait which now bears his name. Knowing nothing of what lay before him, and in spite of meeting with a hostile reception from the aborigines, he boldly sailed on; and for the first time European sailors entered the Pacific and reached the Spice Islands from the East.

power of the cities of the Malabar coast, she was drawn almost inevitably into military intervention and empire building.

The Moslems soon hit back at the trespassers upon their Indian trade, and fleets came from Egypt against the Portuguese. The great Alfonso de Albuquerque, who became governor of India in 1509, realized that Portugal could hold her new commerce only by sea power, and that the "Moors" must be pinned back in the Red Sea or the Persian Gulf. This required a strong fleet in the Indian Ocean. Thus Goa in western India became the centre of the Portuguese Empire in Asia, an empire that widened with the capture of Malacca, the penetra-

tion of the Malay archipelago, the reaching of the Spice Islands, the Moluccas, and the arrival of Portuguese ships in China and Japan. Portugal might now lay claim to the whole periphery of the Indian Ocean. But the very vastness of the empire made it precarious. Portugal could not hope to colonize the East as she had colonized the Azores and Madeira, and her resources were gradually wasted by numerous wars in India. Finally, in 1580, her crown passed to Philip II of Spain and she acquired the enemies of Spain, who soon made inroads on her oriental possessions.

The Portuguese Empire in the East was built up with astonishing speed. Within

Various handwritten annotations appear on the illustration:

D. fernan
ma put *da. cor tes montesu*
rador *chiliguil, nieto del enpe*

D. diego
de mendosa de *montesuma*
higo li ge timo. de D. fernando cortes,
mon te su ma guichiliguil.

de guichili
y de lacche
enperado
y reyes,
fueron d
niudaes

se fundose ni pique porbenias
de necayualcoyol, como descendire
safarereal

D. baltasar
de mendosa,
montesuma
higo ligitimo d
Don diego, den
donsa. de aus
montesuma
del emperado
montesuma

AZTEC GENEALOGY

Portion of a manuscript genealogy of Montezuma, who was Aztec emperor at the time of the Spanish conquest of Mexico. After welcoming Cortes with presents he eventually became a virtual captive in his own city of Mexico. When in 1520, the Spaniards were attacked by the natives of the city, Montezuma, on appealing to them to lay down their arms, was set upon by his own people and so seriously wounded that he died three days later.

twenty years of Cabral's expedition, the Portuguese were trading in China and had made themselves strong in Goa and had conquered Malacca. Twenty years after Columbus's discovery, the Spaniards had only begun to establish themselves on the American mainland, founding their first town at Darien on the Isthmus of Panama in 1509. They had, it is true, entrenched themselves in the Caribbean Islands, but their main effort had been to explore the American coasts in the hope of finding a passage through to India. Coasts were found in plenty not only by the Spaniards, but by Cabot, sailing from Bristol, and the Portuguese Corte-Reals, who visited Labrador. The seekers were encouraged by the discovery of the Pacific Ocean by Vasco Núñez de Balboa who crossed the narrow Isthmus of Panama in 1513. Balboa at once claimed the shores of the new ocean for Castile. But it was not until 1520 that Ferdinand Magellan (Fernão de Magalhães), a Portuguese sailing under the Spanish flag, discovered the strait that bears his name, and sailed into the Pacific.

Magellan crossed the Pacific and discovered the Philippine Islands, where he was killed in a skirmish. His companions visited the Spice Islands, which the Portuguese had already reached from the West, and went on to complete the first circumnavigation of the world, one of the most hazardous and magnificent exploits of a great age. The possession of the Spice Islands, the source of the much-sought merchandise of Asia, was the subject of a dispute between Spain and Portugal. In 1529 the islands were adjudicated to Portugal in return for a payment of money.

By this time, however, the Spaniards had somewhat altered their purpose. The desire for spices had been tempered by the discovery of precious metals in the New World. Discovery for the purpose of commerce gave way to empire, and navigators to conquerors. While Magellan was still encompassing the globe, a Spanish adventurer, Hernan Cortes, marched into the interior of Mexico and captured the emperor of the Aztecs, Montezuma, and his capital. Having laid low the highest civilization in North America, Cortes sent out his captains to reduce what is now Central America and laid the foundations of the Viceroyalty of New Spain. A few years later, Francisco Pizarro, an illiterate soldier of fortune, brought down the Inca Empire in Peru, and his companion, Almagro, carried Spanish arms into Chile. Jiménez de Quesada penetrated the Andine valleys of what is now Colombia in 1536, and founded the city of Bogota. Both in Mexico and Peru the Spaniards found precious metals in quantities comparable with the wealth attributed to Asia. By 1580, when the town of Buenos Aires was first founded, they had staked out an empire twice the size of Europe and had founded some two hundred towns.

Spanish Emancipation

The imperialism of the Spaniards in America was different in nature from that of the Portuguese in Asia. The Portuguese were confronted by a number of peoples in all states of civilization, some much more advanced than themselves, others recently converted to Islam, and therefore profoundly hostile. By contrast with the high civilization of India and China, most of the Americans were as children. The civilizations of the Aztecs, Mayas and Incas were remarkable, but on a material plane they were ignorant of the use of the true arch and even of the wheel, and of iron, despite their great achievements in architecture, astronomy and crafts. Phonetic writing was almost unknown, but the Mayas and Aztecs used pictographs.

Spanish nationalism was ripe for empire, and Spanish Catholicism was ready for the opportunity to proselytize. The basis for a Spanish Golden Age had been laid with the union of the two states of Castile and Aragon in the persons of Ferdinand and Isabella in 1474. A few years later, changes in the administrative system laid the foundations of Spanish bureaucracy. The monarchy won prestige in Spain and in Europe, and embarked on the dynastic alliances which brought the crowns of Spain and the Holy Roman Empire together in the possession of the Emperor Charles V. As an imperial power, Spain attempted to do for the New World what Rome had done for Spain. She gave colonists, her architecture, administration, laws, language, peace and religion. Rome had imprinted her civilization indelibly on Spain in two centuries: in three, Spain almost did as much in the Americas.

Appointment of Viceroys

In theory the possessions of the New World were kingdoms belonging directly to the Spanish Crown, not to the Spanish nation. At first the "conquerors" were licensed by the king to conquer, colonize and administer the New World. This implied the implantation of a feudal system, and the early institutions of Spanish America were strikingly feudal in nature. But the distance between the king and his new territories made it difficult for him to exercise any effective control over the conquistadores. As a result, the Crown had to protect its interests by appointing its own representatives, viceroys or captains-general, who received a copious stream of instructions from the royal council concerned with the affairs of the New World. Even so, the examples of ambition and avarice set by the early conquerors were not forgotten, and neither the Crown nor the Church proved capable of saving the Indians from the abuses of a system of forced labour. The enslavement of Indians was forbidden, while that of Negroes was permitted.

It is, perhaps, understandable that the colonists should not have appreciated the theological distinction, and when the efforts of priests such as Las Casas resulted in the modification of the laws, the practical result of their struggle was small. During the seventeenth and eighteenth centuries, therefore, the Indian remained in a position of feudal subordination as a hewer of wood and drawer of water. Although protectors or guardians were assigned to the Indians in the sixteenth century, their usefulness was limited by the fact that the Spaniards were dependent on Indian labour for the mines and for agriculture, and this labour could be obtained only under duress. Forced labour took a heavy toll of Indian lives and resulted in the depopulation of certain areas or the retirement of the Indians to remote and infertile mountain ranges or to the forests.

Inca Rebellion

So the first intention of saving the souls of the Indians for Christ was perverted by the need to exploit their bodies for silver, and the Indians became a subject race. Yet where there were no mines, the Indian stood a fair chance of responsible and paternalistic treatment. The Spaniards had little prejudice against intermingling with the natives, and there was no policy of deliberate extermination such as was practised in North America. It has been said that Spain gave her American empire three centuries of peace, and it must be granted that major disturbances were rare. In Peru Indian unrest simmered from time to time; as late as 1781 a great Inca rebellion broke out which was subdued only after there had been much fighting and bloodshed.

Even apart from the question of the Indians, which inevitably made the Spanish-American social structure differ from that of Spain, distinctions of class developed between the Spaniards themselves. The Spaniard born in Spain came out to the Americas with the king's commission, and whether as an official or as a soldier, had every intention of enriching himself and then returning to Spain. The American-born Spaniard, or creole, found himself debarred from the highest and most remunerative offices in the administration, and was indeed regarded as an inferior by the Peninsular Spaniard. The distinction between the two classes widened as immigration, which had been quite free until the middle of the sixteenth century, was more strictly controlled As time went on, the proportion of creoles in the population naturally increased, and in the course of the eighteenth century in particular they multiplied greatly in numbers and wealth. But the Peninsular Spaniards continued to enjoy the plums of office.

In this respect the Spanish system of government in America cannot be said to have provided the same allowance for natural evolutionary processes as the ancient Roman system in Spain. In fact, the government showed little change between the middle of the sixteenth century and the middle of the eighteenth. The pivots of the administration were the two viceroyalties in Peru and New Spain (Mexico). The Viceroy of Peru governed the whole of Spanish South America except Venezuela, though in practice the captaincy-general of Chile and six other regions enjoyed varying measures of administrative autonomy. The Viceroy of New Spain was responsible for the rest of Spanish possessions between the Philippines and the Caribbean Islands, though in fact a number of governors were again virtually independent of the viceroy.

Council of the Indies

Royal *audiencias*, or courts, acted partly as administrative councils and partly as courts of appeal with jurisdiction over wide areas. Under these, administration was based largely on the township. Here alone was there representation of the people, and even here seats on the town council which had originally been elective were soon regularly sold to the highest bidder. The method of government was thus autocratic, and the means of government were as centralized as circumstances allowed. From the Council of the Indies in Spain a flood of royal orders emanated, dealing alike with general policy and with the most trivial matters of bureaucratic routine. Instructions were accordingly passed on by the viceroy or, if inconvenient, were pigeon-holed. Official papers were voluminous and circulated slowly. Although every official from the viceroy downwards was required to face a public inquiry at the end of his term of office, it was generally understood that men went to the New World with the object of enriching themselves, and corruption was rife.

For three hundred years the Spanish possessions in America were kept isolated from the rest of the world. Even in the eighteenth century Spain was still seeking to assert monopolies of trade, navigation and colonization similar to those claimed by Prince Henry or Ferdinand and Isabella. The severe regimentation of commerce was partly accounted for by the need to protect the merchandise of the New World from the attacks of pirates or of the king's enemies. To this end only two fleets sailed annually from Andalusia across the Atlantic, the one to pick up the goods of New Spain at Vera Cruz, the other to Cartagena in modern Colombia. This second fleet received the goods of South America, the silver of Peru being brought by the Pacific route to Panama. At first even goods from Buenos Aires were carried overland to Peru: but from 1620 there was a small direct trade from the River Plate to Spain. The strict control of commerce at a few points and its concentration on long and uneconomic routes raised the price of ordinary European goods to exorbitant heights in Spanish America, especially in places remote from the authorized ports. High prices were tolerable in the bullion-producing areas of Peru and Mexico, but they made exchange difficult in the agricultural regions and put a brake on the development of commerce. Strict control and high prices encouraged smuggling

EARLY SIXTEENTH-CENTURY SHIP IN FULL SAIL

The blazing sun and shoal of flying fish pursued by porpoises were used by a cartographer of 1520 to show that the Tudor ship was in tropic seas. Such embellishments served both to suggest the wonders of foreign places, and helped to conceal the cartographer's ignorance.

EGYPTIAN SHIP, ABOUT 1250 B.C.

EARLY BRITISH CORACLE,
1st CENTURY B.C.

13th CENTURY; KING'S SHIPS SHOWIN
"CASTLES" AT BOW AND STERN

TRANSPORT ON LAND AND SEA
TO A.D. 1400

PACK PONIES, A FORM
OF TRANSPORT WHICH
IS STILL EMPLOYED

ROMAN MERCHANT GALLEY

SCANDINAVIAN LONG SHIP,
THE VIKING WARSHIP

11th CENTURY: FARM CART

14th CENTURY: HORSE LITTER

which increased enormously with the expansion of American population and wealth in the eighteenth century.

Nevertheless, the transatlantic galleons were preserved from excessive depredations at the hands of the pirates who infested the seas, especially the Caribbean. In spite of Spain's wars with other European powers in the seventeenth and eighteenth centuries, she was able to keep the whole of her American empire with the exception of Jamaica, which was captured by the English in 1656, Louisiana, Florida and a few islands.

While the Spaniards were consolidating their American empire, the Portuguese embarked upon the development of Brazil. Pedro Alvares Cabral's discovery of what he called the "Land of the True Cross" in 1500 did not lead to an immediate occupation, for the Portuguese were at that time far too busy in the East to pay much attention to a country where precious metals had not been found, and where the principal merchandise consisted, apart from dyewoods, of monkeys and parrots. Apart from their interests in Asia, the Portuguese had also established themselves at various points in East and West Africa, at once regions of greater strategic importance than Brazil, since they covered the sea route to the Indian Ocean, and of more political interest since, having identified the ruler of Abyssinia with the fabled Prester John, they felt obliged to concern themselves with the affairs of their fellow Christians in Africa. However, the visits of French ships to Brazil to collect cargoes of dyewood served to remind Portugal of her rights, and in 1531 an expedition was sent to establish a colony.

Coastal Colonization

In succeeding years the rest of the Brazilian coastline was split up into captaincies, which were granted to persons selected by the king. Such persons were given almost absolute rights to colonize, to found townships, to govern and to trade. Under this system, the captaincies attained various degrees of development, some remaining almost untouched, while others began to produce sugar, the crop with which

the Portuguese had been particularly successful in the Azores and Madeira. This coastal and sectional method of colonization has indeed left its mark in the development of Brazil, which still consists of a series of thickly populated coastal strips, sometimes almost isolated from one another, behind which lies a vast interior with only a sprinkling of inhabitants.

In the middle of the sixteenth century the Portuguese Crown found it prudent to strengthen and unify the colony by placing a governor in charge of the whole, with headquarters in the northern city of Bahia. This step was rendered necessary by the continued intrusions of the French, and these intrusions also made expedient the founding of a city in the southern part of the territory. The settlement of St. Sebastian, established in 1567, later became the city of Rio de Janeiro, and succeeded Bahia as the capital of Brazil.

Portuguese Independence

During the period when the Spanish and Portuguese Crowns were united, from 1580 to 1640, Brazil was exposed to the depredations of the Dutch, who succeeded in holding the city of Olinda for twenty-four years. With the restoration of Portuguese independence in 1640, however, the Brazilians not only succeeded in driving the Dutch out of their own territory, but also recovered part of Portuguese West Africa, of capital importance to them as the source of the slaves on whom the sugar industry depended. The Portuguese were at this time much less successful in recovering their oriental possessions from the Dutch, and they therefore turned their attention away from the East and towards the exploitation of Brazil.

Brazil amply rewarded their attention. In the last years of the seventeenth century, gold and precious stones were found in the region known as the "General Mines," and a veritable gold rush began, not only from Lisbon, but from the northern parts of Brazil. The colony passed rapidly from an economy based on the exploitation of the sugar-cane into one based on gold and diamonds. As in Spain, the Crown claimed a fifth part of the bullion that was mined, and

SPAIN'S "INVINCIBLE ARMADA" IN THE ENGLISH CHANNEL, 1588

The tapestry from which this engraving was made was at one time in the House of Lords, but has been destroyed by fire. Ships of Philip II's armada are shown in battle array, while the few English ships are being reinforced by others from Plymouth. The battle lasted a week, after which, with the aid of fireships and a favourable wind, the armada was utterly routed.

though the royal share was much reduced by evasion and fraudulence, it sufficed to raise the Portuguese monarchy from penury to magnificence. In throwing off the Spanish yoke in the movement of 1640, Portugal had certainly gained glory and regained sovereignty over herself: she had also found herself impoverished and weak. In these circumstances the influx of wealth from Brazil was providential.

The mines drew Portuguese of all classes and conditions to Brazil. But the fact that so small a power could colonize so vast an area was partly due to enforced immigration—the importation of slaves from the Portuguese stations in Africa. The involuntary African and the ambitious Portuguese together laid the foundations of Brazil. The former worked the sugar mills and the mines, while the Brazilian creoles, and especially the inhabitants of São Paulo, forced their way through the forests and up the rivers of the interior. The pioneering bands would consist of a leader with his household, dependants and slaves and a party of Indian followers. These would set out on an exploration of the backwoods that might last several years. Yet the pio-

neers had a rough hand. They did not hesitate to raid the reservations of the Jesuits who alone of the missionary orders seriously endeavoured to build a civilization for the Indians. The Jesuit "reductions" were inhabited only by the Indians and the priests, who set up their own paternalistic and theocratic form of government. There were in Brazil no natives of a relatively high degree of civilization such as the Incas or Aztecs. The Brazilian Indian did not survive as a conquered race servile to the conquering Europeans. He was in fact incapable of the heavy labour of the sugar field or mine, and he survives today in the north, where the Negro was introduced in large numbers to bear the brunt of manual labour, and in the interior where he has managed to keep his distance from the white man. In the south, where the creole pioneers had their way, Indian blood is relatively uncommon.

The eighteenth century saw a considerable development of Spanish America in wealth and population. After 1700 the restrictions on colonial trade were somewhat relaxed, and ships sailed from Cadiz to the Pacific ports of Peru and Chile.

SOURCE OF SPANISH WEALTH

No time was lost by the Spaniards in exploiting the natural resources of their South American possessions. In this woodcut in de Bry's "Voyages" (1591), aborigines are seen under armed supervision delving into the hillside for gold and silver, while others pile up the excavated earth before a seated Spaniard. The precious metal was later sent to Spain in great treasure convoys, which were frequently attacked by privateers.

The creole class grew rapidly in number and the total population of the Spanish New World is estimated to have risen from some five-and-a-half millions, plus an uncertain number of unassimilated natives in 1600, to about fifteen millions in 1810. The series of wars with Great Britain and other powers in which Spain was engaged in the course of the eighteenth century undermined Spain's position in Europe without seriously impairing her authority in the New World.

What aroused discontent and a sense of political detachment in the New World was partly the attempt by the Spanish monarchy to modernize the traditional institutions of the empire and partly the infection of a restless and revolutionary feeling bred elsewhere.

Among the Bourbon kings of Spain the outstanding ruler was Charles III, who endeavoured to promote a series of far-reaching reforms between 1759 and 1788. This attempt to replace the familiar lax administration by a modern bureaucracy with power to demand obedience and enforce taxation disturbed and upset the colonials. Thus in 1781 a serious revolt against the authorities occurred in New Granada (now Colombia) caused by the high rate of taxation. There was no doubt of the rebels' keen sense of local interests, but there was no question of their loyalty to the Spanish Crown.

When Charles III expelled the Jesuits from the Spanish New World, he removed the backbone of tradition and education in the colonies and perhaps the stoutest prop of the monarchical tradition. Moreover, Spain set her own colonies the worst possible example by siding with the thirteen British colonies of North America in their rebellion against the Crown. The success of the American Revolution provided Spain's own colonies with an obvious precedent; and through the United States of North America the revolutionary ideas of French thinkers of the eighteenth century filtered through to the creoles, despite the official prohibition of the circulation of such works. The French Revolution added its disturbing influence in the last decade of the eighteenth century.

Napoleon Invades Spain

However, active revolutionary ideas were entertained by only a minority of creoles. Most of Spanish America respected the monarchical and imperial tradition until, and even after, the crown of Spain was juggled away from the Bourbons by Napoleon. When the first important attempt to revolutionize South America was made by a Venezuelan, Francisco de Miranda, in 1806, it failed completely of its purpose. In the same year a British expedition against Buenos Aires led to the temporary capture of the town. The Spanish viceroy fled, and it was left to the inhabitants themselves to drive out the invaders, thereby winning a moral victory over both the British and Spanish. The creoles had not only gained self-confidence, but discovered how easily Spanish trade barriers might be broken down.

In 1808 Napoleon invaded Spain, and removing the Bourbons from the throne, placed his brother Joseph in their stead. The French sent commissioners to the New World as representatives of their monarchy in Spain. These were in some cases received by the Spanish authorities, but they were almost universally rejected by the creoles, and there began to appear governing councils (*juntas*), whose object was ostensibly to hold the New World in trust for the legitimate Bourbon King of Spain: in practice these *juntas* soon passed into the hands of extremists committed to the task of winning independence.

Movements of independence appeared in three areas—in the River Plate, in northern South America and in parts of Mexico. The struggle lasted from 1808 until 1824, and during the first half of this period it may be said to have failed everywhere except in the River Plate area. Simon Bolivar, the inspirer and crusader of independence in northern South America, was ejected and driven into exile in Jamaica and Haiti. The movement in Mexico led by the priest Hidalgo resulted in the arming of the Indians, whose inability and unwillingness to distinguish between creoles and Spaniards frightened the former into siding with the latter, until the movement collapsed. It even seemed that the Spaniards might threaten Buenos Aires from their stronghold in Peru.

But after 1816 the fortunes of war changed. Spain, devastated by the Napoleonic wars and torn by political divergencies, herself no longer had the resources to wage effective war upon her colonies. Bolivar returned to the mainland of South America and freed Venezuela and Colombia. In the south General San Martin crossed the Andes from what is now Argentina into Chile, whence he invaded Peru with a sea expedition.

New Sovereign States

The two movements, north and south, met later on in Ecuador, and San Martin, considering his task done, retired to Europe leaving Bolivar to complete the victory and organize the independent states of Latin America. The last important battle of the Wars of Independence was fought at Ayacucho in 1824 and ended with the rout or capture of most of the royalist forces in South America. By a more circuitous route Mexico reached the same stage of independence in the same year.

The Spanish Empire had disappeared after 330 years of existence. Despite the efforts of Bolivar to hold its parts together, it disintegrated and formed new and

SLINGER AND
ARCHER 1220

A NORMAN KNIGHT – 1066

DEVELOPMENT OF
ARMOUR AND WEAPON
BETWEEN 1066 AND 185

SOLDIERS
OF THE
15th CENTURY

A KNIGHT OF ABOUT 1320
SHOWING CHAIN MAIL REINFORCED
WITH PLATE ARMOUR

LATE 15th CENTURY
WAR HARNESS FOR
MAN AND HORSE

A CUMBERSOME
THREE-QUARTER
SUIT OF THE
17th CENTURY

A FUSILIER
1745

ARTILLERY ON FIELD SERVICE
IN INDIA 1857

separate states. These new states, though they corresponded closely to the administrative divisions of colonial days, nevertheless rejected everything that savoured of Spanish imperialism and set their political course by the rising star of the United States, the shining example of a group of colonies successfully erected into a sovereign state by their own efforts.

Conflict with Tradition

Hence the new states declared themselves republics, and committed themselves to theories of democratic government based on representative constitutionalism, which subsist with surprisingly little modification today. Nevertheless, those theories of government conflicted with three centuries of Spanish tradition. Spanish America was authoritarian, centralist and paternalistic by tradition: the system that had been gradually developed from North American experience for the United States could not suddenly, for the mere wishing, be made to fit Spanish America. The history of the Spanish-American republics since the gaining of independence is largely explicable in terms of the conflict between the Spanish authoritarian tradition and North American democratic theory.

But although the new states had a common heritage of three centuries of colonialism and underwent the same political influences in their formative years, they have now developed sharply differing personalities of their own, in which geographical, racial and economic divergencies have played their part. The new states originally numbered a dozen (including Portuguese Brazil), but already in the first half of the nineteenth century the unions of Central America and Greater Colombia dissolved into their component parts, and the Latin America of today consists of a score of republics.

Putting aside Brazil, which is a little larger than the United States, these republics range in size from Argentina, almost twelve times the size of Great Britain, to Haiti, smaller than Belgium. Some are peopled almost entirely by descendants of Europeans, such as Argentina, Chile, Uruguay and Costa Rica: some have a largely Indian population, such as Mexico, Guatemala, Peru, Bolivia and Paraguay; some are predominantly *mestizo*, or mixed-blooded, as Colombia; some have Negro stock, and one, Haiti, is almost entirely black or mulatto. Brazil, just as much as the United States, may be described as the melting-pot of all races.

Differences of climate are no less striking than differences of race, while the exploitation of local resources has contributed to the growth of new national characteristics. But the salient feature of the last hundred years has been the rapid development of the temperate areas of South America and especially of the region of River Plate, where alone in Spanish America there has been immigration on a scale comparable with that to the United States. The pampas of Argentina, for centuries a fertile wilderness, have been fenced off, stocked with cattle or tilled, penetrated by railways and roads, and made to deliver their produce to markets overseas. Their prosperity has been built up by several millions of European settlers, who have helped to make Argentina the richest, most developed, most urban and most European of the daughter nations of Spain, and who have made Buenos Aires the third city of the western hemisphere.

Military Dictatorship

In the north, Mexico, the most populous of the Spanish-American nations, has undergone many violent wars and revolutions in solving the racial and economic problems presented by the age-long spoliation of an illiterate and feudalized Indian peasantry. Liberalism was the solution sought by the great Indian president Benito Juárez, and economic development was the aim of the long dictatorship of Porfirio Diaz. Since 1910 the Mexican Revolution has followed both paths in trying to bring the Indian into the national life. Between Argentina and Mexico, there are states in all degrees of development: some like Colombia and Chile, distinguished for their stable governments and democratic practice; some, more remarkable for the turbulence of their revolutions or the length of their dictatorships. But there can be no

PROCESSING SUGAR

Native workers on a South American sugar plantation are depicted in this print from Theodore de Bry's "Voyages" (1591), cutting, crushing and boiling sugar-cane and ladling the sugar into pots for shipment to Spain—an example of the way the Spaniards developed the natural resources of their colonial possessions.

doubt that at present overt military dictatorship as a form of government has gone out of fashion, and that revolutions have become respectable. Neither authoritarianism nor corruption has disappeared, but the experience of recent years has been to prove that good government is both possible and practicable in Spanish America.

Brazil gained its independence from Portugal in the same period as Spanish America from Spain, but by a different method, that of gradual fission. When Napoleon invaded Spain, the Portuguese monarchy decided to take refuge in Brazil. Portugal was overrun, and Brazil was elevated to the rank of a kingdom. With the monarchy the institutions proper to a

kingdom were installed, and when the Napoleonic wave receded and the time came for the monarchy to return to the mother country, Brazil was no longer prepared to return to the status of a colony. Serious conflict was, however, avoided, and the Portuguese dynasty, the House of Bragança, continued to rule in both countries. Brazil retained its monarchical institution until 1889, and thereby secured peace during the transitional period between colonial status and nationhood.

The Wars of Independence were, for Spain, the ebbtide, as it were, of the great wave of conquest and colonization which began in 1492. After Ayacucho, she still retained Cuba and Puerto Rico in the Caribbean and the Philippines, all of which were lost in the Spanish-American conflict of 1898. The present Spanish Empire is limited to a strip of Morocco and a few small possessions in West Africa. Portugal, though equally weakened by the Napoleonic wars and the loss of Brazil, was able to form a third empire—or a fourth if we include her fifteenth- and sixteenth-century ventures in Morocco—by returning to her possessions in Africa. By the end of the nineteenth century she had consolidated her possession of two large colonies, Angola in West Africa and Mozambique in East Africa, which form the mainstay of her colonial empire of today. Fittingly she retains traces of her far-flung empire in four continents—the Azores and Madeira which now form part of European Portugal: Portuguese Guinea, the earliest colony of the modern world, and two groups of islands off West Africa, possessions in India and the peninsula of Macao in China, and half of the island of Timor in Oceania.

Loss of New World Possessions

Finally it remains to glance at Spain and Portugal themselves, the originators of the great movement of European discovery, conquest and settlement. Both were devastated by the Napoleonic Wars at the beginning of the nineteenth century; both suffered serious economic difficulties through the loss of their possessions in the New World; and both were deeply divided for and against nineteenth-century liberalism and involved by the commingling of ideological and dynastic issues in disastrous civil wars.

In both cases the substitution for the old absolutist monarchical system of the eighteenth century of that of constitutional government and party politics was attended by unrest, corruption and intrigues, which at length discredited the monarchy and led to its replacement by republican systems. But here the resemblance ends.

Portugal, despite the fact that she has a problem in the limitations of her natural resources, has gradually built up her new empire in Africa, restored her financial stability, and under the leadership of Dr. Antonio de Oliveira Salazar, has experienced a period of reconstruction which, though impeded by war, provides at least a beginning for the future.

Problems of the Spanish Republic

Spain, now as ever a land of violent contrasts, has suffered many forms of political torment. Political action has done little to solve her problems: direst poverty and disproportionate wealth exist side by side; blind anti-clericalism faces sometimes fanatical piety, sometimes blind superstition; politically minded generals are always at the service of opportunism. Yet sane and liberal Spaniards have not been lacking. When, in 1931, the monarchy crumbled away, the Spanish Republic was born peacefully, and it seemed hopefully. Five years later those hopes were dashed: Spain, hopelessly and passionately divided against herself, plunged into the bloodiest civil conflict of her history and, under the pretence of non-intervention, the German and Italian dictators carried out a cynical experiment in military dissection on her tormented body.

Test Yourself

1. What causes led Europeans in the sixteenth century to take an interest in other parts of the world?
2. Compare the work of the Spaniards and the Portuguese as discoverers.
3. Sketch the organization of the Spanish conquests in the New World.
4. Suggest motives for the movement for independence in Spanish and Portuguese colonies in South America.
5. Summarize the similarities and differences of the Latin American nations of today.
6. Compare the relative situations of modern Portugal and Spain.

Answers will be found at the end of the book.

CHAPTER VII

BALANCE OF EUROPEAN POWER IN THE MERCANTILE AGE

DURING the period with which we are going to deal, Western European humanity was faced with two problems which have again cropped up in the years between the two world wars. There was the difficult relationship between sovereign states, and the equally difficult relationship between the ordinary citizen and the chief of state with unlimited powers.

The great King Louis XIV, who ruled France from 1661 to 1715, has been called the Hitler of an older Europe. The parallel does not apply without a number of reservations, but it is striking enough to make the modern reader sit up and take notice. To understand the age of Louis XIV we must study these two problems of inter-state relations and of unrestricted state authority. We shall find that they are closely connected, that they are, in fact, two aspects of the same historical development. To see this clearly is to understand the period.

What strikes us most, when we look at the second half of the seventeenth century, is the intense activity of international relations. Negotiations, treaties of alliance, wars during which negotiations went on merrily, conferences, congresses, peace treaties, followed each other in rapid succession. There was no novelty in this: what was new was the regularity of it all, the growing concern of statesmen with foreign affairs, the increasing tendency to entrust professionals with the representation of their countries' interests abroad. System, even science, crept into state relations, as also into military art.

If we look, now, at the individual states of Western Europe, the states that were so actively preoccupied with each other, we find that, with the exception of England and the Dutch Republic, they were governed by a system which has become known as ripe absolutism. Absolutism is the system of government in which the monarch is completely identified with the state. His will, which is supposed to represent the Divine Will, is subject to no control or limitation. Should we say that such a system deserves no other name than that of tyranny? Not necessarily. The absolute monarch may be conscientious and well advised, and his rule may be a blessing to his people. There is one, and only one proviso. The power of the absolute monarch must answer to a need existing in his own time, and the time for absolutism is over by now. No one can hope ever to understand history if he forgets that what is wrong today may have been right in times gone by.

Respect for Royalty

Absolutism arose because the nobility had performed its task and refused to leave the stage where it was no longer needed. The strong monarch alone was able to give his subjects the unity of government, the centralization, the rule of law and order which the self-seeking high nobility did not care to achieve. The end of the Middle Ages and the beginning of the modern era witnessed the rise of absolute rulers whose appearance was well received.

In France, which is in many respects the model of all political development on the European Continent, royalty had curbed the high nobility and was keeping it in check. By the time the middle of the seventeenth century had been reached, only one more step had to be taken in this direction. Obedience, still the result of fear inspired by the king's power, must become an automatic habit. Respect for the royal figure must become the mainspring of submission, especially on the part of the high nobility.

The two great cardinals who had ruled France before the accession of Louis XIV

TIME CHART

A.D. 1501—1700

A.D.	
1501	Partition of Naples between France and Spain.
1503	Marriage of James IV of Scotland and Margaret of England.
1504	Guilds and companies placed under state supervision by Henry VII.
1509	Spanish conquests in N. Africa.
1511	Henry VIII joins Holy League against France.
1516	Portuguese begin trade with China.
1517	Syria and Egypt conquered by Ottoman Empire.
1519	First voyage round the world by Magellan.
1520	Henry VIII and Francis I of France meet at Field of the Cloth of Gold.
	Charles V Emperor over the larger part of Europe.
1521	Martin Luther excommunicated for defying the Pope.
1522	Turks capture Rhodes.
1525	Spain acquires ascendancy in Italy.
1526	Tyndale's translation of the Bible admitted into England.
	Invasion of Hungary by the Turks.
	Mogul dynasty founded at Delhi.
1528	First Protestant martyrs burned in England.
1529	Turks invade Germany and besiege Vienna.
1530	Spinning wheel invented in Germany.
	Malta given to the Knights of Rhodes by Charles V of Spain.
1534	Ignatius Loyola founds order of Jesuits.
	England breaks away from Roman Church. Henry VIII makes himself head of the English Church.
1536	Dissolution of the English monasteries.
	Unification of English and Welsh systems of government.
1538	Charles V forms alliance with France against Turks.
1541	Knox begins reformation in Scotland.
	Turks overrun Hungary.
1542	Christianity introduced to India by Francis Xavier.
	Commercial treaty between Portugal and Japan.
1543	Henry VIII allies with Charles V against Francis I.
1548	Turks invade Persia.
1549	Introduction of first English Prayer Book.
1553	Restoration of Roman Catholicism in England under Mary Tudor.
1555	Philip of Spain acquires the Netherlands.
	Protestants tolerated in Germany under Peace of Augsburg.
	Charles V resigns Italy and Netherlands to Philip of Spain.
1556	Abdication of Charles V. Possessions divided between his brother and son.
	Akbar, Mogul Emperor, raises empire to its greatest splendour.
1558	England loses Calais to France.
1559	Protestantism re-established in England under Elizabeth.
	Decrease in influence of German Hansa towns.
1562	John Hawkins starts slave trade between Africa and America.
	Massacre of Vassy opens French Wars of Religion.
	Religious liberty granted to the Huguenots in France.
1565	Spain occupies Philippines.
	Turks unsuccessfully besiege Malta.
1569	Mercator's map of the world founds modern cartography.
1571	Cyprus reduced by Turks; defeated by Don John of Austria off Lepanto. End of Turkish naval power.
1572	Huguenots massacred in France on St. Bartholomew's Eve.
1576	Dutch provinces unite against Spain.
1577	Sir Francis Drake sails round the world.
1579	Dutch Republic founded.
1580	Portugal under Spanish dominance.
1581	First trading relations established between England and the Ottoman Empire.
1582	Gregorian reformation of the calendar.
1584	Potatoes first imported into Europe.

A.D.	
1586	Tobacco first introduced into England.
	Disputes over the French crown by Henry of Navarre and Henry of Guise.
1588	Destruction of Spanish Armada by the British fleet.
1590	Coal mining begins in Ruhr district of Germany.
1592	Portuguese settle in Mombasa.
	Presbyterian system established in Scotland.
1595	Dutch begin to colonize in E. Indies.
1596	English raid Cadiz; England, France and Netherlands ally against Spain.
1598	Toleration granted to Protestants in France by Edict of Nantes.
1600	East India Company incorporated by Elizabeth.
1601	Persians win back territory from the Turks.
1602	Persecution of Protestants in Bohemia and Hungary.
1603	Union of England and Scotland by accession of James VI of Scotland to English throne.
1604	Authorized Version of the Bible commenced; published 1611.
1605	Gunpowder Plot. Attempt to blow up English Houses of Parliament.
1606	Commercial treaty between England and France.
1609	First English Embassy to India.
1610	German Catholic League founded by Maximilian of Bavaria to counteract Protestant Union.
1611	Dutch trade with Japan.
1618	Start of Thirty Years War.
1619	Emigration of Pilgrim Fathers to America.
	Batavia founded by the Dutch.
1621	Conflict between English and Dutch East India Companies.
1622	First weekly newspaper in England.
1624	Ministry of Cardinal Richelieu in France.
	First English settlement in India.
1627	England at war with France in support of the Huguenots.
1628	Petition of Right in England.
1640	Portugal revolts from Spain: War of Independence.
1642	Tasmania and New Zealand discovered.
	Civil war in England.
1643	Accession of Louis XIV of France: Ministry of Cardinal Mazarin.
1648	End of Thirty Years War.
1649	Charles I tried and executed.
	Cromwell establishes the Commonwealth in England.
1650	Tea first imported into England.
1652	Naval war between England and Holland.
	Capetown founded by Dutch.
1653	Cromwell made Lord Protector.
1660	Restoration of the monarchy in England.
1665	Great Plague of London. Second naval war with Holland.
1666	Great Fire of London.
1667	Louis XIV of France invades Netherlands. Dutch fleet sails into the Thames.
	Peace of Breda between England and Holland.
1668	Triple Alliance, England, Sweden and Holland against France.
1670	Secret Treaty of Dover allying France and Britain against Holland.
1672	Declaration of Indulgence ends persecution of non-conformists in England.
1678	Beginning of the party system in British Parliament.
	Peace of Nijmegen makes France most formidable power in Europe.
1685	Revocation of the Edict of Nantes. Huguenots flee to England, Germany and America.
1687	French Huguenots settle at Cape of Good Hope.
1688	Louis XIV begins war against Germany and Holland.
	Abdication of James II. Mary and William of Orange become joint sovereigns.
1694	Foundation of the Bank of England.
1697	Peace of Ryswick between France, England, Holland and Spain.
1699	Power of the Ottoman Empire broken.

to power, Richelieu (1622-42) and Mazarin (1642-61), had laid the foundations upon which Louis was able to build. Thus, in its ripe old age, could absolutism become the natural form of government, could the law rule instead of the sword, and could Western Europe move towards new forms of government more consonant with progress and human dignity.

Coached by Mazarin, who, during the young king's minority, was his tutor as much as his prime minister, Louis XIV was well aware of the task that awaited him. When, at the age of twenty-three (1661), he took over the direction of his country's affairs, he knew that it was his royal duty to be the centre and pivot of government. He may not always have lived up to his great obligations. Pleasure often caused him to neglect his work. But the very fact that the king's presence, his semi-divinity, was being accepted more fervently every day by the very people whom it deprived of the last relics of their former influence, made these lapses less important. Developing a trend which his predecessors had started, he wisely decided to give the high nobility a substitute for the political influence and the territorial power of which he was depriving them. He gave them glory and kudos, and, most important, he made their greatness consist primarily in their close association with his daily existence.

King-worship

The opportunity for enjoying this priceless privilege of personal contact with the Sun-King—it was Louis himself who chose the sun as his emblem—was provided by court life. A fitting background for king-worship was the immense and beautiful palace at Versailles, constructed by the architect Le Nôtre. With its magnificent gardens and its lake which stretches where once no water was to be found, it proclaimed the triumph of tidiness born of planning, the supreme significance of controlled immensity, and of a calmness that seemed more than human. There the king would hold his petty and grand levees, when his noblemen were privileged to witness the details of his personal toilet. So it came about that administration was

no more a nobleman's concern than work or trade. His task was king-worship.

The secret of the king's power over his environment resided partly at any rate in his personal magnetism. At the beginning of his reign, he was, undoubtedly, a strikingly handsome young man. It was a pleasure to listen to his fine voice and his beautiful diction. Royal in every movement, he managed to convey to those around him the conviction that it was a rare privilege to be in his presence. He knew how to exploit his charm: there was nothing spontaneous in his behaviour.

Use of Professional Administrators

Total success crowned his endeavours, and before long his personal ascendancy was accepted by all who knew him. His noblemen acquired the habit of consulting him at every important step in their existence. No marriage was arranged in court circles before the king had personally investigated all its advantages and disadvantages. Soon, instead of asking the king's advice, the noblemen craved his permission. By his rulings the king taught his nobility to look upon matters of race and blood with a severity that would have put the most thoroughgoing Nazi to shame. He made them feel that they were made of an essence different from that of other men. Thus notions of honour and of race filled their minds, the puzzling out of questions of ancestry, precedence and dignity occupied their time, and, meanwhile, their ambition ceased to pursue power and to be dangerous to the state.

The business from which the high nobility was so carefully kept away was handled by various councils over which the king himself presided. They consisted of high-ranking civil servants belonging to the upper-middle class. An exception was made in favour of the Princes of the Blood, who partook of the semi-divine royal essence, and were therefore allowed a share in government.

Instead of governors belonging to the high nobility, the provinces were given professional administrators, *intendants*, who reported regularly to the council and received their instructions from it.

Prosperity was, after law and order, the principal concern of the absolute monarch's centralized administration—we shall presently see how this came to pass. There can be no doubt that this policy met with considerable success, and that for a long period the French were given efficient, wise and successful government.

Such, then, was the machinery of ripe absolutism, the system by which the unlimited monarch was able to substitute the habit of total obedience for the practice of submission inspired by fear. The French system was copied in many European countries. The Austrian territories of the House of Habsburg, whose head was also German Emperor; the Spanish monarchy; Brandenburg, which was soon to blossom out into the Kingdom of Prussia; and a number of Italian principalities, were all passing through a period of ripe absolutism, less thorough-going than that of France, but inspired by the same principles.

Now, it is essential that we should bear in mind that all these monarchies which existed side by side had grown from small beginnings, by a process in which force was the main element of success. The gradual establishment of order and sound government in the place of administrative chaos and economic disruption was effected by conquests, by the fact that one stronger territorial ruler had slowly established his authority over his neighbours. The units owned by these successful rulers increased in size, till they formed those monarchies, France, Spain, and so forth, whose populations were developing a loyalty to their rulers, a loyalty which was later to develop into national consciousness. Sooner or later these different expansionist movements were bound to meet and to clash. Between the French and the German monarchies, for instance, lay much territory that was no more indicated by Nature as the perquisite of the one than of the other. Disputes must arise over these border zones. Sometimes also one monarchy grew so powerful that it became a menace to its neighbours.

Thus the House of Habsburg, which at the beginning of the sixteenth century had acquired not only the hereditary lands of

Austria, but also the Low Countries, Spain, and a portion of Italy, hemmed in France and threatened its very existence. The French kingdom fought back, and saved itself from absorption. By the time Louis XIV began his personal rule, France had achieved its security. But was it going to rest, now that it was safe? It would be asking too much from human nature to expect this. Expansion had for centuries gone hand in hand with centralization and the improvement of administration. The kings of France had looked too long upon the offensive as a form of defence, and could not bring themselves to give it up. Now France became a danger to the neighbours who once threatened her.

Warfare was, moreover, second to king-worship, the best way of keeping the unemployed nobility out of mischief. They were professional soldiers by origin and by tradition. At the same time war, at least if it were successful, increased the glory of the monarch. Conquest added to the fascination which was an essential part of the moral power it was his business to exercise. In this business morality had no say. The doctrine which provided absolutism with its basic outlook on life was the invention of Italian thinkers, who had argued that the sole consideration which must direct a ruler's actions was "reason of state." According to this doctrine, morality was valid for private individuals only. A ruler must ignore morality and act exclusively in the interest of the state, that is, in his own interest.

Thus it was that power, which can be defined as force held in reserve, became the prominent preoccupation of all absolute rulers. To be powerful was the aim of all government. Even the task of centralizing the administration and making it more efficient, which was, after all, an historical necessity, was looked upon as a method for increasing a country's power. More than this, the economic policy pursued by the absolute governments was entirely subordinated to considerations of power. We call the seventeenth and eighteenth centuries the age of mercantilism. The word mercantilism suggests merchant

OMMEGANCK PROCESSION IN BRUSSELS, 1615

Part of one of the large canvases, now in the Victoria and Albert Museum, painted by Denis van Alsloot for the town hall in Brussels, shows a section of the great procession, in which the whole of the city's civic pomp was displayed, similar in many ways to a Lord Mayor's Show in London. The Ommeganck procession, which originated as far back as 1348, commemorates the subject of numerous legends—the arrival of a boat from Antwerp with a statue of the Virgin Mary. Many of the costumes and banners were destroyed by the Nazis during their occupation of Belgium in the Second World War. Those now used represent only a part of the selection previously held in Brussels.

FIGHTING A FIRE IN SEVENTEENTH-CENTURY NUREMBERG

Two types of fire pump are shown in action in this engraving of 1658. Both are worked by hand, each engine being supplied with water from large butts drawn on runners. In the foreground the largest pump (A) is being operated by sixteen men. Two others replenish the tanks and a third directs the hose. Beyond, is a smaller pump (B) operated by one man, and light enough to be carried upstairs, while shown at (C) is a pump being used to play water on to the burning house from an adjoining property.

calculation, that is, a preoccupation with money and trade. It is a fact that statesmen of the seventeenth century professed doctrines known as mercantilism, which preached a system of organized prosperity, of state interference in favour of trade and industry; a method, in short, which aimed at increasing a country's wealth. It is a fact, also, that France, in particular, carried this system to great lengths. Colbert, who was Louis XIV's minister of finance from 1661 to 1683, gave the mercantilist system its alternative name of Colbertism. He was a thorough protectionist, and encouraged new industries.

The whole system, however, was con-

cerned with prosperity merely as a means, never as an end. Its aim was to increase the king's power. In olden days kings had a war chest in which they collected treasure against the day when they would go to war. But it had been discovered, before the days of Colbert, that this system was faulty. Wealth ought not to be immobilized in the king's treasure house. Let cash circulate, instead, and multiply. Whenever it was needed it could be extracted from the subject by taxation. Of course, it must not leave the country or it would be lost to the exchequer. This is the origin of the mercantilist doctrine that a country's wealth consisted in its stock of precious metals, and that the aim of foreign trade was to have a favourable trade balance, i.e. so that there was a flow of gold into the country.

Now we are in possession of the formula of the age: power unlimited! Unlimited power for the central government which, as preachers and prelates never tired of explaining from the pulpit, represented God on earth. There must be one religion in the state, for men must think alike, and their thoughts must be of obedience. No subject should be allowed to withdraw from complete participation in the life of the state into a religion which was not that of his fellow-subjects truly a striking anticipation of twentieth-century totalitarianism. Power, also, had to be the aim and inspiration of the state's relations with the outside world. Here, indeed, power could hardly be unlimited: the limit of one's power was the power of one's neighbour.

If, ideally, the power of France was to be unlimited, it is not surprising that those who wielded it, the king and his close advisers, should dream of extending it over other countries. They thought out a system, which became known as Bourbonism, from the family name of the royal house of France (the Bourbons). According to this system the king of France was destined to share power over the whole of Christian Europe with the German Emperor and the Russian Tsar. France's share was to be Spain and Portugal, with their colonies, Italy and all the Low Countries. This compact state could then, it was fondly imagined, live at peace with its German neighbour. England would probably be a vassal state, ruled by a Catholic Stuart under French supervision.

France and the Spanish Succession

Now, it happened that the King of Spain, Charles II (1665-1700), was an ailing man, not likely to leave any descendants. Allied by marriage to the House of Spain, Louis XIV looked upon himself as the heir of the Spanish monarchy. Throughout his reign he was mindful of the possibilities implied in this claim to the Spanish succession. Sometimes he was content to help himself to minor portions of the Spanish possessions to the north and north-east of his kingdom. From time to time, when Charles of Spain was reported to be more ailing than usual, the dream of raking in the complete succession would take substance and shape, and all considerations of immediate gain had to give way while the master plan was allowed to mature.

French Threat to Europe

With its increasingly efficient administration and its growing resources, the France of Louis XIV, guided by principles such as these, was fast becoming a menace to Europe. Its king was clearly aiming at what the English and the Dutch, with some exaggeration but nevertheless with good reason, called "Universal Monarchy." They saw this Universal Monarchy as a system under which absolutism would rule over the whole continent, with compulsory Catholicism and a complete lack of freedom for the individual conscience. The fight was joined, first of all, by the Dutch, though not of their own choice (1668). About twenty years later the English entered the fray and this meant the end of Louis's dream of universal domination. But the end was long in coming.

Neither the Dutch Republic nor England corresponded to the pattern of government prevalent in the age of Louis XIV. Both had moved beyond absolutism, though in different ways and for different reasons. In 1648 England became a commonwealth. At the time of Louis XIV's accession to personal power, it is true, England had just restored the monarchy (1660), but the king's power was limited by that of Parliament. Power was henceforth shared by the king, the landed aristocracy, and the merchant classes. The Stuart kings, Charles II (1660-85) and James II (1685-88), attempted to restore absolutism, but it was too late for this. Safe behind the protecting seas, England had been able to hasten the course of its evolution. The task of absolutism was terminated, and instead of being progress, as it was in France, absolutism in England was pure reaction. With absolutism, certain modes of thinking, familiar upon the Continent, were also disappearing. Reason of state was not the guide of all English policy, and the statesmen of that country pursued prosperity for its own sake, although they were not blind to considerations of power.

The Dutch Republic, which was called upon to offer the first resistance to the Bourbonism of Louis XIV, was even more advanced in its evolution than England. It was born of a revolution against absolutism, in the sixteenth century, and now, in the seventeenth century, it was governed by the upper-middle class. This was a stage reached only in the nineteenth century by the rest of Western Europe. The Dutch State was unique in Europe. It was a federation of seven sovereign provinces, and in each province the sovereignty resided with the States or Assembly of the province. An assembly of delegates from each province, the States General, represented this sovereignty toward the outside world.

Regents of Holland

In theory, at any rate, any province had the right to veto any proposal which was before the States General. Yet the Dutch Republic was not in such a chaos as one might have expected judging from its queer constitution. This was due to the fact that the province of Holland, in which most of the big towns were situated, was wealthier than all the other provinces put together, and could, as often as not, get its way merely by the threat of withholding its financial contribution. There was another element making for unity. In recognition of the immense services rendered to the Dutch Commonwealth during the first years of the fight against Spain by the Prince of Orange, known as William the Silent, the successive heads of the House of Orange were appointed to several key positions in the Republic. They were commanders-in-chief of the armed forces of the whole Republic, and they were chief executive officers in most of the sovereign provinces. This was the office of stadtholder, a word which one might translate as lord lieutenant. These princes were not sovereigns. Their office was not

hereditary, but their appointment, upon the death of the previous stadtholder, became a matter of custom, and there was a fair chance that sooner or later they would rise to be the undisputed masters, perhaps even the sovereigns, of the country.

The regents or professional administrators, a narrow group of men who dominated the province of Holland, were not interested in the system of power politics which was the main preoccupation of statesmen in other countries. They were descended from wealthy merchants, and remained interested in trade by holding directorships in big overseas enterprises, or by being sleeping partners in some important business. They retained all the virtues and shortcomings of a merchant class. Power as such did not interest them: they wanted the Dutch State to protect navigation and commerce, and their concern was first and foremost for the prosperity of the country. Moreover, they were tolerant, because merchants are in the habit of rubbing shoulders with men from many climes and professing different religions. This caused them to protect those who did not belong to the dominant Calvinist Church.

The regents of Holland came in conflict with two groups of people. In the first place there was the mass of Calvinists, who were strongest among the lower-middle class and the working class of the towns. These people agreed with their ministers who demanded the repression of Nonconformism and Catholicism. The ministers wanted the Dutch State to be another Geneva, ruled according to Holy Writ, and they looked upon the Dutch nation as a second Israel. They loathed the tolerance of the regents. For very different reasons, the princes of Orange equally disliked the policy of the regents. They were professional soldiers, who throve by war, while the regents realized that peace is better for a country's trade, and avoided anything that might bring them in conflict with foreign nations. At the same time the princes of Orange were always trying to increase their power in the Republic, and to achieve their ends they encouraged every tendency towards

SEVENTEENTH-CENTURY TAILOR

Painted by van Brekelenkam about 1650, this picture, now in the National Gallery, shows a Dutch tailor and his assistants at work in the corner of his living-room, sitting cross-legged upon their work tables in the traditional manner. The woman, presumably the tailor's wife, with her baby, adds a note of domesticity to the scene.

centralization. They disliked the sovereignty of the provinces, and their endeavour was always to increase the power of the States General at the expense of this sovereignty. The regents, on the other hand, supported the system of provincial sovereignty, under which their stronghold, the Province of Holland, dominated the Republic by the power of the purse.

The Calvinist democracy and the princes of Orange had long since (in 1618) concluded an alliance, based upon their common dislike of the regents' power. Usually, a subtle balance was preserved between the two parties. But now and

then some issue divided them very sharply, and then the Prince of Orange, who had the support of the masses and who disposed of the armed forces, had little difficulty in imposing his will on his opponents. Such a conflict occurred in 1650, when the young stadtholder, William II, who objected to a plan of the Holland regents to retrench on military expenditure, imprisoned several leaders of the regents' party and tried to take the wealthy town of Amsterdam by force. It is probable that he would have succeeded in carrying through his programme, but he died unexpectedly of the smallpox. His heir, the

TRANSPORT ON LAND AND SEA FROM THE FIFTEENTH TO NINETEENTH CENTURY

15th. CENTURY; THE "SANTA MARIA" IN WHICH COLUMBUS VOYAGED TO AMERICA

17th. CENTURY; PRIVATE COACH

18th. CENTURY; SEDAN CHAIR

16th. CENTURY:
BAGGAGE WAGGON

16th. CENTURY:
THE "GOLDEN HIND"
IN WHICH DRAKE
SAILED ROUND THE
WORLD

DUTCH EAST
INDIAMAN,
1740

EARLY 19th. CENTURY:
STAGE COACH

CYCLING IN THE
EIGHTEEN-SEVENTIES

future King William III of England, was born a week after his father's death.

Here was the opportunity of the Holland regents. They decided to do without a stadtholder, and introduced a new system in which their own preponderance was made secure. This was the so-called stadtholderless period of Dutch history. The chief officer of the province of Holland, the Grand Pensionary, became in fact the Prime Minister of the republic. He had charge of its foreign policy, and saw to it that the principles of prosperity and retrenchment were scrupulously observed. Most of the time, from 1653 to 1672, this office was held by John de Witt, one of the greatest Dutchmen who ever lived. But de Witt was not able to give his country the peace for which it longed. Yet it was not from France, which was fast growing into a permanent threat to the independence of the Dutch, that the first challenge came.

Relations between the Dutch Republic and England were governed by two contradictory and indeed incompatible principles. From the point of view of England's safety, the Low Countries occupied, as indeed they still do, a very special position.

Opposite the dangerously open eastern shore of England lie the Low Countries, with wide estuaries from which a hostile fleet could easily sally unperceived to begin an invasion. For centuries English statesmen have rightly considered that it was vital for the safety of their country that the dominant power on the European Continent should have no footing in those Low Countries. To defend them against any possible disturber of the European peace has therefore always been a primary object of English statesmanship.

Against this consideration, which tended to make England and the Dutch Republic natural allies, there stood another set of factors which worked in the opposite direction. Both the Dutch and the English were enterprising seafarers and colonizers, and their interests clashed in many parts of the globe. The Dutch, moreover, were somewhat ahead of the English in their economic development, especially as the quarrels between kings and parliaments, which filled the first half of the seventeenth century, prevented English governments from taking sufficient care of the economic well-being of their subjects. The Dutch,

DUTCH MUSKETEERS IN THE SEVENTEENTH CENTURY

This portrait group, now in the National Gallery, of Amsterdam musketeers, is of historic interest since it portrays a variety of local military costume and equipment. Each member of the company subscribed towards the cost of the painting and expected equal prominence.

who were no lambs, made full use of this temporary backwardness on the part of the English. They elbowed them out of many markets, and showed themselves ruthless in their methods of competition. The commercial classes of England, and in particular the merchants of the City of London, clamoured for strong measures by which the Dutch would be put in their place. Thus trade competition was leading to war, and was causing English people to forget that in the interests of their own safety they ought to live on terms of friendship with the Dutch.

War broke out for the first time after the English had settled their internal disputes by establishing a commonwealth. From 1652 to 1654 an epic sea war was fought between the two republics. The English had the better of it, but a reasonable peace was made owing to the fact that Cromwell, then the master of England, was aware of the community of interests that existed between the two countries. In 1665, after the Stuart kings had been restored, war broke out afresh. The Dutch were somewhat luckier than in the previous war, but once more peace was made on satisfactory terms after two years' fighting. This time the two enemies were brought together by a sudden increase of danger from France.

Louis XIV had embarked upon his policy of conquest. After the death of Philip IV of Spain, in 1665, he claimed a portion of Belgium, which was a Spanish possession, as due to his wife under some obscure law which his legal advisers had conveniently unearthed for the occasion. The Dutch had no desire to have the powerful French as their neighbours, and the English were very conscious of the disadvantages of a French settlement in Belgium. Already Louis was fighting his War of Devolution (1667-68), so called from Louis's claim that the rights of the Spanish in the Low Countries had devolved upon his wife, who was the elder daughter of the late king. The English and the Dutch hastily patched up their quarrel. More than that: the next year (1668) de Witt made an alliance with England and Sweden, the purpose of which was to arrest Louis's progress in the Belgian provinces. Louis realized that he could not face this alliance and made his peace with Spain, contenting himself with but a fraction of the conquests which he had intended to make. Here was the first instance of the application of a new principle in international affairs: the co-operation of threatened countries in the defence of their safety and independence against a strong country that threatened the peace of Europe. We shall see what a prominent part this principle was going to play. But the threat was not yet potent enough, and the victims were not yet sufficiently aware of the importance of collective security. The people of England did not realize that the trade war with the Dutch could be fought successfully by peaceful methods.

War With the Dutch

Louis XIV, the glorious monarch, was furious because a republic of merchants had dared to place itself in the way of his ambition. He swore to revenge himself. Slowly, with the utmost cunning, he set to work to break the Triple Alliance and to establish in its place a conspiracy of self-seekers who would help him in his enterprise of humiliating the Dutch merchants. It was not difficult to win over Charles II to his side. The Stuart king was always in need of money. His parliament did not trust him, and refused to provide money which he would have squandered on his mistresses. Louis bought him out with a pension. Meanwhile, his gold was at work in other directions. He obtained the neutrality of Sweden, and purchased allies among the ambitious German princelings whose territories bordered on the Dutch Republic.

By 1670, Charles II of England had agreed to a scheme by which the Dutch Republic was to be attacked, conquered and divided by the joint effort of France and of England, while the Catholic religion, disliked by the majority of his subjects, was to be imposed upon them. With the help of his fleet and of his armies Charles II was therefore going to enable Louis

XIV, the strongest potentate on the European Continent, to establish himself in the heart of those territories which English tradition and wisdom looked upon as their continental bastion.

The years 1670 and 1671 were devoted to a systematic preparation of the attack. At last, early in 1672, the kings of France and of England declared war on the Dutch. The Dutch Navy was ready. But the land defences had been sadly neglected. When, by the middle of the year, Louis marched his armies into the territories of the republic, the Dutch fortresses fell like ninepins. There was panic among the Dutch. They clamoured for a leader. The son of the late stadtholder had reached the age of twenty-one. He was untried, because the Holland regents and John de Witt had kept him away from all public business. But the people were sure that he alone could save them. They rose in their towns, and everywhere demanded that the young prince should be raised to the dignities and offices formerly held by his ancestors. The regents submitted, and the prince became Stadtholder William III.

Critical Position in Holland

John de Witt knew that his days were over. He had always looked upon simultaneous hostilities with France and England as the worst evil that could befall his country. De Witt was beaten. His story is one of neither folly nor bad faith. He was defeated by circumstances beyond his control. Soon after his resignation he was murdered in gruesome circumstances by the mob of the Hague. Meanwhile the young stadtholder was organizing the defence of the country. The large tract of land reserved for this purpose, east and south of the Province of Holland, was flooded. This water line arrested the onslaught of the French. At the same time the Dutch fleet under Admiral de Ruyter was keeping the English fleet at arm's length and was preventing an invasion from the west. But more than half the country was overrun by the French and their German allies.

During the second half of 1672, and during the year that followed, the Dutch wrote some of the most thrilling pages in the book of history. Political quarrels were set aside: high and low collaborated with complete self-denial in the defence of their country. The fleet continued its successful defence against English attacks.

Alliance With Empire

On land, there was no hope of offensive action. The Dutch knew that they were too weak for anything but defensive operations. These they carried out with skill and devotion. Once the French onslaught was arrested it was not allowed to advance a further inch. The prince, no great soldier, led the fight, and his negative success was due entirely to the self-sacrifice of the common men of Holland who dug trenches, mounted guard, and waited for salvation with the simple faith inspired by their loyalism.

The prince, meanwhile, realized that the only way to expel France's unbeaten army was to accumulate in its rear such a host of enemies that it would have to operate a strategic withdrawal for the sake of its own safety. If he were no military genius, William III was a born diplomat. He was eminently successful in carrying out his plan. In the middle of 1673 he made an alliance with the German Empire, and early in 1674 he persuaded King Charles of England to withdraw from the unholy alliance. The latter task was not very difficult, because the English people, with the sense of reality that has always characterized them, had by this time come to see that the independence of the Dutch Republic mattered more to them than commercial jealousy. In making peace with the Dutch, Charles II for once committed an act that was popular with his subjects. Soon afterwards Louis XIV withdrew his armies from Dutch territory, and the republic was saved.

A real success had been booked for the policy of collective security, but much remained to be done. England still stood out, and soon enough Charles II was once more accepting subsidies from the monarch whose purpose it was to impose his will on Europe. Nevertheless, the way was clear. Henceforth, William III devoted all his energy to the building up of an

DUTCH MARKET-PLACE IN THE SEVENTEENTH CENTURY

Berck-Heyde (1638-98) painted this picture, now in the National Gallery, of the market-square of Haarlem in 1674. It is dominated by the fine Gothic church, whilst on either side are seen the tall brick-built houses with picturesque gables so typical of the period. Near the church is a low range of shingle-roofed market booths.

alliance which would safeguard his country and the whole of Europe from aggression. Every one of his subsequent actions must be looked upon in this light. To build up a balance of power, in which the crushing preponderance of the French scale was neutralized by heaping up into the other scale the forces of all those whom France threatened—such became William's self-imposed task.

Up to a point, as we shall see, but only up to a point, William was successful. What he would have liked to establish was the preventive balance of power, a system which would have eliminated war once and for all. All nations of Christian Europe were to join in a kind of league, whose task would be to prevent aggression, and to turn its collective armament against any member which, instead of submitting its cause to a conference, resorted to force.

This idea sounds surprisingly modern. Even today it offers the one and only chance of eliminating war from the affairs of men. The name "collective security" was not used by European statesmen of the age of William III. They acquired the habit of speaking of "the indivisibility of the peace." As the words indicate, they meant the same thing.

William was unable to build a lasting league which included France. Louis XIV was bent upon conquest, and the selfishness of his intended victims blinded them to their own interest. But twice more, when the danger from France grew to dimensions that could not be ignored, William found it possible to form an alliance which successfully halted the French king. By the end of Louis XIV's reign, France had ceased to be a threat to the safety of Europe. No single state

COURT OF KING LOUIS XIV

Seeds of discontent which culminated in the French Revolution were being sown even in the days of the Sun-King—Louis XIV. In these contemporary engravings by Philippoteoux, the king is shown above, surrounded by his gentlemen of the bedchamber, each of whom,

took over the role of bully number one, and for nearly three generations, till the advent of the French Revolution, there was no call for men to stand together in defence against the ambitions of a single enemy of international order.

The War of the First Coalition (1673-78) against Louis XIV went the normal course of the wars of those days. Every spring, large armies took the field. They were manœuvred slowly and carefully across the plains of Europe. In all their actions the generals kept in mind the fact that the training of soldiers was slow and expensive and that efficiency must therefore not be wasted. War was rather like a game of draughts: the great art consisted in interposing one's own forces between the enemy and his magazines. When this happened, the enemy commander was in danger of losing his armies of mercenaries by wholesale desertion, because it was impossible to preserve discipline among underfed soldiers. Now and then a fortified town, which could not be left behind one's front lest it threatened one's own communications, had to be besieged. Here, too, the rules of the game were rigorous. The town was surrounded, zigzag trenches

were dug which gradually crept nearer to the walls. As artillery carried only a few hundred feet, and musketry even less, there was little danger in this operation. At last the day came for the general assault. Usually one began by blowing a breach in the enemy's walls by means of a concentration of artillery. When preparations were ready, the governor of the town was solemnly asked to surrender. The code of honour of the period left him free to decide whether he had a fair chance; if not he surrendered.

Usually, in the course of a campaign, one or two pitched battles were fought. In these, the main objective was to break the cohesion of the enemy army by dividing it into unconnected units, over which the enemy command had no further control. On these rare occasions all thoughts of economy in manpower went by the board, but apart from them a soldier's life was one of hardships rather than of danger.

At the end of the campaign, towards September or October, both sides withdrew into winter quarters. The troops were re-equipped, refitted, and drilled, and the generals returned home to participate in a round of pleasure and intrigue.

—AND HIS SUBJECTS

according to court etiquette, had his particular duty to perform. In contrast, the miserable plight of the French peasants, portrayed in the above print, is hard to believe. In a state of starvation they are shown contending with the dogs for bones or dying from malnutrition.

The generals of Louis XIV were victorious on several occasions. But they were unable to impose their master's will upon his united enemies, and in 1678 and 1679 a peace was made, in which the Dutch suffered no losses at all, and the German Empire had to sacrifice a few towns only. There followed ten years of uncertainty and tension. Louis, as ambitious as ever, used legal quibbles to absorb small slices of neighbouring territory. He irritated everyone, and seemed bent upon keeping every mind in Western Europe alive to the danger that threatened from France.

It has been noted that some time during the 1680s the character of Louis's government changed. The king grew more tyrannical, he seemed unable to stand the slightest criticism, he became impatient of anything that savoured of independent thought within the kingdom. In 1685 he abolished the privileges which his ancestor King Henry IV had granted to the Protestants, and began an open persecution of this prosperous and peaceful section of the French community. The Huguenots, as the French Protestants were called, emigrated in large numbers, and settled in England, in the Dutch Republic, and in

Prussia. Everywhere they carried with them their skill and enterprise, but also their tales of oppression and of atrocities, everywhere they strengthened the sense of insecurity and of impending doom. Not only foreign domination threatened: if Louis were victorious in a subsequent war, ancient and cherished liberties, and in particular religious freedom, would be abolished. The English nation felt more and more disgusted with the pro-French policy of its king. In 1685 Charles II died, and was succeeded by his brother James II. James was an open adherent of the Catholic Church, and his people felt themselves threatened in their dearest spiritual possessions.

The system of Colbert was still providing Louis XIV with the sinews of war, but prosperity was ceasing to be one of its fruits. Less and less did the splendours of the royal court find a counterpart in the well-being of the subjects at large. Historians have searched for an explanation of the deterioration that was taking place about this period. A decline in the king's health, the allegedly baneful influence of Madame de Maintenon, a mistress whom, after his queen's death, Louis married in 1685, the rise of new and unenlightened

2000 B.C.

AN ANCIENT
EGYPTIAN POTTER

A LOOM OF THE LATE BRONZE AGE
IN EUROPE ABOUT 750 B.C.

A MEDIEVAL WATER WHEE

TOGGLE JOINTING USED FIRST IN ENGLAND
AT STONEHENGE (1750 B.C.) WAS AN IMPORTANT
BUILDING DEVELOPMENT; IT ENABLED STONES
TO BE FIXED IN POSITION, NOT MERELY PILED
ONE ON ANOTHER

AN EARLY EGYPTIAN
OX-DRAWN PLOUGH

INVENTIONS WHICH HAVE CHANGED THE PATTERN OF SOCIAL LIFE

15th. CENTURY WINDMILLS

A PRINTING PRESS ABOUT 1470

A 17th. CENTURY LANTERN CLOCK

advisers, have been adduced in turn as an explanation. None of them bears careful examination. No special events need be called to aid if we wish to explain what was an inevitable development. We have seen that at the beginning of the personal reign of Louis XIV ripe absolutism was progress. The unchallenged rule of law had to be won for France by the dignity and glory of its absolute ruler. Now this task was fulfilled. The country was ready for new developments; fresh administrative and political experiments had to be made. But the system had acquired a death-like rigidity; the king's semi-divine person could not be challenged, there was no opening for improvement and novelty. The law of history that the good thing of yesterday becomes a bad thing today had been at work once more. And yet, for such is the power of inertia in human affairs, the

system was going to survive for another thirty years. Each year poured new poison into the life-stream of France.

In 1686 the growing usurpations of Louis XIV brought about a new coalition among some of the victims of his aggression. Spain, Sweden, and several German territories formed the League of Augsburg for the defence of their common interests. William III would have liked the Dutch Republic to join this league, but the Holland regents, though not hostile to his purpose, deemed that the moment for action had not yet arrived. Louis and his friends were themselves hard at work to strengthen the League of Augsburg. While Louis continued to help himself to German territory in full peace-time, the Catholic King of England, James II, was making rapid moves toward the establishment of a Catholic supremacy in his country, and

LOUIS XIV PLAYING BILLIARDS

This engraving by A. Trouvain, dated 1694, from the Bibliothèque Nationale, Paris, shows the King of France, accompanied by the Duc de Chartres, the Comte de Toulouse, the Duc de Vendôme and two gentlemen-in-waiting, playing a game very similar to the modern Continental form of billiards, against his eldest son, the Dauphin.

toward the establishment of royal absolutism on the French model. In the end leaders of the two political parties in England appealed to the Dutch stadtholder, who was both nephew and son-in-law to the English king, to come over and restore the constitution and the established religion of the realm.

Here, at last, was William's great opportunity. He did not accept the invitation in the hope of acquiring a royal crown. It was by no means certain, early in 1688, that he would ascend the English throne as the outcome of his intervention. He was sure of one thing only: the restoration of Protestantism and Parliament in England would mean that this powerful country would at last take its rightful place in the coalition for the protection of collective security. Without any further hesitation the Dutch regents agreed to co-operate in the enterprise. They gave unstinting help, and it is well known that the expedition which they supported was crowned with success. James II fled to France, William and his wife, Mary, became joint sovereigns of England, Scotland and Ireland, and the Glorious Revolution ended the Stuart system of subsidized submission.

Spanish Territory Partitioned

Louis XIV declared war on England and the Dutch Republic. He was already at war with the members of the League of Augsburg. From 1688 to 1697 the Nine Years War, or War of the Second Coalition, was fought. It ended with the Peace of Ryswick, in which Louis recognized William III as king of Great Britain, and restored his unlawful peace-time conquests. By now William III was acknowledged throughout Europe as the man who directed resistance against the perpetual disturber of the peace. The system of the balance was recognized as the only means of curbing aggression.

Now, as the seventeenth century was drawing to a close, the two protagonists were exhausted. France had suffered much in the course of the Nine Years War, and its king was open, as he had been at no previous stage, to a reasonable compromise. The health of the king of Spain, Charles II,

was more precarious than ever. Louis knew that at his death it would be impossible for France to help herself to the whole of his dominions, and stay at peace. He agreed therefore to an arrangement whereby the Spanish territories were to be partitioned among the various claimants to the heritage.

War of Spanish Succession

The details of these partitions—there were two of them, in 1698 and in 1700—need not detain us here. What matters about them is that, although the contrary has been asserted, Louis was in earnest with them, because he wished to end his reign without further bloodshed. The king of Spain, however, made a will in which he left all his dominions to Philip of Anjou, grandson of Louis XIV. He made it a condition that this prince should accept the whole inheritance intact. Unless he did, the inheritance was to go to the German Emperor, who was the other claimant. The main concern of the dying king was to prevent the sharing out of his dominions, because Spanish pride objected to this.

Louis accepted this will, and allowed his grandson to become king of Spain, under the appellation of Philip V. Curiously enough, the one-sided action of Louis XIV, who discarded the solemn partition treaty of 1700, six months after it had been signed, did not cause a general war to break out. The opponents of Louis were, as we have seen, as war-weary as he. They acquiesced in the new arrangement, and both England and the Dutch Republic recognized Philip V as king of Spain. Only the Austrian Emperor, who lost his chance of obtaining a share of the Spanish possessions for his own family, objected and went to war (1701). But now Louis XIV's old enemy, his lack of a sense of proportion, got the better of him. Louis had grown used to adulation, his courtiers had drummed the tale of invincibility and unlimited power into his ears till he believed that nothing could stand in his way. Flushed by his success, he treated Spain and its possessions not as the kingdom of a member of his family, but as his own private property. He sent his royal commands to Madrid, where his grandson had been received with joy by the Spanish people—and his commands were obeyed All the extensive trading privileges, once possessed by the English and the Dutch, were withdrawn from them by the Spanish Government and granted to Frenchmen. Spanish Belgium was occupied by French troops and administered, infinitely better than it had ever been under its Spanish masters, by representatives of Louis XIV. Now the Dutch saw their nightmare come true. The French were their neighbours. Even so the English nation was reluctant to allow its king to lead it into a new war. But Louis committed the supreme blunder of recognizing the son of the dethroned King James II, known as the Old Pretender, as king of Great Britain and Ireland. At this, the cup overflowed and war became inevitable.

At this juncture William III died, and was succeeded by his sister-in-law, Anne. She and the Duke of Marlborough, who was her chief adviser, continued the policy of William III. England, the Dutch Republic and the Empire formed an alliance and went to war with France, for the purpose of preventing the eventual union of the Crowns of France and of Spain. This became the War of the Third Coalition, usually called the War of the Spanish Succession. Though William III was not there to conduct the diplomacy of his two countries, his system had prevailed once more, and a long and bitter war was waged for collective security and the indivisibility of the peace. The war ended in 1713 by the compromise Peace of Utrecht. The major objective of the Grand Alliance was achieved. Henceforth, at any rate till the 1790s, no single nation was able to threaten the tranquillity of Europe.

Strengthening the State

In September 1715 Louis XIV died. His successor was his great-grandson Louis XV, a child of five, who was placed, till 1723, under the regency of Philip, Duke of Orleans. Europe was by now a very different place from the continent that had witnessed the grandeur of the Sun-King and had been goaded into resisting his lust for domination. The main difference was the complete divorce between domestic and foreign policy.

We have seen that at the period of ripe absolutism a tradition had been established of strengthening the state by two complementary methods: one was the centralization of administration in the hands of a monarch with unlimited power, the other was the extension of the monarch's power through an active and even aggressive foreign policy. Now the days of absolutism were over.

Political Corruption

Everywhere, in Europe, in Prussia, in Austria, in Spain, in many of the Italian principalities, and even in Russia, a new system was adopted. The ruler ceased to be the owner of the state. He became its first servant, and looked upon himself as such. It has been said that this was the death-bed repentance of absolutism. Its essential aspect was that the power and glory of the ruler was no longer the very purpose of government. The happiness of the subject became, in theory at any rate, the leading preoccupation of the state. We can say that this development was consonant with the general course of events, with the gradual increase of the importance and the dignity of the human individual, with the spread of more enlightened doctrines about man and his destiny.

Curiously enough, there was one country where this natural development did not take place. In France the clock was put back at the very time when other countries took a step forward. The nobility seemed completely tamed under Louis XIV, and yet it rose, immediately upon his disappearance, to claim many of its ancient and almost forgotten privileges. Had Louis failed in his task to inaugurate the reign of law, which made obedience to the state an automatic reaction? No, and the proof is that at his death there was no armed revolt by the nobility as there had been at the end of several previous reigns. But the excesses of the last decades of his reign brought the whole system into disrepute. As a result, the death of the Great King was followed by a return to government by the nobility. France gave itself

WILLIAM III AT THE HAGUE

The Grand Alliance against Louis XIV was organized by William III of England. R. de Hooche made this engraving which shows the king's entry into The Hague in 1690, with the royal coach about to pass under the huge triumphal arch.

the system known as Polysynody, under which the task of ministers was performed by councils consisting of grandees. The system was a complete fiasco: the period of the Regency was characterized by the utmost moral and political corruption as well as by incompetence, and the new regime was discarded after a few years' time. It had a remarkable result, however. Absolutism, which was becoming out of date in other countries, appeared to the French so much better than the regent's reactionary experiment, that they resumed the yoke and submitted to government by the methods inaugurated under Louis XIV. France, henceforth, was out of step in the march of progress, and there is little doubt that this must be counted among the causes of the French Revolution, about which more is said in another chapter.

Here, then, were the states of Western Europe, no longer in fear of a conqueror.

But although power was ceasing to be their primary concern, other preoccupations kept them divided among themselves. The eighteenth century was much more keenly aware of economic factors than the seventeenth. Gain was becoming the leading object of every state. Each was out to acquire all it could get, and each grudged the slightest success on the part of its neighbour, in the mistaken idea that the world's resources were limited, and that no nation could thrive except to the detriment of all the others.

A new conception of the balance of power was taking shape under the influence of these economic jealousies. Every government persuaded itself that for the slightest gain of territory, the meanest little agreement by which some commercial advantage was obtained by one of its neighbours, it must obtain an immediate equivalent, if it did not wish

Paris Cher Monf*-Trolaria   Sold by C.Dicey & Cain Aldermary Church

EIGHTEENTH-CENTURY COFFEE HOUSE

In France, as in England, coffee houses were gathering-places of writers, artists and intellectuals. This contemporary engraving, from the Douce Collection in the Bodleian Library, Oxford, shows a Parisian coffee house in 1740, which, though less elegantly appointed, is obviously the forerunner of the modern café. The presence of writing materials indicates that the place was used for work as well as refreshment.

to be left behind in the race. There is a family game called demon patience, in which three or more people build up their pile of cards, in competition, from a common pool. To play this game properly one has to have eyes like those of a prawn, and turn them in every direction, remaining intent not only upon one's own gain, but also on thwarting the efforts of every other player. Such became the game of diplomacy. Each against all, instead of all against the aggressor, was henceforth the leading principle in matters of international policy.

The system of William III contained possibilities of international co-operation, of work for the building up of a genuine comity of nations in which even the former aggressor might take his place. Though William's ideals did not materialize, the old conception of the balance of power

was not without nobility. Now all was narrow and petty.

Alliances, in the eighteenth century, were not long-lived. There was a continual reshuffling of the cards, and cardsharpers took the seats of honour in the European Casino. The new game began at once. In 1716 England and Austria formed an alliance for the mutual defence of their interests. England and the Dutch Republic formed a similar alliance. The following year England and the Dutch Republic formed an alliance with the ancient and traditional enemy, France. A year later Austria joined this alliance and in 1718 these allies went to war with Spain. But by 1721 England, France and Spain had concluded an alliance! Thus it went on, a petty game which destroyed all chances of stability. One of the worst influences in European diplomacy was the fact that the new king of England, George I, who had succeeded Queen Anne in 1714, happened also to be the ruler of the German principality of Hanover. For a long time he used the power and prestige of his new dignity to further his aims as a German ruler, although his British subjects had no interest whatever in the extension of his European territories.

There would be little point in pursuing the capricious course of European diplomacy and warfare in the eighteenth century. Let us note that by concentrating upon the pursuit of the will-o'-the-wisp, by chasing that elusive thing, the new balance of power, France forfeited an empire in America and in the Indies. Thereupon she hastened to support the rebellious colonies of Britain, just "to restore the balance." It was a crazy system which ended in the general European wars of the French Revolution. These wars, which began in 1792, continued with hardly any interruption till the final defeat of the Emperor Napoleon in 1815. A striking aspect of these wars was the fact that they did not begin as a fight by conservative Europe against a new and dangerous doctrine which threatened to upset the foundations of social order. No, in 1792 Prussia and Austria went to war against France in the hope of grabbing some of its territory while it was weakened by internal dissension.

First Total Wars

With the beginning of the wars of the French Revolution two characteristic aspects of the so-called Old Regime disappeared from Europe. The first to disappear was the divorce between domestic and foreign policy which characterized the period that followed upon the death of Louis XIV. Once more states and nations fought for objects that mattered supremely in their eyes. Whether this was an unmixed blessing is another matter. But henceforth rulers, before they embarked upon war, had to appeal to their subjects for support, and to make out a plausible case. No doubt they usually did this by telling a pack of lies. But the principle that war was the business of the people was recognized. The other thing that disappeared was the conception of war as the sport of kings. The clean, gentlemanly war, with its rules and limitations, with its economy of manpower, with its respect for the non-combatant, passed into history. It was a fairly novel conception in any case. It appeared only after the Thirty Years War. Now it made way for the new idea of war, which, to use an expression that was born in our own time, we may call the total war. For let there be no mistake about it, the wars of the French Revolution and of Napoleon were the first total wars, and they were less frightful than the wars of the twentieth century only because the technique of destruction had not yet reached the high level known to us who live in the twentieth century.

French Nationalism

In 1789 the French rose against outdated absolutism. Their chosen representatives proclaimed the sovereignty of the nation, and to the French who at that time already were so fascinated by abstract ideas this was no empty word. In less than no time they became used to looking upon themselves as the owners of the French State. When, therefore, the Austrians and the Prussians threatened them, when their National Assembly declared war upon Austria, and Prussia joined in the war as Austria's ally, the French began a people's war, a war which was the concern of everybody. They accepted compulsory universal military service with enthusiasm, and the strength of this enthusiasm was such that their conscripts swept the professional armies of the monarchs from their country and followed them across the frontier. To the strains of that inspiring marching hymn, the Marseillaise, they braved death and conquered half Europe.

All this is beautiful and inspiring. But it has one enormous drawback. From that time onward, war became the business of nations. In the past a defeat was a blot on the escutcheon of one man, and national pride was not involved in the issue of war. Monarchs gained territory and lost it, as a gambler rakes in the stakes or pays them out. Now the nation, that is, the ordinary citizen and his neighbour, became concerned in all that happened in the international field, not only when there was fighting, but when negotiations went on. The nation fought, the nation lost or triumphed, and the morbidly sharpened sensitiveness of the nation degenerated into one of the most dangerous passions which threaten the modern world, nationalism. Nationalism is the perversion of patriotism, for it places the interests of the nation above all other values, religious, moral and intellectual.

The French Revolution has given mankind much that is beautiful and of eternal value. But it gave them nationalism, too, which is a poisoned gift. From the defence of their country and their revolution, the French people passed imperceptibly to the attack on other people's freedom. After some years of warfare and of internal chaos the French gave themselves a leader, Napoleon Bonaparte, who began by being their consul or president, and who became emperor in 1804. From the point of view of foreign policy nothing was changed: the Empire, like the Republic before it, was aggressive, and renewed the threat which Louis XIV had once held over Europe. Once more Europe resisted. It was the task of Britain to organize collective security. Britain initiated several coalitions, and in the end a coalition consisting of Britain, Russia, Prussia and Austria proved successful.

The resistance against French aggression was, however, not merely a matter for the rulers of the endangered states. The peoples of Europe took an active part in it. The movement began in Spain, which Napoleon took by trickery from its legitimate king, and gave as a kingdom to his brother, Joseph. The Spaniards thereupon began an out-and-out resistance, similar in many respects to the heroic underground movements in occupied countries during the Second World War. Like the French whom they resisted, the Spaniards developed a nationalistic frame of mind, and they too acquired the outlook which makes state affairs and the often imaginary honour of the country everybody's concern. In Prussia, humiliated and crushed by Napoleon, there was a similar development. When, in 1812, Napoleon launched his armies into Russia because it refused to do his bidding, the whole Russian nation rose against the invasion. Territory was sacrificed without hesitation, because what the Russians wanted to preserve was not the country but the people. Finally, stifled by the hug of the Russian bear, Napoleon was defeated. But in Russia too he left behind him the ambiguous gift of nationalism.

The nineteenth century tried to restore war to its honourable position as the sport of kings. The attempt was vain. Democracy was knocking at the gate, and, for better or for worse, insisted on taking charge of international relations. More and more, war became the clash between masses, and the affair of Everyman. It is perhaps a consolation to think that, as a result, the prevention of war has also become the concern of Everyman.

Test Yourself

1. Discuss the place of monarchy in the Europe of Louis XIV.
2. What do you understand by " mercantilism " ?
3. Discuss the reasons for the decline of Holland after its seventeenth century greatness.
4. How far were European wars in the eighteenth century a product of the struggle for colonies?
5. How do you account for the rise of Prussia?
6. Discuss the impact of the French Revolution upon international relations.

Answers will be found at the end of the book.

CHAPTER VIII

ADVENT OF RUSSIA

DURING all the time when the civilization of Western Europe was crystallizing into the glitter of unified kingdoms which was to last until our own days, the eastern frontier of that polyglot continent was closed. For all practical purposes this frontier may be said to have marched with the River Dnieper. It was guarded and fought over by people who looked westward, and the life of the obscure and legendary forest-dwellers on the eastern bank, though familiar enough to their immediate neighbours, some of whom shared their blood, had little or no effect on the groupings which were shaping the face of Europe proper. Muscovy was the great nothing. Bounded on the north by the frozen Arctic seas and on the south by barren deserts, her western frontiers were screened, often impenetrably, by the Swedes, the Teutonic Knights of the Holy Roman Empire, the Poles, the Lithuanians and the Turks; while her perpetual and overriding preoccupation with the nomad invaders from the heart of Asia kept her facing east and south.

Barriers Between East and West

Towards the end of the fifteenth century the Grand Prince of Moscow, Ivan III, the Great, who was also the first real aristocrat of the modern Russian state, went to Italy for his bride, Zoë Paleologus, niece of the last of the Byzantine emperors, and at the same time took what he could from the new life of the Renaissance. There was, however, no reciprocity. Russia took, but she gave nothing; and what she took, notably architects, artists and scholars, was soon absorbed into the body of her own inward-growing life and its origins forgotten. Nothing, for instance, could be more Russian than the immense and lowering complex of the Moscow Kremlin, the earlier parts of which, nevertheless, were raised by Ivan's Italian architects. The barrier of hostile peoples standing between Muscovy and the West made free intercourse most difficult and at times impossible; and the need for securing her own Asiatic frontier, or, rather, for pushing it slowly east and south into the depths of the great vulnerable Eurasian plain was still imperative.

Russian Expansion to the West

Only in the middle of the sixteenth century do we find Ivan IV, the Terrible, making the first sustained and really determined effort to break out to the West by securing means of access to the Baltic. In the end he failed, in spite of some striking victories. And although he expanded his empire eastwards into Siberia, and southward to the Caspian, fifteen years later the Tartars of the Crimea made a great raid across the steppe as far as Moscow itself, which they burnt to the ground; and when Ivan at last died, Muscovy remained still blocked from the sea—except for her new back door on the estuary of the eastern Dvina where it flows into the White Sea, discovered in 1563 by an English merchant adventurer, Richard Chancellor, and pertinaciously exploited thereafter by England in search of trade and by Muscovy in search of munitions of war and political support from the far West.

It was not, however, until the beginning of the eighteenth century, after the arrival of Peter the Great, that the ambitions of Ivan were realized and the Swedes made to loosen their hold on the Baltic, so that, with the establishment of St. Petersburg, an immense and unpredictable power, about which nobody knew anything, made itself disturbingly felt in the councils of the European great. Even then, Russia had to wait for Catherine for her final conquest of the Black Sea steppe and the clearing away for ever of the Turks from the northern Black Sea coast.

Russia had not always existed in isolation. The political history of the Russian

RUSSIAN ICON FROM A MONASTERY NEAR MOSCOW;
EARLY 15th. CENTURY

RUSSIA—TIME CHART

A.D.	
800	Varangians from Scandinavia begin to penetrate and plunder.
860	First Varangian expedition against Constantinople.
862	Rurik, the Varangian, invited to rule in Novgorod traditional date.
988	Baptism of Vladimir; Russia "converted" to Christianity.
1223	First Mongol invasion inspired by Ghengiz Khan.
1252	Reign of Alexander Nevsky which ended in 1263.
1380	Dmitri Donskoy defeats Tartars at Kulikovo.
1462	Ivan III (The Great) becomes Grand Duke of Moscow.
1480	End on Mongol yoke.
1547	Ivan IV assumes power, and title of tsar.
	Ivan IV commences to regularize system of military service based on land.
1553	Richard Chancellor, English explorer, opens White Sea route.
1581	Yermak begins conquest of Siberia.
1598	Election of Boris Godunov as tsar begins "Time of Troubles."
1610	Poles occupy Moscow; national resistance under Minin and Pozharsky, lasting until 1612.
1613	Election of Michael Romanov as tsar creates Romanov dynasty.
1667	Truce of Andrusova: Russia acquires Kiev, Little Russia and Smolensk.
1689	Peter the Great seizes power.
1760	Russians enter Berlin during war with Frederick the Great.
1762	Catherine II (The Great) becomes tsarina.
1772	First Partition of Poland.
1783	Russia annexes Crimea.
1807	Peace of Tilsit with Napoleon.
1812	Napoleon enters Moscow but is forced to retreat.
1825	Decembrist Rising.
1830	Polish Insurrection defeated; Poland declared Russian province.
1853	Crimean War against Turkey, lasting until 1856.
1861	Alexander II emancipates the serfs.
1863	Reforms in Law and Administration.
1864	Russian conquest of Central Asia; completed in 1885.
1877	Russo-Turkish War concluding in 1878.
1904	Russo-Japanese War; concluding in 1905.
1905	General Strike—October manifesto grants limited franchise.
1914	Germany declares war on Russia.
1917	Russian Revolution.
1918	Treaty of Brest-Litovsk with Germany and her allies.
1918	Civil War.
1919	Founding of Communist International.
1923	First U.S.S.R. Constitution comes into force.
1928	First five-year plan.
1934	Russia admitted to the League of Nations.
1939	Soviet-German non-aggression pact. E. Poland occupied.
1941	Germany invades U.S.S.R.
1942	Anglo-Soviet alliance.
1945	Germany defeated.
1947	Russia denounces the Marshall Plan. "Cold War" begins.
1948	Jugoslavia expelled from the Cominform.
1953	Death of Stalin.
1955	"Cold War" gives way to economic competition.

ELABORATELY DECORATED
STOVE IN A CORNER OF A
NOBLE'S HOUSE IN THE
17th. CENTURY

RUSSIAN PEASANT DANCE;
FROM AN 18th. CENTURY
PAINTING

J. HAMBURGER

state opens in the year A.D. 862. In that year the Varangians, river Vikings of the kind who figured so energetically in early British history, settled themselves, in the persons of the three brothers, Rurik, Sineius and Truvor, in the neighbourhood of Novgorod, as rulers over the Slavonic inhabitants of the Volkhov basin. Rurik himself became the founder of a multifold dynasty of princes, one line of which was to grow and harden into the royal house of Muscovy, persisting until the first decade of the seventeenth century. For a long time these Varangians had been using the Dnieper as a highway between their native Scandinavia and the Black Sea, which was the open road to Constantinople and the isles of Greece where they had constant dealings in the mixed capacity of invaders, blackmailers and traders.

For much of the way their route passed through virgin forests inhabited by a branch of the Slavonic family, who, having largely absorbed the indigenous, non-Aryan Finnish elements of these lands, lived the lives of hunters, trappers, fishermen, foresters, beekeepers and traders, keeping always close to the great rivers, which intersected the forest and afforded them both their natural highways and a great part of their livelihood. Their society seems to have been far from primitive. It tended, as far as one can make out, towards a series of close communities of an equalitarian nature, which, in the big centres such as Novgorod the Great and Pskov, attained to a species of republican free city, which developed and flourished exceedingly under the early Ruriki (who brought them increased trade with the Baltic lands), and persisted for many centuries until finally overthrown by the Grand Princes of Muscovy, then engaged in a unifying programme, and notably by Ivan III, to whom we have already referred, who found that such separatist republican pretentions did not accord with his plans for a united autocratic Russia, and, in 1478 put Great Novgorod to the sword.

But although even in the ninth century the eastern Slavs knew how to run small communities of an enlightened constitution, they showed no signs of any centralizing instinct. On the other hand, the very readiness with which the ancestors of the Russians seem, with certain important safeguards, to have accepted the supremacy of the Ruriki, is in keeping with the most marked characteristic, and perpetual feature of the Russian temperament, so often to be underlined through their history, the need for some kind of overlord, a species of protector-cum-tyrant whom all, without loss of face or dignity amongst themselves, could regard as their superior.

The Ruriki came and they ruled, and founded, among others, the House of Moscow. But the House of Moscow meant very little in the early days of Russian history, which was made first in Novgorod, then, most aboundingly, in Kiev, which soon became the seat of the Grand Prince. From Kiev the Russian rulers raided deep into the south, campaigning extensively against Bulgaria, against Byzantium, and against the Greeks. To Kiev, in 988, the Grand Prince Vladimir brought Christianity back from one of the familiar campaigns against Byzantium. In Kiev were raised, particularly in the time of Yaroslav the Wise (1019-54), buildings which are as glorious as the contemporary fabrics anywhere in Europe. The first codified law was closely in sympathy with contemporary western codes. It was not superseded until Ivan the Great brought out his rather harsh and arbitrary code in 1497, and the difference in spirit between these two codes is the story of what happened to the dawning state of Russia.

What happened was first that the ruling princes developed to the point of insanity the appanage system, whereby their land was divided among their always numerous sons, so that what should have been a gradually expanding princedom became broken up into a welter of fraternal strongholds, perpetually at strife. There were moments when it looked as though this disintegrating process would be checked and Kiev assumed something like its old importance, notably during the reign of Vladimir Monomakh (1113-25); but the appanage system was too strong. Brother continued to war on brother. In 1169, Prince Andrew Bogolyubsky of Vladimir-

Suzdal sacked and pillaged Kiev and wrested from it, its last pretensions to supremacy. Chaos ensued, until in 1224, while the rival princes combined against each other in perpetually fluid coalitions, there appeared from the east the swift, barbaric Tartar horsemen of Ghengiz Khan, in a horrifying progress of blood and fire. Fourteen years later, in 1238, with a deeper bite and a longer range and with the force of a tidal wave, came the Tartar invasion proper, led by Batu, the successor of Ghengiz. All Russia was engulfed, with exception of the far north. The wave passed on deep into Europe, only to recede to the banks of the Dnieper, which marked the approximate limits of durable and established conquest. All Russia east of Kiev now lay beneath this flood.

Byzantine Influence

The Tartar hold on Russia was not finally broken until 1480, when Ivan III, the Great, Grand Prince of Moscow, declared the end of Muscovite subjection and refused further tribute. And for a century after that, until the end of the reign of Ivan the Terrible, the ever-present menace, ready to flood in from the limitless steppe, kept the eyes of the Muscovites toward the East. What went on during those two hundred and fifty years of domination by an alien and oriental absolutism was a radical reorientation of the development of the Russian people and their rulers, who, in the eleventh century, in spite of their Byzantine connexions and their dissociation from Rome, were developing along lines similar to those of other nascent European states, such as, for example, England. Further, whereas we enter on this period speaking of the Russians or eastern Slavs, we conclude it speaking of the Muscovites. The Novgorod-Kiev-Vladimir period is finally done with.

It is impossible to overestimate the magnitude of the consequences of this long period of subjection, a period equal in length to the years that divided Elizabethan and Victorian England. It is not in the least merely a matter of such superficial things as how many Tartars intermarried with the Slavs, how many Tartar words were incorporated into Russian, or even to what extent Tartar institutions affected the development of Russian institutions. These are all important matters, especially the last. But even had there been no fraternization, no exchange of vocabularies, no intimation of the ways of violent tyranny, the very fact of Russia's isolation from Europe at precisely the time when Europe was forming herself would be enough to create the most striking divergencies between the development of Russia and the development of the West. For Russia *was* isolated, and what energies she had over and above the business of daily living were expended in struggling against the periodical outbursts of savagery on the part of her masters, fruitless efforts to break their thrall, and in building up her own previously aborted unity with the aid of the Tartars and in the Tartars' despite. No people could have stood this strain without a narrowing of their horizons, without turning inward upon themselves, without receiving the imprint of the methods of their so successful conquerors, and least of all a receptive and plastic people like the Russians. Even their religion was alien to most of Europe. Russia was indeed isolated, and as if to set the seal on her unique and self-sufficing destiny, in 1453, the Turks took Constantinople, the second Rome. The first Rome had apostatized; the second Rome had fallen to the Moslem; the third and eternal Rome had, evidently, to be Moscow (to which city the Metropolitan had transferred himself from Vladimir in 1326). So that by the time liberation came, Muscovy herself had developed her own haughty, self-centred and Byzantine tradition of superiority to all the rest of the world, which materially assisted in the preservation of her at first involuntary isolation.

But what was Muscovy? Muscovy was all those lands ruled over by the Grand Prince of Moscow, who, in the person of Ivan the Terrible, became the Tsar of All Russia. If the Tartars completed the disintegration of the Russians and delayed the development of the new civilization by many, many years, in the end they also

CATCHING STURGEON ON THE VOLGA

Russia's most famous river and greatest highway of communication, the Volga, is renowned for its sturgeon. This engraving from Struy's "Voyages," published in 1681, shows the method used in those days to catch this fish. A vast series of palisades (B) in which the great fish are trapped zigzags across the entrance to the Caspian Sea (C). The fish are then brought to the villages (A) and distributed, methods of transport varying considerably.

brought about the unity of Russia, and a closer knit and more rigid unity than would ever have been achieved without them. The unifying factor was Moscow, whose princes, for long unimportant, developed a strain of statesmen and diplomatists who took every advantage of the uniquely central situation of their city near the confluence of a great river system, achieved grand-princedom in 1318, and, in spite of certain set-backs, never relinquished a supremacy which steadily became more real. In the person of Ivan Kalita (1325-41), Moscow received from the Tartar Khan the privilege of collecting and delivering all the tribute of the other princes. This gave her a weapon and a

shield, and although in the last resort force had to be used to overcome the strongest of her rivals, by the end of the reign of Ivan III (1462-1505), he was able to bequeath to his successor a unified Russia, known as Muscovy, which was never again to be broken.

Ivan the Great, as we have said, was the first real autocrat of Russia and the portent of things to come, although he did not call himself tsar. His successor, Vasily III (1505-33), was another strong prince who held steadfastly to his new dominions and added to them the last free city, Pskov, in 1510, and, in 1514 regained from the Lithuanians the district and city of Smolensk. His successor, Ivan IV, the Terrible, was an infant. But the new Muscovy survived the regency of his mother, and in 1547 Ivan crowned himself the first tsar, or cæsar, of all Russia, and proceeded with his immense and life-long task of establishing the tsardom as an absolute autocracy and carrying the borders of the state into the territory of his neighbours.

Thus Muscovy, started on the road to supremacy in the first half of the fourteenth century, had the extraordinary luck of a succession of three strong and long-lived rulers, covering a period of one hundred and twenty-two years. With the death of Ivan the Great, Russia was virtually synonymous with Moscow. With the death of his grandson, Russia was virtually synonymous with the tsar. It was in this condition, the condition of an absolutism unparalleled in the history of modern Europe, that she regained contact with the West, above all with the greatest contemporary of Ivan the Terrible, Elizabeth of England.

That auspicious event was the outcome of a chance discovery, pressed home with the utmost boldness and imagination, by an English merchant adventurer, Richard Chancellor, the survivor of three sea captains who sailed round the North Cape looking for China, and who found himself in the White Sea at the estuary of the eastern Dvina. He was an ideal example of the English people to set before a mighty king, the possessor of resolution, courage, vision, observation, tact, and a prose style worthy of the age in which he lived. He got on very well with Ivan and paved the way for the formation of the Russia Company. For it was characteristic of England that her one and only interest in Muscovy was in the trade it offered; and it was characteristic of Ivan that he began at once, overjoyed by the news of the discovery by strangers from England of this unsuspected backdoor to the outside world, to dream of a military alliance with this independent sea power which would help him in his struggle for the Baltic, and which could give him moral support. So, with the utmost pertinacity he set himself to the task of wooing England, to the point of seeking, and all but obtaining, an English bride.

Elizabeth, however, wanted trade, not alliance, with obscure and passionate barbarians, however powerful. Although she got herself into trouble with the Poles by

EARLY NINETEENTH-CENTURY TARTAR VILLAGE

The Tartars were excellent horsemen and led a nomadic life on the steppes of Asia and south Russia. Their tents, covered with woollen cloth or felt, fastened to a frame of thin wooden laths, had only a small door close to the ground. This drawing is from Atkinson and Walker's "Picturesque Representations of the Russians," published in 1812.

pursuing that trade and arming the Muscovite tsar so that he could strike the harder, on the alliance question she hedged, until it was too late, until Ivan was dead. Then she changed her mind, but the successors of Ivan were not visionaries and backed away from Elizabeth's advances, deep into the obscurity of their forested plain. And when the time came, with Peter the Great, to admit the influences of the West, the West by then meant not England but Germany.

Trade With the West

If Ivan failed to break out directly into the West via the Baltic, which was his dream and his constant aspiration, he at least established a life-line to the freely breathing West, by his backdoor in the White Sea, hard by the present site of Archangel. This, short-circuiting the imposing barrier of his land frontier, took his thoughts and his embassies by a wide outflanking movement far beyond his immediate Baltic preoccupations and offered him a haven of refuge on the other side of Europe should his burdens prove too much for him, which, more than once, he feared. And thus this life-line, provided by the English, remained the chief link with the West until Peter secured the Baltic ports at last and Archangel sank into relative obscurity.

Thus, too, from 1563 onwards, Russia belongs once more to European history, but still mainly, as far as the far West was concerned, as a limitless emporium of furs and wax and train oil; not, however, to her immediate neighbours, the Swedes, the German knights, the Lithuanians, the Poles and the Turks. These at last had genuine cause for alarm. After centuries of sporadic warfare these Baltic lands found themselves on the defensive and had to rearrange themselves accordingly.

The Baltic plain in the sixteenth century presented a complex and fluid picture, and to understand the position of sixteenth- and seventeenth-century Muscovy it is necessary to glance beyond her frontiers.

In the far north was Sweden, which occupied Finland and confined Muscovy's contact with the sea to the narrow Ingrian inlet upon which Leningrad now stands. In Livonia and Esthonia were the Teutonic Knights of the Holy Roman Empire, whose power had been permanently on the wane since their defeat by the combined Poles and Lithuanians at Tannenburg in 1410, but who still formed a formidable enemy for Muscovy.

Then came Lithuania, a curious conception. During the Mongol occupation of the great Russian plain and before the rise of Muscovy, she presented what was in effect the major Russian province, the apparent heir to Kiev Russia. There were Lithuanians in the north, but beneath their grand duke there also coalesced the Russian principalities of the extreme west, which had escaped the permanent yoke of the Tartars, and which later hardened into the White Russians (Minsk) and the Little Russians, or Ukrainians (Kiev). The capital was Vilna, and right up into the sixteenth century it was a common thing for Muscovite nobles to transfer their allegiance from the Grand Prince of Moscow to the Grand Duke of Lithuania, and vice versa. By 1450 this strange and loosely knit grand duchy stretched from the Baltic in the north to the Black Sea in the south and, by perpetually striving herself to annex more of the Russian lands, was the real screen which pressed the eastern Slavs back in upon themselves.

Union of Lublin

West of Lithuania lay Poland; and it was the pressure first of the Teutonic Knights in the north, then of increasing Muscovy in the east which threw this great gangling, half-Russian, half non-Russian state of Lithuania into an ever more absorbing union with the Catholic Poles. It could no longer act as an indeterminate buffer between the East and the West, and so it turned West. And, under pressure of Ivan the Terrible, there occurred in 1569 the crowning act of combination, the Union of Lublin, which made Poland and Lithuania finally one, with the Poles preponderant. So that, from now on the east-west division is marked by the borders of Russia and Poland, a closely knit Catholic state stretching from the Baltic to the Black Sea,

THE KREMLIN, MOSCOW, 1815

Moscow's life and history have always been centred on the Kremlin, or Citadel. Its ancient walls and towers enclosed the Great Palace of tsars, the arsenal, which is now a museum, the residence of the metropolitan archbishop, monasteries, churches and three cathedrals. In spite of modern improvements it still retains its ancient aspect, as may be seen from the illustration on the opposite page. It is now the headquarters of the Soviet Government.

from the Oder to the Oka. The broad picture of the Baltic lands in the sixteenth and seventeenth centuries, then, is of an immense triangular struggle between Russia, Sweden and Poland. At first the Poles prevailed, then the Swedes, and finally the Russians, not Muscovy, but St. Petersburg Russia.

It was the wars of Ivan the Terrible which reduced a complicated and desultory struggle into a simplified and more intensive one. He fought the Swedes, the Teutonic Knights of Livonia, the Lithuanians, Polish Lithuania, impartially. He extended his eastern borders to Kazan and his southern limits to Astrakhan at the mouth of the Volga. He also strove for an alliance with England, wooed and nearly gained an English bride, created the Oprichniki, the forerunners of the Ochrana and the G.P.U., savagely broke into little pieces the flower of his nobility, the hereditary grandees, or boyars, and established an order of service to the crown which was the

immediate cause of serfdom. But at the end of all this, and after considerable successes in his wars, he failed in his main object, the conquest of the Baltic, and when he died in 1584 the situation of Muscovy was much as it had been before. But he had left the title of Tsar of All Russia and an autocratic tradition which was to survive the occupation of the throne by an imbecile son.

The imbecile was Feodor (1584-98), with whom the dynasty died. There was not much difficulty about his successor, for his brother-in-law, Boris Godunov, had been acting as a species of regent or lord protector for some years, and in 1598 he was unanimously confirmed as tsar by the Assembly of the Land. Boris was a strong ruler who, however, had his hands more than full with domestic troubles, and when, after a flurry of civil war, he committed suicide, the country fell to pieces. From 1605 to 1613 Muscovy was a welter of tsars and pretenders, and the Swedes and the Poles took advantage of her internal weakness to strike at her sovereignty.

Novgorod fell to the Swedes. The spirit of the people was broken by famine. In 1610, the Poles crowned their own tsar in Moscow and it looked like the end. Poland, strengthened by her recent absorption of Lithuania, was for the moment a strong and unified state, already containing all the Russians of the western lands, and with strong ties with the enlightened West. Muscovy, the creation of the princes of Moscow beneath the Tartar yoke, had fallen to pieces. In the year 1611, however, the shattered unity of the new autocracy of the Ivans was pulled together by Minin, a tradesman from Nijni Novgorod (Gorky) and Pozharsky, a member of the nobility, acting in the happiest coalition. The Poles were driven from Moscow, the Assembly of the Land was called, and in 1613 a new tsar was elected, Michael Romanov, who gave his name to a dynasty that persisted, in spite of interruptions, until the abdication of Nicholas II in 1917

The most illuminating aspect of this whole affair was the behaviour of the Assembly in putting all power into the hands of their chosen anointed. The very people who might have been expected to welcome this moment as the chance of curbing the absolutism of the tsar, an absolutism about which, after the exploits of Ivan the Terrible, they can have had no illusions—these very people gave all power into the hands of Michael Romanov without reservations or safeguards of any kind whatsoever, not because of an innate subservience but, on the contrary, because they were naturally independent to the point of anarchy and yet perceived the need for a central authority which must be above themselves. By placing the tsar apart and making him above all laws, thereby ensuring that each and every one of them was equally subject to his arbitrary rule, honour was satisfied. All Russians were still equal—under God and the tsar, and they were free to go about their business. This new dynasty, established in

NIJNI NOVGOROD, 1880
For centuries famous for its fairs, Nijni Novgorod, now Gorki, was founded in the thirteenth century. A glimpse of the town is shown with its market-place and church, and beyond, is the Chasovoi Hill, surmounted by the walls of the Kremlin, which dates from the early sixteenth century when the city was a busy cosmopolitan halting place on the land route to the East.

such interesting circumstances, was destined to last until the twentieth century, surviving imbeciles, criminal intrigues, assassinations, palace revolutions, as well as the attempts of Peter the Great to bully the nobility into taking a share of the burden and the successful reversion of Nicholas I to the principles of the great Ivans. All the revolts, whether acts of desperation by the peasant or carefully planned intrigues on the part of the nobility, were revolts not against tsarism as such but against individual tsars (on the part of the nobility) or against the nobility (on the part of the peasantry). And when the dynasty at last did fall, it was not because it was tyrannical, but because it was weak, incompetent and not tyrannical enough.

But we are a long way ahead. From the accession of Michael Romanov in 1613 to the accession of Peter the Great in 1682, for sixty years after her temporary disruption, the pressure of Muscovy on the western world continued intermittently, without the intensity inspired by Ivan the Terrible in his striving towards the sea.

There were habitual wars with Poland and Sweden, culminating in the important Truce of Andrusovo in 1667, whereby Muscovy gained possession of Kiev, Smolensk and the Ukraine. There was the conquest of Siberia from scattered Asiatic tribes by Yermak the outlawed Cossack, who was financed by the Stroganovs, a powerful and visionary mercantile family, many years in advance of their time, who combined something of a vision of a Rhodes with the acquisitiveness of a Rockefeller and the culture of a Rothschild. There was a peasant revolt led by the Cossack, Stenka Razin, which assumed tremendous proportions and indicated the growing discontent of the peasantry with the increasing rigour of the system which bound them to the land. It was also the type of the peasant revolt which was to be the Russian speciality, a non-political uprush of pent-up passions, dying down as swiftly as it had arisen when the immediate game was lost, because it was not sustained by any idea of liberty or political change but only by the desire for easier living.

It was this revolt which led to the curtailment of the autonomy of the Cossacks, originally a grouping of untameable spirits who had fled southward into the steppe of the western lands (now the Ukraine) where they organized their own equalitarian society.

The most important internal event of this period was the schism in the Orthodox Church, provoked by the reforms of the Patriarch Nikon (1654), a genius of intolerant character. This schism resulted in the formation of a sect called the Raskolniki, the Old Believers, and it is characteristic of Russia that her great and solitary dissenting movement was non-conformity in defence of orthodoxy, not, as in every other country of the world, away from orthodoxy. They dissented from Nikon's revision of the letter of the liturgy, corrupted by faulty transposition through the centuries, to accord with the Greek original. This was tampering with the holy, the unchangeable. The Church and the State had, henceforward, not simply fallen from grace. They were the embodiments of anti-Christ.

The Old Believers, scattered throughout the vast plain, cut off absolutely from the body of the Church and dividing in time into local sub-sects, remained a powerful leaven in orthodox Russia up to the time of the Revolution, remarkable for the strength and purity of their convictions and their stubborn resistance to persecution. In them we can observe the Russian character in the nearest thing to active dissent it ever achieved, save in moments of hot-blooded revolt. The Old Believers may be found all over Russia to this day.

Russians Drive Southward

The most portentous external event of this period was the war with Turkey, which dragged on into the reign of Peter the Great and ended unsatisfactorily for Russia with the Treaty of Bakchi-Serai in 1681. The Turks had been in Constantinople since 1453 and now spread all over the Danube basin. Russia, since the days of the Ruriki, had always felt a latent proprietary interest in this city, first because of its riches and its command of the gates

of the Mediterranean, later as the seat of their religion. Sooner or later the southward drive was bound to begin again, and with this first round with the Turks we have the first act in the interminable drama of the eighteenth and nineteenth centuries which was to harden into the Eastern Question. This, however, did not present itself with force to the western world (and notably Great Britain) until long after Catherine the Great at last succeeded, where Peter had failed, in establishing a secure foothold on the Black Sea, and, with the Treaty of Kutchuk Kainardji in 1774, securing for Russian ships the right of passage through the Straits and for herself and her successors an official title as protector of all Christians resident in Turkish lands, thereby gaining a highly moral pretext for peaceful penetration.

Western Culture Sought

We are again too far ahead. We return to the year 1682, and the reign of Peter the Great, which began amidst all the uproar of a palace revolution, so that Peter had to seize his inheritance by force, and continued until 1725 with all the characteristics of a national revolution—carried out, in the Russian manner, from above. For during those forty-three astonishing years Russia not only transformed herself from solitary, brooding Muscovy into a first-class European power and master of the eastern Baltic, but also suffered a revolution which turned her inside out and upside down and transformed what had been an Asiatic culture into, at least so far as the nobility were concerned, a colourable imitation of a western one.

Peter the Great was a genius of the first order with a revolutionary vision, an obstinacy, a ruthlessness, a singleness of purpose, and a practical sense, which has so far not been met with outside Russia, and not often there. In effect, detesting the stuffy Byzantine, Tartar, dense-forest gloom and stiffness of the Russian court, thirsting genuinely for enlightenment, and seeing clearly that his great land of unparalleled immensity would never be a match for the pocket-handkerchief countries of the West unless it was dosed with some of the revivifying spirit of the West, he picked up Russia by the scruff of her neck and threw her head first into the lap of that same dazed and bewildered West— which he then proceeded to bully and cajole into helping him build up his country so that it would be a match for the West.

Treaty of Nystadt

It was an astonishing performance, paralleled in all history only by the prodigies so recently performed by another Russian ruler, Generalissimo Stalin. It produced a new Russia, but a Russia most bitterly divided between the "progressives" and the "reactionaries," a division which was to be the determining factor in her government for fifty years after the death of Peter. But although great numbers of his subjects resisted in the Russian manner (that is mainly with sulks, but occasionally with reckless and unconsidered violence), to suggest that Peter turned Russia upside down against her will is as wrong as to suggest that in every Russian he found a happy collaborator. Russia was ripe for one of those sudden and shattering changes which mark her irregular progression through the centuries. And Peter was the man to provide it.

Peter's warlike achievements were also considerable. Against the Turks he failed, succeeded, and failed again, disastrously at Pruth in 1711, so that Azov was still in their hands when he died. But against the Swedes, led by the magnificent but criminally reckless and irresponsible Charles XII, he was (after an initial defeat which would have broken the spirit of a less purposeful man, the smashing of the Russian Army at Narva in 1700), entirely successful; the defeat of Charles at Poltava in 1709, was the beginning of the end of Sweden as a great military power. The end was implicit in the terms of the Treaty of Nystadt of 1721.

Russia now had, in name as well as in fact, possession of Livonia, Estonia, Ingria and Karelia. In the south-west she also had the Ukraine, which lost its autonomy as the result of the troubles of Poland, with whom Peter was in alliance during the Great Northern War against

Sweden. Poland put up a disastrous performance, so that the Swedes were in both Warsaw and Cracow. She was never to be the same again. As for the Cossacks of the Ukraine, these, under their Hetman Mazeppa, had fought against Peter and with the Swedes; so that was the end of them, too.

Peter's succession was complicated by four facts. First, he had his own elder son put to death for joining in a revolt against his authority. Second, he had in his lifetime decreed that henceforward the tsar should appoint his successor—but had omitted to do so himself. Third, he left a bitter legacy in the divided reactionaries and progressives. Fourth, the power of the hereditary nobility was upset because of his introduction of a table of ranks, which were the only ranks to be recognized in future, and which had to be *earned*. The easiest way to earn high rank was, of course, to become a court favourite. Peter also introduced Germans in large quantities, and German methods, into the government of the country. Thus, from his death in 1725 to the accession of his youngest daughter Elizabeth in 1741, St. Petersburg was the scene of perpetual palace intrigues for the throne, and the governing of the country was done by the favourites, usually German.

Seven Years War

This was not an edifying or constructive period, and it was a relief for the Russian people when Elizabeth took the throne by storm, drove the Germans out and proceeded to run the country as a responsible part of the world on the lines laid down by her father. Moscow University was founded in her reign, which also saw the beginning of the national theatre and the creation of the Russian language as a literary medium of extreme richness and delicacy. Elizabeth fought the Swedes, as usual, and, in the Seven Years War, she fought with France and Austria against Prussia, the new and sinister power, Russian troops entering Berlin for the first time in 1760. Had it not been for her death and the accession of Peter III, who was an admirer of Frederick the Great, this Frederick would have been in a disastrous position and Prussia might never have recovered.

Peter III was the husband of the Princess Sophie of Anhalt-Zerbst, who took the throne when Peter was done away with by her own plotting, and called herself Catherine II (1762-96). He had less than a year in which to make trouble but in that brief period he achieved two momentous acts: the *rapprochement* with Prussia and the freeing of the nobility from their obligations to the throne without freeing the serfs from compensatory obligations to the landowners. Thus, with the accession of Catherine the Great, we find Russia, the great power, linked for good or evil with Frederick's Prussia, and Russia, the state, based on a population of slaves supporting a caste of wholly irresponsible landowners and nobles. There was also a Germanized civil service which interpreted the loose harsh decrees of absolutism with a rigidity, a pedantry and a thoroughness entirely foreign to the spirit of the plain.

The serf system was not a relic of the Middle Ages, it was roughed out by Ivan the Terrible and regularized by Boris Godunov. It had its roots in necessity, and although it was not an ideal system, in theory it was reasonable in a rough and ready Muscovite manner. Ivan, to fight his enemies effectively and to stop perpetual defection of his boyars to the Lithuanian Grand Duke, had to demand service from them in exchange for land. He could not get the service unless they were well established on convenient land. They could not be well established if there were no labourers to work the land and to march with the boyar to the wars. But labour was difficult to come by. Russia was so vast, her laws so harsh, and the spaces and adjacent freedoms so beckoning, that there was a perpetual movement of peasants into the deep plain or into the estates of the more prosperous landowners. There had to be laws to restrict these migrations. But still the peasants wandered. Whole villages, preceded by path-finders, would set forth on interminable voyages of discovery. So, in 1594, Boris Godunov issued his celebrated decree binding the peasants to the land upon which they were born. This was the formal establishment of serfdom, which

RUSSIAN REVOLUTION—NOVEMBER, 1917

Large numbers of soldiers are prominent among this vast crowd of demonstrators in Petrograd, now called Leningrad, demanding the overthrow of the provisional government which wished to continue the war at the side of the Allies.

PRINCIPAL NATURAL RESOURCES
OF THE U.S.S.R.

ARCTIC OCEAN

Anadirsk

ikha

Volosyanka

Shigansk

Omdonsk

CIRCLE

Yakutsk

OKHOTSK SEA

Vitim

Nezametui

Kha

Nikolayevsk

Dui

Komsomolsk

MANCHURIA

Khabarovsk

Irkutsk

MONGOLIA

Vladivostok

Expansion of Russian Territory
1689-1945

RUSSIAN EMPIRE

1689

Additions
1816-1854

Additions
1905-1945

Additions
1690-1815

Additions
1855-1904

slowly tightened its hold upon the peasants until Peter III, seeking to propitiate his nobles, released them in 1762 from all obligations to the crown while taking no steps to do the same for the peasants.

This was the signal for a wave of revolt greater and more widespread than the Stenka Razin revolt, and more particularized, for the peasants would not believe that a tsar would cheat them in this way; and when, after Peter had been done away with, the Cossack adventurer Pugachev announced that he was the deposed tsar come to regain his rights and free the peasants, they were ready to believe him, and a major civil war ensued, upsetting the liberal ideas of Catherine the Great, and lasting from 1773 to 1775.

This, then, was the domestic background of Catherine the Great, who, to the outside world, appeared as a splendid and glittering figure at the head of a new and mighty power whose strength was inestimable and whose policy was unpredictable. With Prussia she broke the power of Turkey on the Black Sea in a war which introduced the Russian fleet to the incredulous eyes of the British who had helped Peter to build it, the said fleet proceeding down the Straits of Dover under the admiralty of the Scottish sailor, Grieg, on passage to defeat the Turks at Chesme. In 1774, Catherine acquired Azov, Kerch and Kinburn, and in 1783 she annexed the Crimea.

The Eastern Question was now beginning to take shape, but in spite of the apprehensions of Pitt, the British, whose main preoccupation it was later to become, did not for the time being take the danger to the Mediterranean very seriously, nor for that matter did Catherine.

The Powers of Europe from now on were to be France, Austria, Great Britain, Prussia and Holy Russia, which was learn-

RUSSIA DURING THE REVOLUTION

Grim indeed were the events which accompanied the overthrow of Kerensky by the Bolsheviks in November, 1917. This picture shows an incident outside the Winter Palace at Petrograd, where the crowd in the square was mown down by machine gun fire during the fighting with supporters of Kerensky's Government.

ing its diplomacy in the new school of Frederick the Great, who did not believe in diplomacy as hitherto understood, but only in force. From Catherine onwards, then, until 1917, the history of Russia is also the history of Europe. In 1812, the new arrival was also to be the saviour of the world, in the person of Alexander I, whose subjects broke Napoleon and who in his own person, while afraid to liberate his serfs at home (though anxious to do so), crusaded up and down the Continent forming the crowned heads into an enlightened union of despots which was to redeem the world in accordance with Christian principles, but which in fact, and particularly under his successor, Nicholas I, became a confederacy of blackest reaction. Alexander, of course, was an enlightened despot, as despots go. For the first part of his reign it looked as though Russia would be a good deal happier under him than it had been under his father, Paul, who loathed and detested his mother and set about the reversal of all her acts.

Russian Tsardom

Commonly called the Mad Tsar, Paul has long been an underrated character. He had vision. He called for peace and stability; but he himself was the most unstable of beings, joining the coalition of England, Austria and Turkey against revolutionary France, and then subsequently, feeling himself left in the lurch by his allies, joining hands with France and concocting a fantastic scheme for a joint Russo-French invasion of India. He was strangled by his own chief of police, Count Pahlen, before this scheme could be tried. Paul may have been mad; but in fairness to his memory we should recall his original gesture in challenging all the sovereigns of Europe, each with his prime minister, to meet him and his own prime minister in a series of duels, so that a quarrel engineered by statesmen and of profit only to princes, could be settled without spilling the blood of the people.

Alexander, his son, was not mad; but he took fright at his own liberal impulses and, dismissing his minister Speransky on the eve of great reforms, turned to Arakcheyev,

the type of cruel and tyrannical Russian functionary as popularly imagined by the West. It was, indeed, the regime of Arakcheyev, running straight into the reign of Nicholas I (1825-55), which gave the West its whole idea of Russian tsardom.

Crisis of Eastern Question

About Nicholas, there is nothing that need be said in fairness to his memory. He came to the throne through a welter of blood in December, 1825, when the future Victoria of England was a little girl of six. The blood belonged to the pick of his young nobility, who, taking advantage of a certain ambiguity about the succession, decided that now or never was the time to transform the autocracy into a constitutional monarchy. This revolt of the "Decembrists" was the first constructive revolt of *principle* (as distinct from hunger and despair) in the history of Russia. It failed completely, and its leading spirits, whom Russia could not spare, were, with all their relatives, treated by this bleak and narrow monarch with a cold and pursuing ferocity peculiar to himself. In him the bold, savage, impulsive arbitrariness of old Russia was revived and made intolerable by the superimposition of Teutonic inflexibility and narrowness. Throughout his long reign the budding intellectual life of Russia lay under a blight, and the automatic banishment of choicer spirits struck a new note even in a land where oppression and censorship had become habitual.

It was this Nicholas who also went to extreme lengths in the policy of forcible Russianization throughout his mighty and embittered empire, which was to be continued by his successors. His Polish policy was particularly atrocious. Beneath his rule, too, the Eastern Question hardened into a first-class standing crisis, which was to produce the Crimean War, the "Balkanization" of the Danubian provinces, and, with the assassination of Ferdinand at Sarajevo, was to help precipitate the First World War.

In its acute form the Eastern Question arose from the rapid disintegration of the Ottoman Empire, which the powers of the West were determined to retard at all costs so that Turkey might continue to act as a counterweight to Russia.

Up to the London Convention of 1840, the fate of the Straits had been determined by the relations of Turkey with individual powers, and with the Treaty of Skelessi of 1833, Russia had contrived to be the individual power that mattered most, so that the Straits were to be closed to the warships of all other powers. The 1840 Treaty of London, however, for the first time made the Straits an international responsibility; and, bowing to the new state of affairs, Russia (much more interested in keeping the West out of the Black Sea than in gaining access to the Aegean for herself) changed her line with the not unreasonable suggestion that the rotten empire of the Turks should be carved up among the Powers and Europe finally cleared of the Moslem influence.

The Christian West, more interested in their own economic and political manœuvres than in the fate of the small peoples of the Danube basin, resisted this suggestion with moral indignation, and when Russia, rebuffed, quietly continued unilaterally with the task in which the West had refused to co-operate, successfully penetrating into Moldavia and Wallachia (later united to make Rumania), the swift outcome was the Crimean War (1853-56).

Russia and the Balkans

This dreary conflict, which benefited nobody, ended in the defeat of Russia and the complete exposure of the bankruptcy of the internal policy of Nicholas, who died at once. By the Treaty of Paris, Russia was excluded from the Danube basin and Turkey in Europe became subject to the same international supervision as the Straits themselves. Russia, however, refused to recognize finality and continued in her task of grouping round her the small Slavonic peoples and protecting the interests of the Christians in the Turkish lands, thereby outraging the interests of one continental Power after another.

After a successful war with Turkey, waged by Alexander II, came the Treaty of San Stefano (1878), which was a triumph for Russian Balkan policy. But the counter-move was immediate. It came in the shape of the Congress of Berlin in that very same year, a Congress which had no other purpose than to resuscitate the "sick man of Europe" at Russian expense, and which successfully modified the San Stefano Treaty to Russia's disadvantage without the slightest regard for the welfare of the Christian, European and often Slavonic peoples of Bulgaria, Rumania, Montenegro and "gallant little Serbia." This was the famous "peace with honour." And it was only fitting that this sort of behaviour should end in what was then the greatest conflict of all time.

Impressive Reforms

Crisis followed crisis in this wholly immoral and mutually destructive struggle of the Christian Powers (a familiar example being the annexation of Bosnia-Herzegovina by Austria in 1908); but these belong to the history of Europe, not of Russia, which was now the grand protector of the Serbs and, in the last decade of the nineteenth century, had secured her old enemy France as an ally. In July, 1914, came the Sarajevo assassination, the Austrian ultimatum to Serbia, the consequent Russian mobilization—and, for the Romanov dynasty, the final test, proving it wanting.

For while Russia had been making an imposing front in Europe, at home she was in a bad way. The Crimean War had shown up Nicholas I, but Alexander II, his successor (1855-81), was a far more reasonable and enlightened creature, and his reign was marked with a series of impressive reforms, beginning in 1861 with the emancipation of the serfs, and passing on to the reforms of the Press censorship, education, law, municipalities, and, most important, the creation of the Zemstva, or local governments (1864). It looked as though the hollow colossus might yet come alive; but the times were moving too fast and the reforms were too late.

Although the Zemstva did magnificent work, they were hampered by the long traditions of absolutism on the part of the government, narrowness on the part of the officials, irresponsibility on the part of the land owners, and distrust of all forms of

LUNCH-TIME ON A RUSSIAN FARM

The vast grain-producing plains of Russia are worked for the most part by collective farms. At meal times in summer the workers gather together in the open air taking their food in picnic fashion while entertainment is provided by one of them.

government on the part of the peasants. Although the serfs were liberated at a blow, the main immediate effect was to create a land-hungry peasantry and a landless proletariat pounced upon by the new industrialists, who were now, with the coming of railways, belatedly putting Russia through her industrial revolution. Although the country seethed with good works and glowed with good intentions, it was slow in getting forward, and the assassination of the tsar in 1881 by a revolutionary terror group did not help matters, confirming the new tsar, Alexander III (1881-94), in his natural feebleness and reaction.

In 1894, with the accession of the weak and almost imbecile Nicholas II, all hope of a rapid modernization of the bankrupt autocracy was at an end, a fact made plain inside Russia to everyone but the tsar himself by the growing success of revolutionary movements and, to the outside world, by the complete breakdown of the military power of Russia in the Japanese War of 1904-05. The bloody repression of peaceful demonstrations of discontent before the Winter Palace led to full-scale popular risings and the forced inauguration of the first national parliament, or Duma, in 1906. With Stolypin's great agrarian reforms the autocracy made its final uncomprehending bid to catch up with the times. But the Duma had already had its teeth drawn at the first signs of independence, and the assassination of Stolypin in 1908 confirmed Nicholas in his natural autocratic faith.

The outbreak of war in 1914 brought about a final popular rallying round the throne; but repeated defeats in the field, the shocking deficiencies of supply, increasing internal confusion and hunger, and the subjection of the ridiculous tsar to the will of the German-born tsaritsa and her evil adviser, Rasputin, all contributed to make it plain to the nobility and the industrialists that Nicholas would have to abdicate, and they were able to use the popular discontent and the troop mutinies in early 1917 to force this issue for their own ends. On March 15, 1917, the Romanov dynasty came to a dispirited end.

The autocracy was immediately replaced by a provisional government headed at first by Prince Lvov and containing a strong representation of the capitalist interest. But the discontent of the people was not appeased by the abdication of the tsar, and the new government was pushed rapidly leftward, when Kerensky, who belonged to the Social Revolutionary Party, jumped first from Minister of Justice to Minister for War, and then in July to Prime Minister.

All the time the Germans were advancing the peasants grew increasingly out of hand with their cry for land and peace, and Bolsheviks, headed by Lenin who had just returned from his Swiss exile in the famous sealed train, made an increasing nuisance of themselves while they waited, with tranquil foresight, for the moment when the Kerensky Government would fall and give them their chance. As winter approached, Lenin decided that the slightest push would bring it down, and on November 7, and with very little bloodshed, he turned the government out of the Winter Palace in St. Petersburg, and sat down in its place. This was the real revolution; but for the Bolsheviks it was only a beginning. It was one thing to seize power, quite another to hold it, and they, a minority party, had arrayed against them a formidable opposition which embraced the greater part of the people, from the army officers and the industrialists to the embittered Social Revolutionaries. Lenin had been successful so far because his party, which was the Bolshevik half of the Social Democrat Party (the Mensheviks being the other and less uncompromising half), though numerically insignificant, was disciplined in the highest degree and was the only body of men in all Russia which knew precisely what it wanted and was prepared to go to extreme lengths to get it. This purity of ideology and singleness of purpose

it owed to the peculiar genius of Lenin himself, who, in the years of exile, had savagely resisted all attempts from within and without to dilute the party by amalgamation with other revolutionary bodies. The success of the "October" Revolution provided the proof of his wisdom and the justification of his rigidity. The retention and consolidation of the power of the party against shattering odds during the ensuing years was the proof of his genius.

Civil War

The first thing that Lenin had to do was to bring the war to an end, and this, with the Treaty of Brest-Litovsk, which lost Russia all the productive wealth of the Ukraine, he did, reluctantly, in March, 1918. Already he was fighting the rapidly organizing Whites and the terroristic tactics of the Social Revolutionaries, of which he himself was later to be a personal and calamitous victim; but now, with Russia out of the war, he was suddenly faced with a first-class civil war, backed by the troops of the outraged Allies, who saw in Russia's defection something like a guarantee of Germany's victory over them. But in spite of the inconceivable suffering, chaos and ruin of the next three years, this concerted attack on Bolshevik power was also the salvation of Bolshevism, since it united beneath the leadership of Lenin all the masses of the great plain, who were not interested in socialism, but only in peace and land, and who bitterly fought the men who had broken their newly found peace and had come to take away their land. In this crucible Trotsky's Red Army was formed, and out of the chaos sprang the *Cheka*, the new security police, so that when all the fighting was over, the new revolutionary government were in possession of overwhelmingly powerful weapons for internal use as required.

New Economic Policy

It was not until the end of 1920 that peace was finally restored and the Russians were once again masters of their own land. Lenin had triumphed; and the Bolsheviks were in a position to go ahead. They started from scratch in a devastated land

and with a famine which swept the whole of Russia and forced the men who had successfully defied the world to appeal to that world for help; and they started with a strategic retreat which was hailed by the world as Lenin's admission of the impotence of socialism—the introduction in 1921 of the new economic policy, which allowed private enterprise in trade, subject to limitations. But Lenin knew what he was doing. Trade agreements were soon concluded with a variety of recently hostile governments, the bourgeois-minded business men were used to put socialism on its legs, and the outside world was placated. In 1924 the year of Lenin's death, the Soviet Government was recognized *de jure* by Great Britain and numerous other lands, and, although, as a result of western fears of communist infiltration, Russia's diplomatic history for the next twenty years was to be chequered and violent, she was never to be quite alone again. The end of the new economic policy came suddenly, when the government was ready. It came as soon as Stalin, then secretary of the Communist Party of Russia, had secured ascendancy over the party by the defeat of Trotsky, with whom he had been engaged in a savage and public conflict since the death of Lenin. That was in 1927. In 1928, Stalin feeling himself secure, and the country sufficiently stable to be committed to a programme, the new economic policy was repealed and the first five-year plan was announced, which was another way of saying: "Let battle commence," the battle being nothing less than the fulfilment of the industrial and agricultural revolution long planned by Lenin. The slogan now was "Socialism in one country." In 1930, Stalin, officially secretary of the Communist Party of Russia, became, *ex-officio*, the leader of the Russians.

This third revolution came to an end in June, 1941, when Germany attacked and Stalin transformed himself overnight from the leader of a revolutionary party to the protector of the embattled Russian fatherland. That was half-way through the third five-year plan. During the intervening years, the Russian people had suffered constant hardship and privation and inter-

mittent suffering of the cruellest kind for the success of the revolution, which involved doing without all the graces of life in order to turn a backward, illiterate, and primitive agricultural community into an industrialized state with an efficient agriculture, materially strong enough to stand up to the armoured columns of the capitalist world. It was a gruelling race with time, and it was only just won. Stalin drove the people to the point of exhaustion, but managed to inspire them with an idea which was a substitute for bread.

The pace was, from the start, terrific, and the first acceleration came with the Japanese seizure of Manchuria in 1931. In 1933, Hitler came to power in Germany, and in that same year the Soviet Government was at last recognized by the U.S.A., and in 1934 admitted to the League of Nations. Abroad there was a feverish drive to establish the principle of collective security. At home the industrial programme was accelerated by every means and all who could be accused in any way of retarding the productive effort were done away with. These included multitudes of so-called kulaks, who raised objection to being collectivized.

In 1936, Germany reoccupied the Rhineland and signed the anti-Comintern Pact with Japan. And now, in the same breath as the introduction of the New Constitution, which looked like the end of Stalin's revolution, came the opening of the tremendous purges, which went on for three years, and which, carried out wastefully and savagely to the point of hysteria, wiped out the potential fifth column and made Stalin's personal position unassailable. In 1938 came the Munich agreement, and belatedly following the example of Great Britain and France, Russia abandoned all ideas of collective security and set to work to pad her own person against German attack and, if possible, to make sure that Hitler would strike first in the West. The crowning success of this policy was the Soviet-German Treaty which shook the world in August, 1939, and was the signal for the German attack on Poland.

But the success held the seeds of failure. And the failure was the dire miscalculation which led Stalin to believe that he had lastingly insured himself and his country and to ignore all warnings from the West about "Barbarossa"—the German plan for the invasion of June, 1941.

The Red Army, badly deployed, inadequately led and insufficiently equipped was at once thrown back and largely overrun, until Leningrad, Moscow, and the Caucasus seemed about to fall.

Then patriotism began to tell. The weight of industry was transferred from the West to the Urals; the high command was reorganized; order was restored; and Stalin, forgetting about Communism for the duration of the war, invoked the moral support of the Russian Church and the patriotic traditions of the fighting Tsars. After heroic efforts, amid scenes of desolation and privation unimaginable in the West, and with the aid of Anglo-American Lease-Lend, the tide was turned, and, in 1945, the Soviet Army occupied Berlin. The terrible experience of "the great patriotic war," instead of breaking the Soviet Union, welded it together and endowed it with a new national consciousness.

But not for long. Instead of allowing the people to relax and lick their wounds and slowly find their feet as citizens of a new society which had proved itself in ordeal by fire, Stalin committed himself deliberately to future policies which were bound to bring the Soviet Union into direct conflict with his Western allies. Not content with the territorial acquisitions arising out of the defeat of Germany, he decided to exploit to the limit in the interests of Communism, or the Soviet Union, the "revolutionary situation" inherent in the chaos of post-war Europe. This entailed the deliberate refusal to co-operate with the West in restoring Europe to peace and health, led directly to the strains and tensions of the Cold War.

At first the aggressive policy seemed to meet with unmitigated success from the point of view of Moscow's immediate interests. Acting determinedly in face of a swiftly disarming West, the Kremlin extended its sway over Poland, Czechoslovakia, East Germany, Hungary, Bulgaria, Rumania, Jugoslavia and Albania. It was not until 1947 that the West, with the promulgation of the Truman Doctrine, showed any signs of reacting. It was not until the defection of Marshal Tito in 1948 that Stalin had his first serious set-back— which only intensified his oppression elsewhere. It was not until the Korean War in 1951 that the West was provoked into retaliatory action and into rearmament on a scale to match the Soviet effort.

This led to a sort of deadlock, ruinously expensive to both sides, ultimately disastrous in its consequences to the prosperity of the Soviet Union. The deadlock remained until Stalin, rigid in old age and unable to adapt his policies to changing needs, at last died, in March, 1953. His successors were faced with the task of bringing Soviet policy into line with the facts of life in the atomic age.

Test Yourself

1. Explain the origin of the Russian State giving dates of the main events in its growth.
2. What forces caused Muscovy to develop on lines different from those on which Western Europe developed?
3. How do you explain the autocratic character of tsarism?
4. How do you account for the origin and development of serfdom? When did it in effect begin? When did it reach its climax? When was it abolished?
5. What was the particular mission of Peter the Great?
6. What was the fundamental purpose of Lenin? To what extent did it coincide with the desires of the people and how far was it realized by Stalin?

Answers will be found at the end of the book.

CHAPTER IX

THE RISE OF NORTH AMERICA

An earlier chapter has traced the development of the Spanish and Portuguese Empires in South America into the Latin American Republics of the twentieth century. Still more remarkable is the story of the rise in North America, out of the rivalries of English, French and lesser imperialisms, of the two great nations we know as Canada and the United States of America. It is more usual to treat of Canada in connexion with the history of the British Commonwealth of Nations in which its part is second only to that of the mother country herself. But to do so is to read history backwards; for the modern political configuration of the North American continent is not one predestined by Nature, and is one indeed which some of its inhabitants have at different periods sought to frustrate.

Because the political history of Canada has been so largely a history of its relationships with Great Britain, it must take a secondary place in this narrative to the history of the United States whose national and constitutional development has dominated so much of the political thought of our times. But the United States and Canada should be thought of and studied together, and it is not without significance that their respective origins should lie so close together in time. The first permanent settlement in what was to be the United States was made at Jamestown, Virginia, in 1607; the French settlement at Quebec dates from 1608.

Neither Virginia nor Quebec was clearly marked out for future greatness. England and France were late-comers on the transatlantic scene. The encouragement of the Cabots by Henry VII had little sequel in the reigns of his successors, when the struggle for national unity and independence absorbed all energies. It is too often forgotten that Queen Elizabeth was the only British sovereign since the Norman Conquest to possess not a foot of soil outside these islands. The brilliant achievements of the early French explorers, like those of their successors, were deprived of their due reward by the indifference and continental-mindedness of their rulers. While Spain and Portugal rose to imperial greatness, the English and French played pirate and interloper on the fringes. The glamour attaching to the exploits of a Drake and a Hawkins must not blind one to the fact that they were bleeding an Empire, not constructing one. It was only when the heroic age was over and the commercial magnates of London began to have their say in national policy that the era of British expansion overseas began.

Causes of British Emigration

The search for markets which took Englishmen to the East Indies, to the Levant and to the White Sea also took them across the Atlantic. Their arrival perhaps prevented the Spaniards from adding North America as well to their Empire; but at first it looked as though the North American mainland and its barbarian inhabitants would provide neither an outlet for trade nor a source of goods as precious as those from the lands to the south. Indeed British and French strength, and the energies of minor competitors such as the Dutch and the Danes, concentrated for most of the seventeenth century not upon the North American continent but upon the sugar islands of the Caribbean, in whose waters a many-sided game of international rivalry went on until the islands' value and importance declined in the early part of the nineteenth century.

If the condition of England in Tudor times, with its great social evil of vagrancy, had continued unchanged, and if Englishmen had continued to believe that their country was over-populated, North America might have been valued for its suitability for white settlement. But in the seventeenth century English economists and statesmen, increasingly obsessed with the commercial competition of the Dutch,

PERU: THE INCA AND HIS CONSORT;
FROM A MANUSCRIPT c. A.D. 1300

AMERICA

A.D.	
1000	**Discovery** of America by Leif Ericsson (?).
1492	**Discovery** of America by Christopher Columbus.
1494	Treaty of Tordesillas; partition of New World discoveries between Spain and Portugal.
1497	John Cabot discovers Newfoundland.
1498	Columbus reaches S. America; discovers Venezuela and Trinidad; Cabot discovers Labrador and east coast of N. America.
1500	Pedro Alvarez Cabral discovers Brazil for Portugal.
1507	New World named America by Waldseemuller after Amerigo Vespucci.
1513	Balboa crosses Isthmus of Panama and reaches Pacific: Florida discovered.
1516	Diaz de Salis reaches mouth of River Plate.
1519	Cortes begins conquest of Mexico.
1520	Discovery of Magellan Strait, during first circumnavigation of world.
1526	Sebastian Cabot sails to River Plate.
1530	William Hawkins's first expedition to Brazil.
1531	Portuguese colony established in Brazil.
1532	Pizarro begins conquest of Peru.
1534	St. Lawrence River discovered by Cartier.
1549	First Jesuit missionaries in S. America.
1562	John Hawkins starts slave trade between Africa and America. French attempt to colonize Florida.
1565	Spaniards destroy Huguenot colony in Florida.
1567	Founding of San Sebastian (Rio de Janeiro).
1572	Francis Drake attacks Spanish harbours in America.
1573	Drake sees Pacific from Isthmus of Panama.
1579	Drake proclaims English sovereignty over New Albion (California) during his circumnavigation of the world.
1580	Buenos Aires founded; Dutch occupy part of Brazil.
1583	Gilbert founds first English colony in Newfoundland.
1584	Raleigh discovers and annexes Virginia.
1585	Unsuccessful attempts to colonize Virginia. John Davis tries to find North-West Passage; discovers Davis Straits.
1604	French settlement in Nova Scotia.
1607	Virginia Company makes first permanent settlement in America.
1608	Samuel de Champlain founds Quebec City.
1609	Henry Hudson, in Dutch employ, discovers Hudson River where the Dutch form a settlement.
1619	First American Assembly meets in Virginia.
	Negro slaves first imported into N. America.
1620	Pilgrim Fathers establish colony in New England.
1624	Dutch found New Amsterdam. England occupies Barbadoes.
1654	Portugal reconquers Brazil from Dutch.
1655	Cromwell attacks Spain in the West Indies.
1664	British take New Amsterdam from the Dutch and rename it New York.
1670	Hudson's Bay Company founded.
1673	"King Philip's War."
1682	La Salle reaches mouth of Mississippi.
1690	Indians raid English settlements.
1731	English sack Portobello in Panama and Spain declares war.
1739	War between English and Spaniards in West Indies.
1754	Hostilities between English and French colonists in N. America.
1759	English capture Quebec from the French.
	Accession of Charles III of Spain.

CALIFORNIA: STATE BUILDING A.D. 1900

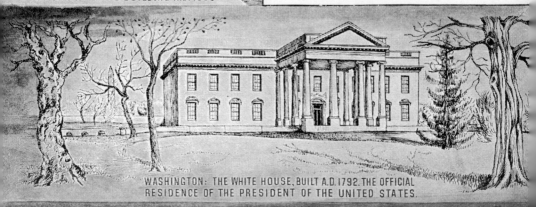

WASHINGTON: THE WHITE HOUSE, BUILT A.D. 1792. THE OFFICIAL
RESIDENCE OF THE PRESIDENT OF THE UNITED STATES.

TIME CHART

A.D.
63	France loses Canada and Spain loses Florida to Britain at Peace of Paris.
73	Boston Tea Party.
75	War of American Independence begins.
76	The thirteen colonies adopt Declaration of Independence.
78	France allies with colonies and declares war on Britain.
79	Spain declares war on England.
83	End of the American War; France and Spain make peace with Britain.
89	George Washington takes office as first President of U.S.A.
91	Quebec Act grants representative government to Canada.
ca	Expansion of cotton cultivation helps firmly to establish
00	slavery. Jefferson elected President of U.S.A.
08	Napoleon invades Spain.
10	Spanish colonies declare themselves independent of Spain: mainly unsuccessfully.
12	American War with Britain; invasion of Canada.
14	Peace of Ghent between U.S.A. and Great Britain.
16	Spanish colonies of S. America again revolt and seek independence.
18	Definition of frontier between Canada and U.S.A.
20	Revolution in Mexico.
21	Peru declares its independence.
23	Monroe Doctrine—a protest against any European power intervening in S. American republics.
24	Last Royalist forces in S. America routed; end of Spanish empire on American mainland.
28	Andrew Jackson elected President of U.S.A.
35	Independence of Texas.
37	Revolt in Canada.
39	Durham Report.
40	Union of Upper and Lower Canada.
45	Annexation of Texas by United States leads to war with Mexico and her defeat.
47	Thousands of immigrants land in N. America from Ireland as a result of Irish famine.
	Responsible government begins in Canada.
48	Discovery of gold in California.
60	Lincoln elected President. Secession of South Carolina leads to civil war on slavery issue.
62	Lincoln proclaims emancipation of slaves.
65	Defeat of the Southern States ends civil war.
66	Civil Rights Bill for the protection of Negroes.
67	Dominion of Canada established by British North America Act.
77	Federal troops finally evacuate South: end of "Reconstruction."
81	Building of the Canadian Pacific Railway started.
98	Spanish-American war—defeat of Spain and annexation of Philippines.
04	Construction of Panama Canal begins.
12	Woodrow Wilson elected President.
17	America enters the First World War.
20	America rejects the Versailles Treaty.
29	Slump on New York Stock Exchange inaugurates great depression.
33	President F. D. Roosevelt's New Deal begins.
41	Entry of U.S.A. into Second World War.
45	Death of President Roosevelt. First atomic bomb.
49	North Atlantic Treaty Organization set up.
52	Election of President Dwight D. Eisenhower.
56	Re-election of President Dwight D. Eisenhower.

CENTRAL AMERICA: CLAY IDOL c. A.D. 1500

HONDURAS: CARVED STONE IMAGE
ERECTED TO RECORD THE DATE,
8th. CENTURY A.D.

MEXICO: MAYA TEMPLE OF THE
PLUMED SERPENT AT CHICHEN ITZA

COLUMBUS LANDS IN AMERICA, 1492

The landing of Columbus on the soil of the New Continent in 1492 is seen in this picture from Gottfried's "Historia Antipodium." While the natives greet the discoverer with signs of friendship, a cross is erected on the sands to symbolize the establishment of Christianity.

were prone to think of under-population as the evil, and emigration was, generally speaking, frowned upon. The peopling of the British colonies was therefore for the most part, an unplanned consequence of domestic stresses. The northern or New England group of colonies in particular owed the dominant section of their early population to the Puritan dislike of the ecclesiastical policy of Charles I.

The Quakers of Pennsylvania represent another group whose motive for migration was primarily religious, and in the eighteenth century, the colonies provided a haven for certain persecuted religious groups from the European continent. It

may be hazarded that the French failure adequately to people their New World territories owed something to their insistence that the monopoly of the Roman Catholic religion should be maintained in the French Empire as rigidly as in the motherland.

By the middle of the eighteenth century, the New England colonies were thriving on a combination of fisheries, trade and shipbuilding. Farther south, New York—conquered from the Dutch, its original settlers—and the other "middle colonies" were important producers of foodstuffs, exporting these and other commodities to the sugar islands of the Caribbean.

Farther south still, on the basis of the labour of Negro slaves imported from Africa, tobacco, sugar and other plantation crops were making the fortunes of a New World squirearchy.

The "second hundred years war" between England and France was the occasion of a series of conflicts on American soil. But there were local as well as general causes for friction. The area of French domination swept in a single mighty arc from the mouth of the St. Lawrence to the mouth of the Mississippi. Early in the eighteenth century France had lost the struggle for Newfoundland and the neighbouring coastline—the future maritime provinces of Canada—although disputes over fishing rights in these coveted waters did not find a final solution until the twentieth century. The French empire of the mainland—apart from some close settlement in the region of Quebec and Montreal, was mainly a fur-trading domain —like that of the still more sparsely inhabited empire of the British Hudson's Bay Company to the north.

Imperial Government

Such an economy was easier to combine with good relations with the native Red Indians than the land-greedy ambitions of most of the English colonists. But the fur-traders of New York had their Indian allies, too, and the participation of Indian auxiliaries added a particular ferocity to the struggle. The military advantage proved to lie with the more thickly populated English colonies, and the French ring which threatened to cut off further expansion to the interior was broken. By the Peace of Paris in 1763, the French abandoned their empire on the mainland of North America and the British Crown found itself in possession of all the land up to the Mississippi, with the mainly unexplored territory beyond ceded to the shadowy power of Spain.

The war against France was of crucial importance in developing a sense of independent nationhood in the British colonies and the disappearance of the French danger made it easier for this sense to find political expression. Although the local concerns of the colonies and particularly the levying of taxes had from early on been the responsibility in each colony of a locally elected assembly, the executive government and matters concerning the Empire as a whole, had continued from London, where, in the seventeenth and eighteenth centuries, power had passed from the Crown to a parliament in which the colonies were unrepresented.

American Independence

A variety of causes contributed to make the Americans regard this system as one of constraint. They felt that the imperial economic regulations, based on the theory of a closed commercial empire, hampered their growing industry and commerce, and restricted them unduly to producing for the British market; the claim of the home government to tax them for the expenses of the late war added to the irritations which had accumulated between the administration and the colonial leaders during its conduct; the home government was thought to oppose the American desire for rapid expansion into the interior because of its undue subservience to fur-trading interests masquerading as protectors of the rights of the Red Indians, and because of the influence of land companies unwilling to see the value of their holdings diminished by the opening up of new areas. These suspicions were increased when much of the newly conquered territory was attached for government to Canada, instead of to the original British colonies. The extreme liberality of Britain's treatment of her new French subjects, whose laws and religion were untouched, was also a source of suspicion to the Americans whose strong Protestant prejudices were aroused, and who feared that the home government was seeking to fortify itself against them by securing Canadian support.

The demands of the colonists which were at first only for more extensive local rights and privileges, became in the course of a decade a movement for outright independence. The principal reason for this was the inability of either side to visualize a bond between the mother country and the colonies without involving sovereignty on the one side and subordination on the other. On the British side, efforts to seek a solution by conciliation either came too late, or were frustrated by the feeling of nearly all British statesmen that there could be no compromise on the root problem of sovereignty. On the American side also, extremists gained the upper hand. The reason here was largely a matter of internal politics. Radical elements were hoping to see an increasing tendency towards democratic government in colonial society, once separation from England had been achieved, and were suspicious of mercantile and other wealthy elements, who in many cases had a strong, vested interest in the maintaining of the imperial connexion, as well as the sympathies with England born of a common upbringing and outlook with the dominant classes.

But the war (1775-83) might not have come at all, and would hardly have ended in the complete defeat of the British, had not the Americans' struggle for independence become involved in the next phase of world politics, the effort of the French to turn the tables upon Great Britain. From the military point of view, American independence was the by-product of Anglo-French rivalry. But it would be unjust to lay too much stress upon this fact.

Early Difficulties

The conclusion of peace in 1783, eight years after the outbreak of the struggle, saw none of the combatants fully satisfied. The independence of the United States was recognized internationally and was never again seriously challenged. But Great Britain remained in Canada—a Canada where in the Maritimes and in Upper Canada, north of the Great Lakes, there was an important new element in the population, "loyalists" from the United States, with memories of ill-treatment to help keep alive their fidelity to the British connexion. In the interior, and south along the shores of the Gulf of Mexico, was Spain. The breaking of the imperial tie lost the Americans the advantages as well as the disadvantages of the imperial commercial system. Henceforth their commerce had to bargain for entry where it could. Politically and strategically also, the responsibilities and burdens of independence had to be endured. Nor was the world in which the new-born nation had to make its way, a simple one. After less than ten years of uneasy peace, the wars of the French Revolution again menaced the quiet of the oceans and even of the New World. Diplomatic and political skill were required by the first generation of American statesmen

The Age of Washington

In these circumstances, the survival and prosperity of the United States, which surprised many contemporaries, has often been treated by historians as though it presented elements of the miraculous. Such accounts minimize certain favourable elements in the situation. The United States were fortunate in possessing what was still a fairly homogeneous population accustomed to the free transaction of its affairs. It had a well-balanced economy to which was soon added, in the form of cotton, yet another staple commodity for which world markets were ever eager.

For a neutral, there were in that age advantages as well as disadvantages to be gained from the strife of the great Powers. But most important of all was the quality of leadership which the new republic managed to secure for its service. While the role of Washington was almost as important in peace as it had been in war it would be incorrect to suggest that he created the republic single-handed. His work, and that of his great contemporaries, was possible because in the national government and in the United States, they could rely upon a whole generation with a strong civic consciousness and great civic capacities. Their capacities are the best tribute to the system which they had spurned, for they were based on that system's devotion to the principle of local responsibility and to the education which they shared with their English counterparts, with its strong roots in the common law and in a limited but significant appreciation of the classics and hence of the political thought of the ancient world.

The political problem before them was essentially the same as that with which the statesmen of the British Empire had been confronted before the American Revolution. How could the jealously cherished autonomy of the colonies, now independent states, be combined with the granting of powers to central institutions which were necessary to the prosperity and even to the survival of the newly enfranchised nation? The question was one to which experience and history gave no obvious answer, for although the notion of federation had a respectable ancestry in the classical world, it had never been practised on so large a scale, and the only two contemporary federations, those of the Netherlands and Switzerland, were also the products of totally different circumstances.

The movement for permanent federal institutions was a natural outgrowth from the improvisations evolved to meet the exigencies of the war. The Articles of Confederation—the first American Constitution—which came into force in 1781 did little more than formalize existing procedures. The energies of constitutional statesmanship had very largely gone into framing constitutions for the separate states. In these, the main task was to find substitutes for the governor and other executive agents of the imperial government; the assemblies or other legislative bodies could largely be taken over unchanged. As a result of this, nearly all the state constitutions embodied the principle of the division of powers. The executive—the governor—was separately elected by the people, and he neither owed his place to the legislature nor was he responsible to it. Furthermore, the mistrust of all government which was a permanent legacy of the constitutional conflicts of the colonial period of the country's history, led to the inclusion in the state constitutions of "bills of rights," statements as to the rights and freedoms of the individual which were thereby guaranteed.

The summer of 1787, during which the Constitutional Convention sat at Phila-

DRAKE LANDS IN CALIFORNIA, 1579

Francis Drake being presented with a feathered headdress in the presence of a group of the natives of the country. His followers, deployed in great strength and armed with muskets and spears, plant a standard and name the land New Albion.

delphia under Washington's chairmanship, was of crucial importance for the nation's future and the constitution which emerged, and which was based largely on the work of James Madison, was an ingenious and, it proved, a surprisingly lasting compromise between the conflicting interests of the participating states which differed widely in their size, economic structure and social outlook. The struggle for popular ratification which followed was accompanied on both sides by able propaganda, in which the very foundations of popular government were probed. This propaganda produced one literary work of major consequence, the *Federalist*. Its two principal authors were Madison himself and Alexander Hamilton, a precociously brilliant lawyer and politician whose own constitutional scheme, which confessedly owed much to the British example, had been turned down by the Convention as too aristocratic and even monarchic in its tendencies; and the book has remained the classical source of arguments in favour of federalism, whether on the national, imperial or international level.

New Constitution

Although the new constitution provided machinery for its own amendment, this has been surprisingly little used, and as far as its formal provisions go, the constitution of the Union of Forty-eight States in the twentieth century is almost identical with that of the Union of Thirteen States for which it was framed. Its endurance and stability have been due partly to the fact that its adoption was followed by a period of peace and prosperity which enabled it to acquire credit not wholly its own, and partly to the fact that it became associated in the popular mind with the prestige of Washington and other heroes of the Revolutionary period. But twentieth-century criticism of its inadequacies should not blind one to its genuine merits, even though its actual working, as in the direct election of the President, does not correspond altogether to its authors' intentions.

The most arresting feature from the point of view of British constitutional practice was that which reproduced in the federal government the complete separation of executive and legislature—in this case of President and Congress. From the American viewpoint, the main feature was the compromise by which in the lower house— the House of Representatives—the states were represented in proportion to population, while in the more important Senate, they were represented equally. Important, too, was the concession made to the constitution's chief critics, the inclusion in the form of the first ten amendments, of a Bill of Rights, comparable to those of the states.

Equality of New States

But the item of most significance was that providing for the future admission of new states on a footing of complete equality with the original members of the federation. This provision, which was bitterly opposed by some of the aristocratic leaders of the older seaboard regions, was the best guarantee for the nation's future. It meant that the overflow of population from the original areas of settlement and the great influx of European immigrants in the following century could go ahead with the settling of the interior of the continent, while retaining or acquiring all the political rights and individual freedom of American citizens. It was a pledge that on its continental territory—at that time there was no thought of any other— the United States would not practise colonialism or imperialism as the world had hitherto known it.

It is important for the understanding of later American developments to appreciate the extent to which the institutions of the United States, and the rights of American citizens, were based from the beginning on carefully drafted written constitutions. This formed a striking contrast to the position in Great Britain whose common law the Americans had inherited, but whose constitutional law was the outcome of separate decisions of Parliament and the courts, and of customary practices worked out over a period of centuries. It also meant that American constitutional development in the nineteenth and twentieth centuries could not follow British lines. Great Britain was to see a series of peace-

Their rype corne

Their greene corne.

Corne newly sprong

Their sitting at meate

The place of solemne prayer

The house wherin the Tombe of their Herounds standeth.

SECOTON

AMERICAN INDIAN VILLAGE IN 1585

John White's drawings of American Indians, now preserved in the British Museum, show clearly that the Indians had an organized community and were aware of the need for rotation of crops. Unmarried braves lived in communal houses seen in the centre, and the ritual of the dance before the sacred fire is also portrayed.

ful revolutions carried out by the unquestioned authority of a sovereign parliament. In the United States, Congress was not sovereign. Its power lay in the document to which it owed its authority, and its actions were tested by their conformity to it, just as the actions of state authorities had to pass the double test of conformity to the State and the Federal Constitution. This gave a great deal of power to the body entrusted with the interpretation of the constitution. Although the location of this power was nowhere specifically laid down in the constitution, it was rapidly acquired by the chief judicial organ of the Federal Government, the Supreme Court. This was challenged in some quarters as undemocratic and contrary to the rights of the states, but there can be little doubt that this development had been regarded as natural by the framers of the constitution, although they can hardly have foreseen all the uses to which this power was to be put.

Washington, the first and inevitable President (1789-97) under the new constitution, endeavoured to make his adminis-tration as representative as possible of the main sections of the country and of all its politically active classes. The two key posts, those of Secretary of State and Secretary of the Treasury, were given to Thomas Jefferson, the author of the Declaration of Independence, and leader of the planters and farmers, and to Alexander Hamilton, the representative of the commercial interests. But the tendency of the legislation needed to clothe the bare bones of the new constitution and to give the new government adequate resources was largely in the hands of the latter and, even before his retirement from office, Jefferson's position was becoming that of an opposition leader.

The trend towards a two-party system was accelerated by the outbreak of the French Revolution and the Revolutionary War. Hamilton and other close associates of Washington were accused of sympathy with Great Britain, while Jefferson and his partisans were regarded as embodying the full revolutionary creed. In spite of the treaty which had bound the United States

LOG HOUSE OF A CANADIAN PIONEER

In the steady advance of civilization westward the early settlers in Canada, having reached their location, first had to clear timber and build a substantial log house, such as that seen in this early etching. The peacefulness of the scene is emphasized by the figure of the pioneer and his dog emerging from his house, and the two children playing on a see-saw.

to France since the Revolutionary War and of certain important differences with Great Britain, Washington managed to keep his country to a neutral position. By retiring after two terms of office, that is eight years, Washington set a precedent which no one was bold enough to disregard until President Franklin Delano Roosevelt did so in the perilous times of the Second World War.

Jeffersonians in Power

An even more vital guide to future generations was embodied in the document which is known as Washington's Farewell Address (1797). In this he warned his countrymen that, for the sake of maintaining peace and their own internal unity, they should beware of political involvement in the affairs of Europe, a continent which seemed to Americans of his and later generations for ever predestined to be the source of wars. An obstacle to following this counsel was the rapid growth in American overseas trade and shipping. French interference with this commerce brought about an undeclared naval war with France during the presidency of John Adams, Washington's immediate successor (1797-1801). Adams's administration was an admittedly party one relying on the Federalists, as the partisans of a strong and conservative central government were then termed. His strong measures against sympathizers with the French helped to alienate support, and in the election of 1800, Jefferson was returned to power at the head of the party known as the Republicans—the party from whom the Democratic Party of today claims direct descent.

Jefferson's creed was one of peace and retrenchment. "Entangling alliances," as he termed them, were to be avoided, and the armed forces were to be reduced. At home his followers stood for the minimum of central control over the affairs of the states. Not for the last time in American history did things work out differently from what was intended by the party "platform." Although Jefferson himself managed to avoid war to the end of his presidency (1801-09), his efforts to secure, by the exercise of economic sanctions, respect for

America's rights as a neutral, proved of little avail against Napoleon who was fighting for world mastery, and against Great Britain which was struggling for survival. War came in the time of his successor, Madison (1809-17), whose political and administrative talents proved inferior to his great theoretical powers. Grievances over British interference with American shipping, and over the impressment from American merchantmen of sailors claimed by the British Navy, combined with a renewal of hopes for the conquest of Canada—believed to be assisting the Indians in their efforts to prevent further expansion of American settlement —to produce a new warlike majority in Congress against which the older Republicans were powerless. The "War of 1812" did little to bring credit on either side. It is perhaps symbolic that its principal battle, the American victory at New Orleans (1814), was fought in the interval between the signing of a peace treaty at Ghent in the Netherlands and the receipt of the news of it in America.

Nationalist Tendencies

The peace treaty itself, notable for its provisions for the disarmament of the Great Lakes frontier between the U.S.A. and Canada, did not settle any of the issues which had been the nominal cause of war, and left open certain frontier questions which were not settled until the signature of the Webster-Ashburton treaty in 1842. Its importance was indeed greater on the Canadian than on the American side, since it marked a final check to the hopes of the merchants of Montreal (by now mostly of British descent), that the St. Lawrence might continue to compete with the Hudson as the main route to the American interior, and to the fur-trading empire, which was henceforth divided between the Americans and the Hudson's Bay Company which controlled the Canadian west.

But the war itself was of great significance in the internal history of the United States. It marked the bridge between the cautious federalism of the revolutionary period and the full-blown nationalism of modern America. The new leaders of the

Republican Party, which acquired a political monopoly at the expense of the Federalists who had been finally ruined by their factious opposition to the war, were conscious that the country's future lay with the national idea, rather than in attachment to states' rights as their predecessors had conceived of them. Some of them, like Henry Clay, came from the new lands of the West where state loyalties never acquired the same hold as on the seaboard with its history going back to colonial days. As the national centre of gravity shifted across the Alleghany Mountains to the valleys of the Mississippi and its tributaries, the national sentiment grew in strength. The breach with Europe, brought about by the war which had suspended the movement of immigrants as well as of goods, created a new feeling of cultural independence and a demand that the industries built up to replace the lost sources of supply should not be allowed to disappear when peace returned. Nationalism was thus bound up with a policy of protection for industry and, for a time, with a demand that the Federal Government should help in improving the internal communications of the country and so assist in achieving its economic integration. These nationalist tendencies received powerful support from the Supreme Court under its remarkable Chief Justice, John Marshall, whose constitutional interpretations were consistently directed towards strengthening the federal authority.

The buoyant self-confidence of the political leaders of this period, best personified in the figure of Clay, was not wholly justified by the country's external position. For the defeat of Napoleon had given power in Europe to sovereigns and statesmen to whom American principles were anathema and who had a very pressing interest in the New World because of the necessity of resolving the problems caused by the dissolution of the Spanish and Portuguese Empires. The greatest of these powers, the Russia of Alexander I, was also a potential menace in the North American continent, since from its Alaskan outpost its fur traders were pressing southward in competition with the Americans, for whom

NATURAL RESOURCES
of CANADA and
THE UNITED STATES
of AMERICA

CITY OF BROOKLYN IN 1816

In 1816, when Francis Guy painted this picture, Brooklyn had a population of only 4,500. In 1839 it became a city and now has a population of about 2,300,000. Now in the Brooklyn Museum, New York, the picture shows the narrow streets and frame houses so characteristic of many similar American towns of that period.

the Pacific coast was an important stage on the Cape Horn route to China. In the Pacific north-west, in what are now the American states of Oregon and Washington and the Canadian Province of British Columbia, there were the makings of a three-cornered contest between the United States, Russia and Great Britain.

The United States' success in extricating itself from these perils was due to the fact that in the most important question, the future of Latin America, its interests and those of Great Britain were largely identical. Neither could gain by the reincorporation of these territories into the closed commercial empire of Spain, still less by having some more vigorous power replace her. The successful enunciation of American policy known as the Monroe Doctrine (1823), which owed much to the diplomacy of President Monroe's able Secretary of State and successor, John Quincy Adams, owed still more to the fact that it coincided with the policy of what was now beyond question the dominant naval power on an issue in which naval power was bound to have the last word. That part of the Monroe Doctrine which referred to the

possible transference of political power in Latin America was made possible by the British attitude and the consequent abstention of the European Powers from intervention; that part which related to Russian designs in the north-west—the non-colonization doctrine—was rendered irrelevant by the collapse of Russian expansionism in this area for reasons unconnected with American opposition.

But this was not the end of the Monroe Doctrine which, although allowed to lie dormant for a time, was successively revived and reinterpreted during new crises in relations between the United States and Europe, and remained a persistent strand in the make-up of American foreign policy. For almost the whole of the remainder of the century, American foreign policy outside the North American continent was largely dependent upon the unspoken implications of Monroe's action as well as upon adherence to the oft-quoted warnings of Washington and Jefferson against meddling in European affairs. Great Britain's command of the ocean meant that the United States had no need to fear any foreign power, so long as its relations with Great Britain were secure.

Foreign policy meant simply relations with Great Britain; and for long periods, when no particular issue with Great Britain was in the air, Americans could feel that they alone among nations could afford the luxury of having no foreign policy at all. This sense of isolation was bound up with the conviction that the absence of the burdens which the ever-present threat of war involved for the countries of the Old World, was one of the secrets of the rapid American material progress. Americans could and did feel a strong sense of being set apart from other nations in order to set them the example of peaceful and ordered development. This sense of dedication helps to explain the continued moral appeal of the isolationist principle even after the conditions which gave rise to it disappeared, and it provided yet another reason for millions of people from war-torn tax-burdened, conscript Europe to seek a haven in the United States.

Party System Perfected

The presidency of John Quincy Adams (1825-29) marks the high tide of the new nationalism and the beginning of its ebb. The policies with which it was connected, particularly protection, bore hardly on certain sections of the country, especially in the south, whose main economic concern was with the export of raw materials to a Europe in the midst of its industrial revolution. Even more important was the feeling that the advantages which accrued from these policies went too exclusively to the wealthier classes of the eastern states whose power was still to some extent buttressed by franchise and other political distinctions. Under the impact of these divergences in outlook, the Republican Party split, and in the election of 1828, comparable in its importance to that of 1800, the democratic wing and its candidate, Andrew Jackson, was successful against the Nationalists. Jackson, the hero of the Battle of New Orleans, a skilful and attractive politician, was to a far greater extent than Jefferson the founder of the Democratic Party, which under him rested, as it has mainly done since, upon a combin-

ation of southern and frontier agrarian elements, with the underprivileged groups in the great cities. The measures of Jackson's presidency (1829-37) are less important than the spirit which inspired them. Neither his frontier supporters nor his following in the cities were willing to accept the leadership of the class which had inherited its power direct from its colonial predecessors. The last obstacles to complete political democracy were removed.

The final victory of the American democracy, the extension to state and federal affairs alike of the principle of the direct responsibility to the electorate of those elected—a process completed later in the century and early in the next, when senators became directly elected—carried with it certain consequences of unforeseen importance. In spite of the characteristic Jacksonian belief that the operations of government and administration were so simple that anyone could perform them, and that in a healthy democracy there would be constant rotation in office, the vast and increasingly divergent electorate could no longer act on the basis of personal knowledge or neighbourly ties. The party system with its local and state machinery, its conventions and large-scale propaganda apparatus, became an essential part of the American political system, with the president as important in his role of party leader and spokesman as he was in that of national executive which the Founding Fathers had assigned to him.

Jackson versus the Bank

At the time of Jackson's re-election to the presidency in 1832, there was among the wealthier elements considerable ill-feeling towards him, owing to attacks he made against the Bank of the United States in the course of an address delivered during his first presidency. Encouraged by his re-election, however, Jackson continued to wage war on the Bank and in July, 1832, he vetoed its new charter passed by the Senate during its previous session. He later attempted to have all public deposits in the Bank transferred to certain state banks as an experiment to ascertain whether these smaller banks could act as financial agents on behalf of the Government. During its next session, the Senate passed a resolution condemning Jackson's action. Assisted by some of his friends, Jackson strongly protested and, after a bitter struggle, the resolution was, in January, 1837, ordered to be removed from the records.

The effects of the great impetus given by Jackson to American democracy were evident even on the far side of the United States' northern border. The maritime colonies of the Canadian seaboard lived fairly detached and peaceable lives, linked by their commerce with the eastern seaboard of the United States and with the British colonies in the Caribbean. But the region around the St. Lawrence and the Great Lakes was the scene of political developments ominously reminiscent, though in very different circumstances, of those which had led to the break-away of the original American colonies.

Canada Divided

The old Province of Quebec had been divided, in 1791, into the two colonies of Upper and Lower Canada—the latter dominantly French in population and law, the former, the modern Ontario, demonstratively English. Both these colonies had been simultaneously endowed with representative institutions, with the result that their constitutions and their relationship to the British Government resembled very closely those of the old colonies, in spite of the British renunciation of any rights of direct taxation over them. This system of divided authority produced the inevitable friction which was made worse by the fact of the difficulties of securing agreement between Upper and Lower Canada on the matters involved in their joint dependence on the St. Lawrence artery. In Lower Canada, the sense of separate nationality, in Upper Canada, important social cleavages, added to the gravity of the situation which in 1837 culminated in two separate but equally abortive risings, whose ringleaders significantly sought asylum in the United States.

The quiescence of the greater part of the population of both colonies expressed the feeling that separation from the Empire would be only the prelude to absorption in the United States, whose increasingly conscious nationalism—cultural as well as political—could not permit the survival of the markedly individual characteristics of the two major Canadian groups. The direct result of the rebellions was therefore a further step in constitutional development within the imperial framework. The Canadian situation was analysed with care and shrewdness in the famous report of the Government's commissioner, Lord Durham, who visited Canada in 1838. His recommendations sought to solve the constitutional problem by granting responsible government to the Canadians, leaving the Crown as the sole formal link with the government of the mother country, while preventing this concession from being made the prelude to secession by French Canada by merging the two colonies once more into one. The latter recommendation which gave Canada an English-speaking majority was accepted in 1840; for the implementation of the former Canadians had to wait until the governor-generalship of Lord Elgin in 1847-54.

It was thus a responsible Canadian ministry which guided Canada's destinies through the challenging period of the late 1840s and 1850s, when American expansionism seemed once again likely to culminate in an attempt to incorporate the entire North American continent into the United States. And it was a Canadian ministry which, with the aid of the southern states of the Union, carried through the commercial reciprocity treaty of 1854, which for a time quieted the demand for annexation.

The opposition of the southern states of the Union to the incorporation of Canada in the United States, was one symptom of the principal feature of the course of American history in the 1840s and 1850s—the growing dominance of the slavery issue. Much that went on which was of the utmost consequence for the United States and its future had nothing to do with slavery in the first instance. There was a great burst of industrial enterprise in the north-eastern states and of railway-

WAR VESSELS IN THE AMERICAN CIVIL WAR

Steam-propelled monitors and armoured mortars approaching a position known as Island Number Ten during the war of 1861-65. The vulnerability of wooden sailing ships against the recently developed rifled gun firing long-range high-explosive shells, prompted the development of armoured vessels against which minefields were later used.

building in the north-east and in the new states of the still predominantly agricultural mid-west. The development of the sailing vessel in its latest stage—the clipper-ship—gave the American mercantile marine a place on the world's oceans such as it had not had before, and was not, for nearly a century, to have again. The 1840s saw the onset of a tide of human migration from the Old World to the New, which was to continue unabated until the closing of the gates after the First World War. The sources and intensity of this migration varied with political and economic pressures in Europe; and it was sensitive to the violent movements of the business cycle which continued to mark the upward movement of the American economy.

The influx of new population as well as a high rate of natural increase gave the required impetus to the continued territorial expansion of the United States. Much of the new land, particularly in the north-west, where the frontier of settlement was reaching out over the prairies, had been gained by the old piecemeal process of pushing back the Indians. Bloody conflict with the Indian tribes

marked each stage in the process and the last Indian war of the United States' Army was not fought until 1886. In the 1840s, the settlement of the Oregon dispute with Great Britain, the annexation of the Republic of Texas, which had thrown off Mexican rule a decade earlier, and the war with Mexico, gave the United States new and desirable lands in the south-west and on the Pacific coast. The Californian gold rush which began in 1848, gave peculiar significance to the youngest of these acquisitions.

It is against this background of an expanding territory and an expanding economy that the slavery issue must be considered and its importance explained. In a country of such great geographical and climatic diversities, uniformity of economic structure was not to be expected. Indeed, the American political and party system was in the early half of the nineteenth century, and has to some extent remained, primarily a method for harmonizing the interests of the different regions or "sections," which far more than the individual states, have been the real constituents of the American nation. Of the sections, the South was from the beginning

AUCTION OF NEGRO SLAVES IN VIRGINIA, 1861

Sale of Negro slaves was a common practice in America until the Civil War. At such sales whole families were sold "separately or in lots," to the highest bidder, as may be seen from this contemporary sketch. In 1834, the British Parliament passed an act abolishing slavery in the Colonies, but it was not until thirty years later that America followed suit.

the one with the most clearly marked individuality, and with the most striking peculiarities of interest and outlook. Its characteristic institution—plantation slavery—was an inheritance from the slave-trade of colonial times which the new republic joined with the rest of the civilized world in putting down, in the first decades of the nineteenth century. But the hopes of most of the enlightened men of the early period of independence that slavery itself would die out were rendered obsolete by Eli Whitney's discovery of the cotton-gin (1793), and by the consequent development of large-scale cotton production in the South to meet the growing demands of the textile industries of old and of New England.

By the middle of the nineteenth century, southern cotton growing occupied a position of unique importance in American and world economy. And although the use of slaves in large numbers for the production of cotton and the other plantation crops was the monopoly of a comparatively small class of planters, these had contrived to make themselves the unchallenged leaders politically as well as socially, of the whole section and to make the defence of slavery the essential element in the southern attitude to national politics.

Although Negro slavery was upheld largely on economic grounds, the problem was not and could not be primarily an economic one. The advocates of gradual emancipation along some such lines as the British West Indian colonies were to follow in the 1830s, with their apprenticeship scheme for the transition period to freedom, had to face the inevitable question of whether they were to proceed from legal to political and social equality which might mean in some parts of the South the acceptance of rule by a Negro majority.

Alexis de Tocqueville, a young Frenchman of genius whose *Democracy in America* (1835), based on a visit to the United States during the Presidency of Jackson, did much to interpret the new country to Europeans and to itself, rose to sombre heights of prophecy when he developed the theme that the Negro problem would by no means be solved with the ending of slavery.

New Republican Party

A preliminary skirmish in 1819-20, over the admission of Missouri to the Union as a slave state, caused the ageing Jefferson to remark that the raising of this issue was as ominous as "a fire-bell in the night," since the Union could not survive if political passions were to coincide with geographical lines of demarcation. From about 1830 onwards, two new trends came to the fore which threatened to make this forecast true and which frustrated the hopes of those statesmen who, like Clay, had hoped to see the great Mississippi artery act as a bond of union between North and South. The first such trend was the growth in the North of a straightforward abolitionist movement advocating total and immediate emancipation. The second trend was the building up in response, both to this propaganda, and to the feeling that the economics of expansion and the growing tide of white immigration were working against the South, was the development of a specifically southern ideology.

In the late 1850s, Jackson's own Democratic Party split into a northern and southern wing and the new Republican Party, based on opposition to any further extension of slavery, was, in the election of 1860, victorious by virtue of its overwhelming strength in the north and north-west. The new president, Abraham Lincoln, was thus a sectional representative and his election was taken by the South as the signal for the long-awaited secession.

The problem of whether or not to allow the southern states to secede in peace was one to which the American political and constitutional tradition gave no unambiguous answer. There were those who had argued that the American nation was a single body which no portion could disown

and that it was compatible with democratic ideals to fight for the preservation of the Union. There were those who argued that the Union was simply the product of a compact entered into by what were originally sovereign states who could resume their rights if the majority infringed them. Close business ties between northern manufacturers and traders and the southern planters provided an economic foundation for a strongly marked tendency towards compromise among the older states of the north-eastern seaboard. But the north-west, whose outlet down the Mississippi would fall into foreign hands if the secession were allowed to endure, and whose vigorous nationalism was not rooted in a particularist colonial past, stood firm for upholding the Union. And a direct challenge to the Union, in the form of a southern attack upon a federal fortress, was answered by Lincoln with war.

The American Civil War (1861-65), bitterly fought out in four years of merciless campaigning, is the great watershed in American history. The South's challenge to a North which numbered more than twice its population, even if the slaves were taken into the reckoning, was in many respects foolhardy. The skill of Robert E. Lee and other southern generals was greater than that of the succession of northern commanders-in-chief who followed after George B. McLellan, when that unfortunate soldier fell victim to the impatience of his political chiefs and their adherents.

Emancipation of Slaves

For a time it seemed as though the sympathies which the South possessed among the upper classes in European society, particularly in Great Britain and France, and the irritation caused by the northern blockade might acquire foreign allies for the southern confederacy. The North in this critical period owed much to the patience and confidence of its chief executive. Slowly the tide turned. The emancipation of the slaves, proclaimed by Lincoln in 1862, largely as a military measure, evoked a wave of sympathy from the British working class, even from the

Lancashire textile workers hard-hit by the cotton-famine, and dispelled any fear of foreign intervention.

In spite of southern privateering, the northern grip on the seas tightened, and on land, McLellan's policy of delay was justified by events. For, as the war went on, and drew to itself all the human and industrial resources of the two communities, the northern advantage became more and more clearly marked. It was the first war fought by a modern industrial society, and its lessons were unmistakable. General Grant's victories on the Mississippi, and the northern domination of the entire West were a prelude to the further bisection of the confederacy by Sherman's march through Georgia, and to Lee's inevitable surrender. Manpower, industrial strength and railways, had been the three keys of victory. The South lay prostrate and exhausted, while northern industry boomed and expansion continued unabated.

Effects of War

Just as the emancipation of the slaves had not ended the Negro problem but merely changed its form, so the surrender of the South did not end the problem of the relationship between the section and the rest of the nation. The constitutional issue was settled indeed. There was to be no further talk of secession; the indissolubility of the Union was generally recognized. Although the vocabulary of States Rights was not to disappear from the mouths of American politicians, it was henceforth largely a cloak behind which particular interests desirous of escaping federal control might seek protection. The real problem was not a constitutional one but a political one—how to reintegrate the defeated South in the nation. Here the nation suffered for decades from the murder of the great president in the moment of victory (1865).

Lincoln had shown that he was determined that the wounds of the war should be healed as rapidly as possible and that the road back should be made as easy as possible to southern pride. His departure removed the floodgates of northern radicalism. Holders of doctrinaire views on the possibility of immediate and total Negro equality, combined with elements seeking for easy profits at the expense of the vanquished, and with Republicans determined to make a permanent party monopoly of the appeal to patriotism, to inflict upon the conquered South the long drawn-out ordeal of reconstruction. Federal troops maintained in power governments composed of Negroes, imported northerners, and what our generation would term southern "quislings." Under their management, any hopes of finding a solution for the economic and social problems created by the wartime devastation, and by emancipation, disappeared. It became inevitable that when, after a decade, the whole country revolted against these proceedings, and the federal troops were finally withdrawn, leaving the South free to govern itself, its leaders should come to their task with re-establishment of "white supremacy" as their primary objective. The safeguards for Negro equality which the victors had written into the Constitution, were of no avail against the determination of the southern whites to set them aside. And southern concentration upon this single issue long hindered the tackling of the South's other great problem, that of its poverty relative to the nation as a whole. Only with the advent of a new generation towards the end of the century did the memories of war and reconstruction fall into the background, and new common interests recreate the psychological bonds of union.

Confidence in the North

If the South in the post-war decades showed the neurosis born of defeat, the North, whose own great losses had been of relatively lesser consequence and were materially compensated for by migration, and which had hardly known war on its own soil, could exult in a mood of new-found confidence resembling that which had accompanied and followed the War of 1812. The significance of the Monroe Doctrine was reasserted when American support for the Mexican republicans under Juarez helped to bring to an end the rule of

Napoleon III's ill-fated puppet, the Emperor Maximilian (1867). For a time it looked as though nothing less than the surrender of Canada would be accepted as satisfaction for certain British departures from strict neutrality during the war. This threat and the failure to renew the Reciprocity Treaty, as well as the consciousness that Lord Durham's Union of Upper and Lower Canada had not made one nation out of the two, led to yet another drastic reorganization of the Canadian polity.

Canada and the United States

In spite of the fact that the early railway system of Canada, like its major waterways, had tended to ignore the political frontier, and to create a series of links at different places along it, the decision was now taken that the future of Canada lay in the development of a single east-to-west axis. This led to the creation of Canada's own transcontinental railways which reached from ocean to ocean by the mid-1880s. The political solution involved the redivision of Canada into the two provinces of Ontario and Quebec and their federation with Nova Scotia and New Brunswick in 1867. The great inland territory of the Hudson's Bay Company, the old fur empire of the north, was purchased by the Dominion in 1869, and the Province of Manitoba, which was formed out of part of it, joined the federation in 1870. British Columbia, on the Pacific coast, and Prince Edward Island, the last of the Atlantic Maritimes, joined in 1873.

The continuation of prairie settlement led to revolts by the half-breeds of the north-west in 1870 and 1885, but the territory involved eventually became part of the federation as the province of Saskatchewan in 1905, in which year the lands still farther to the west were admitted as the last of the prairie provinces, Alberta. Into these territories came, among other settlers, a very large number of Americans, from the adjacent prairie and Pacific states. Thus the intermingling of the peoples in the east of the continent through a southward movement was paralleled by an intermingling in the west through a movement northwards. With the consoli-dation of the Canadian confederation in the last third of the nineteenth century, and with the great economic growth of the Dominion both then and later, the question of its political relations with the United States receded into the background. Canada acquired a new status as the senior member, after the mother country, in the partnership of the British Commonwealth and showed its consciousness of the significance of that role in both world wars and their aftermaths.

The rapid development of Canada as an industrial nation provided new links with the United States, and both capital and labour organizations found the political frontier no bar to their unity. By the 1940s the technical problems of the hemisphere's defence were bringing the two nations into a close partnership without raising the question of their incorporation in a single unit. The continued emphasis of the United States upon a single nationhood, cultural as well as political, was not matched in Canada, where the special problems and attitudes of the French Catholic minority continued to tax the resources of Canadian and imperial statesmanship.

Growth of Modern Industry

If the twentieth century saw a new Canada, it saw as emphatically a new United States. As industrialization swept forward on its all-conquering path in the decades after the Civil War, the conflict of geographical sections while not wholly in abeyance, was less obvious than the struggle between new and powerful interests. A series of political revolts by agrarian interests who felt the tide running against them strained but did not break the two-party system; and in men such as W. J. Bryan, American democracy found spokesmen who gave a new, more emphatically economic accent to its historic doctrines.

Industry also had its problems. The so-called "closing of the frontier" in 1890, when it was officially accepted that the empty lands were filled up and the three centuries of continental expansion ended, may have had less effect on the fortunes of the common man than was at one time believed. But the psychological effect of the feeling that the great opportunities enshrined in the idea of going west were now at an end, cannot be too strongly stressed. The growth in the scale of business was actually of far greater consequence in checking the previous exceptional fluidity of American society. And, although many an individual career showed that the era of opportunity was not over, it was obvious that America would have to face the old-world problems of permanent labouring and middle-class urban populations.

In their American setting, the familiar problems of capital and labour, and of social reform, particularly in the cities, possessed a marked character of their own. The constitutional system acted as a brake upon the action both of the states and of the Federal Government, and the believers in a policy of absolute non-interference fought a long rearguard action through the courts. The lack of a common background among large sections of the population, and the newness of many of the great urban communities, gave violence and corruption a place in the national life, and particularly in the relations between capital and labour whose dramatization served to conceal its more constructive aspects.

The speed with which what remained of American land was brought under cultivation reproduced in many of the most newly settled areas the same conditions of exhausted soils and denuded countrysides which had been found in over-exploited districts in the older states. The colourful career of President Theodore Roosevelt (1901-09), and his attempts to assert a more positive role for government in the nation's economic life, left no legacy more lasting than the heightened awareness of the need for the conservation of natural resources. And thirty years later, the Tennessee Valley Authority scheme, carried out under the ægis of President Franklin D. Roosevelt, made conservation no mere protective policy, but a positive attempt to secure for the people the fullest possible advantages from the natural wealth of their inheritance.

While the United States was wrestling with new problems internally, a vast change was taking place in her relations with the outside world. The abundant nationalism of the 1860s had left no permanent trace other than the acquisition by purchase of the Russian colony of Alaska, the significance of which was revealed only in the Second World War.

America as a Great Power

But in the closing years of the century, new and far-reaching developments took place. The acquisition of Hawaii set America on a career of expansionism in the Pacific to which the growing activity of her traders and missionaries had formed a prelude. The new imperial age was confirmed when the war with Spain in 1898 gave her the Philippines as well as Puerto Rico in the Caribbean. The Monroe Doctrine ceased to bear a purely defensive significance and American intervention in the affairs of Latin America, culminating in the transactions which made the long-dreamed-of isthmian canal at Panama, a purely United States concern, became an accepted feature of the American scene. Thus the United States was deeply involved by the beginning of the century in both South America, and in the Far East where Russia and Japan met her as rivals, and Theodore Roosevelt, to a greater extent than any of his predecessors, was regarded as a statesman of world significance. But the change which had occurred in both the position and the responsibilities of the United States was not yet widely understood among Americans. The reforming wave which brought President Wilson into power in 1913 concentrated upon pressing internal matters, and it was with reluctance that president and people found themselves forced into war by Germany's indiscriminate pursuit of her objectives.

The First World War marked the end of a major phase in American history even though the effect of the war itself was much smaller than that of the Civil War. America became finally and inescapably a great Power. On the economic side, the long period of indebtedness to the old world ended, and the United States acquired a new creditor status. Internally the existing trends favouring industry against the farmer came into play once more after the wartime boom. Post-war legislation closed the door to mass immigration with serious consequences for the whole world. Inside the United States there were major shifts in population, notably the northward trek of the Negroes to regions of greater economic opportunity, and of less blatant, if still severe, social discrimination. The attempt to deal with economic and social problems according to the formulæ of the preceding hundred years appeared to have collapsed with the great depression of 1929 to 1932. The return to isolation, marked by the repudiation of President Wilson and of the League of Nations, with which his policy was identified, appeared more successful. But here, too, the path could not be retraced completely.

The "New Deal" initiated by President Roosevelt in 1933 owed much to the inspiration of Wilson. It attracted the world's attention because of the determination with which the President attempted to tackle the great economic and social problems of the time by methods which did not involve too fundamental a departure from the American tradition of individual enterprise and popularly controlled government. Nevertheless, extension of Federal activity once again produced a struggle with the Supreme Court. Although the immediate result seemed favourable to the court rather than the president, it was seen when the tumult died down, that in fact the Federal Government (and the presidency in particular) had further advanced its powers, and some close observers of the American system wondered whether the new accretions of federal power did not imply a final abandonment of the idea of federalism in favour of that of a unitary state of the familiar kind. Since much of the New Deal's economic (as distinct from its social) legislation was based on not wholly consistent theories of the causes of the depression, and was for this and other reasons abandoned, it may well be that it is in the sphere of government and administration, and in its effect upon the climate of opinion, that the historical significance of the New Deal must be sought.

But in this field, the parallelism with Wilson holds; for changes in the inter-national scene caused Roosevelt to depart further and further from his original assumption that the American problem could be treated in isolation. The fall of France in 1940 and the possibility that Britain might fall, too, leaving the seas to a power whose ideology was essentially hostile to everything for which the United States had stood, caused a rapid transformation of the American attitude. Assistance to the Allies was given by the exchange of destroyers for Caribbean bases and by the Lend-Lease Act of March, 1941. American naval activity in the Atlantic increased, and her attitude towards Japanese aggression in the Pacific—a matter on which Americans had long felt strongly—hardened.

America and Second World War

Japan's attack on the U.S.A. in December, 1941, which was followed by declarations of war on the part of the other two Axis Powers may be regarded as the inevitable result of the U.S.A.'s growing appreciation of her role as the arsenal and citadel of democracy. The American contribution to victory was not made in purely military terms, and the importance of her position in formulating plans for post-war reconstruction and security was made manifest in the vital series of conferences on American soil which marked the last period of the war. As leading members of the United Nations and its associated international bodies, both the U.S.A. and Canada appeared in 1945 to be on the threshold of a new and vital period in the rise of North America.

It was, however, not necessarily obvious that North America could continue its stupendous material progress if the rest of the world failed to recover from the ravages of war, and it was not at once clear whether the United States, despite its formal commitment to the United Nations, would accept those responsibilities in the political and economic fields which it had repudiated after the previous world conflict. Despite American generosity through UNRRA to the homeless and hungry and despite short-term economic aid to replace the hurriedly wound-up machinery of lend-lease, the question where Europe was concerned remained undecided for almost two years. In the Far East, the position was different. General MacArthur became, as head of the American forces of occupation, the real ruler of Japan and set on foot an elaborate programme designed to "democratize" that country's life and institutions. In China an attempt was made to bring about a peaceful agreement between the Kuomintang and the Chinese Communists struggling to fill the vacuum caused by the collapse of Japanese power.

The real change in United States policy was the outcome of a new challenge, that of Soviet Communism. This had been foreshadowed in the angry exchanges between President Roosevelt and Stalin over the future of Poland which marked the last weeks of the President's life. His successor, President Harry Truman, was involved from the first in a series of differences with the Russians over the shape of the post-war world, and although the temporary American monopoly in atomic weapons after August 1945 seemed to indicate American superiority in any ultimate conflict, the issues had to be fought out in more local and limited terms. With the declining strength of Britain and the weakness of France, American power was the only available check to the ambitions of world communism. In successive stages—the "Truman doctrine" which committed the United States to the defence of Greece and Turkey, the "Marshall Plan" which brought in American aid on a large scale to bolster up the ailing economies of Europe, and make possible major efforts at reorganizing

them, and with, finally, in 1949, the setting up of the North Atlantic Treaty Organization, in which Canada, now clearly a "Middle" rather than a "Small" Power was to take a major role, the historic American isolationism was reversed.

In Europe, the position was stabilized though the United States was disappointed in its hopes of integrating Western Europe in its own image. In the Far East, there was, however, a major set-back as the Kuomintang regime disintegrated under Communist pressure and was thrown back on to the island of Formosa where it owed its survival to the cover of American naval power. President Truman also committed American forces to the defence of the South Korean regime against its Communist rival in the north. But there were later fears that some American leaders wished the war to be carried into Communist China.

These difficulties and uncertainties led to the defeat of the Democrats in the 1952 election, and the choice for President of America's great wartime general and later NATO commander, Dwight D. Eisenhower. Although Republican foreign policy in effect turned out to differ little from Democratic policy, the Republicans did their best to exploit past disappointments for political ends and for a period the "loyalty" drive and the attempts to enforce a rigid ideology of anti-Communism upon the nation were the most striking features of the internal scene, but by the end of President Eisenhower's first term of office these febrile symptoms had largely disappeared.

Test Yourself

1. To what do you ascribe the different course which colonization took in North America as compared with South and Central America?
2. What have been the main characteristics of American democracy?
3. What historical forces have prevented the absorption of Canada by the United States?
4. What influences have brought the United States out of its isolationism?
5. How far was the "New Deal" a departure from the existing political traditions of the United States?
6. Trace the stages through which the Negro problem has passed in the course of American history.

Answers will be found at the end of the book.

CHAPTER X
EUROPE IN REVOLUTION

NINETEENTH-CENTURY Europe struggled with the ideas of political democracy, national self-determination and all the implications of a belief in the equality of man. These ideas were the legacy of the French Revolution. But they were ideas which Europe had to work out in a century of enormous social and economic changes.

In England, where the Industrial Revolution started earliest, the changes in the social and political order were soonest apparent. In Continental Europe the need for revolutionary philosophy to take account of economic and social changes was not always realized. In the minds of European statesmen, the ideas of eighteenth-century Europe were still valid; for the nineteenth-century revolutionaries their struggle was essentially an attempt to carry out the destruction of governmental systems which refused to adapt themselves to a Europe which had witnessed the French Revolution. Not all the nineteenth-century revolutionaries made the same thing of the French Revolution; they each selected what they considered to be its most important lessons. But in every case they were opposed to any attempt to regard it as an abnormal development. It was their starting point.

Eighteenth-century Background

The French Revolution was influenced by certain aspects of the rationalist philosophies of the eighteenth century; the ideas with which it worked were the protests of thinkers against eighteenth-century institutions. In this way nearly every revolutionary development in the nineteenth century inspired by the French Revolution, was linked ultimately with the eighteenth century. Yet the social and economic changes of the nineteenth century—the rapid and painful growth of industrialism—had hardly been anticipated by the revolutionary idealism of the eighteenth.

Eighteenth-century Europe relied on hereditary autocracy as its political system. The centralized despotism of Louis XIV, who died in 1715, was imitated by Frederick the Great in Prussia (1740-86), by the Emperor Joseph II in Austria (1765-90), and by Catherine II in Russia (1762-96). It is an age which has been called the age of the enlightened despots because these last three rulers and others in smaller states, tried to associate their attempts at unified centralization in government with enlightened ideas of benevolent improvement from above.

Class Distinctions

There was much in common between the social systems of most Continental European states in the eighteenth century. In each there was a marked division between the privileged and unprivileged. The monarchs had gained their power by their defeat of the feudal aristocrats; they had compensated them for their loss of political executive authority by allowing them social privileges. The nobles and clergy were largely exempt from taxes paid by the unprivileged. Their life at court was unproductive and extravagant. The higher ranks of the army and the Church were in some cases the monopolies of the nobles. The social condition of the people, in spite of local variations, presented a fairly uniform picture. Upon the peasantry fell a great burden of taxation; and even when they owned their lands their proprietorship was limited by their need to pay feudal dues which no longer expressed their social relationship with the nobles. A proportion of the produce of the peasant owners was paid in dues, and taxes on their houses and lands, even when they were not crippling economically, symbolized a social stigma.

It is the position of the French middle class in the eighteenth century which shows the lack of relationship between the political system and the social facts, and accounts for the character of the revolutionary thought. From 1740 until the Treaty of Paris (1763), a maritime and

FALL OF THE BASTILLE, 1789

The fall of the Bastille on July 14, 1789, celebrated as a national holiday in France, has always been regarded as symbolic of the Revolution, although, at the time, it was a largely irrelevant demonstration of the power of the Parisian populace—a key factor later on.

colonial struggle was fought between England and France and Spain which in its demands for money, skill and enterprise in every area where it was fought—in North America, in Europe, in India—gave to the growing, largely mercantile middle class a chance to feel the worth of its talents and wealth. Those who organized and administered the trading companies and the banks; the army contractors, the merchants who had created and shared in the five hundred per cent increase of foreign trade from 1715 to 1780 were without political rights and social position. During the century, property passed into their hands and wealth was no longer with the socially privileged classes. To this prosperous middle class it was inexcusable that privilege should be the prerogative of the unproductive. The middle class demanded for itself a share in government commen-surate with its wealth. It was through this class that the revolutionary thought of the eighteenth century took shape.

Monarchy could not solve the problem of privilege; the middle class demanded political rights and economic freedom; the peasants wanted security. There was no industrial proletariat with a case against capital and ownership, but there were urban populations, principally that of Paris, which were often short of bread owing to unscientific methods of agriculture, a mass of internal customs duties, and frequent exploitation by speculators who bought up corn supplies in anticipation of bad harvests. Behind the middle-class protest against privilege there was a mob which could be inflamed for political purposes.

Fénelon, tutor to the grandson of Louis XIV, advised that government ought to be referred to moral standards, that the

212

secular power should be separated from religious authority so that toleration might be practised. He advocated a constitution to remedy arbitrary power and, although he believed that a more active aristocracy would serve as a check on the king, he realized the need for a code of law to which the king was subject. Education and acts of wise local and central assemblies, he believed, would make men responsible and even, in time, good.

The belief of Fénelon in the utility of a code of law and his hope for moral improvement became typical of French philosophy. English institutions were rationalized by French writers. The works of the English philosopher John Locke who explained and justified the English Revolution of 1688 in terms of civil government being founded upon the consent of the governed, the essential need for religious toleration, the inviolable rights of property based upon industry, became the test of French institutions. Voltaire spent three years in England, and in his *Letters on the English*, published in 1733, he held up English constitutional monarchy as an example to France.

Montesquieu, who came to England, also used English institutions as a measuring stick for France. In his *Spirit of the Laws* (1748), he reconciled monarchy with reform in proposing the separation of the judicial, executive and legislative functions in government. Like Fénelon he thought monarchy could be preserved by aristocracy; this was what he believed made England more stable than any possible republic. Although he attacked privilege and wanted greater equality in taxation, he held no theory of democracy.

In the career and changing opinions of Turgot (1727-81), there is a summary and symbol of the conflict of rational philosophy with religion. He first studied to be a priest, but became an administrator for the monarchy. His theological studies led him to believe that growth and progress was the law of human life; his administrative experience convinced him that economic changes must be made. In his philosophy the past meant imperfection, and, therefore, escape from the past was necessary for progress. This over-simplified view became typical of the revolution. It was possible to hold it because eighteenth-century interpretations of religion ignored all possibilities of development in man and insisted upon his degeneracy.

Turgot turned away from the Church and became a freethinker. He joined the contributors to the *Encyclopædia*, a great French work which, in thirty-four volumes, published in 1751-52, carried the test of reason to every European institution, and endeavoured to give the scientific and political information which its authors believed would make men reasonable and responsible. The fierce anti-religious attitude of some of its contributors drove Turgot away, and he joined a group of critics of the economic principles of state regulation, the Physiocrats. This group clearly represents the rational and the middle-class character of eighteenth-century revolutionary thought. They tried to base political theory on the new science of economics. Man's first property, they argued, was his labour. He must be free to use it and so a society must have a minimum of economic regulations, and the land, as the ultimate source of wealth, should bear the whole burden of taxation. Interferences with trade were injurious to prosperity. Nature, left to herself, could bring wealth to all. These truths would be proclaimed by popular education although they would have to be served by a strong, even absolute government, capable of overcoming all obstacles to a change from regulation to freedom. Such belief indicated the commercial aspiration of the French middle class.

Turgot himself became a minister to Louis XVI for thirteen months; his proposals to abolish the guilds and free the corn trade were frustrated. His failure in office, however, can be measured against the fact that during the revolution several of the doctrines of the Physiocrats were incorporated among the reforms.

With Jean Jacques Rousseau, the belief in Nature, which was for the Physiocrats an economic law of unrestricted trade, became a philosophical principle. He preferred Nature to civilization. Men were born free, innocent and equal. The only good society would be one where men made their individual wills conform to the general will which infallibly sought the good of all. In *The Social Contract* (1762), Rousseau argued that the people were sovereign and infallible. He abstracted his political theory from the practice of the Geneva Republic, and himself saw that direct democracy with every virtuously educated citizen participating in affairs was practicable only in a small state. But in making the people sovereign in government, in denouncing all intermediate bodies in society, and above all in declaring that the state which expressed the general will was beyond the right of criticism, he left a body of doctrine as fatal to the French Revolution as it was to the monarchy. For, as with the rationalists who saw man capable of perfection by reason and so attacked religion which stressed man's evil inclinations, Rousseau in giving man's natural innocence an almost religious emphasis, left it possible for reformers to believe that changes in institutions would automatically reveal man's goodness.

Opposition to Reforms

All these ideas were tested in the French Revolution; its nature and work revealed their limitations in practice. Nevertheless, the French Revolution did not happen simply because men sought to put into practice philosophical ideas.

Louis XVI, who came to the throne in 1774, was amenable to humanitarian ideas but lacked decision and purpose. His wife, Marie Antoinette, an Austrian, became a popular symbol of courtly frivolity as well as of an un-national foreign policy. The opposition of the court to Turgot's scheme for reform, equitable taxation and free trade, an opposition in which the queen played a part, was taken as a sign that reform could not come from the monarchy. The dismissal of Necker, a skilful financier, largely because of his open publication of the financial state of the country, further demonstrated the unlikelihood of fundamental reform. France was not uniquely impoverished. The financial deficit could have been met by an additional tax of seven

francs (seven shillings) per head, but no minister could press taxation upon the privileged nobility and clergy. Calonne, his successor as Finance Minister, summoned an Assembly of Notables in 1787 (i.e. one confined to the privileged classes). They declined to accept taxation of their order and recommended a summoning of the States General, a body representative of the clergy, nobility and commons, which had not met since 1614.

On August 8, 1788, Louis summoned the States General; they met at Versailles in May, 1789. The States General had never possessed legislative power; the three estates, meeting separately, could each make only a general statement of their wishes. Each member brought a summary of grievances mostly urging some kind of constitutional reform and the need for popular consent to taxation. One, drafted by Talleyrand, outlined a constitutional monarchy. The king had no plan for reform to present before the States General; he had taken no decision how they were to debate and vote. If they voted in separate estates, the two privileged groups would outvote the Commons; if all as one body, then the Commons with six hundred representatives against three hundred in each of the other estates would probably tip the scales for reform. The Commons refused to co-operate until the three estates were in one chamber and a vote by heads granted. In seven weeks they made effective the first step of the Revolution. On June 19 the Commons declared themselves to be the National Assembly. The Commons had claimed sovereignty despite the king and the privileged. On June 20, meeting in a tennis court, the Commons swore on oath to remain united until they had made a constitution. On June 22 more than a hundred of the clergy joined them.

The National Assembly, with constitution-making as its programme, became the Constituent Assembly and was composed of the middle class, mainly merchants and lawyers. They had clear political aims for themselves; their knowledge of social questions beyond their interests was vague and expressed in sentimental generalization. Outside and apart from their constitution-making, was the Paris mob. The revolution was made between them. The attack on the Bastille on July 14 by the mob became to Europe a symbol of the attack on tyranny; in France it was a demonstration of the divorce between the constitution-making and the passions of a mob which might be exploited for almost any purpose. The Revolution became Parisian. On August 1, 1789, the Constituent Assembly drew up the "Rights of Man," three clauses of which suffice to show both its importance in all revolutionary thought during the nineteenth century and its practical insistence on the rights which the middle class who framed it wanted established for themselves:

1. Men are born and remain free and equal in rights. Social distinctions can only be founded on public utility.
4. Liberty consists in being allowed to do whatever does not injure other people.
17. Property being an inviolable and sacred right, no one can be deprived of it except when public necessity, declared by form of law, makes it clearly necessary.

The declaration was affixed to the Constitution of 1791. This Constitution limited the franchise by a property qualification which excluded the peasants and most of the artisans. When a minority in the assembly declared for the deposition of the king and the Paris mob was used to back up a petition for this purpose, the National Guard, a citizen militia used to defend the constitutional revolution, opened fire on the crowd. This massacre of the Champ de Mars (July, 1791), emphasized again the gap between the revolution which meant rights for the middle class, and the revolution which could take the doctrine of the sovereignty of the people as the basis for any change.

It was war which conditioned the course of the Revolution. It became impossible for the middle-class constitutionalists represented as a majority in the Assembly to be representative of a France which felt itself threatened by the Declaration of Pillnitz (1791), in which the Emperor Leopold and the King of Prussia declared that the maintenance of order in France was a European concern; it became impossible for a man like Lafayette, a romantic liberal aristocrat, to express the excitement of a nation defending itself. It was possible for the Girondists, a group of young men from the Gironde (south-west France), who believed passionately in the virtues of a republic, to see war as a way of

ENGLISH FAIR IN THE SEVENTEENTH CENTURY

Contemporary prints, such as this from the Douce Collection at the Bodleian Library, show the simple excitements which satisfied our forefathers. A stage is erected on the village green where feats of wrestling, juggling and acrobatics are being rehearsed.

raising feeling to a republican pitch; it was possible for moderates to seize war as an escape from the difficulties to which theories of natural right in practice led.

The extreme revolutionaries, the Jacobins, at first opposed war. Yet it was war which, demanding a strong executive, gave them their chance; it was war which could point to the danger of internal treachery as long as the king remained alive.

The Legislative Assembly, elected under the new constitution, was attached in origin to the idea of monarchy; the Jacobins, for the safety of France and the Revolution were ready to seize power as a minority, dispense with monarchy and supply the control and decision for a successful war. The Jacobins were extremists, but not working class; their support came from the mob of Paris. With them revolution became dictatorship.

Revolutionary Dictatorship

In August, 1792, the palace of the Tuileries was attacked; the king's only protection was the Assembly. Lafayette, attempting to raise troops to support the monarchy, found that he had to take refuge outside France. The Paris "Commune" replaced the Assembly as the source of authority. As news from the front was news of defeat, in Paris suspicion and fear brought a search for enemies of the Revolution. Suspects were tried in batches; hundreds were massacred in September, 1792. In the same month at Valmy the revolutionary army gained its first victory. In Paris, the Convention, a new body elected on a much wider franchise, abolished the monarchy and by a majority of one decided to execute Louis XVI, unanimously found guilty of plotting against the nation. It produced a more democratic constitution with a new Bill of Rights, but this was not enforced. Events moved too rapidly.

French armies crossed the Rhine, and invaded Belgium. In November, 1792, revolutionary France offered brotherhood and assistance to all peoples wishing their liberty. By February, 1793, France was at war with all Europe. Internally, there was a counter-revolutionary movement in the district called La Vendée, where the peasan-

try remained devoted to the Church and attached to a gentry with strong local roots, and refused military service. Against danger from without and within, the revolutionary Government determined upon further concentration of executive power. In April, 1793, the Committee of Public Safety was appointed. With this and other committees meeting in private, and a thorough system for enforcing the decisions of the central government throughout France, the Revolution had begun to emulate the centralization of the monarchy it had overthrown. In June, 1793, a Paris mob seized the Hall of the Convention, demanding the arrests of Girondists as enemies of the Revolution. The Reign of Terror began.

Robespierre replaced Danton as the leader of the Committee of Public Safety. His ferocious idealization of the sovereignty of the people in a state resting upon virtue and justice brought in a France at war the Law of Suspected Persons, the Revolutionary Tribunal, the conscription of all between eighteen and twenty-five, and the law of "forty sous," which gave this money to all who attended political meetings of the Paris wards. It was a dictatorship using terror, cruelty, force and bribery, seeking what was logical and uniform. It brought in the decimal system of weights and measures, a new calendar beginning with the declaration of the Republic in September, 1792, a new religion, the worship of deified Reason celebrated in Notre-Dame. It resulted finally in differences in the Jacobin Party, in which each group endeavoured to use the Paris mob as its chief support. Robespierre's support came from a law which confiscated, for the relief of the poor, the property of all arrested on suspicion. In April, 1794, Danton was executed. In June, the worship of Reason was replaced by the acknowledgement of the Supreme Being. The Revolution had reached a stage where the ruthlessness of a group dictatorship went hand in hand with theoretical unity and imposed belief.

This stage of the Revolution provides an early modern example of one-party rule. Throughout France the network of Jacobin

MARKET PLACE AT THE HAGUE

Painted in 1760 by La Fargue, and now in the National Gallery, this picture of a scene in the vegetable market at The Hague, reveals how shopping was done in those days. Under the trees is an animated crowd, at the back are the booths, while in the foreground are cabbages, leeks, carrots and baskets for sale. Through the trees may be seen the tower of the Great Church.

clubs interpenetrated and inspired the governmental machine. The Law of the Prairial (June, 1794), asked anyone to denounce traitors, and members of the Convention became open to arrest. Robespierre's attempt to keep power in this way left members of the Convention uncertain which one of them was to be guillotined next, and the following day (Thermidor 9), he was refused a hearing and arrested. The Commune released him; the Convention attacked the Hotel de Ville where the Commune met. Robespierre, injured in the fight, was dragged off to the guillotine. The dictatorship of terror had been defeated by the only method to which it had itself given sanction, the use of force and violence.

With the fall of Robespierre and the increasing successes of the French army, it became possible for the Convention to possess authority over separate groups and mob politics. The Terror had been initially a military measure; military success brought a change; henceforth order was maintained against the mob. In April, 1795, the Paris mob rioted after a winter of shortages, the Convention used military force against the rising. The middle-class National Guard was reformed; property of the guillotined was restored to relatives. In May, 1795, the Convention was saved from a further revolt by the intervention of regular troops. A new constitution of the same year added the "duties of the citizen" to the rights of man; and it limited the number of citizens by taxation assessments. Two Houses were instituted both of which could meet outside Paris. Once again when a mob rising threatened the Convention's ruling in October, 1795 (Vendémiaire), military force was used; the defence of the Convention's meeting place was made effective by Napoleon's use of artillery.

Each revolutionary stage from 1789 had been marked by violence; perhaps a theory of natural rights implies violence. Napoleon represented the stability of controlled violence and the efficiency of the revolutionary armies. The theoretical will of the people had found little expression in the Assembly, the Convention, or the Committee of Public Safety. Equality could be measured by the Terror, Liberty by continuous political controversy, Fraternity by the guillotine, the cruel fighting in La Vendée, and the outraged Paris mob. By 1795, the greatest successes of the revolu-

tion seemed to rest with the armies. It was possible for Napoleon to say: "I am the Revolution," as Louis XIV had said: "I am the State."

The new civil government—the Directory—failed to establish peace and order. There were signs of a recrudescence of Jacobinism, and the demand was for stability even at the price of liberty. Napoleon capitalized the demand. In November, 1799, at Napoleon's orders, Republican troops turned out the constitutionally elected government of France. Three consuls, Napoleon, Siéyès, and Ducos, were appointed to revise the Constitution. Napoleon was distrustful of popular government, resentful of popular discussion; he believed in order from above,

CAPTURE OF LOUIS XVI AND MARIE ANTOINETTE

The last dramatic episode in the career of Louis XVI as King of France is seen in this engraving published in 1804. On June 20, 1791, having stolen away from the Tuileries in the dead of night, the king, with Marie Antoinette and family, were compelled to halt at Varennes. While eating a meal, the royal fugitives and their entourage were arrested by revolutionaries and taken back to Paris as prisoners. Louis and his queen were separately confined in prison until eventually they both suffered death on the guillotine in 1793.

obedience from below. He was appointed as First Consul; a nominated State Council was to initiate legislation, a "Conservative Senate" was to appoint all the bodies which would debate whatever proposals were presented to them. A plebiscite was held on the new constitution; 3,012,000 voted for it; 1,562 against. The revolutionary principle of popular sovereignty was recognized in the plebiscite; the people of revolutionary France chose a centrally appointed personal government resting upon military success and guaranteeing order, security, and freedom from revolutionary politics.

Napoleon as Emperor

Personal power became identified with stability. In 1802, Napoleon was made consul for life with the right to choose his own successor, and of appointing a Privy Council with the sole right of initiating legislation. The strengthening of the hostile European coalition, and the discovery of plots against Napoleon, further strengthened his position. In 1804, he became Emperor. But he perpetuated the Revolution and harmonized it with elements of the old world in a way which made it impossible for its work to be wholly undone. In 1801 he came to terms with the Pope; the Church in France, scorned and attacked by the Revolution, was again linked with Rome.

The codification of French laws in 1804 systematized a fusion of past and present, in which tradition and revolution were inseparable. The Civil Codes defined a society based upon the ideas of the Revolution, yet with a structure of discipline and order achieved by centralization as rigid as that of the old regime. Civil equality, religious toleration, public trial, an ordered family life, and the full rights of private property were guaranteed; the idea of civil marriage and divorce was given legal sanction. Many revolutionary ideas found no place, for Napoleon chose arbitrarily; but enough were embodied to make the codes a standard of liberal and secular achievement for all Europe.

Even the centralization of the Empire did not cancel out the Revolution. There was little democracy, and institutions of the old regime like the Council of State and courts of appeal were reintroduced; but the servants of centralization in every department were children of the Revolution; talents were used wherever found and a civil service dependent upon the State was created. A body called "The University" and controlled by the State, was set up in 1808, to provide all grades of education; there was no freedom, but again a revolutionary idea of opportunities for the many was put into practice. Napoleon was an enlightened despot, but his enlightenment was the confirmation of the Revolution.

It was because Napoleon consolidated the Revolution that after his downfall it became so difficult for sovereigns and ministers to pretend that Europe was as it had been before 1789. Napoleon's armies had taken revolutionary ideas and laws to almost every country in Europe; the Empire had incorporated in the codes a pattern of liberal ideas; even where French occupation was resisted, it was in the name of French ideas. Constitutionalism and national self-determination became European demands.

Effect on Other Countries

In 1810, under popular pressure in Spain, the Cortes, or parliament, was called and formed into a Constituent Assembly which drew up a constitution modelled on the French one of 1791, and declared for the sovereignty of the people expressed in a single legislative chamber elected by complete male suffrage. In Prussia, where the government was the harshest example of the type of government overthrown by revolutionary France, a complete social and military reorganization was carried out which used many of the revolutionary ideas for Prussia's own purposes. A national army was created in which foreigners could not serve and in which room was made for recognition of ability. Serfdom was abolished although those who had been peasant-serfs remained military conscripts. Much feudal jurisdiction was also abolished and peasant ownership of land increased. The establishment of the University of Berlin marked a growing state concern for

LIBERTY OF THE SUBJECT

Gillray's caricature dating from the wars with Revolutionary France shows how, in England, in order to man ships of war, the press gang roamed the streets of the ports, compelling unwilling recruits to join the ranks. Two sailors with cudgels have captured a hapless tailor, and, followed by a crowd, are seen escorting him through the streets.

education. Italy had tasted under French rule a measure of unity and became conscious of the possibilities of national independence. In Poland, Napoleon in 1807 had set up a Duchy of Warsaw, which however fictitious it was as an independent state, gave to large numbers of Poles who still lived under foreign rule a temporary base for potential independence. Everywhere in fact, French ideas of national self-determination and the Napoleonic Empire, not least where it was resisted, had made a different Europe.

The settlement of 1815 made little allowance for the new factor of national feeling. The principle of legitimacy (that long possession gives right to rule) was its basis. The Bourbons returned to France with Louis XVIII; Austria was given further territory in Italy, Russia more of Poland. Holland and Belgium were united into one nation; territorial changes were made in Germany to achieve a balance of power between Austria and Prussia. The attempt of the Tsar of Russia to proclaim a Holy Alliance in which rulers would bind themselves to preserve the principles of absolutist government further associated the settlement with the forces of reaction.

In 1820, revolution in Spain forced the king to accept a constitution. Further revolutions in Portugal, Naples and Piedmont, each demanding a constitution, emphasized the difference in point of view between the Powers which had defeated Napoleon. Russia, Austria and Prussia bound themselves to regard the peace settlement as involving their right to decide the political forms of European governments. Britain differentiated between the territorial settlement and internal political changes. For European revolutionaries wishing either to assert national rights against the territorial settlements of 1815, or to gain constitutions even without territorial changes, it became impossible to separate the 1815 settlement from the absolutist ideas of the Holy Alliance. Until 1848, revolution in Europe took the form of protest against the arrangements of 1815; it was the continued life of the French Revolution with delayed effect.

In the States of Europe, where people speaking different languages found themselves under the same rule, national movements became based on language; some became nationalists because, if a nation gained political power, they hoped there would be jobs for all who spoke that language. The rulers who defended their power to govern over different nations often exiled the revolutionaries. The national movements of nineteenth-century Europe were thus frequently organized by exiles who became a strange fraternity of the century, mostly packed in London or Paris, all advocating the exclusive claims of some particular national group in Europe or protesting against established autocracies.

In 1821, Austrian troops crushed the revolutions in Italy and restored monarchs in Naples and Piedmont. A revolt of the Greeks against the Turks, in the name of nationality, was viewed by Metternich as a dangerous movement against monarchy. In 1823 French troops invaded Spain, restored the king and abolished the constitution. In Germany, regulations controlling the Press and muzzling the universities were enforced by a secret police system organized by Metternich which prevented the birth of any kind of liberal or constitutional movement. The idea of German unity encouraged in the opposition to Napoleon was stillborn; because of Metternich's policy of repression it was possible in the end for Prussia to identify her own expansion with German unity. Everywhere the national and liberal ideas of the French Revolution were suppressed.

It was in France that the post-Vienna reaction was first tested. The restoration of the Bourbons was combined with an experiment in constitutional monarchy. But the issue was between monarchy with its traditions and the enlargement of the experiments of the Revolution. Reaction sought to guarantee the monarchy by

pushing it to the Right. Property was restored to those who had fled, land was returned to the Church, the Press was corrupted, Parliament controlled, the tricolour abolished. Charles X, crowned in 1824, tried gradually to restore the old regime.

Closer links between monarchy and the Church suggested the old regime to both middle and working classes; a measure to compensate with money those who had lost land during the revolution threatened the Napoleonic land settlement; the restoration of the principle of the unequal division of land alarmed the peasantry which had solid interests founded in Napoleon's legal confirmation of the revolutionary destruction of much previously concentrated landed wealth. In the deadlock between monarch and parliament, Charles X issued ordinances which altered the franchise to the advantage of landed wealth, established Press censorship, dissolved the chamber elected in 1830, even before it had met, and ordered elections under a new limited franchise. Rioting began in Paris the next day. On July 28, part of Paris was in the hands of the revolutionaries.

" 1830 " Revolution

The predicament was one determined by the earlier revolution. The Jacobin days were still a vivid memory, the middle class feared a republic; Europe feared another revolutionary France. Yet if the middle class were to assist in the overthrow of the 1830 revolutionaries, they would strengthen a monarchy which had already broken the constitution and, if successful against revolution, would be completely in the control of revengeful royalists. In an effort to avoid extremes, Louis Philippe, Duke of Orleans, son of a Bourbon, Philippe "Egalité," who in 1789 had joined the revolutionary cause, was invited to become king of the French. The mob marching on Saint-Cloud, the palace of Charles X, as once they had marched on Versailles, forced him to abdicate. Lafayette, hero of revolutions, embraced Louis Philippe in front of the revolutionary mob as though past and present approved of each other. A republic was avoided; an elaborate constitutional show was devised to make clear that Louis Philippe ruled not by revolution but by the invitation of moderate men. In fact the pressure of popular sovereignty, the principle of the Revolution, had overthrown the settlement of 1815.

In Belgium, revolution followed within a month. It was a movement for both national independence from the Dutch, and for constitutional rule. The Dutch king insisted that, while negotiations for administrative independence took place, Dutch troops should occupy Brussels; their entry was resisted in three days' street fighting. The Belgians proclaimed a provisional government, summoned a national convention and declared their country's independence. Holland, looking to the guarantee given at Vienna to the settlement of 1815, invited the Quadruple Alliance to intervene. The solution, suggested by England, was found in a Five Power guarantee of the neutrality of Belgium announced in 1831, and embodied in the Treaty of London, 1839. Leopold of Saxe-Coburg, an uncle of Queen Victoria, was offered the crown of Belgium. A Dutch attempt to resist the settlement, a French advance to Brussels to assist the Belgians and to provide for possible French claims, were both frustrated by English hostility. Belgium began her independence under constitutional rule. Nationality and constitutionalism had breached the 1815 settlement.

Nationalism and Liberal Ideas

In Portugal and Spain, constitutional monarchy walked a tightrope because in each country child queens, whose advisers professed liberal ideas, were threatened by claimants to the throne who advocated absolutism. England offered alliances to the child rulers and with this aid the Portuguese Pretender was expelled in 1834, the Spanish Pretender in 1839. But in each country constitutional government was haphazard, having no traditional basis.

The principle of nationality took a violent form in Poland. The 1815 settlement had once more divided Poland into three. The Tsar, Alexander, had given his share of Poland a constitution, had spoken of it as a National Kingdom. The Poles scorned a Russian gift; their hostility made Russia limit the constitution as soon as it was made. The death of Alexander in 1825 was followed by a conspiracy in Russia against his successor, Nicholas, in which some Poles were implicated. But the national antipathies of the conspirators proved stronger than their liberalism.

Influence of Secret Societies

The French Revolution of July, 1830, produced an increase in the activity of Polish secret societies. The Tsar was preparing to use Polish forces to help defeat the revolution in France when an insurrection in Warsaw took place in November. It was a revolution organized by officers and landowners in the name of nationality. Warsaw was taken, the Tsar declared deposed; the Poles held out until September, 1831. Thereafter all forms of a separate life for Russian Poland were blotted out by an autocratic and military rule. But the 1815 settlement had been challenged, and the ferocious attraction of the principle of nationality had been demonstrated in a country where little effort was made to associate it with political or social change.

In Italy there was constant secret activity against the domination of Austria. The revolutions of 1820 and 1821 in Naples and Piedmont had been suppressed; but the most influential secret society, the Carbonari, continued to plot and to propagate. Mazzini (1805-72) who had met the conspirators of 1821, and who became, exile and patriot, the idealist propagandist for a united Italy, seeing the way in which protests against Austrian rule tended to be movements for republican independence by single cities which were easily suppressed, as were the outbursts in Italy in 1830, gave Italy the inspiration of a national republican movement. In 1831 the Young Italy movement was founded.

The movements for national union and for liberal constitutions in Europe were often self-contradictory. They were complicated by the rise of modern industry which in the end transformed the revolutionary idea but was itself always associated with both liberalism and nationalism.

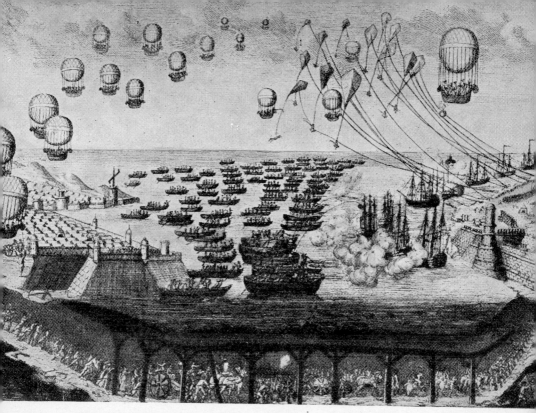

FRENCH PREPARATIONS FOR INVASION OF ENGLAND

Although Napoleon's threat in 1798 to invade England was very real it did not prevent the satirists of the time from making light of the possibility, as this drawing clearly shows. The idea of an air-umbrella—balloons and man-carrying kites—to accompany invasion ships, is interesting in the light of experiences in the Second World War. It appears that the possibility of constructing and making good use of a Channel tunnel was also considered.

The rise of industry was uneven in Europe. In the German Empire of 1870, there were few large towns with industrial populations. In 1850 the industrial development of the Ruhr and Rhineland had hardly begun; not until 1871 did the German industrial revolution really begin. But revolutionary movements were, from 1848, everywhere influenced in some degree by the political theories of industrialized society. Between 1815 and 1848, only two towns in France grew rapidly; yet the demands of workers as a class were felt in the revolution of 1848. The development of railways accounted for political growths. Prussia was able to become the driving force of German unity partly because her economic stability rested upon a carefully planned railway system designed to conform to strategic needs. Revolutionary movements were linked with industrial changes, but because those changes were not experienced simultaneously in Europe so often the revolutionary idea remained primarily a demand for national self-determination or for a written constitution.

The year 1848 was one of widespread European revolution in the history of which it is possible to see each variety of revolutionary faith in action, and in particular to see the liberal movement in conflict with revolutionary nationalism. In Germany, the demand for national unity was based upon a liberal idealism. It was a faith of professors, lawyers and students that a free Press, a parliamentary government based upon universal suffrage, and a national constitution would solve all problems. In the

Austrian Empire national movements, associated with liberalism, fought for freedom from the tyranny of Metternich, a freedom in which it became possible for each national movement to assert itself against all others.

In March, 1848, all over Germany princes were accepting liberal constitutions. In Vienna, a revolution in which the troops joined the mob forced Metternich to flee. It was a symbol like the fall of the Bastille. The Emperor promised a liberal constitution, a free Press, a Parliament, and a committee for the defence of popular rights set itself up in Vienna. A National Guard was organized.

In Pressburg (Bratislava), a Hungarian Diet, which had pressed for the use of the Magyar language, demanded also the responsibility of ministers to the Lower House, a free Press, a National Guard and a proclamation of the autonomous independence of Hungary. Magyar nationalism preached by Louis Kossuth was infectious; Hungary's non-Magyar races, Croats, Serbs, Slovaks and Rumanians, asserted their own national rights.

German Ideals

In Berlin, the King of Prussia, Frederick William IV, granted a representative constitution, a free Press, a Liberal Ministry. The German Parliament met at Frankfurt. A National Assembly followed in the May. It was a revolution inspired by a faith in ideas, and the delegates at Frankfurt were men who clung to the ideals of the German war against Napoleon in 1813. They were liberals, middle class and academic, believing in the power of discussion; those who were radical enough to believe in force had little idea of political authority. For them revolution was an end, a satisfaction in itself, not the beginning of a problem of where authority should rest in a State. The educated middle-class revolutionaries appealed to the great mass of the people but did not understand their needs. There was no working man and only one peasant in the National Assembly; there was no programme of agrarian reform; the only authority to back the declarations of the Assembly was the oath to the constitution

taken by the German princes. The attempt of the National Assembly to incorporate the provinces of Schleswig-Holstein in the new Germany meant reliance on the army of Prussia; when the Prussian army made a truce with the Danes who fought to retain the provinces it implied a defiance of the Frankfurt Assembly. Finally, Prussian troops had to restore order when the news of the acceptance of the truce by the Assembly caused riots. The Liberals were learning that ideas were not enough.

Revolution and Reaction

In Hungary, Kossuth proclaimed the abolition of serfdom and a comprehensive land reform; but national rights were denied to Serbs, Croats and Rumanians. The Emperor fled from Vienna. In Prague the Czechs of Bohemia fought for national rights against Germans, demanding an independent legislature. Constitutionalism was clothed in national dress. The Czechs summoned a conference of Slav peoples; Austrian Germans who were ready enough for a liberal German Empire resented both the Czech movement and the Hungarian demand for a separate foreign policy, army, and currency. Austria took advantage of the confusion.

Windischgrätz, the Austrian commander, forced the Czechs to surrender in June, 1848. Jellacic, the Governor of Croatia, encouraged a Croat national movement against the Magyars and invaded Hungary in the September. Windischgrätz and Jellacic moved on Vienna; a Hungarian army which attempted to reach Vienna was defeated. Count Schwarzenburg, brother-in-law of Windischgrätz, became Chief Minister in Vienna; the constitution was ignored, the revolution defeated, and Russian aid was gained for the final defeat of Hungary in August, 1849.

In Prussia, Frederick William followed up the defeat of revolution in Vienna by dissolving in December, 1848, the parliament he had authorized in March. The Frankfurt Parliament, faced with the problem of authority, offered the crown of Germany to Frederick William. He refused to "pick up a crown from the gutter." The German revolution, embodied in the deliberations of the Frankfurt Assembly, frustrated by its inability to deal with the non-German national movements, putting into law universal suffrage and a secret ballot without an economic programme, unable to decide upon the shape of the new Germany, found finally that it possessed no authority. When, after the Prussian refusal to give that authority, the Frankfurt Assembly tried to appeal to the mass of the people for further revolution, Prussian troops put down risings in Baden, Saxony and Hanover. By the end of 1849, Prussia and Austria had absolute executive authority in Germany. It was their rivalry, not further revolution, which determined the character of Germany. Nationalism had defeated liberalism; constitutionalism was discredited and authority was again respected.

In Italy, too, nationalism found the need for institutions and organized power as well as ideas. Most educated Italians in 1848 believed that a reformed Papacy could lead Italy to unity. A gifted publicist, Gioberti, advocated an alliance of democracy and the Papacy. In 1846 the newly elected Pope Pius IX, a man of liberal ideas, seemed to embody these hopes. The ecclesiastical character of Papal government was modified, a municipal council was established, and a constitution was granted in March, 1848. Revolutions in Milan, Florence, Pisa and Naples struck against Austrian authority. A revolution in Sicily forced the King of Naples and Sicily to grant a constitution; popular

pressure resulted in the granting of a constitution in Piedmont-Sardinia. Austrian governments were driven from Parma, Modena, Venice and Milan. The problem was to find an authority which would link all revolutionary movements in a united national cause against Austria. The Pope, in April, 1848, announced his refusal to participate in war against Austria. The Italian national movement lost its belief in a democratic Christian Italy united under a liberal Pope, and sought the most effective authority to lead to success.

The Sardinian army, composed mostly of Piedmontese, gave assistance to the revolutionaries in Lombardy and Venetia. Attempts to form a league of Italian states failed. Mazzini tried to turn the revolution towards a republic; like the liberals of Germany he believed in the force of ideas. But, when the Austrians attacked, every ruler who had granted a constitution hesitated between Austria and Mazzini's call for a people's war. Austria triumphed against Italian disunity. Rome, where Mazzini and Garibaldi had established a republic, was occupied by French troops. Venice, which Daniele Manin had proclaimed an independent republic, was subdued last. Disunity among their leaders, and the inability of those inspired by Mazzini's faith in an Italian Republic to defeat Austria, left disappointed revolutionaries ready to accept liberation through the agency of Sardinia whose army had offered the most effective resistance. When

ROCKET AS A WEAPON IN THE TIME OF NAPOLEON

Before the days of incendiary shells and other methods of setting fire to enemy towns, rockets were discharged from special craft manned by marines. This coloured aquatint in the National Maritime Museum, Greenwich, shows the method of operation about 1814.

EPISODE DURING THE FRANCO-PRUSSIAN WAR, 1870

Pierre Petit-Gérard has here depicted an incident in the Franco-Prussian War. The war, planned by Bismarck, culminated in the Siege of Paris, during which beleaguered troops and inhabitants suffered extreme privation.

the new ruler, Victor Emmanuel, left in force the liberal constitution of his father, the kingdom of Sardinia became the focus of revolutionary effort.

In this way the struggle for Italian unity became one for expansion of the kingdom of Sardinia under the House of Savoy. The nationalism of Mazzini was a moral idea seeking the freedom of peoples in a republic; the nationalism given Italy by the House of Savoy, was dynastic policy using the ordinary technique of international relations. Count Cavour, an admirer of English ideas of government, was the architect of this policy. The kingdom was modelled on approved liberal lines; ecclesiastical establishments were decreased; civil marriage was enacted; commercial treaties were made with England and France; loans were obtained from the Rothschild banks; railways were developed; a cotton industry built up. Piedmontese troops fought against Russia in the Crimean War so that at the Congress of Paris in 1856, Cavour was able to present Italian grievances to England and France. He obtained a promise of help from

Napoleon III; in 1859 Piedmontese and French forces were in battle with Austrian. There were spontaneous risings throughout northern Italy; Garibaldi organized irregular troops. A separate peace between France and Austria, which freed Lombardy but not Venetia, once more crushed revolutionary hopes of a republic, but what measure of freedom had been gained had been due to Cavour's policy. Central Italy declared for incorporation with the Kingdom of Sardinia.

Mazzini protested against this way of bringing about national liberation, but Cavour cleverly associated Sardinia with the republican movement by sending Garibaldi, the hero of the revolutionaries, from Genoa to assist a rebellion in Sicily, organized against the King of Naples and Sicily by a republican conspirator, Crispi. Garibaldi went in the uniform of a Piedmontese general. He liberated Italy from the south and entered Naples. Plebiscites in Naples and Sicily declared for union with Sardinia in 1860. In 1861 the first Italian Parliament met in Turin, and the constitution of Sardinia became the constitution of Italy. Only Venetia and Rome were still outside the unified Italy. Venetia was acquired by an alliance with Prussia during the Austro-Prussian War of 1866; Rome, which Garibaldi tried unsuccessfully to conquer in 1862 and 1867, was taken in 1870, when the Franco-Prussian War forced the French to withdraw troops which protected the Papal States. National unity in Italy had been accomplished less by popular revolt and the force of the gospel of revolutionary republicanism than by the careful political intrigue of the Kingdom of Sardinia. Nationalism, as in Germany, proved a greater force than liberal theories of political change.

"1848" in France

In France where there were the beginnings of an industrial society, where there was no problem of national liberation and unification, the revolutionary idea continued to find new political expressions. In 1848, in France, the politics of the dispossessed took a conscious form; but everything was related to 1789. Louis Philippe was the bourgeois king; the limited franchise dissatisfied republican memories; frock-coated citizenship seemed dull compared with Napoleonic dreams; commercial prosperity was not accompanied by improvements in workers' conditions. In 1840, out of every 10,000 men called up for military service from ten districts, predominantly industrial, 9,000 were rejected as unfit; in predominantly agricultural districts only 4,000 were rejected. In 1840 the average wage of a workman in France was between 1s. 4d. and 1s. 7d. a day. The working day was between eleven hours and thirteen hours. Political changes had produced no economic programme; the safe constitutional monarchy of Louis Philippe had shown no concern with social welfare. The state abstained from economic regulation. The workers in 1848 were faced with a middle class, established by the revolutions of 1789 and 1830, in as privileged a position as the nobles had been in under the old monarchy. In 1846, of a population of over thirty-five millions, less than 300,000 had the vote.

By 1848, socialist reformers in France were applying the political ideas of 1789 to economic affairs. Saint-Simon had advocated the international organization of labour; Fourier had suggested self-contained units of co-operative workers; Proudhon, anarchist and anti-clerical, attacked property in the name of justice. Louis Blanc published in 1837 The Organization of Industry; socialism was given a scientific form with a clear statement that the state must be the means of obtaining social justice, "the state is, or ought to be, the banker of the poor"; the fundamental right of the worker was the right to work. But though these ideas had caused ferment, they had not produced a practical socialist programme.

In France, the revolution of 1848 came almost by accident. A liberal leader, Barrot, failing to secure a promise of electoral reform from the government, began a campaign of propaganda which took the form of public banquets. The proposed reforms would have benefited only a section of the middle class. The police refused permission for a banquet in a working class district in Paris; an unofficial demonstration was held. On the next day a procession on its way home was refused permission to pass the Foreign Office; shots were fired; revolution began. Again a Paris mob took control. The Chamber of Deputies was invaded. The king abdicated. Two provisional governments were chosen; one approved by the mob in the chamber, the other selected by men in the offices of the newspaper Réforme. Louis Blanc was included on the second list. These groups merged but were, from the beginning, divided into a radical and a socialist camp.

National Workshops

The socialist group proclaimed a republic. In France this action suggested the dictatorship of a Paris mob, and, because every French revolution was in a sense retrospective, it revived memories of the Terror. Louis Blanc in order to give practical expression to the right to work, set up national workshops to which the unemployed came from all parts of France, and where they received wages even if no work was available. The workshops, experiments in guild socialism, became instruments of relief. The provisional government declared for universal suffrage, and the results of the elections for an Assembly were that a conservative peasantry and a property-conscious provincial vote returned a majority opposed to the social revolution of Louis Blanc. France imposed its will on Paris. A Paris mob invaded the chamber and declared its dissolution. The government with an executive of middle-class radicals used the National Guard against the mob. The national workshops were closed. Louis Blanc retired into exile. For four days the National Guard fought in the streets of Paris against the unemployed thrown out of the national workshops. Scared by the threat of revolution of the unemployed, France elected Louis Napoleon Bonaparte, the emperor's nephew, as President.

Working-class Movements

The rift between the working-class and middle-class republicans remained. Social and economic change had become an inescapable part of revolutionary programmes in an industrialized society. The defeat of the working class in France gave to European socialism a hostility towards all middle-class governments whatever their political colour. Industrial issues made it possible for revolution to provide itself with a theory based on an attempt to understand the particular position and needs of industrial workers. With Marx and Engels, socialism claimed to become scientific with a theory of history based upon the class war, an analysis of the nature of capitalism, and predictions concerning the ultimate development of society and the state. In 1867, Volume I of *Das Kapital* was published. The First International Working Men's Association was formed in 1864; it broke down largely over the clash between Marx and the more humane if less practical revolutionary anarchist, Bakunin. The Second International, a Marxist body, was founded in 1889. In Germany, Ferdinand Lassalle made socialism a political movement with the formation of the Universal German Workers' Association in 1862.

It was in France again that the new revolutionary issue between workers and governments, which, in the view of the "scientific socialists" and "communists," always protected the interests of capitalism, became clear. The Second Republic with Louis Bonaparte as President had become the Second Empire in December, 1852.

Paris Commune: 1871

The Empire's social policy had made some acknowledgement of the needs of industrial society; attention was given to housing, and until 1870 there was consistent economic progress with little unemployment. Government subsidies to shipping and building were clear efforts to abandon an uncontrolled liberal capitalism. But there was little political liberty. When in 1870 the Empire collapsed in war with Germany, a Government of Defence at Bordeaux signed an armistice and prepared for new elections. It was an Assembly of which more than half the members desired a restoration of the monarchy. Paris, with its republican revolutionary tradition and its memory of militant patriotism in defence of the revolution, questioned the decision at Bordeaux. The Paris Commune came into being. It drew to itself every kind of revolutionary. The numbers in the movement were swelled when the government stopped the pay of the National Guard; republican Paris faced the royalist provinces. The Commune had to bid for the government of France. Elections to a municipal council in Paris gave a majority of left-wing revolutionaries who wanted France to become a federation of Communes. Their view was that of revolutionaries in an industrial society who suspect any strong centralized government in a national state as being a protector of capitalism; it was the view of the First International.

This aspect of the Commune was the development of the revolutionary attitude since the defeat of the workers in 1848. It was selected by Marx as the fundamental feature of the Commune; but it is difficult to see it as such. The Commune was not set up to overthrow the economic power of the bourgeoisie; it was a Parisian protest against a government which had accepted a harsh peace and might try to restore monarchy. It behaved in the spirit of Danton rather than of Marx. It was anti-German rather than international in feeling.

The Commune, violent itself, was suppressed in a week of bloody fighting. The Third Republic, while it suffered during the century from the bitterness of 1871, became the safeguard against fears of reactionary monarchy, revolutionary Paris and opportunist Bonapartism. In 1889, General Boulanger, who half-heartedly sought to become another Napoleon, was forced out of France; in 1895, a Jewish army captain called Dreyfus was wrongfully accused of selling secrets to Germany, and military reactionaries sought to discredit a "corrupt" Republic, but when his innocence was proved in 1899, Republican prestige was increased. In 1892 a papal encyclical advised the clergy to accept the republic. By 1900, Republican France was clear of the nineteenth-century forces of reaction, but faced with the need for greater economic change if the republican tradition was to fit the needs of industrialized society in the twentieth century. This was the legacy of nineteenth-century revolution. Everywhere eighteenth-century rationalism, transformed into political democracy by the French Revolution, gave peoples the determination to share in their governments. Europe sought constitutions to safeguard political rights. Since these rights had to be gained against foreign governments often the political struggle for freedom became a fight for national independence. In 1848, in Germany, revolutionary nationalism defeated revolutionary liberalism. In 1871, in France patriotism became an opportunity for revolutionary socialism. In 1914, international socialist movements were powerless in the face of hostile nationalisms. Because political nationalism was a defence of revolution in France in 1791, because it was associated with political change in nineteenth-century Italy, Germany and Poland, it has remained a more powerful force than the doctrine of international class war which emerged from the industrialization of society.

At the close of the nineteenth century Europe remained in revolution. The political freedoms had still to be related to the economic opportunities of industrial society. Republican France, a product of continuous revolution, represented the need to achieve economic justice within the political security of the democratic national state. Imperial Germany represented the triumph of nationalism over possibilities of revolution from below. Bismarck's State Socialism attempted to recognize and direct the needs of an industrial society, but it had been conferred by a military state, just as German unity had been gained by Prussia's conquest of Germany. United Italy exhibited the same triumph of national unity over the possibilities of republican revolution. The twentieth century has done no more than try to resolve the contradiction between these two legacies of nineteenth-century Europe. It remains to be seen whether, in fact, freedom and justice are compatible with nationalism.

Test Yourself

1. What were the main features of the French Revolution?
2. Discuss the motives of the revolutionary efforts to break up the settlement of 1815.
3. Discuss what truth, if any, there is in the statement that all French history in the nineteenth century is a drama of the French Revolution.
4. What can be learnt from the revolution of 1848?
5. Explain why nationalism has confused revolutionary efforts to change industrial societies.

Answers will be found at the end of the book.

CHAPTER XI

INTERNATIONAL RELATIONS IN THE INDUSTRIAL AGE

THE Industrial Revolution in England did little to alter international relations during the first half of the nineteenth century. It did much, however, to enable Great Britain to maintain her position of leadership. During the wars against revolutionary and Napoleonic France she had withstood alone the threat of the greatest and most powerful army the continent of Europe had seen in modern times. Her persistence had been made possible by her island position and by her economic stability. Deserted by her allies time after time, she had continued the struggle alone; Britain's unyielding obstinacy was sustained by British wealth.

Yet the spread of knowledge of the new machinery and techniques of industry outside Britain was slow. Before the defeat of Napoleon, British statesmen had been content to use the wealth of Britain to pay subsidies which put Prussian, Austrian and Russian troops into the field against him. After Waterloo they became more concerned to secure the peace of Europe and to guard against a second widespread revolutionary outbreak than to exploit the potential power of industrial development. Canning, it is true, understood the commercial needs of Britain and based much of his foreign policy on them; but, generally speaking, the interplay of the European Powers in the first half of the nineteenth century was not greatly affected by the industrialism which after 1850 had always to be taken into account by Cavour, Bismarck and Disraeli.

Castlereagh, British Foreign Secretary from 1812 to 1822, saw no reason to deviate from the eighteenth-century conception of British foreign policy. He was in part justified, since the fundamental interests of a nation in its foreign relations change very little; geography, the habits and economic needs of the people and the requirements of security all remain more or less constant factors in national policy. Time and development may shift the emphasis or lead to new interpretations of known facts, but little more. Ironical as it may seem, the dominance of Great Britain, her success in forcing upon her quarrelsome allies a united front against Napoleon in the Quadruple Alliance signed on March 9, 1814, and in prolonging its life into the post-war period by means of its renewal after Waterloo in the Treaty of Paris, of November 20, 1815, were all the fruits of that Industrial Revolution which seemed to be happening independently of the international events of the time. Although Great Britain had always been rich through her commerce, she was about to become the richest nation in Europe because of her industrial potential.

From War to Peace

Castlereagh was a great Foreign Secretary because he understood the permanent factors in foreign policy but he failed to foresee the future development of events and movements outside his own immediate province of foreign affairs. Byron, Shelley, and Cobbett all attacked him because he acquiesced in a reactionary home policy. In 1815, as always after great wars, there was more concern for reform at home than for the re-settlement of Europe. In 1815, too, there was in Britain all the ferment, all the social injustice and all the poverty that accompanied the double change that was taking place; the change from twenty years of war to conditions of peace was being made more difficult by the change from an agricultural and commercial economy to industrial capitalism in a society which encouraged a maximum of freedom and a minimum of governmental control.

In 1817, Castlereagh himself admitted some of the difficulties; three hundred thousand demobilized sailors and soldiers flooded a labour market already over-crowded despite miserable conditions. Canning's recognition of the Spanish South American colonies as independent republics satisfied the demands of British merchants for protection of their trading rights in wider markets. But usually these were not the first concerns of British Foreign Secretaries, who cared more for the final settlement of Europe and the establish-ment of a lasting peace through some sort of international co-operation.

Vienna Settlement

The settlement reached at Vienna, where the dominant figures besides Castlereagh were the Tsar Alexander I of Russia, Metternich, Foreign Minister and later Chancellor of the Austrian Empire, and Talleyrand, Foreign Minister of France, was to last for nearly fifty years without serious alterations and was to remain the basic framework within which a hundred years passed without a general European war. If one remembers the sincerity of Castlereagh in the pursuit of peace and his fatalism when he declared that what had been patched up at Vienna might last for seven years, one can view with greater appreciation his courage and perseverance in attempting to compel recognition of the community of interest of the Powers.

If the economic circumstances of the peacemaking period were still to bear their fruit, this period itself contains all the beginnings of the European system which lasted up to 1914, and which only finally began to give way to an entirely new state of affairs in 1939. Even the impact of the industrial changes on the whole of Europe did not shake the continent's foundations until a world-wide war which brought the rise of two great non-European Powers, the U.S.A. and Japan, and world-shaking revolution in semi-Asiatic Russia, all of which unhinged the whole framework of the organization of power.

In the first quarter of the nineteenth century the Powers became recognized in the order of their importance. It is significant that the word should have been applied as it was; size, military potential and the extent of their interests in Europe determined that the four great Powers of the Alliance should be the leading nations of the continent, during the eclipse of France. Upon their unity depended the future of Europe; and it was their unity which was the greatest triumph of Castle-reagh, although it did not last. They had been united only by a temporary need to defeat the French; in victory they saw advantages for themselves which each one knew would have to be disputed with the others. Castlereagh brought each to realize that the real basis for European security lay in international solidarity.

He was the first modern European statesman to put into practice a system openly acknowledging the existence of great and secondary Powers. The great Powers of the Quadruple Alliance were Austria, Great Britain, Prussia and Russia. Britain alone had begun her industrial development and possessed wealth, a strong fleet and a system of representative govern-ment. Austria and Russia were great land Powers, ruled by absolute sovereigns, whilst Prussia was still suffering from her defeat by Napoleon in 1806, though she, too, had the traditions of absolute monarchy and of the military successes of the reign of Frederick the Great.

Aims of the Four Allies

The achievement of Castlereagh was as much the result of his moderation and good sense as of his favourable position as the representative of the Power footing the military bills of the others. He pitched the demands of Britain in the post-war settle-ment low; yet he asserted them firmly. They were, in fact, simple. Britain insisted that the maritime laws which had been devised and were operated by herself to maintain her commercial and naval supre-macy at sea should be left untouched and undisputed by the other Powers. Secondly, she demanded that the River Scheldt, the gateway into Europe for her goods, should be controlled by an independent Power strong enough to protect itself but unlikely to be in a position to enter on a career of European domination. Lastly, she required the setting up and maintenance of a system

TIME CHART

A.D. 1701—1800

A.D.	
1701	Act of Settlement provides for Protestant succession of House of Hanover in England.
	War of Spanish succession.
	Grand alliance of Holland and England and the Empire to prevent union of France and Spain.
	Prussia becomes a kingdom under Frederick.
1702	France invades Holland.
	England at war with France and Spain.
1703	Portugal joins Grand Alliance.
1704	Marlborough enters Germany, defeats French at Battle of Blenheim.
	Gibraltar taken by English.
1705	English Navy takes Barcelona.
1706	Battle of Ramillies. Marlborough defeats French and conquers Spanish Netherlands.
	French driven from Italy by Prince Eugene.
	English and Portuguese enter Madrid.
1707	Act of Union of England and Scotland. First united Parliament of Great Britain meets.
	All Spanish possessions in Italy seized by Allies.
1708	French defeated at Battle of Oudenarde.
	Sardinia and Minorca captured by British.
	Unsuccessful attempt by Pretender to land in Scotland.
1709	Defeat of French at Malplaquet.
	Sweden at war with Denmark.
	First mass emigration of Germans to America.
	Coke first produced and used to smelt iron.
1710	Turkey at war with Russia.
1712	Philip V of Spain renounces claim to French throne.
1713	Peace of Utrecht; crowns of France and Spain to be separate.
	England acquires colonial possessions.
	Pragmatic Sanction vests succession to Austria in daughters of Charles VI.
1714	Accession of George I of Hanover to English throne.
1715	Unsuccessful Jacobite rising in Scotland.
	England at war with Sweden.
	Austria obtains Spanish Netherlands.
	Turks seize Corinth.
1717	Triple Alliance between England, France and Holland.
1718	Quadruple Alliance: England, Holland, France and Germany against Spain.
	Turks advance in Hungary.
1719	South Sea Bubble.
1721	Sir Robert Walpole's ministry begins in England.
	Defensive alliance between England, France and Spain.
1722	Persia under Afghan rule.
1723	Turks and Russians attempt to dismember Persia.
1725	Treaty between England, France and Prussia.
	Treaty of Vienna between Spain and Austria.
1733	War of Polish succession.
	Treaty of Escorial between France and Spain against Britain.
1739	Turks besiege Belgrade.
1740	War of the Austrian succession.
1741	French and Bavarians overrun Austria and crown Charles VII Emperor.
1742	Large part of Silesia ceded to Prussia at Treaty of Berlin.
1744	France declares war on England and Austria.
	Hostilities between English and French in India.
	North Italy occupied by French and Spanish.
1745	Failure of last Jacobite rebellion.
1746	French overrun Austrian Netherlands.
1751	Clive, in India, takes Arcot and defeats French.
1752	Franklin makes discoveries in electricity.
1755	Britain and France at war in India.
1756	Seven Years War between Austria and Prussia; Austria makes alliance with France.
	Calcutta taken by Surajah Dowlah of Bengal.
	Treaty of Westminster between England and Prussia.
	Massacre of Black Hole of Calcutta.
1757	Clive wins Battle of Plassey and takes Calcutta.

A.D.	
1758	Threshing machine invented.
1762	England at war with Spain; English conquests in West Indies.
1763	Peace of Paris between England France, and Spain; Canada ceded to Britain.
	Peace of Hubertsburg between Prussia and Austria.
1764	Jesuits expelled from France.
1765	Bengal ceded to British East India Company.
	Clive reforms Indian administration.
1766	Lorraine annexed to France.
	Occupation of Falkland Isles by English.
1767	Spinning jenny invented by Hargreaves in England.
1768	Captain Cook's first voyage of discovery.
1769	Arkwright makes spinning frame.
	Australia discovered by Captain Cook.
1772	First partition of Poland among Russia, Prussia and Austria.
1774	Accession of Louis XVI of France.
	Priestley discovers oxygen.
1775	Watt invents the steam engine.
	Beginning of American War of Independence.
	England hires German mercenaries for service in N. America.
1776	America declares herself independent of Britain.
1778	America in alliance with France.
	Captain Cook discovers Sandwich Isles.
1779	Spain allies with American colonists.
1780	Sunday schools established in England.
	Gordon anti-Popery riots in London.
1783	Independence of United States acknowledged at Peace of Versailles.
1784	Pitt's India Bill—Indian affairs placed under Board of Control.
1787	First convicts transported to Australia.
1789	French Revolution; arrest of the king; States-General meets for first time since 1610. Storming of the Bastille.
	Austrian Netherlands declare independence as state of Belgium.
1791	French king accepts constitution.
1792	France declared a republic.
	War declared by France against Prussia and Austria. France annexes Savoy and Nice.
1793	First coalition against France. France declares war on Britain and Holland.
	Execution of Louis XVI and Marie Antoinette.
	Reign of Terror begins in France.
	English seize French settlements in India.
	Second partition of Poland by Russia and Prussia.
1794	Execution of Robespierre. Reign of Terror in France ends.
1795	England at war with Holland; Cape of Good Hope seized.
	French Directory set up.
	Peace of Basel. Prussia recognizes French conquests on the Rhine.
	Popular insurrection in Paris suppressed by Napoleon Bonaparte.
	Holland conquered by France—Batavian Republic proclaimed.
	Final partition of Poland—extinction of kingdom.
1796	France invades Italy. Bonaparte enters Milan.
1798	Bonaparte's expedition to Egypt.
	Nelson wins victory at Battle of Nile.
	Revolution in Switzerland. French erect Helvetian Republic.
1799	Pitt imposes income tax in England.
	Second coalition against France.
	Bonaparte made First Consul in France.
	Bonaparte invades Syria and storms Jaffa. Repulsed at siege of Acre. Defeats Turks at Aboukir.
1800	Union of England and Ireland effected.
	Malta captured by British.
	Bonaparte defeats Austrians at Battle of Marengo and conquers N. Italy.

to ensure that no one of the great Powers should be able to embark on a programme of aggression and conquest such as had been the final programme of revolutionary and Napoleonic France.

During the wars, the British had made considerable colonial conquests at the expense of France and her dependencies, particularly Holland. Castlereagh was willing to restore many of these and to pay compensation for others, provided that the Allies agreed to these three main British requirements. He thus put Britain in the advantageous position of a bargainer whose demands are the most modest at the conference table, for all three other Allies had definite aims of territorial expansion in Europe. Prussia, the smallest and weakest, was anxious to regain the position she had enjoyed before the disaster of 1806; and Alexander I had agreed to support her attempts to do so. Austria wanted to acquire or regain provinces in northern Italy (Venice and Lombardy), and to hold the nominally independent states in the middle and south of the peninsula under her direct influence.

Alexander of Russia realized that the defeat of the French invaders by his armies in 1812, had marked the beginning of Napoleon's fall from power over the whole continent. He desired to follow up this advantage by making Russia, with her vast population and complete subjection to himself, the deciding influence and ultimately the supreme controller of the destinies of Europe. In this, his aims were threefold. He desired to make Russia decisive in the affairs of Europe; he became, towards the end of his life in 1825, determined to crush the spirit of liberalism, which he felt the nineteenth century had inherited from the revolutionary period; he wished to increase the western territories of Russia by taking the crown of a restored Poland for himself.

Such, very briefly, were the aims and intentions of the four allies after the defeat of Napoleon. The nature of these four Powers was to determine the political development of the nineteenth century. Prussia, Austria and Russia were essentially continental land Powers, important

because of their military strength and ruled by sovereigns absolute in their authority. Frederick William III of Prussia and Francis I of Austria depended in fact on their advisers; the Tsar, Alexander, was by nature and by the tradition of the Russian state an autocrat, taking his own decisions and making his own laws, whatever his ministers might advise. He ruled supreme over vast territories, with a huge population obedient to his will. Britain, the fourth great Power, differed from the other three in possessing a constitution of which the monarchy was an integral part, functioning within and not above it. The king of England could not take any action without the consent as well as the advice of his ministers. In other respects, however, Britain bore outward resemblance to two of her allies.

Problems of Nation-states

Like Austria and like Russia, Britain and her empire comprised peoples of different races, creeds and (in the case of Russia) colours. She was a nation-state, but not a national state in the sense in which France and Prussia were national states. After 1815, Prussia, too, gained territories with a different culture and a different language from her own; but until the Congress of Vienna, Prussia alone shared with the enemy, France, the nature of a national state whose people were bound together by language, soil, economic interests and cultural traditions held in common. The diversity of territories and subjects under the British crown had no real effect upon British policy, whilst the whole life-work of Metternich was founded upon his appreciation of the varied character and special interlocking and overlapping interests of the Austrian Empire.

The majority of the population of Austria proper was German in language and culture. In the rest of Francis I's dominions there were Germans only in Bohemia, where the German-speaking upper classes outweighed, though they did not outnumber, the Czech peasants and artisans, and in Hungary where there were small German settlements. At the Congress of Vienna, Austria renounced her claims

WESTERN EUROPE, 1815

to the parts of north-western Europe, especially Belgium, where she had ruled until dispossessed by the French victories of 1791 to 1806, and sought compensation in Italy. Thus she added to her collection of German, Czech, Hungarian (Magyar), Polish, Ruthenian and Southern Slav subjects yet another foreign and highly discontented people in the shape of the Italian inhabitants of Lombardy and Venetia. By her insistence on dominating the small duchies and principalities of the rest of Italy over which she did not rule directly, as well as the Papal States and the kingdom of the two Sicilies (Sicily and the southern half of Italy itself, with its capital at Naples), Austria kept alive those feelings of Italian nationalism first stirred up by French invasion and occupation.

It has been said with a great deal of truth that Metternich knew the weakness of Austria and knew, too, that she had found herself on the winning side in 1814, through a combination of lucky chances which no Austrian statesman could expect to recur. The Austrian Empire was obliged to act as a great Power and a nation-state in a world becoming increasingly conscious of nationalism and of power; but it was in fact a state whose very composition made it vulnerable to all the influences of such a world. Austria was strong because of the large numbers of her peoples but those peoples, once they felt the urge of nationalism, would fall away like ripe fruit from a tree, each nationality taking up its ideal of a separate national existence. Metternich's whole career from 1815 to 1848 was, therefore,· devoted to the creation and maintenance of a European system which would consolidate the delicate yet essential position of Austria; for the Austrian Empire occupied the geographical heart of the Europe created by the Treaty of Vienna.

The problem of diverse nationalities within the nation-state was not so difficult for the Tsar of All Russia. The autocracy and the very size of his empire, which was being vigorously expanded to the south-east during the first half of the nineteenth century, enabled him to conduct Russian policy in relation to other states as if Russia were in fact a national whole. Indeed, Alexander I and his successors were able to encourage the nationalist idea in the Balkans by appealing to the Slavs of Serbia and Bulgaria and the Orthodox Christians of Greece, subjects, or recently subjects, of the Turk, to consider the Russians, really a great mixture of peoples as varied as those of the Austrian Empire, as their kinsmen, protectors or co-religionists as the case might be. The attractions of this kind of appeal were considerable both to those who broadcast and to those who received it.

Of the two most completely national of the nation-states, Prussia, except for the Polish province of Posen (Poznan), had a wholly German population. She embodied the German ideal of the national state and appeared to the rest of Germany as a great Power created in and through the German tradition. Of all the Powers, Prussia was the most conscious of her military past and of the military possibilities of her present and her future. The army built up by Frederick the Great's father and used by Frederick himself to make Prussia a great Power had been defeated at Jena; but it had avenged itself at Leipzig and in the campaigns of 1814. It had fully vindicated its reputation at Waterloo. From 1815 onwards the generals and the classes from which army officers were drawn were to guide the policy of Prussia until she became the Greater German State. The German nation was born out of the defeat of German nationalism by Prussia; absorbed into the Prussian state, Germans were to become so enthralled by their unity that they failed utterly to see their transition from being Germans to becoming Prussians. In 1815 much lay

WESTERN EUROPE, 1871

hidden in the future; one of the buried truths which was to emerge from the passing years was that the Allies had created a new and greater danger for Europe in the small and comparatively weak Power they set down upon the Rhine to guard against a second French aggression.

France was in no position to contemplate a repetition of her attempt to dominate Europe. Her people were tired of the apparently ceaseless warfare of the Empire which they had been forced to sustain. The "blood tax" of conscription had weighed too heavily upon them. The Tsar had obliged Louis XVIII to grant his people a "charter" or constitution which provided for two chambers more or less on the English model. Theoretically at least. Louis was a constitutional monarch, and constitutional monarchs are not often in a position to embark on a career of conquest. Louis had, in any case, no desire to do so. He was the one king in Europe who had never for an instant relaxed his hostility to republican and imperial France. He desired above all things to enter into the respectable company of the Allies and to take his country with him. So, paradoxically enough, until 1830, when the Bourbon family was chased from the throne, France was the one purely national great European Power—a state containing none but Frenchmen within her frontiers, yet appearing to want only stability and the opportunity to recover her prosperity without fundamentally changing the arrangements of the Vienna Treaty.

This combination of circumstances in France gave Talleyrand the opportunity to dominate the Congress and to set the tone of the settlement. He was able to exploit differences between the victors to the advantage of France, whose government was, after all, one which could hardly be considered hostile by the Allies who had supported it in exile and placed it in power after the defeat of the Revolution in the person of Napoleon.

Talleyrand's ability brought France back to the ranks of the great Powers. Once he had pledged French aid to Britain and Austria in the event of Prussia and Russia combining to seize Saxony and Poland respectively, he had won his position, though this pledge, made in a secret treaty on January 3, 1815, was contrary to the will of his king.

Castlereagh had already aimed at creating "the germ of future international government" in Article VI of the Treaty of November 20, 1815. The Powers had "agreed to renew, at fixed periods . . . reunions devoted to the great common interests and to the examination of the measures which . . . shall be judged most salutary for the repose and prosperity of the peoples, and for the maintenance of the peace of the State." Although the bond holding the Allies together was their determination that France should not renew her attempt to dominate Europe, coupled with their hostility to and fear of "Jacobinism" —the doctrines, the appeal and the spirit of the French Revolution—their first reunion at Aix-la-Chapelle in the autumn of 1818 ended with their acceptance of France as one of their number. The allied armies of occupation were withdrawn and France paid her full war indemnity with the help of a loan made to her through the London banking firm of Baring Brothers.

The Congress of Aix-la-Chapelle marked the emergence of that difference of approach between Britain and the three eastern Powers which was to end the experiment of the congress system. The Tsar wanted "a general union of sovereigns against revolution," especially in view of the revolt of the Spanish colonies in South America, whither he proposed the dispatch of an allied force. Castlereagh successfully opposed this suggestion, which implied that the alliance of the Powers was a general combination of authority, as it had been conceived at Vienna, against any attempts at internal change or reform in any country. In fact, the difference which was emerging between the autocracies of the east and Britain was based upon their varying interpretation of the dangers of revolution.

Throughout the nineteenth century, revolution meant the French Revolution. This event, as has been seen, left a legacy which the world has found at once attractive and uneasy. Its three watchwords, Liberty, Equality, Fraternity, held out a hope and an ideal to the peoples of Europe. But, possibly more significantly, the Revolution aroused the force of nationalism. Nationalism, far more than the Industrial Revolution, determined the policies of the Powers from 1815 to 1870; for it led to all the disturbances in Germany, in Italy and in south-east Europe, which make nineteenth-century diplomacy so complicated at first sight. Nationalism owed its existence and its appeal to the political ideas of the French Revolution, but nationalism proved to be the rock upon which the Revolution foundered.

Metternich's name is associated with the conservatism of the period between 1815 and 1848, because it was he above all who stood for the maintenance of the territorial settlement of Vienna and for the co-operation of the Powers in combating the dangers of the Revolution. He tried to reconcile the increasingly authoritarian views of Alexander I with those of the British statesmen, representatives of a country whose whole political and social structure rested upon acceptance of the revolution of 1688, when the crown of England came to William of Orange and Mary on terms—the Declaration of Right—which became the touchstone of British constitutional principles.

Castlereagh thought of the reaction in the House of Commons to any acceptance of Alexander's proposals for a union of the Powers against the Revolution wherever it should raise its head; Metternich, sympathetic to the Tsar's point of view through temperament and training, tried to run with the autocratic hare whilst he slowed down the pursuit of the constitutional hounds. Only his personal relationship with Castlereagh and his respect for the other's integrity and wide knowledge of European affairs could make this possible.

Towards the end of Castlereagh's life the situation was, in fact, becoming impossible. Revolutions in Italy, where Austria had vital interests, and in Spain, which was too near home for the restored French king to tolerate, were forcing Metternich into Alexander's arms. Nationalism had found a firm foothold among Turkey's subjects in the Balkans. Greece had rebelled against the Turks and Alexander was torn between his hatred of revolution and his desire as a Greek Orthodox Christian to help his co-religionists, thereby gaining for Russia a sphere of influence in the south-east which would see her some way towards fulfilling the age-old longing of the Tsars to recapture Constantinople and to re-establish

CONGRESS OF VIENNA, 1814–15

Chief result of this meeting of the principal European Powers was the redrafting of the map of Europe after the Revolutionary and Napoleonic upheaval. Around the conference table are seated the Tsar of Russia, the Emperor of Austria, the kings of Prussia, Denmark and Bavaria. Wellington, Castlereagh, Talleyrand and Metternich were also present.

MASSACRE OF CHIOS

The war for Greece's independence from Turkish rule was waged with remarkable ferocity by both. In 1822, after heavy bombardment by the Turks, the Greek island of Chios was captured and 30,000 of its inhabitants brutally murdered or sold into slavery. This graphic representation of the scene was painted by the contemporary French artist, Eugène Delacroix.

the Eastern Empire. Thus revolution and nationalism combined to defy the foreign rule of Austria in Italy, to raise resistance to the Turks in south-east Europe and to challenge the tyrannical rule of the restored kings of Spain, Naples and Portugal.

The frantic worry of his position drove Castlereagh to suicide on August 12, 1822. His successor, George Canning, mistrusted the eastern Powers and disliked the Congress system which had proved to be little more than a trade union of autocrats.

At Troppau in 1820 and at Laibach early in 1821, the British had done no more than send their Ambassador in Vienna as an observer to report helplessly whilst Metternich and Alexander issued threats against rebellious Spaniards and Italians and declarations of their own solidarity against all revolutionary attempts to change the internal government of other countries. In January, 1821, Castlereagh had felt compelled to make public the attitude he had already taken up in a Cabinet Paper of

May 5, 1820. Britain considered herself free to intervene if the territorial arrangements of Vienna were violated; she was in no way and by no means a guarantor of the particular kind of government set up in each separate country. Immediately after Castlereagh's death the whole problem was presented to Canning in its acutest form.

At the Congress of Verona, on October 30, 1822, the British representative, the Duke of Wellington, rejected the proposal that the Allies should interfere in the revolutionary situation which had existed for nearly three years in Spain. Acting on direct and explicit orders from Canning he walked out of the conference. It was left for the French delegation to decide whether or not France should execute the desires of Metternich and Alexander. Swayed by his ultra-royalist advisers and fearful lest if he did not act Russian or Austrian troops might demand to cross French territory, Louis XVIII laid aside his role of constitutional monarch. In the spring of 1823, the French armies crossed the Pyrenees into Spain in order to restore the absolute power of the cruel and treacherous king, Ferdinand VII.

Canning's Policy

This episode marks the end of the attempt to order Europe through a crude kind of international assembly. Canning appealed for the first time and with great success to British public opinion; he declared that ". . . the immediate object of England" was to "take care that the war should not grow out of an assumed jurisdiction of the Congress"; he published documents and pointed out that the power of Britain was not to be used for mere abstract causes. Yet on December 31, 1824, he completed the arrangements which ended in the recognition as independent republics of Spain's rebellious South American colonies.

Canning explained, and where necessary defended, his policy with masterly logic; yet he never intended that Britain should come to be regarded as the champion of liberalism on the continent, as in fact happened under his successors at the Foreign Office between 1828 and 1850.

Canning mistrusted Metternich's policy of attempting to control all European events and developments. But Canning died in August, 1827, while engaged in approaches to Russia about the Greek revolt against the Turks. This rebellion was the first major problem of that eastern question which vexed the statesmen of the whole nineteenth century and which was eventually to prove the immediate cause of the First World War. While Canning had always distrusted Austria, his successors shifted their hostility to Russia, largely because of the eastern question with its implications of danger to the eastern Mediterranean, to the routes to India and ultimately to the security of India itself.

Egyptian Forces Intervene

Though the Russian Tsar may have been anxious about the incompatibility of his dislike of revolutions in general and his desire to aid the Greeks as the protector of the Greek Church, the Greek cause made great headway in the West. With the death of Alexander I in 1825, and the accession of his brother, Nicholas I, Russian policy became even more hostile to the Turks.

Yet the Greeks were not simply the cultured and oppressed descendants of those who had inspired the writings of the classical historians, philosophers and poets. The war was waged with incredible barbarity on both sides and the massacre of the whole population of the island of Chios by the Turks, which so shocked the whole of civilized Europe, had its counterparts on the Greek side. Canning originally agreed with Metternich that the Russians must not be allowed to intervene alone; but after 1825 the situation changed. The Sultan of Turkey in that year called upon his Governor in Egypt to help him to crush the five-year-old revolt. This Governor, Mehemet Ali, an Albanian adventurer who had risen high in the Turkish service, had created a powerful Egyptian army and fleet, part of which was sent to the Morea (the Peloponnese), thus cutting off the Greeks from their vital seaborne supplies and bringing disaster to their troops.

Nicholas could not allow this situation to remain without Russian action. Nego-

tiations and disagreements ending in the
Treaty of London, signed in July, 1827,
at last procured a combination of the
powers to press the Turks to make peace.
But Turkish obduracy brought about the
annihilation of the Egyptian fleet by an
Allied squadron at Navarino, and this
"untoward incident," coupled with the
British Prime Minister's dislike of the
Treaty of London, encouraged the Tsar
to declare war on Turkey who accused the
Powers of bad faith.

Effects of Turkey's Weakness

This was the first of a series of Russo-
Turkish wars which led to disunion and
hostility between Russia and the Powers.
Henceforward the peace of Europe often
turned on the weakness of Turkey, the discontent and nationalism of her Christian
subjects in the Balkans and Russian designs
on the Straits. In fact, in 1829, Nicholas
was persuaded that the maintenance of a
weak Turkey was preferable to her disappearance, since the latter might involve
the creation of small but strongly nationalistic Balkan states which would prove
hostile to Russian ambitions in the south-
east and might also earn for Russia the
permanent hostility of the Powers, especially Britain and Austria. Britain's interests
in the eastern Mediterranean were obvious;
Austria, Russia's nearest and most suspicious neighbour, was anxious to extend
her dominions into the Balkans and still
more anxious to prevent Russia from doing
the same thing.

When, therefore, the ambitious and
powerful Mehemet Ali revolted against his
overlord the Sultan on two occasions, in
1831 and 1839, Russia assumed the role of
protector and supporter of the Sultan
against his Pasha. On February 20, 1833,
for the only time in history, a Russian
naval squadron anchored at Constantinople by Turkish invitation. Britain, preoccupied with events in western Europe
and engaged above all in ensuring that
Antwerp did not fall to the French, who
were nominally assisting the Belgians in
their rebellion against Dutch rule, was
obliged to allow Russia to land troops from
her fleet and to take the whole glory of pre-

serving the Turkish Empire. From the
eventual settlement the Russians gained a
treaty of alliance with Turkey which contained a secret clause virtually giving
them control of the Straits (the Dardanelles
and the Bosporus) joining the Black Sea
with the Mediterranean.

In 1839 it was the Sultan who commenced
hostilities against the Pasha, in the best
traditions of "preventive war." Britain
now acted promptly, for her hands were no
longer tied. The Foreign Secretary, Lord
Palmerston, struggled to unite the Powers,
especially after the defeat of the Turkish
armies by Ibrahim, Mehemet Ali's son.
This time it was the French who hoped to
gain a foothold in Egypt and Syria by supporting Mehemet Ali; Palmerston turned
to the three remaining Powers, Austria,
Prussia and Russia, who signed a convention with Britain at London, on July 15,
1840, presenting an ultimatum to Mehemet
Ali. France was excluded; but Palmerston
had gambled correctly on her not being
ready in the last resort to declare war.
The Powers now intervened directly in
Syria and the Pasha at length capitulated
to their naval force. On July 13, 1841, the
five Powers, including now a chastened
France, signed a convention which regulated the control of the Straits.

Treaty of Paris

This apparently secondary, but really
most important issue, lay at the root of the
great mid-century crisis in the Near East.
The Crimean War of 1854-56, was the
product of British and French opposition
to Russian efforts to secure influence and
power over the declining Turkish Empire.
It marks, too, the triumph of Britain in the
counsels of the Sultan. It can be regarded
as one of the most unnecessary and useless
wars ever fought but, more significantly, it
was the last war between the great Powers
in which the old conception of warfare
persisted. So far as the Crimean War is
concerned, the Industrial Revolution and
the resources of rapidly developing science
might never have existed. One reason
which caused Great Britain and France to
fight with the Turks against Russia was
found in that truly nineteenth-century

FORERUNNER OF THE MOTOR OMNIBUS

This Ackerman print shows the Enterprise Steam Omnibus, built in 1833, for the London and Paddington Steam Carriage Company. The picture reveals some of the excitement of Londoners when this novel vehicle started running to and from Paddington and the City.

phenomenon: nationalism. Since 1832 Greece had been recognized as an independent kingdom; by 1850 the Bulgarians, the inhabitants of Moldavia and Wallachia (now called Rumanians), and the Serbs, who had won partial independence in a series of wars, assassinations and revolts from 1804 onwards, all responded to the urge to assert their national ambitions. To the north-west, Austria, long the bulwark of European civilization against the Turks, watched anxiously the attempts of the Russian Tsars to establish their claim to be the protectors of the eastern Christians and the champions of the Balkan peoples.

Nevertheless, the Austrians kept out of the war in the Crimea. France, an empire once again under Napoleon III, was eager to regain the military glories of the first Napoleon. Lord Palmerston, with his hatred of the Russian autocracy and his suspicions of the aims of the Tsars, played upon British public opinion until it forced Britain into war and himself to the premiership. Austria was to look south-eastwards with increasing intensity as her interests in Germany and Italy became less through force of circumstances. The end of the Crimean War with the Treaty of Paris in 1856 began a new stage in the slow dissolution of the Turkish Empire and also, because of the cleverness of Count Cavour, the Prime Minister of the Kingdom of Sardinia, the decline of Austria as a dominant force in the states' system of Western Europe dates from the same time.

Cavour was determined to end Austrian rule in Italy and to unite her under his own king. Having built up in Piedmont, the main portion of the Kingdom of Sardinia, a small but sound industrial economy, Cavour saw in the Crimean War his chance to further his aims in the international sphere. A contingent of Sardinian troops, therefore, fought with the Allies in the Crimea; Sardinia secured the right to sit at the Peace Conference in Paris, and so to influence Britain, and especially Napoleon, in her favour. Thus Austria's remarkable recovery after 1848, the year of revolution throughout her dominions, was counterbalanced by Cavour's astuteness and, not for the first time, the eastern question definitely affected developments in Western Europe.

Austrian recovery in Germany and at home lasted only until 1859, when Cavour began his direct struggle to unite all Italy, with the military assistance of Napoleon III, who saw in the defeat of Austria the

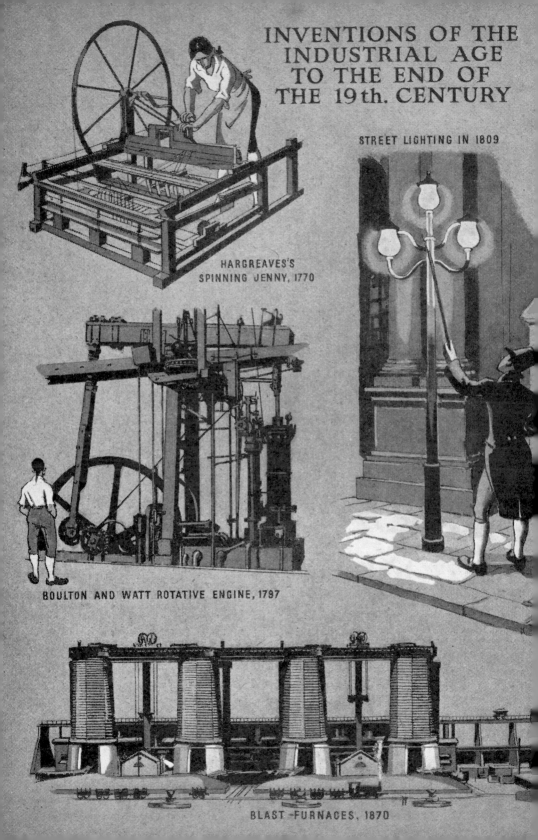

INVENTIONS OF THE
INDUSTRIAL AGE
TO THE END OF
THE 19th. CENTURY

STREET LIGHTING IN 1809

HARGREAVES'S
SPINNING JENNY, 1770

BOULTON AND WATT ROTATIVE ENGINE, 1797

BLAST-FURNACES, 1870

PHOTOGRAPHER, ABOUT 1860

TYPEWRITER, 1874

BRUSH DYNAMO, 1878

TELEPHONE EXCHANGE IN 1885

means of establishing France as the leading Power of the Continent. All the administrative reforms in Austria after 1848 failed to create a military force able to resist the combination of French troops and Italian bitterness against the hated "Germans"; nor could they create any unity of purpose or spirit between the Germans and Magyars and the other, more suppressed, minority groups. Thus Austria's history from 1848 onwards falls into four distinct periods.

German Confederation

After the revolutions of 1848 until 1859, the stabilization of the internal situation, started by the cynical and ruthless Schwarzenberg, whose motto was, "One can do anything with bayonets, except sit on them," was followed by the resumption of Austrian leadership in the German Confederation. The next period is one of struggle for domination in Germany, beginning with the loss of all the Austrian provinces in Italy except Venetia, in 1859, and ending with the lost war against Prussia in 1866. Between 1867 and 1873, the Empire was finally re-organized as the dual monarchy of Austria and Hungary, in which the Magyars at last gained political equality with the Germans and control over the internal affairs of Hungary.

In 1873, the last period begins; by then Germany, united by the aggressive expansion of Prussia under Bismarck, had initiated the League of the Three Emperors. Germany, Austria and Russia combined for the protection and advancement of their especial interests in Europe. Until the final collapse of the Empire as a result of the First World War, Austria was the partner of Germany, not always completely subservient, and despite her weakness increasingly indispensable to a German policy which successively alienated the other major Powers.

The German Confederation in the last half of the nineteenth century was vastly different from that desired by Metternich at the Vienna Congress in 1815. Then, as a result of the victories of Napoleon I, Prussia was weak by comparison with Austria. The internal reforms of 1807-13 helped to restore Prussian strength; but

these reforms were carried out in order to create a state of affairs in which revenge for Jena should become possible. Baron vom Stein, the only Prussian statesman who might have made Prussia a really progressive country, held power for only a year. The generals and ministers who were the reorganizers of the Prussian army made reforms only where they promised to improve the quality and numbers of their intake of recruits. Gneisenau, who with Scharnhorst, was the leading military member of the group, argued that feudal and politically backward monarchies such as Prussia had much to learn from the equality of opportunity presented to all citizens by the revolution in France, but was disregarded. The landlords of Brandenburg and Silesia freed their serfs only to ensure a cheap and steady flow of labour at the same time as the army was receiving a larger supply of recruits.

The German Confederation was originally designed to enable the Powers to ensure that France was bordered on the east by an organization which could dispose of sufficient troops, swiftly assembled, to counterbalance any potential French armies. At the same time the Confederation, composed as it was of some thirty-eight states, was not likely to interfere with Metternich's conception of Austrian influence. Prussia under her romantic and indecisive king, Frederick William III, was still intimidated by the traditional authority of the Austrian emperors and by the actuality of Austrian triumphs over Napoleon in diplomacy and war. So the situation in Germany was moulded by the relationship between the two largest German Powers.

Influence of Bismarck

The revolutions of 1848 suddenly altered that relationship. The fall of Metternich and the prolonged preoccupation of his successors with the internal difficulties of the Austrian Empire, combined with the reaction of German liberals against the repressive and often brutal methods of Metternich to turn their attention towards Prussia. Prussia seemed to be destined for the leadership of Germany; she was, by comparison with Austria, a truly German power. Moreover, by the Vienna settlement, she stood with her new Rhineland provinces as the military protector of Germany against the possibility of a renewal of French aggression.

As has been seen, Frederick William IV of Prussia refused the crown of Germany offered by the Frankfurt Assembly. German nationalism conflicted hopelessly with German liberalism, especially when the allegedly liberal German National Assembly demanded that troops of the Confederation should force the two provinces of Schleswig and Holstein away from Denmark, whose king was the Duke of Schleswig-Holstein, into the German Confederation. This conflict, coinciding with the recovery of Austria, resulted in the ten years of Austrian supremacy. Prussia submitted her German policy to Austrian demands and her internal administration to those conservative landowners and soldiers

who saw in German nationalism the ally of the liberal tendencies they dreaded.

In September, 1862, three years after the Austrian defeats in Italy, Otto von Bismarck-Schönhausen became the Minister President of Prussia. The new king, William I, was determined to build up a Prussian army of greater strength and with more trained reserves than ever before. The Prussian Chamber refused to vote the necessary money; Bismarck, a conservative landowner, had experience of diplomacy and of the Austrian methods of controlling Germany in the years of her triumph, for before working in the Prussian embassies in St. Petersburg and Paris, he had been the Prussian representative in the Diet of the German Confederation. He now urged the king to dissolve the chamber and carry on with his army reforms; he was determined to defeat the liberals who thought that representative institutions

GLADSTONE'S FIRST ADMINISTRATION

Portrait group by H. Barraud, showing W. E. Gladstone, surrounded by ministers of his first administration, 1868-74, including Lord Hatherley (Lord Chancellor), Earl de Grey (Lord President of the Council), Earl of Kimberley (Lord Privy Seal), Robert Lowe (Chancellor of the Exchequer), and John Bright (President of the Board of Trade). This Government was noted for the Disestablishment of the Irish Church in 1869, and the Irish Land Act, 1870, also Forster's Education Act and Cardwell's Army Reforms.

FIRST GERMAN EMPEROR

William I succeeded to the throne of Prussia in 1861 and, on the successful conclusion of the Franco-Prussian War of 1870, was proclaimed German Emperor at Versailles on January 18, 1871. He is seen here with his sister, the Grand Duchess, Alexandrine von Mecklenburg-Schwerin, at Bad Ems.

should settle affairs of state and control expenditure of public money; and he despised and ignored those German nationalists who believed that Germany should be united by the will and for the good of the people. His success was the triumph of his genius and perseverance and the beginning of the Bismarckian era for the whole of Europe.

Prussia already had one great advantage against the day when she should become the mistress of Germany. Although the industrial revolution did not make rapid progress in Germany until after 1871, the widely spread territories of the Prussian crown, stringing out from East Prussia to the Rhine, caused Prussian civil servants to devise a system whereby goods could be exchanged with other German states, whose territories were interspersed among the Prussian provinces. This system, incorporated in the Prussian Customs Union (Zollverein), unified all customs and excise duties through all the member states. Although created for purely administrative convenience and for economy in the carrying on of trade, it actually provided a framework within which it was possible for Bismarck to carry out his schemes for making his master the German Emperor.

These schemes depended on war. By 1864, Bismarck was ready and he utilized the revival of the complicated question of Schleswig-Holstein to launch his first aggressive war. Denmark was attacked by Prussian and Austrian troops, acting nominally on behalf of the Confederation, because her king had threatened to break his pledge, given in the Convention of London in 1852, that the two duchies should never be incorporated directly into the Danish kingdom. After a campaign which proved not quite so easy as the Prussian General Staff had hoped, the Danes were defeated and the two provinces occupied. Prussia went into Schleswig and Austria into Holstein. The stage was set for Bismarck's second war. He could now force a quarrel on Austria and gain Prussia's revenge for the humiliation of the ten years' Austrian supremacy.

Prussia began by establishing herself in Schleswig. When the Austrians protested against the removal of the Prussian naval base from Danzig to Kiel, Bismarck replied that Austria had an equal right to transfer her warships from Pola on the Adriatic to a port in Holstein. He forced a crisis over the administration and the future of the two duchies.

Subsequent Prussian tactics seem very modern in the light of the German manœuvres of August, 1939: Austria began to mobilize in self-defence and Bismarck issued an ultimatum requiring immediate demobilization without mention of any Prussian concession in return. At the same time he surprised all Germany, and especially the liberals, by sending to the Diet of the Confederation a demand for reform of the whole constitution, proposing universal suffrage and the virtual elimination of Austria from Germany. Austria countered by accusing Prussia of breaking the peace treaty with Denmark and her word to Austria; Austria therefore demanded the mobilization of the federal army against Prussia and received a majority of nine votes to six in the Diet. Prussia thereupon declared Austria's action unconstitutional and announced the end of the Confederation. On June 14, 1866, Prussia declared war on Austria. By August 23, Austria had been defeated, and on that date she signed a treaty of peace in Prague.

With a facility for making immediately useful allies which German diplomatists have tried to emulate in modern times, Bismarck had secured the support of Italy before war broke out. He had taken full advantage of Italian eagerness to include Venetia in their newly formed kingdom; at the same time he had played with success on the needs and ambitions of Napoleon III, who desired above all to make France the leading European Power; to this end Napoleon had supported the Italians against Austria and had suggested many times that a European Congress should meet in Paris to discuss the outstanding problems of the day.

Bismarck's Policy

The Treaty of Prague is interesting if only for the fact that a nation whose army and navy had lost every action in which they took part, gained handsomely by it. Austria ceded Venetia to Napoleon III, who handed over the province to the Italians, whose own armies had been decisively beaten and whose navy had proved unequal to the Austrian fleet. Austria renounced all share in the future organization of Germany; a North German Confederation was to be formed under Prussian leadership; the southern German states were to form an association; Schleswig and Holstein were both to become Prussian.

Bismarck's peace policy towards defeated Austria was masterly: he saw that he must at all costs avoid the intervention of Napoleon III, which might prevent the localization of the war. He therefore made peace at the earliest possible moment after the first conclusive victory over the Austrians at Sadowa, although in doing so he had to overcome the resentment of King William and of the Prussian generals. He saw, too, that he must not antagonize Austria permanently because she was to play an important part in his plans for the future; he demanded no territorial concessions apart from Venetia, and he so engineered the surrender of that province that Napoleon III's action was resented both by Austria and by the Italians.

War With Prussia

Finally, Bismarck reorganized Germany so that it would be easy, when the time came, for the southern states to join the North German Confederation. He made treaties of military alliance, offensive and defensive, with them before the Treaty of Prague was actually signed; consequently the provision that the North German Confederation should be "north of the line of the [river] Main" was already void in view of Prussia's influence with her new allies to the south of it.

Two obstacles only remained in the way of the unification, or, perhaps, more accurately, the submergence in Prussia, of Germany. The first was France; Napoleon III could not afford to see a united and powerful state standing in the centre of Europe; France could never be the leading Power in a continent thus dominated from the heart. The second, far less important, obstacle lay in the difficulty of attracting the southern states of Germany into the framework of the Prussian-controlled North German Confederation. Only war could remove these hindrances; and war was ideally suited to do so, provided a European conflagration could be avoided as Bismarck had managed to avoid it in 1864 and 1866. His next move, therefore, was to engineer a quarrel with France over the comparatively unimportant question of a candidate for the vacant Spanish throne. Bismarck gave his approval to a candidate whom he knew to be unacceptable to the French Government. From their opposition and by means of a quick-witted alteration in the presentation of a

OTTOMAN EMPIRE, 1871

The principalities of Serbia, Wallachia, Moldavia and Montenegro were autonomous though under Ottoman protection. In 1861 Moldavia and Wallachia became the Principality of Rumania; in 1878 Rumania gained her independence, though she lost southern Bessarabia to Russia in return for the Dobrudja, the Kingdom of Rumania being proclaimed in 1881.

telegram to the press, Bismarck created the semblance of French aggression and Prussian innocence. He was even able to provoke the ministers of Napoleon to declare war against Prussia; a Napoleon could not afford the suspicion of an insult.

William I Becomes Emperor

The Prussian victory in the war of 1870 —a victory won despite French superiority in manpower and equipment—was the culminating triumph of Bismarck's planning. Prussia's position was now unassailable. Her South German allies shared in her military glory; she was the undisputed military master of the Continent. Bismarck persuaded the king of Bavaria to offer King William of Prussia the crown of the German Empire, inducing his master to accept it. William would have been content to see Prussia assimilate all Germany without the change in his own title; but Bismarck wished to ensure the completion of his work by its general acceptance in Europe. So William I was proclaimed German Emperor in the Hall of Mirrors at Versailles on January 18, 1871.

With the entry of Germany into the ranks of the great Powers, the balance of the European situation was altered. From 1830 onwards, Great Britain had been content to preserve this balance, to continue to develop and enjoy her own industrial prosperity and to safeguard her especial interests in the East. Between 1840 and 1870, industrialization spread to Europe at large, though German activity before 1870 was almost entirely confined to the building of strategic railways and a canal system, which Prussia showed skill in using in the war. The French indemnity provided an immediate impetus to an industrial expansion of unparalleled magnitude into which went the entire energies of the German middle class, backed by the practical concern of government.

Britain had avoided entangling alliances since the Crimean War. During the long period when her conduct of foreign affairs was in the hands of Palmerston and Lord John Russell, her policy on the Continent had been to support all movements which seemed to aim at achieving a replica of the British constitution; to assert British contempt for, and defiance of, tyrants wherever possible; to maintain a balance against the power and ambitions of Russia by preserving the integrity of the Austrian Empire, even though this meant opposing revolutionary movements within Austria-Hungary proper whilst encouraging the men and actions leading to the unification of Italy in defiance of Austria; and, most consistently of all, to continue British support of Turkey against Russian attempts to advance towards the Straits. Thus in Spain and Portugal, as well as in Italy, Palmerston and Russell encouraged the hopes, and, often, the absurdities of liberals.

In 1864 the Queen and public opinion had been in favour of Denmark, one of whose princesses had recently married the Prince of Wales. Yet Russell had written that Britain would only consider war "if . . . the safety of Copenhagen or the existence of Denmark as an independent kingdom should be menaced." The Powers, Britain and Russia especially, had a great interest in preserving the state of affairs at the entrance to the Baltic. Palmerston wrote after the victory of Prussia and Austria over Denmark: "Prussia is too weak as she now is . . . and . . . it is desirable that Germany, in the aggregate, should be strong, in order to control those two ambitious and aggressive powers, France and Russia, that press upon her east and west." Palmerston could not foresee that the strengthening of Prussia would mean the obliteration of "Germany in the aggregate," and that the result would be to make Britain an ally of France and Russia.

Pro-Prussian Sentiment

Similarly in 1870, the British reaction to the war that Bismarck so carefully localized was unsuspecting of the future. Queen Victoria always had great affection for anything German, and the sentiments of the middle and upper classes at least were almost entirely pro-Prussian. When Russia took advantage of the war and of Bismarck's need for Russian neutrality to denounce those clauses of the 1856 Treaty of Paris, which forbade her to fortify her Black Sea ports or to maintain a Black Sea

IRON CHANCELLOR

The determined and successful foreign policy of Prince Otto von Bismarck, seen above at his desk in the German Foreign Office, was mainly responsible for the important place which Prussia achieved in European affairs during the second half of the nineteenth century, and for the establishment and consolidation of the German Empire.

fleet, Gladstone and the Foreign Secretary, Lord Granville, insisted on regularizing this undoubtedly illegal act by calling a conference of the signatories of the Paris Treaty, but were unable and probably unwilling to do more.

Bismarck secured Russian acquiescence to his attack on Denmark in 1864, and to the war against Austria in 1866, by forbidding the Polish refugees from the insurrection of 1863 to cross the Prussian frontier in their flight from the cruel punishment which awaited them at the hands of the Tsar. He had assured Austria's friendship after 1866; but the hatred of France, deprived of Alsace and Lorraine by the Peace of Frankfurt of 1871, remained implacable. All German diplomacy from then until Bismarck's fall from power in 1890, was directed towards preventing a French revenge. In 1879 Bismarck

encouraged the French to send an expedition to Tunis, intending them to seek compensation for their European losses in the acquisition of colonies. He formed his alliances with Austria and with Italy; he countered every attempt by the French to initiate a policy which might end in readjusting the European settlement.

Germany's predominance on the Continent was publicly acknowledged in 1876-78, when the Russian wars with Turkey were resumed; massacres of Christians in the Balkans, and Russian desire to set up a satellite state in Bulgaria caused a war in which Turkey was defeated. So sweeping were the Russian terms in the Treaty of San Stefano that the Powers demanded their revision in a European Congress. A Russian-dominated Balkan Peninsula was unthinkable to Disraeli and Bismarck. This was Bismarck's opportunity to fulfil in

Berlin for Germany the ambition that Napoleon III had never been able to attain for France in Paris. The Congress of Berlin, therefore, presented Bismarck and Germany to Europe as host and mediator.

Russian demands were reduced to more or less acceptable terms; Britain gained a protectorate over Cyprus; the Turkish Empire submitted to further control by the Powers; Germany consolidated her European position and exploited Austrian apprehension of Russian advances in the Balkans to bind the Dual Monarchy still closer to her side.

Under the Bismarckian Empire, Germany completed her development into one of the world's leading industrial nations. Heavy industry and shipping, as well as great advances in the textile industries, helped to extend German trade throughout the world. Germany became, not only a market for British semi-manufactured goods, such as cotton yarn, but also a rival in the manufacture of machin-

THREE NINETEENTH-CENTURY STATESMEN

Nicholas de Giers, Russian Foreign Minister; Prince von Bismarck, German Chancellor, and Count Kalnóky, Foreign Minister of Austria-Hungary, meet together for a conference between their respective sovereigns held at Skierniewice, Poland, in September, 1884.

ery and in shipping. After 1870 the industrial age became a European epoch.

In this epoch the gioupings of the powers which preceded the First World War were made. Iron and coal measures, railways and heavy industry, not only supported large populations but in their turn created them. France, with about forty per cent of her population still engaged in agriculture, watched the rise of Germany with fear and hate; Russia became more and more jealous of Austria's use of the German alliance to bolster up her determination to allow no Russian expansion towards south-eastern Europe. Britain slowly emerged from her preoccupation with the colonization of Africa and her suspicion of French intentions there.

At Berlin in 1884 the partition of Africa was arranged between the Powers; for Germany, too, was conscious of the appropriateness of colonial possessions to a great Power. Colonies were a source of prestige as well as of raw materials; the British, French and Dutch Empires, all acquired early in the history of these peoples, already had most of the raw materials. Germany had to concentrate on prestige. Even colonial markets were a delusion, for more German goods were sold in British than in German colonies.

Thus Bismarck realized that the future for German security and prosperity lay rather in the alliances he could make than in adventure overseas. He had had his day of aggression; he was ready to become a peaceful European, provided that his achievement remained safe and unquestioned. It is conceivable that had he not been dismissed by the ambitious and erratic young William II, Germany might have eschewed the disaster of 1914-18. Yet in many ways his own actions show that he recognized the seeds of trouble in his treatment of France. His own statement that he was forced on by the generals to the annexation of Alsace and Lorraine is not borne out by anyone else. His own act in forming the Triple Alliance of Germany, Austria and Italy shows that he realized in advance the need to shelter from the storm of French and Russian hostility, however far off it seemed. This is the background to the eventual division of Europe into the "armed camps" from which the First World War was fought.

Great Britain alone was outside these armed camps; under the guidance of Lord Salisbury the slogan of British foreign policy was "drift," which meant an absence of European entanglements. Britain was content to see power balanced in Europe —if necessary by delicate adjustments in Africa or Persia—and to pursue her commercial and industrial avocations. But with the rise of Germany and the decay of the Turkish Empire she was obliged to take action to suit the changing situation. The economic results of the spreading industrialization of the Continent were such as to bring Britain's gaze more fully to bear upon it; but although she was willing to settle her differences with France on African and other overseas questions, she was not yet ready to commit herself to an "understanding." Bismarck had prepared an advanced position in the bastions of the Triple Alliance.

Test Yourself

1. Why did the Congress system not develop into a form of international government?
2. Why did British foreign policy desire to maintain the Austrian Empire?
3. Why did Prussia win leadership in Germany from Austria?
4. Did the Industrial Revolution affect the attitude of (a) Britain towards the continental Powers, and (b) of the continental Powers to one another?
5. To what extent was Bismarck at once the creator and the destroyer of Greater Germany?
6. How far did British relations with other Powers in the nineteenth century reflect the permanent features underlying British foreign policy?

Answers will be found at the end of the book.

CHAPTER XII

THE BRITISH EMPIRE AND COMMONWEALTH

THE loss of the American colonies by Britain marked a new stage in the evolution of a unique political organization —the British Commonwealth.

Three years after the close of the American War of Independence, another breach with the past, the campaign against the slave trade began. This lasted for twenty years and ended in 1807 when the trade, which had once been considered a mainstay of British commerce, was made illegal to British subjects altogether. Revolution and disruption in one part of the Empire, social and economic convulsions in another, created a widespread spirit of scepticism in Britain about the permanence of the colonial connexion. In general it was assumed that colonies of the New England type would inevitably became independent, and for some years after the close of the American War there was, therefore, an inclination to favour tropical plantation colonies rather than colonies of settlement. The possessions that remained in North America were generally believed to be of little value.

Colonies as Liabilities

While tropical and sub-tropical colonies were viewed with greater favour the attitude to them was not one of unmixed approbation. Even they could be a great nuisance to the Mother Country and possibly in the long run a source of serious economic loss. After the slave trade was prohibited, and when the demand for emancipation was raised, this was the belief of many planters and others whose fortunes were tied up in the Caribbean colonies. Later, when the Free Traders climbed into the saddle, colonies were denounced as liabilities. It mattered little to such men where Britons settled when they went overseas, since even in foreign countries they would still require British products, and that was the only respect in which they were significant. The Free Traders repudiated the argument of the mercantilists that colonies might be made sources of strength to the Mother Country, for in the world to which they looked forward trade was to be free, and, as peace would reign, considerations of defence were unnecessary.

Nineteenth-Century Trade

Such were the views of many of those who took the trouble to think about the colonies in the three-quarters of a century subsequent to the American Revolution. There were, however, others whose imperial faith was more robust, and between the two extremes stretched many shades of opinion. Even in 1783 there were some people who did not believe that the misunderstandings which had led to the disruption of the first Empire were inseparable from the relationship between the Mother Country and her maturing colonies. They studied the story of the Revolution and the early history of the colonies in order to discover where mistakes had been made so that these might be avoided in the future. As the nineteenth century advanced this section of public opinion grew in strength, and it may be that the change of heart was helped on somewhat by a growing consciousness among Englishmen that the colonies were not so worthless as Cobbett and others had declared them to be. By the thirties, the furs, timber and other forest products, the ships, the fish and foodstuffs of British North America constituted a considerable volume of trade. The population of these colonies was advancing rapidly and their demand for British products was steadily increasing.

There were other reasons that helped to modify the general disbelief in the Empire. At the end of the eighteenth century the population of Britain was increasing at a rate hitherto unknown. Prohibitions of

COLLINS STREET, MELBOURNE

Melbourne, capital of Victoria since 1850, was first settled in during 1835. It has grown to be the largest city in Australia. Its civic life centres upon the broad length of Collins Street and the changes made within a hundred years may be seen by comparing the aquatint of 1840, above, with the photograph on the opposite page taken in 1940.

the seventeenth century seemed unnecessary, when there were more people than the country seemed able to employ. It was at this juncture that Malthus in his book *Essay on Population*, published in 1798, gave currency to gloomy views about the future of England unless something was done to grapple with the mounting tide of population. Emigration was suggested as one way by which the danger might be lessened though the Malthusians never put it forward as a solution of the problem. Even without Malthus the attitude of the British people and government to emigration was changing and the outward movement from Scotland and Ireland

increased rapidly after the Revolution. It was not until the close of the Napoleonic era that it began on a large scale.

With the defeat of France by Germany and the rise of the German Empire the world entered upon a new period of colonial expansion. Though many in high places in England still viewed the acquisition of colonies with disfavour, the idea of Empire now became popular with the British people. In time, despite misgivings and hesitations, Britain joined in with the others in the scramble and the closing decades of the nineteenth century were marked by a new spirit of imperialism. Of major consequence to the Empire and the world was the independent growth of Canada, which has already been chronicled. But while British North America had thus in a century and a half advanced from a position of colonial dependence and obscurity to one of honour among the nations of the world, progress no less remarkable had been taking place in the Antipodes. Though the existence of a great southern continent was suspected by the ancients and though in the sixteenth and seventeenth centuries various European explorers visited the Australian coasts, the exact whereabouts of the continent and its size were still matters of speculation well into the eighteenth century. Indeed, it was not until its close that much was known for certain about New Holland as Australia was then called.

The American Revolution put an end to the practice of transporting convicts to the continental colonies. This occurred at a time when the population of the country was increasing at an unprecedented rate and the tide of crime was rising. Under the unreformed legal system of the period many offences were seriously viewed which today would be considered of slight importance. So it came about that the prison accommodation of the country was wholly inadequate for the increasing need, and the use of floating hulks provided no solution. It was then the British Government remembered that distant continent

whose eastern shores Captain Cook had explored and so favourably described. In January, 1788, Captain Arthur Phillip with 717 convicts of whom 188 were women, guarded by 191 marines and 18 officers, landed at Sydney Cove. So the history of New South Wales and Australia began. Phillip and his immediate successors had many difficulties to surmount. Convicts did not make the best of pioneers, the officers frequently neglected their duty in pursuit of private gain and the guards were often no better than the prisoners they guarded, while some of the governors themselves had conspicuous defects. After the first few critical years, the colony went ahead. The area under crop was increased and in 1797 Captain Macarthur introduced merino sheep and so laid the foundation of the great pastoral industry of Australia.

Shut in between the mountains and the sea the new settlement was indeed a prison from which escape was difficult, but it was not long before the settlers began to seek a way over the Blue Mountains in order to discover what kind of country lay beyond. At last, in 1813, the mountains were crossed and new rich pasture lands were revealed. Exploration in Australia went on through the greater part of the nineteenth century, but as the Murray and its tributaries were discovered and explored and the rich lands of Victoria, New South Wales and Queensland were made known, it was realized that this new great country was far too good a place to be condemned for ever to the function of a convict station.

Party Struggles

Hobart was founded in 1804 and Tasmania became a separate colony in 1825. Settlement began in Queensland in the same year, but it was not until 1859 that this northern part of New South Wales became a separate colony. Western Australia was founded in the year 1829. Batman arrived in what was later to be Victoria in 1835 and South Australia was established in the following year. Thus, within seventy years after the arrival of Phillip, six separate colonies had come into existence.

During the early years of New South Wales, officials and those who were free of the convict taint tried to monopolize all the leading posts in the colony and to debar ex-convicts and their families from their full social and legal rights. Indeed, an attempt was made to erect a colonial aristocracy on the most insubstantial and unjustifiable of all foundations, presumed superior moral worth. This led to a prolonged struggle between the party which took the name of Emancipist, and the Exclusives, but as the wave of free immigration rose both of these older groups were challenged by the new settlers who were concerned not so much with social or legal rights as with wages, prices and freight charges.

End of Convict Emigration

In 1840 the British Government decided to discontinue sending convicts to the Australian Colonies. Tasmania for the next few years received thousands of felons but when saturation point had been reached in that colony, Western Australia became the sole recipient of prisoners; the last convict ship sailed to that colony in 1867. This system was neither wholly bad nor wholly good. It had the merit of giving many victims of unsatisfactory social and economic environment a second chance of which they took full advantage. It provided cheap labour in the early period which enabled much public work to be done that otherwise might have been neglected. When, however, the foundations of the new community were firmly laid and a free labouring class appeared, its period of usefulness was over.

The economic development of Australia reads almost like a fairy story. At first the settlers' lives depended on supplies brought into the country from other parts of the world, but in a few years the colony was able to feed itself. By 1822 Macarthur's wool was judged to be equal to the best Saxon and thirty years later Australia possessed millions of sheep and cattle, and its merino wool was a valuable export. Then in the fifties came the gold discoveries which not only increased the wealth of those fortunate colonies but attracted to them a free, vigorous mining population which has left its mark on the Australian character. In 1850 the total population of all six colonies combined was about four hundred thousand. Ten years later that number had been trebled. The triumph of the steamer over the sailing ship, the completion of the Suez Canal, and the successful installation of refrigeration plants in ships enabled Australia to send wool, cheese, butter, fruit and mutton through the tropics to England.

Australia and Federation

After a period of autocratic rule under governors sent out from England, the principle of representation was extended to the Australian colonies. Between 1855 and 1857 responsible government as it had been worked out in Canada was established in New South Wales, Victoria, South Australia and Tasmania. Queensland followed suit in 1859, and Western Australia in 1890.

The Federal Council of Australasia which was formed in 1885 was the response of the colonies to French and German activities in the neighbouring islands, and was the first genuine move made by the colonies themselves towards federation.

The federation movement had, however, to face many setbacks, but in 1897-98 a federal convention drafted a bill which, when it had been accepted by the people of the colonies, was sent to London, rapidly passed through its various stages and became law in 1900.

New Zealand was first discovered by the Dutch navigator Abel Tasman in the seventeenth century. It was claimed in 1769 by Captain Cook for George III, but for many years after that no attempt was made to establish a colony there. The place acquired an evil reputation at the beginning of the nineteenth century on account of the savage nature of its inhabitants and the lawless crew of whalers, traders and escaped convicts who gathered in the Bay of Islands to prey upon the natives and each other. Missionary efforts began with the arrival of Samuel Marsden in 1814. Various missionary societies were chiefly concerned to convert the natives and to protect them from lawless intruders. In the twenties faint-hearted attempts were

made to take the colonization of New Zealand seriously in hand. The missionaries, however, were against this movement, and the government in England was opposed to any further extensions of British territory. After indication of French interest in the country the reluctant government at home at last ordered formal annexation, and on February 6, 1840, the Treaty of Waitangi was signed by which in return for the guarantee of their rights the Maoris accepted the sovereignty of Queen Victoria. Most of the difficulties in early New Zealand history arose out of disputes over land. Out of these, violent hostility between the Maoris and the settlers developed which culminated in a series of wars. By 1872 these troubles were over and they left behind them a tradition of courage and chivalry on the part of the Maoris that has become the proud inheritance of all New Zealanders. The remarkable Maori race showed itself as gifted in the pursuits of peace as it was quick to learn European methods of warfare. The happy result is that New Zealand has been more successful than any other country in the world in reconciling the interests of a primitive and an advanced race in the same state.

Farming and Refrigeration

The New Zealand Company, which received its charter in 1841, had a turbulent history of over ten years, but in that time it was able to sponsor two very successful colonizing schemes. The Otago and Canterbury colonies showed the wisdom of choosing settlers carefully, for from the beginning the intelligence and stalwart character of these people insured the success of the undertakings.

In 1852 representative government was established in New Zealand. The country was provided with six provincial legislatures, abolished in 1875, and a semi-federal parliament. Responsible government was not mentioned in the constitution of 1852, but nevertheless came to New Zealand in 1856, and in 1907 New Zealand was recognized as a separate dominion.

The economic and social history of New Zealand is one of extremely rapid advance.

BRITISH COMMONWEALTH

This map shows the method of government operating in the individual areas and the principal British sea and air routes.

AND EMPIRE, 1957

It does not include British claims in the Antarctic. Burma and the Sudan have left the Commonwealth since the war.

Forestry, fishing, mining, arable and dairy farming, and pastoral industries were soon flourishing and, with the successful development of refrigeration, already referred to, New Zealand became the dairy of the Mother Country. This dominion has also been a pioneer in social legislation.

The history of South Africa is more colourful than that of the other dominions and it is richer in striking personalities.

Dutch settlements at the Cape passed into British hands in 1806; they contained some twenty-five thousand Europeans, a large number of Cape coloured folk, that is people of mixed origins, and numbers of African slaves. The original dwellers in the country when the white man first arrived, the Bushmen and the Hottentots, gave comparatively little trouble and for the greater part of the Dutch period there was no native question in the sense in which that phrase would be understood today. Already, however, the danger was threatening before the English arrived, for in the eighteenth century the warlike Bantu invaders began to appear on the frontiers, and in the nineteenth century were continually trying to advance southward. This occurred at the very time when Europeans were pushing into the interior. Thus a clash was inevitable. The story of that clash makes up much of South African history in the nineteenth century for the forces of racial antagonism were always smouldering and were constantly blazing up into war. Between 1779 and 1877 there were nine so-called Kaffir wars, and there were more to come.

Great Trek

At first after the British occupation all went well. The two white races were much alike and there was no barrier of religion to part them. Large-minded and generous views of imperial responsibility, such as those which had influenced British policy towards the French in Canada, found little support in Great Britain at this time. So in 1822 it was decided to make English the official language in place of Dutch. Later the law courts were anglicized and in 1833 the slaves were emancipated.

Even during the Dutch regime some farmers had wandered off into the interior and successive governors were confronted with a dangerous tendency to dispersion which they deplored but could not restrain. The men who took part in the Great Trek of 1836-38, therefore, were not beginning a new phase but merely extending one which had already begun. Though this trekking was natural enough, the causes which gave rise to it were short-sightedness, ignorance and misrepresentation. Some of the best people in the colony quitted their homes and set off in search of new lands where they would be free from British control. These trekkers were, however, pronounced individualists and it was not long before they were split up into a number of weak groups.

Independence of Transvaal

In 1843, after the Dutch and the British had both claimed it, Natal became a British colony and the trekkers were denied an access to the sea. Five years later British sovereignty was extended over the Orange River State without much objection on the part of its people, and further extensions were believed to be imminent. In 1852, however, by the Sand River Convention, the full independence of the Transvaal was recognized and two years later by the Bloemfontein Convention independence was given to the Orange River Colony even though it was little desired. By 1857 there were five small and weak Dutch republics in the interior and three British colonies, as British Kaffraria was still recognized as a separate dependency, on the seaboard.

Sir George Grey, one of the ablest of colonial governors in the nineteenth century, believed that some form of unification was essential and so proposed a federation of all the white states in South Africa, but he was not supported at home, and was recalled in 1859, to be reinstated a few months later. Fifteen years afterwards, the Colonial Secretary, Lord Carnarvon, pressed a federal form of government upon South Africa. Although the end in view may have been desirable, his procedure was tactless. Undeterred by the irritation he had caused, Carnarvon worked for con-

CAPITAL OF BRITISH KAFFRARIA IN 1860

King William's Town (Cape Province), founded during the Kaffir War in 1835, was named after King William IV. It was the capital of British Kaffraria from 1847 until 1865, when the district was merged in Cape Colony. In the foreground is seen an ox-wagon, of the type generally used for transport by the Voortrekkers.

federation and in accordance with his instructions Theophilus Shepstone annexed the Transvaal in 1877, claiming that its condition was unsatisfactory and that its future was precarious because of the native danger. This led later to war and finally to the full recognition of Transvaal independence by the Convention of Pretoria (1881), confirmed by the Convention of London (1884).

In order to understand the history of South Africa in the nineteenth century the economic background must be kept in mind. During the Dutch period the Cape had been mainly thought of as a place of refreshment, where ships were refitted on their way to and from the Far East. Under the English it still discharged this function and annually exported small quantities of wool and hides, some mohair and a little wine, but an entirely new phase began with the discovery of diamonds in Griqualand West in 1867, and the manner in which this area was shortly afterwards annexed to the Cape left bitter memories behind.

In the eighties gold was discovered on the Rand, and the Boer Republic, dominated by Paul Kruger, was provided with the sinews of war which enabled him to challenge Great Britain as the paramount power in South Africa.

But the presence of gold stimulated immigration into the Transvaal, and the newcomers, Outlanders, as the Dutch called them, were refused political rights in the farmer republic. At the same time, Cape Colony's desire to extend its influence northwards found active leadership in Cecil Rhodes. The latter was involved in an attempt to force the issue in the Jameson raid, a foray into the Transvaal by supporters of the Outlanders, made in the hope of securing British intervention. But although Rhodes himself disappeared later on from the political scene, the tension could not be allayed and in 1899 the second Boer War came. Though at first the Boers won some victories, the superior resources and power of Great Britain, once these could be brought to bear, told in the end. It was, however, a struggle heroically maintained by the Dutch burgers and left behind it a mingled inheritance of bitter memories and feelings of mutual respect among many of the leading opponents. The Peace of Vereeniging in 1902 was followed on the British side by a definite attempt at conciliation, culminating in 1906-07 in the grant of responsible government to the Transvaal and Orange River State. In 1909 these two colonies, together with Cape Colony and the largely British Natal, agreed upon a union under a constitution which gave South Africa equal status with the elder dominions. So was handed over to the South Africans the task of solving the still burning issues between British and Dutch, and between both white peoples and the black majority of their fellow-countrymen.

A still more difficult problem was presented by Ireland. The status of that country, conquered by England in the Middle Ages, had never been satisfactorily settled. The problem was rendered more intractable when the Reformation added a difference of religion to the racial and cultural differences between the two islands. The reconquest of Ireland in the sixteenth and seventeenth centuries added a foreign and largely absentee landlord class to Irish grievances. The land problem became far more acute in the nineteenth century. This was due to the fact that the growth of population there was not accompanied by industrialization similar to that which occurred elsewhere. The Irish union was never as successful as the Scottish one had been. Thus Irish nationalism developed along lines familiar in the history of other subject nationalities in Europe. In the course of the second half of the century, Ireland was won for a policy of "home rule" or autonomy within the Empire. Opposition to this in England was fortified by the emergence of a dissident group among the Protestants of the north-east of Ireland.

BOER WAR, 1899-1902

Boer scouts on the veldt near Ladysmith; the iron pot was used generally for cooking mealie pap. The primitive tent is of particular interest.

The threat of civil war was postponed by the First World War. Nevertheless, the home rule movement was transformed into a campaign for the establishment of an independent and a united Irish Republic. Rebellion, suppressed in 1916, flared up again after the war. It was only ended in 1922 when the majority of the southern Irish accepted a dominion status for the Irish Free State. Northern Ireland (Ulster), however, remained within the United Kingdom, although it acquired a measure of local self-government.

Later changes made the status of Eire, as the Irish Free State came to be called, so obscure as to baffle elucidation. The Irish Government of Eamon de Valera, who became President of the Executive Council of the Irish Free State in 1932, evinced a strong desire for Eire to be considered as a community apart from the British Commonwealth and Empire. According to de Valera Eire accepted "external association." The king was eliminated from the constitution, the office of governor-general was abolished, the senate was destroyed and then created again. Eire has continued to demand the unification of Ireland, to which Northern Ireland has remained opposed. Eire was neutral in the Second World War and became a completely independent republic in 1948.

Government Policy

The penetration of India by European powers in the seventeenth and eighteenth centuries came when the overlordship of the Mogul Emperors was breaking up. By the Peace of Paris in 1763, the British eliminated their French rivals from the race for supremacy in India. The British East India Company found itself entangled in a welter of political disputes between the various competitors for the different portions of the Mogul inheritance. They were therefore less and less able to escape political responsibilities.

Visitors to India, both British and foreign, in the first half of the nineteenth century frequently referred to the contrast between the peace and order that prevailed in British territories, and the insecurity and violence that were to be found elsewhere.

Lawlessness and fear became habitual to millions of people and the process of pacification was very slow.

Warren Hastings, Monroe, Mountstuart Elphinstone and other administrators during the first century of British rule were strongly opposed to anglicization. They believed that it was their task to build on foundations that already existed, and to adapt and utilize what they found in India. So long as Indian laws and customs were not incompatible with civilized practice they should be retained. They considered it to be essential that the British Government should preserve an impartiality between Hindus and Moslems; but it was difficult for Indians to grasp this policy.

Rule by Princes

From the eighteenth century onward Britain's connexion with India was of a dual nature. Some parts of the country, such as Bengal after 1772, Madras, Bombay and the other provinces, were ruled by the Company while others were still administered by independent princes, whose rights were guaranteed by treaties or other engagements. These provided that the British, while defending the ruler from external attack and internal revolution, should not interfere (except for gross misgovernment) in the internal affairs of the state. The ruler for his part undertook to accept British suzerainty and to surrender to the paramount power the control of his relations with all foreign states. He also accepted a British adviser at his court, and agreed to provide on request his quota of military aid in the defence of India, and generally to co-operate with the government of India in all matters of common interest. The lands of these princes were not British territories and their subjects were not British subjects. In all, there were about 562 states, ranging in size from Hyderabad with an area of 82,313 square miles to a small estate of a few hundred acres. Generally speaking material progress was less rapid in princely India than in British India, though in some of the states it was very considerable, and in certain particulars was in advance of British India. But, while the Indian states played an important and honourable part in the evolution of modern India, it was in British India that the chief impact of West upon East was felt, and it was there that the development of responsible government was carried farthest.

For several years after the Battle of Plassey in 1757, which gave the British control of Bengal, they failed to appreciate the full meaning of their victory. In 1765 Clive inaugurated a system of dual government but the authority of the nabob grew steadily more shadowy, until in 1772 the Company pensioned him off and assumed full responsibility itself. In 1773 North's Regulating Act was passed, and the Company's activities were brought under some measure of parliamentary control.

Then followed the long and brilliant administration of Warren Hastings as Governor-General. The condition of the people greatly improved but by 1784 the affairs of India had become entangled in British domestic politics. Pitt's Act of that year extended the control of the government over the policies of the East India Company. In 1785 Warren Hastings returned to England to be impeached as the reward for his splendid services, while Lord Cornwallis was sent to govern India in 1786. Under him abuses were ruthlessly suppressed and the Civil Service was strengthened and purified.

Wellesley's Administration

In 1793 the Company's Charter was renewed and five years after that the vigorous administration of Wellesley began. It had been made perfectly clear that wars with Indian rulers were contrary to British policy and that further additions of territory were not wanted. But Wellesley boldly embarked upon what he styled "a forward policy," which at that time was probably the only one that could have succeeded in preserving British power.

The Act of 1833 renewing the Company's charter put an end to its commercial functions, though the directors still retained considerable powers. The Act vested all legislative power in the Governor-General in Council, and laid down the principle that Indians should not be debarred from high office by consideration of race, colour or religion. At that time there was little belief among the British in the permanence of their rule in India, and many of them looked forward to a time when India would assume the control of her own government. By self-government, however, they did not mean parliamentary responsible government on the British model, but some form of autocracy which Indians themselves would direct.

Indian Mutiny

In 1833 all members of the councils were Europeans and many years were to pass by before the promise contained in the Act of that year was carried into effect. By the close of Dalhousie's administration, 1856, the consolidation of India had been completed and a degree of political unity attained such as the country had never known. The rule of law was established, but this did not give the general satisfaction to Indians which Europeans and others might have expected.

High-caste Hindus and proud warrior noblemen considered that the principle of equality before the law was highly objectionable.

Though, judged by modern standards, material improvement of India during the first century of British rule was slow, it was meteoric compared with anything the country had known in the past. The first railway was opened in 1853, the first telegraph came into service in the following year. These things caused great alarm to people deeply attached to the old ways, and even the new postal service seemed to have some sinister significance which they felt but could not express. The year 1857 was the centenary of Plassey and many Indians, knowing that in the past empires had come and gone, believed that the time had now arrived when British power must also pass. In 1857 it was not difficult to fan the smouldering fires of suspicion, wounded pride and religious bigotry into flaming revolt. So the Indian Mutiny broke out and was crushed.

At last the Company's rule ended and Parliament assumed responsibility for India. A new department of state was created, the

HOMAGE TO AKBAR

In this miniature painting, now in the Victoria and Albert Museum, by a Mogul painter of the sixteenth century. Akbar the Great, founder of the Mogul Empire, is receiving the submission and homage of Mirza Shah.

H.E.L.—I*

India Office, presided over by a new minister of full cabinet rank, the Secretary of State for India, who was to be assisted by a body known as the Council for India. In order to reassure her Indian subjects and to emphasize the transfer of authority from the Company to Parliament, Queen Victoria in a famous proclamation promised to respect the religions of India, and to admit Indians who were qualified by their character and abilities to high offices in the State.

Though some representation was conceded in the council of the Governor-General and in the enlarged provincial councils of 1861 there was as yet no thought of election. It was made plain that the parliamentary form of government that existed in England was not to be extended to India. This declaration was made because it was believed that that type of government was wholly unsuited to India.

From 1861 onwards the political consciousness of Indians developed rapidly, and as it did so the wish for further instalments of representative institutions grew stronger. In the year 1885 the All-India National Congress was founded, a body which from the beginning called for the extension of parliamentary institutions to India. For many years after its foundation it was loyal to the British connexion and moderate in its outlook, but as the spirit of nationalism grew in intensity, the Congress became more violent.

Hostility to Great Britain

The last decades of the nineteenth century witnessed enormous advances in India, the population increased as never before, the development of modern industries began, India was linked to Britain by cable, and the completion of the Suez Canal drew the two countries even nearer together. But still the caste system and the joint family remained intact. The peasant, now secure in person and property, seldom looked beyond the circumscribed limits of his village life.

Though the sentiment of hostility to Great Britain was to become more articulate and active in the period after 1919, it was already beginning to manifest itself before the close of the nineteenth century. Prior to 1900 Indian politicians, generally speaking, accepted and indeed rejoiced in the British connexion. They nevertheless demanded that as British subjects they should have the same political rights and the same parliamentary institutions in time as their fellow subjects in the self-governing colonies and in England.

Moslem League Formed

Direct election to municipal boards was introduced by Lord Ripon (1883), but no further important development took place until 1892. The Act of that year, however, greatly enlarged the provincial legislative councils, which were now empowered to discuss the Budget and to ask questions on executive business though they were not to vote on these subjects.

The tempo of political life now quickened. The significance of the rapid advance of Japan to a foremost place among the nations of the world was not lost on India.

As India became more politically conscious, and as the spirit of nationalism grew, the mutual suspicions of Moslem and Hindu also increased. Mr. Gandhi's statement that communal rivalry began with British rule is true but only in this sense: that under the Moguls, Hindus were kept in a position of complete subordination, in which no rivalry was possible with their Moslem rulers. During the early part of the nineteenth century communal riots were rare, though they did occur; but in the years prior to 1906 they were more frequent. Whatever the name of the Congress might be—and it was genuinely intended to embrace all communities—it was clear to Moslem leaders that this organization was largely Hindu. In order to protect the rights of their community, therefore, they formed the All-India Moslem League, which met for the first time in December, 1906. Such was the political situation in India when the Morley-Minto reforms were introduced in 1909. A section of the nationalist movement by that time was violently anti-British, though many of the most respected Indian leaders still believed in the British connexion The Moslem and Hindu communities were openly hostile to each other and determined to secure their respective rights. In 1909 the Moslems were successful in establishing their claim to "weightage," that is, more seats in the councils than they were entitled to on the basis of numbers only, and to have the right of voting in the general constituencies as well as in purely Moslem ones.

By the Morley-Minto reforms the principle of election triumphed in the provinces and at the centre, where a small official majority was retained. Nominated unofficial and elected members, however, were in a majority in the provincial councils, and in Bengal there was a clear majority of the elected element. The admission of Indians to high office was at last conceded.

The new councils were not a success. They gave their members full opportunity of obstruction and criticism but they imposed no sense of responsibility. Debates tended, therefore, to be unpractical and wild, and in the meantime Congress and the leaders of Indian political opinion were demanding further advance. They contended that their country should go through the same process of political development as the dominions, and in time should reach the same position. Then the First World War broke out and India threw herself into the struggle wholeheartedly.

It appeared at first that this great national effort was destined to draw the Hindus and Moslems together. In 1916 the Lucknow Pact was produced by leading representatives of the two communities. This seemed to show that a solution of the communal question was possible and

PALACE OF THE GREAT MOGUL

A Mogul artist of the seventeenth century painted this perspective view which is preserved in the Victoria and Albert Museum. It shows the royal palace of a Mogul prince. The emperor is seen upon a wide raised platform; women of the palace are assembled on rich carpets.

INDIAN BLACKSMITHS AT WORK

Blacksmiths at work are still a familiar scene in almost any Indian village. While five men are busy hammering and fashioning various articles, the one on the right is resting upon a charpoy, or string bed, and smoking his narghile, or pipe.

that both sides were ready to compromise. By this pact the principle of communal electorates was conceded by the Hindus, and the Moslems surrendered various points, but those who produced it made it clear that nothing less than full dominion status in the future and complete parliamentary government on the British model would satisfy them. The response of Britain came in 1917 when the Secretary of State for India, on August 20, made his pronouncement in the House of Commons:

> The policy of His Majesty's Government, with which the Government of India are in complete accord, is that of the increasing association of Indians in every branch of the administration and the gradual development of self-governing institutions with a view to the progressive realization of responsible government in India as an integral part of the British Empire. . . .

This in effect meant a revolution in British policy, for now Britain declared that the form of government which for almost a century she had stated to be unsuited to India was to be extended to that country by gradual stages.

Under the Act of 1919 a legislature was set up which consisted of two chambers—a Council of State and a Legislative Assembly. Though it was given wide powers of legislation, responsible government was withheld. Three members of the Governor-General's first executive council under the new system were Indians. The Governor-General was given special powers which enabled him, when he believed it to be in the interests of India, to certify bills which thus became law in spite of a hostile majority in the legislature. Such action was subject to review by Parliament.

It was in the provinces that the main changes were made. All the provincial councils were greatly enlarged and contained seventy per cent elected members who represented general and minority constituencies. The powers of the provincial governments were divided into two classes which were to be known in the future as transferred and reserved groups respectively. The transferred powers, which included education, public health and local government were placed in the hands of ministers responsible to the Council while the reserved functions, that is to say, law and order, land revenue and famine relief remained in the hands of officials responsible to the Governor.

Indian Federation

This system, known as "diarchy," would have been very difficult to work even with a genuine desire on all sides to give it a fair trial. But with Mr. Gandhi preaching non-co-operation, the Moslems infuriated by the supposed injuries inflicted by the Allies on Turkey, and the effects on India of post-war malaise, conditions could scarcely have been more unfavourable.

The division of the functions of government into separate water-tight compartments was impossible to maintain for long. The functions of ministers and officials overlapped; but worse than this was the widespread belief that the scheme was transitional. Almost as soon as the Councils began their sittings members asked for further advances and demanded the appointment of committees to examine the working of the system. Lastly the Congress, by far the strongest and most politically conscious group in India, set itself to ruin the plan and to force the provincial governors to assume official control of the whole field of administration.

It was such considerations that impelled the British Government to antedate the appointment of the Parliamentary Commission by two years, and so the Simon Commission began its work at the end of 1927. The Commission, which concerned itself with the whole of India, believed that a federation which would include provinces and states was desirable and that in the provinces full responsible government should be established. It considered that other forms of representative government might be more suited to an Indian Federation than the parliamentary model. The constitution should have within itself the capacity to change according to need and in the light of experience. These alterations should be carried through by Indians themselves and there should be no more periodic visitations of British parliamentarians. It rejected adult suffrage because of its practical impossibility, since it would mean the placing of one hundred million voters on the lists instead of six million. At the centre it recommended a two-chamber legislature which should reflect the federal principle and in which representatives of British India and of the Indian States should sit together. Responsible government at the centre, however, was not recommended and pending the coming into existence of the Federation, a Council of Greater India should be set up to discuss matters of common concern. The report reluctantly accepted the principle of communalism which it considered to be an open denial of the existence of a common civic spirit between the two chief communities.

The commission and all its work was anathema to the Congress and before the report was produced a widespread civil disobedience movement began in the spring of 1930 from which excesses the Moslems stood aloof.

In spite of these disturbances, and in accordance with the recommendations of the Simon Commission, a series of Round Table conferences was held in 1930-32.

In March, 1933, the British Government outlined its policy in a White Paper, and in the following month a Joint Parliamentary Committee was appointed to make official recommendations. Finally, after exhaustive debates in Parliament, the great bill became law on August 4, 1935.

Separate Provinces

By this Act, Burma was separated from India, and two new provinces were created in India itself, Sind was cut off from Bombay, and Orissa from Bihar. In some of the provinces the Act made provision for two-chamber, and in the others for single-chamber, legislatures. The electorate was increased to over thirty millions. Separate electorates and "weightage" for minority interests were retained. Except in certain discretionary matters, which included the summoning of the legislature, the appointment of ministers, assent to or reservation of bills and the administration of backward areas, the Governor had to act on the advice of ministers responsible to the legislature.

The provinces acquired a separate personality as distinct from India as a whole and ceased to be purely subsidiary units. Thus the much-discussed principle of federalism to a great extent had triumphed over the unitary conception of the constitution championed by the Congress.

Congressmen in Office

The 1935 Act was never given a fair trial. The princes were perturbed by the openly avowed intention of Congress to destroy them. They therefore refused to accept the federal provisions of the Act, which were never put into force. The Moslems were ready to work the provincial councils and Congress was prepared to do so as a temporary makeshift for the good of India. The elections of 1936 returned Congress majorities in seven provinces and after a long and involved discussion over the use of the Governor's safeguards Congressmen were permitted by the "high command" to take office.

Flushed by its victory at the poll Congress determined to be more open in its policy, so it pressed for more rapid constitutional development in princely India, and announced that, in accordance with its contention that India was one, it would absorb the All-India Moslem League and lesser political groups. This merely hardened the determination of the princes to remain aloof and impelled the League to denounce Congress as a purely Hindu body which was seeking to establish a Hindu state. It is significant that, as Congress claims became more vehement, by-elections in Moslem constituencies went increasingly in favour of the League. That body now charged the Congress ministries with numerous outrages against the Moslems which it proceeded to investigate. Finally Mr. Jinnah, the leader of the Moslem League, denounced the whole principle of democratic rule in India. By the beginning of the war the League stood for a separate Moslem nation, it repudiated federation, and in 1940 adopted the demand for Pakstan or "Pakistan," "land of the pure," as it was later called. [This word stands for *P*unjab, *A*fghan Province (North-West Frontier Province), *K*ashmir, *S*ind and Baluchis*tan*.]

When the Viceroy in 1939 committed the country to war without seeking for the assent of the Indian Legislature, Congress found another stick with which to beat the British lion, and continued to stand aloof from the war, since it declared that India could not fight because she was not free. Its provincial governments resigned and the provinces concerned were again British ruled.

By the beginning of 1942, with the Japanese knocking at her gates, it was more than ever necessary that India should be united. The British Government therefore sent Sir Stafford Cripps out with proposals which it was hoped would have the effect of ending party feuds and uniting all Indians in a common effort.

The Cripps proposals were rejected partly because of the growing demand of the Moslems for self-determination to the point of secession in opposition to the stress laid by Congress upon the unity of a future free India, and partly because of failure to agree upon the composition of an interim government to be set up pending the end of the war and the working out of a new constitution. The result was a renewal of civil disobedience by Congress and a period of necessary repression until the external danger was removed by the repulse of Japan. Negotiations along the lines of the Cripps proposal were renewed in 1946. Agreement was reached upon the calling of an Indian Constituent Assembly and upon the lines on which it could work and eventually an interim coalition government was set up.

Hopes which had been raised by the measure of agreement reached were disappointed when the Moslems refused to participate in the Constituent Assembly. Mr. Jinnah and many of his friends declared that Congress's interpretation of the agreed procedure prejudged the issue of Pakistan. At a time when India was feeling the full blast of the world food shortage and when her own resources were increasingly inadequate to meet the needs of a growing population, Indian statesmanship was diverted from the tasks of economic construction to sterile national and religious strife. Local famines and sanguinary communal rioting darkened the Indian scene.

The long deadlock was broken in February, 1947, when the British Government announced that it proposed to transfer power to Indian hands not later than June, 1948. Further negotiations showed that it was unlikely that any single Indian Government could be made responsible at that date and on June 3, 1947, the British Government announced a plan by which two Dominions could be formed, as an interim measure, and put forward the date of handing over power to August of that year. Negotiations between the Viceroy, Lord Louis Mountbatten, and the leaders of the Hindu, Moslem and Sikh communities produced agreement on procedure; boundaries were demarcated, necessary plebiscites held, and negotiations were entered into with the Indian Princes over whom the paramountcy of the Crown would now lapse. On August 15, 1947, power in British India was transferred to the two new independent Dominions of India and Pakistan, whose peoples were free to pursue their own future inside or outside the British Commonwealth.

Both these Dominions in due course decided to become independent republics within the Commonwealth, whose Head they recognize to be the Queen. Many changes, too numerous to mention here, took place in these countries between 1947 and 1956, but the division of territory led to considerable transfers of population——a process which has left great bitterness behind. Unhappily there have been other causes of misunderstanding between India and Pakistan, the most important of which was the dispute over Kashmir. Despite the efforts of Indians and Pakistanis, assisted by others, within the Commonwealth and without, this knotty problem remained to bedevil Indian-Pakistani affairs in 1956. In some respects the relations of each of these Dominions with the Commonwealth have become closer and more friendly since 1947. India, under Mr. Nehru's dynamic leadership, has played a notable part in Asian and, indeed, in world affairs. Pakistan, now the largest of Moslem States, in the face of very great economic, geographic and other difficulties, has succeeded in winning the respect and admiration not only of the Commonwealth but the world at large. In the days to come she may well be a bridge between the Western world and Islam.

Ceylon received complete responsible government in 1947 and in the ensuing years she made notable political, economic and social advances. After the accession to power of Mr. Bandaranaike in 1956 she decided to follow the example of India and Pakistan by becoming a republic within the Commonwealth. In common with other countries of South East Asia, Ceylon's economic development has been materially assisted by her sister nations of the Commonwealth and the United States through the Colombo Plan.

The Dependent Empire

The population of the dependent Empire amounts to about eighty million. This comprises peoples who differ widely in racial type, in the stage of their evolution and in their social, economic and political capacities. During the seventeenth and eighteenth centuries, Britons, like other Europeans, regarded these countries and the people who inhabited them as material to be exploited for their own economic advantage. Then, as a result of the humanitarian revolution, missionary zeal and traditional ideas of British political right, the conception of trusteeship for the well-being of backward peoples evolved. Article XXII of the League of Nations Covenant gave international recognition to this principle which was first fully worked out in the British Empire. But as it was felt trusteeship by itself assigned to the peoples concerned a role largely passive, partnership has now become the aim of British policy in the dependent Empire.

Partnership, it has been realized, must mean much more than instruction in government, and guidance along the political path. Great Britain has never aimed at standardization in the forms of government provided for her dependencies, though, in general, it has been her aim to encourage their political evolution towards the development of representative institutions. As they differ widely from each other in their practical political experience, they exhibit much diversity in their constitutions, which need not, however, be considered at length here. It will be sufficient for the present purpose if it is understood that these divergencies exist. In the period 1946-56 constitutional advance went on at a rate hitherto unknown in British imperial history. Here it is only possible to touch in a very general way upon the changes that have taken place.

Recent Changes

In the Caribbean area, where are to be found some of the oldest of all British colonies, the dream of federation was brought almost to fulfilment. Throughout this whole period the problem of grouping these widely scattered colonies together was continually under discussion, both in England and in the West Indies. In 1948 a memorable report was produced by the Standing Closer Association Committee, upon which were represented all the colonies that were ready to federate. This document outlined a scheme of federation and, after various modifications had been adopted by successive conferences, the proposed constitution was finally elaborated in 1956. It is proposed that there shall be a bicameral federal parliament, consisting of a nominated senate and an elected house of representatives. The senators shall hold their seats for not more than five years without renomination and they will be nominated in such a way that the federating units shall each be represented by two members, except Montserrat which shall have one. The house of representatives will be elected on a universal franchise without property qualification and distribution of seats will take place according to an agreed plan which is a compromise between representation according to population and representation by unit. There will be a federal judiciary from which appeals to the Privy Council will be allowed.

Residuary powers will reside with the federating units. If the wisdom, moderation and political know-how which characterize the Standing Closer Association Committee's report is any evidence of West Indian statesmanship, then the prospects for this new federation are bright indeed. There is no doubt, however, that this new dominion of the Commonwealth will have many difficulties to surmount.

In Africa and Malaya the rate of political advance has been even more astounding. When the war ended in 1945 representative government in these countries existed only in the most rudimentary form, but by 1956 Nigeria had already been provided with a fully developed system of parliamentary government and was on the verge of independence. In Ghana, then called the Gold Coast, the development had gone further, while in Kenya, Tanganyika and Uganda notable political changes were taking place.

In 1953, after very prolonged discussions both in Britain and in Africa, the three territories of Southern Rhodesia, Northern Rhodesia and Nyasaland combined together to form the Federation of Rhodesia and Nyasaland. This is a multi-racial State on whose success is fixed the hopes of many who believe in partnership between the races. Though difficulties have already arisen, some at least of these have been overcome and the foundation of the University College of Rhodesia and Nyasaland points the way to a brighter future. In contrast with the universities of the Union of South Africa, this institution from its foundation will be open to students of all kinds irrespective of race and within its gates strenuous efforts will be made to attain the ideal of true partnership between African, European and Asian. Meanwhile notable economic developments, such as the Kariba scheme, were going forward and this new future dominion was attracting the interest of the investing public in all parts of the world.

Though some industries exist in this section of the Empire the main concern of the people is agriculture, and British partnership must mean assistance and help to the native farmer. British scientific knowledge and experience, British research capacity and technique, British energy and British capital must be placed at the service of these people even in greater measure in the future than in the past.

Again, partnership entails advance in social welfare. It has been decided that the experience and knowledge which Britain has acquired in grappling with social problems at home will be placed at the services of the colonies.

Scientific knowledge has been mobilized for the prosecution of the war against disease. Nothing, however, is possible unless there is rapid advance in education.

Several universities or institutions of university standard have been established and there is no doubt that in the near future full universities will appear in the West Indies, in West Africa and in East Africa, whilst secondary education and elementary education will continue to develop.

This work costs money, and Great Britain by the Colonial Development and Welfare Act, 1940, made a beginning by undertaking to spend £5 million a year for ten years in the promotion of social improvement and to expend another £500,000 a year for the same period on research work connected with the various tasks to be done. In 1945 a second Colonial Development and Welfare Act was passed by which the parliamentary grant was increased to £120 million in the next ten years. In 1950 the total provision for the ten years 1946-56 was increased to £140 million. By the 1955 Act, Parliament provided £80 million for the five years 1955-60. As £40 million of the sums already voted remained unexpended, this means that for these years Parliament is providing £120 million for colonial development.

The Place of Capitalism

But while the role of government in the financing of economic development is of growing importance, it is still felt by many people that the private capitalist has a part to play. It is possible for him to embark upon promising schemes which a public corporation under government control could never consider. These industrial and economic developments, it is hoped, will cause an ever-increasing additional stream of revenue to flow into the local coffers.

It was widely believed in the nineteenth century that self-governing colonies would sooner or later become independent, and independence at that time meant complete separation from the Empire. In the years between the close of the Boer War and the outbreak of the First World War, the scheme of imperial federation which had been mooted in the eighties and nineties was revived. It called for the creation of an Imperial Parliament in which the self-governing units of the Empire would be represented and which would control imperial defence, foreign policy and the government of the dependencies.

While the imperial federation movement thus waxed and waned, representatives of Great Britain and of the self-governing colonies began the practice of meeting from time to time to discuss matters of common concern, in what were called Colonial Conferences.

In 1907 the Colonial Conference became the Imperial Conference, and the self-governing colonies were henceforward known as dominions.

First World War

When war came in 1914, the dominions and India placed great armies in the field; they expended vast sums of money in their war efforts and so won their national status. During the war the Imperial Conference, which did not meet until 1917, became more truly imperial by the inclusion of Indian representatives, and both India and the dominions took their full share in the Peace Conference at Paris. They signed the Peace Treaty and entered the League of Nations as separate states. In the years after the war the dominions set themselves to sweep away the last vestiges of colonialism. They established their right to negotiate and to conclude treaties; they set up legations in various capitals and in general they acted as sovereign powers. These Imperial Conferences, however, important as they were, had no legislative or executive power. They were purely deliberative bodies where a useful exchange of ideas

ST. HELENA IN 1788

When this engraving was published, the island belonged to the British East India Company, and here is shown a view of Jamestown nestling between rocky headlands, with English ships off-shore. Later the island became celebrated as the place of exile of Napoleon.

between imperial statesmen could take place, but they could only suggest lines of policy. The equal status of the dominions and the mother country was given the force of law by the Statute of Westminster in 1931.

The problem of co-operation was then unsolved but today consultation and interchange of opinions between the Prime Ministers and also the governments of the Empire are matters of everyday routine.

The Dominions Office, established in 1925, and now known as the Commonwealth Relations Office, has done much to facilitate communications between the British Government and the governments of the dominions. This process has been still further assisted by the evolution of Dominion Departments of External Relations. Then again, since the close of the First World War, the prestige of Dominion High Commissioners has grown with the growing dignity of the countries they represent and today they are something more than ambassadors. There are also today British High Commissioners in dominion capitals who are frequently men of full cabinet rank. Thus there has arisen an inter-imperial diplomatic service which not only ensures consultation between Great Britain and her partner nations but between the dominions themselves.

Test Yourself

1. Discuss and account for the successive changes in the British attitude towards the problems of Empire.
2. How far was the movement for Irish independence a typical example of the nationalist movements of the nineteenth and twentieth centuries?
3. Discuss the major economic factors in the development of Australia and New Zealand.
4. What successes and failures in racial co-operation has the history of South Africa to show?
5. What major criticisms can fairly be brought against the history of British rule in India?
6. What lessons in colonial policy can be drawn from the history of the British West Indies?

Answers will be found at the end of the book.

CHAPTER XIII

EUROPEAN EXPANSION IN AFRICA AND SOUTH-EAST ASIA

WITH the partial exception of Asia, all the five continents of the world were ruled in 1939 by Europeans or people of European descent. The stages by which this was achieved in the Americas, in Australasia and in the East, are described in other chapters of this book. Here we are concerned with the establishment of European control in Africa, Ceylon, Malaya and the Dutch East Indies.

The ancient Greeks and Romans knew little of the world that lay beyond the southern coast of the Mediterranean. It is true that they were in close and continuous touch with Egypt. Herodotus visited it in the fifth century B.C., and has preserved for us not only an account of the country as it was in his day, but also a number of the more or less fabulous stories he picked up there concerning the interior of Africa. The problem of the sources of the Nile fascinated him and he went to much trouble questioning witnesses about it. He was also interested in another river farther to the west, whose existence was rumoured in Egypt: the Niger. The search for full knowledge of the course of these two rivers dominated the whole exploration of tropical Africa until the nineteenth century.

Early Exploration

Under the later rulers of Egypt and under the Romans the Red Sea was explored. Traders even ventured out into the Indian Ocean and down the East African coast. One of them wrote a guide-book to this region, in the second half of the first century A.D., describing the coast as far south as Zanzibar; another, Diodorus, sailed on to reach Cape Delgado; a third brought back tales of two great lakes in the interior of Africa. But these were isolated discoveries. They were not followed up. The Romans established themselves in what we now call Tunisia and Libya, but they showed no interest in tropical Africa. Nor did they discover much about the North-west African coast. The ancients, then, had very little reliable information about Africa, and no knowledge of South-east Asia.

Influence of Arabs

In the seventh century A.D., the contact of Rome and Byzantium with the whole world south and east of the Mediterranean was violently interrupted. Mahomet died in 632. Within ten years Arab invaders, sweeping from the east and preaching the gospel of Islam, had subdued Egypt. Their westward surge continued, until by the end of the century the greater part of North Africa was under their control, or at least under their suzerainty. Although they were involved in a continual struggle with the indigenous Berbers, the Arabs succeeded in imposing their religion upon a great majority of the North African peoples. Their influence was much more extensive than ever that of the Romans had been: westwards it reached to Marrakesh and the coast of Morocco, southwards over the Sahara to the middle Niger. Arab merchants developed a considerable trade across the desert, importing West African gold in large quantities. Great cities grew up as commercial centres for this trade: Sijilmasa, for example, on the Oasis of Tafilet in Morocco, Timbuktu and Kano.

Europe had, for a long time, little direct share in this trade. Not that all contact between the northern and southern shores of the Mediterranean had been broken off. Christianity was generally tolerated by the Moslem rulers of North Africa. Something like forty episcopal sees remained, and Carthage continued to be the seat of the Primate. Gradually, too, from the ninth century onwards, Italian merchants began to re-establish themselves at North African ports, building up once more a secure trade, importing gold, pepper, ivory and leather into Europe. Nor were the relations between Europe and Africa confined to trade. In the twelfth century the North African sultans began to hire Christian mercenaries to form their bodyguards, and with the full approval of popes and kings, European soldiers of fortune crossed over in large numbers to serve in Barbary.

Portuguese Expansion

All this is true of the central region of North Africa. To the east and west it was different. In Egypt, Islam was more aggressively self-conscious, more intolerant, and it was the scene of fierce fighting in the later Crusades, especially the Third (1189), Fifth (1217), and Seventh (1248). North-west Africa was inevitably affected by the long struggle between Christians and Moslems in the Iberian peninsula, just across the Strait of Gibraltar; and it was natural, when at last the Moslems were in steady retreat from Europe, that the Christian powers should think of pursuing them into Africa. Besides, much was already known—and a great deal more was rumoured—of the wealth to be drawn from the interior of the continent. Religious zeal and commercial profit thus seemed to go together. They formed a powerful union, more powerful still when a third consideration was joined to them. If the great Moslem port of Ceuta could be seized, it would not only provide a good base for extending the attack more widely on the African mainland, it would in itself be an important strategic acquisition, since it controlled the Strait in much the same way as it is now controlled by the modern Gibraltar. Inspired by these motives— but most of all by the first, for he was a genuine, zealous crusader—King John I of Portugal set his heart on the prize, and after careful preparation he achieved it. A Portuguese army captured Ceuta in 1415.

It proved a disappointing conquest, in the long run hardly justifying the cost of its defence against Arab counter-attacks. Portugal did not go on to found an empire in Morocco: that was to be achieved in the twentieth century by France and Spain.

Nor did Ceuta yield the profits that had been hoped for: the Saharan trade was simply diverted by the Arabs to other Mediterranean ports.

Yet the expedition did show one indirect result, far more important than the capture of the town itself. It determined King John's third son, Prince Henry, who had taken a prominent part in the assault, to devote his life to furthering African exploration, an account of which is given in a previous chapter.

The activity of the Portuguese had not been limited, however, to exploration. They built for themselves forts in West Africa—the greatest of them at Elmina on the Gold Coast—as bases for their trade. Imperial expansion had already begun to pay good dividends: the Portuguese kings drew a considerable revenue from Africa, especially in gold and spices. But all this was a trifle compared to the wealth the Portuguese found in India. The African trade was eclipsed at once, and by the middle of the sixteenth century it was already in decline. Africa was now of value to Portugal mainly for the harbours it could provide for her ships going to and from India round the Cape. They were few and poor: the most important were Ribiera Grande, in the Cape Verde islands, and Mozambique.

First Viceroy in India

The Portuguese established themselves in the East with astonishing speed. Soon after Da Gama's return home in 1499, a large new fleet left Portugal for India, and thereafter these voyages were annual. Quietly and almost at once, Lisbon took the place of Venice as Europe's chief market for Eastern drugs and spices. In 1505 a great expedition was sent out under Francisco de Almeida, who became the king's first viceroy in India. One of his earliest actions was to secure a footing in Ceylon, the only source of cinnamon then known to the world. The Portuguese settled firmly in the coastal plain, leaving the mountainous interior in the hands of the Sinhalese king of Kandy.

The irruption of the Portuguese into the wealthy trade of India did not pass without

PRIMITIVE ART IN THE EAST INDIES

Quaint carvings and, in centre, secret writing, made on bone by islanders in the East Indies.
They are used by the tribal medicine men as magic charms.

challenge. Venice was not the only power whose interests it threatened. The Sultan of Egypt saw at once that if trade between Europe and the East were diverted to the new sea route he would lose the valuable revenue he had previously drawn from transit dues over the isthmus of Suez. And so in 1507 he dispatched a powerful fleet to attack the Portuguese in the Indian Ocean. It won a considerable initial success, after which it was joined by more than a hundred Indian ships; but the combined force was completely defeated by Almeida at Diu in February, 1509. This was one of the decisive battles of Asiatic history, and for a century afterwards the control of the Indian Ocean remained in Portuguese hands

Portuguese ambition did not remain satisfied with the Indian trade. Two years after the battle of Diu they pressed on farther east and took the port of Malacca, the centre of trade with Java, the Spice Islands, China and Japan. They were the masters of an immense commercial empire.

But though trade was their greatest objective, it was not the only one. The second viceroy, Albuquerque, was anxious to encourage colonization. Settlers arrived in Goa (which he established as the capital of the Portuguese dominions in the East): they married Indian wives and made permanent homes there. Nor was the crusading spirit, which had played a great part in Portuguese expansion from the first, by any means dead. Along with the government officials, business men and settlers, came missionaries, the greatest of whom, St. Francis Xavier, began work at Goa in 1542.

This is what distinguishes the imperialism of Portugal from that of the Dutch, the English and the French, who inherited her power in the East. She was engaged from the outset in building up a new state in Asia, a political, not merely a commercial, empire. Her successors were, by intention, traders, and traders only.

The attempt was heroic, but it was bound

The Talipat Tree

MEAL-TIME CUSTOM IN CEYLON

Meals among the Sinhalese in the seventeenth century were frugal, short and unsocial. The head of the family was served first. Seated upon a mat, as shown in this engraving from "Historical Relation of Ceylon," by Robert Knox, 1681, he took his solitary repast waited upon by his wife, who is serving him with curried rice from a chattie or earthen pot, and with drinks from a vessel with a spout. Only when he had eaten did his wife serve the children and then herself.

to fail; for Portugal had not the resources it demanded. Her empire was built up without any thought of the cost. The wastage of men was enormous—far greater than she could afford. So long as she was without dangerous rivals, she could just maintain her position. Immediately she had to fight for it, her power collapsed.

In 1580 King Henry of Portugal died, childless. The successful claimant to his throne was the Spanish king, Philip II; and so, for the next sixty years, the Portuguese and Spanish empires were united. This meant that Spain's enemies, the Dutch and the English, now became Portugal's enemies, too. But whereas Spain was strong enough, militarily and economically, to ward off their blows and to retaliate upon them with some success, that was beyond the strength of Portugal. In 1595 the Dutch began to invade the Portuguese empire, and in the first half of the seventeenth century it seemed almost to shrivel away before them. By 1605 they were established at Amboyna in the Moluccas, the very heart of the spice trade; in 1617 they founded Batavia on the north coast of Java, commanding the very important Sunda Straits; they expelled the Portuguese from Ceylon (1638-56); in 1641 they took Malacca. They commanded the trade of the East Indies.

Their position there was built up at the expense not only of the Portuguese: English and French rivals had to make way for them as well. The English East India Company (founded in 1600), was forced back from the East Indies on to the mainland of India—which was seen in the end as a stroke of good luck, but appeared at the time as a wretched makeshift.

It was at first much the same story in Africa. One by one the main Portuguese bases fell into Dutch hands: Arguin, Elmina, Loanda, St. Helena. In the Indian Ocean they took Mauritius and dangerously threatened Mozambique. At two important points, moreover, they founded new forts. In West Africa in 1621 they bought from the natives the island of Goree, in a vital strategic position just below Cape Verde. And in 1652 they took another step, which was to have momentous consequences in the future. The Dutch East India Company founded a station at the Cape of Good Hope. It was intended to be a calling-point and no more, a harbour, a store for provisions and a garden for growing the fresh vegetables that the ships needed. As long as the Dutch controlled the Cape, they always saw it in that light. For a little while, it is true, at the close of the seventeenth century, colonization was encouraged, and besides the Dutch

278

settlers who came out at this time— "Afrikanders," as they came to be called— there was an important group of Huguenots expelled from France by Louis XIV. But this policy was soon reversed. The Company went back to its old plan of keeping the Cape as a calling-point only, and its governors tried—though in vain—to limit its boundaries. For already, in spite of innumerable regulations to the contrary, the Dutch settlers had become cattle-farmers, wandering ever farther and farther inland to search for good pasture and to evade the irksome control of the Company. The history of trekking in South Africa is almost as old as white settlement there.

In the earlier seventeenth century it looked as if the Dutch were going to succeed, without much trouble, to the entire Portuguese position in Africa. But it did not happen that way. They soon found themselves in the same difficulty as the Portuguese: they, too, were a small people, short of manpower, strictly limited in economic resources, hedged about with jealous enemies. It was now, for the first time, that West Africa began to figure prominently in European diplomacy. White men had one objective there—trade, and above all the immensely valuable trade in slaves. France had already begun to establish herself in Senegal. England had a foothold on the Gambia and several small forts farther down on the Gold Coast, scattered between the rather more important posts held by the Dutch, and others belonging to the Swedes and Danes. Here was a fine opportunity for international disputes. There was heavy fighting on the west coast between the English, French and Dutch in the wars of the late seventeenth century. By the peace treaties, so far as England and France were concerned, the *status quo* was usually restored; but at the end of this fifty years' fighting the Dutch had been obliged to withdraw from all their African possessions except the Cape of Good Hope and a few of their Gold Coast forts. England and France were the dominant powers in West Africa.

The Dutch remained undisturbed, however, in their command of the East Indies. No European rival effectively threatened

them there until late in the eighteenth century. The only danger they faced came from internal revolt. The rule of the Dutch East India Company—like that of the English Company in India itself from Clive's time to Cornwallis's—was harsh, for the directors' sole concern was to raise a revenue. Except for the region immediately round Batavia, Java was not ruled directly by the Dutch, but through native regents. So long as the regents met the requests of the Dutch for supplies they were allowed to rule their subjects much as they pleased and could count on the support of the Company. Their harshness, however, frequently led to trouble. In the middle of the eighteenth century it provoked a rebellion that raged and smouldered in Java for seventeen years.

Ever since their withdrawal from the East Indies early in the seventeenth century, the British had offered no threat to the

WOMEN OF AFRICA IN THE FIELDS

Among the Negroes of Africa, agricultural work in the fields has from time immemorial been the lot of women. Here they are seen hoeing, carrying the grain in baskets and grinding corn in a primitive handmill.

continued supremacy of the Dutch in that region. Late in the eighteenth century, however, they began to take measures in the Indian Ocean that the Dutch regarded with serious alarm.

In the War of American Independence (1776-83), Britain came very near to losing command of the Bay of Bengal, which was essential to the maintenance of her whole position in India. This was due partly to the genius of the opposing commander, Suffren—one of the ablest admirals in French history—and partly to the disgraceful condition into which the British fleet had been allowed to fall during the years of peace since 1763. But it was also caused by a grave strategic weakness.

British Capture Ceylon

Britain had only one naval base in India—at Bombay on the west coast. The Dutch, on the other hand, had an excellent harbour at Trincomalee in Ceylon, not to mention Batavia farther east. Warren Hastings thought of establishing a British base in Sumatra, and approached two native rulers for their permission; but the Dutch saw to it that they refused. In 1786, however, Captain Francis Light succeeded in buying the island of Penang for this purpose from the sultan of Kedah, to which, fourteen years later, was added a stretch of the opposite mainland of Malaya, known ever since as Province Wellesley.

In 1795 the armies of the French Revolution overran Holland and turned it into a republic, which soon declared war on Britain as France's enemy. This offered Britain a great opportunity, and she was quick to take it. The Dutch calling-station at the Cape was captured at once, and before the year was out an expedition was sent to Ceylon. Trincomalee and Colombo were taken. The island passed out of Dutch hands for ever.

For the moment Britain was too much occupied, fighting in Europe, to press home the attack any further. The Dutch used the delay to strengthen their position as much as they could; and the republican government showed its spirit by initiating reforms in its eastern empire. First, and most important, the Company was abolished in 1800, the Dutch colonies passing into the direct control of the government. Then came a whole series of administrative changes, designed to end the misrule that had undoubtedly gone on under the Company. The distinguished soldier Daendels was sent out in 1808 as governor-general, and he entered on the new policy with enthusiasm. But he was not given time to complete his work. He was superseded in 1811. In August of that year the British landed in Java and, without difficulty, defeated the Dutch forces there. Lord Minto, the governor-general of India, who had personally accompanied the expeditionary force, left behind him as lieutenant-governor of the great island a young man of thirty, Stamford Raffles.

Raffles at once set himself to carry on the reforming policy of Daendels, to which he added many features of his own devising. He made a determined attack upon the old monopolies of trade. He did much to improve the conditions of the people, by diminishing the political powers of the regents, starting an inquiry into land tenures, reforming and simplifying the judicial system, and carrying out a multitude of minor administrative changes. Not all his measures were effective—like Daendels, he was given only a few years of power: —some of them were ill-conceived, and many were abandoned by his successors. But he set an altogether new standard of administration for the future. He was passionately interested in the welfare of the Javanese people themselves, and for the first time raised that into a main preoccupation of the government.

British Purchase Singapore

The theories of colonial policy held by Raffles had a considerable permanent influence on Dutch rule. He was extremely indignant when he heard the terms of peace that were settled with Holland in 1814; for though Britain kept the Cape of Good Hope and Ceylon she gave back the rich East Indian colonies she had captured. In 1815, before the actual restoration took place, Raffles was recalled.

He was not left unemployed for long, however. In 1818 he became governor of

Bencoolen, a dilapidated settlement belonging to the East India Company on the southern coast of Sumatra. Here he showed the same vigour as in Java, exploring, botanizing, building schools, establishing personal relations with the chiefs near by. One other thing he did while he was there—the thing for which he is, most of all, remembered in history. He saw the need for a British base in the East, better placed than Bencoolen and more capable of development. He himself discovered a perfect site for it, the almost uninhabited island of Singapore off the southern tip of the Malay peninsula. On his advice the Company bought it from the sultan of Johore in 1819.

Opening-up Africa

By 1713, Britain and France had outrun all their rivals in Africa. They had become —what they remain today—indisputably the leading European powers there, and that meant, above everything else, that they commanded the greatest share in the slave trade.

Ever since Spain had begun to develop her West Indian and South American colonies, a steady stream of African captives had crossed the Atlantic into slavery. Until the Dutch, with their commercial genius, took a hand in it in the early seventeenth century, this trade had been almost entirely controlled by the Spaniards and Portuguese. Now it fell into the hands of England and France, both of whom had important colonies of their own in the New World crying out for labour. In the course of the eighteenth century, these two powers developed the slave trade to a level of efficiency and profit never before reached.

It is impossible to make an accurate estimate of the magnitude of the slave trade, for the statistics are unsatisfactory. When it was at its height in the later eighteenth century, the number of slaves crossing the Atlantic must often have reached 100,000 a year. On the other hand it was an unsteady trade. Its profits were subject to severe fluctuations. They were usually high, but might at any time be diminished or cut off altogether by war, either in the Atlantic or in the interior of

Africa, by disease, by storms at sea, by the carelessness or brutality of the slave-ships' captains.

Perhaps one gains the best idea of the scale of the whole business from a few figures relating to a single English town, Liverpool, which by the end of the eighteenth century had become, beyond question, the greatest slave port in Europe. (They are to be accepted with all the caution due to eighteenth-century statistics, but they are not likely to be very far from the truth.) In 1765—just after the end of the Seven Years War—Liverpool ships transported 24,200 slaves from Africa to the New World. In 1779, the second year of the War of American Independence, the number fell catastrophically to 1,205. In the eleven years of peace, 1783-93, when the trade had recovered, 303,737 slaves were conveyed in Liverpool ships. They brought in a little over £15 million. Deducting all expenses, that represents a profit of more than thirty per cent, or something like £300,000 a year. Then in ten years of war (1795-1804), ships from the three ports of London, Bristol and Liverpool together carried 389,923 slaves, of which Liverpool's share was about eighty-five per cent.

Attack on Slave Trade

As a complement to these figures, we may note that at the census of 1790 the number of slaves in the United States of America was almost exactly 700,000. In 1791 there were a quarter of a million slaves in Jamaica, and about 206,000 in the remaining British West Indies. Two years earlier those in the great French colony of St. Domingo were reckoned at 480,000. A reasonable estimate of the total number of slaves in the whole of North America and the West Indies about 1790 would perhaps be 2,500,000.

There had always been a few people who hated the slave trade and slavery as an institution. In eighteenth-century England, numerous attacks were made upon it, and for the first time they became effective in practice. Motions against the trade now began to come before the House of Commons. They were quickly rejected, but they were true evidence of public disquiet on the subject. In 1787 an effective committee was formed to work for the total abolition of the trade, and William Wilberforce was persuaded to lead the attack in Parliament.

Wilberforce and his friends faced, as they knew they would, a most formidable coalition of opponents. The whole economic system of the West Indies—commercially the most valuable of all the British colonies—was based upon the sugar industry, and sugar demanded a steady supply of slave labour for its cultivation. The West India proprietors were a powerful group in British politics, and the Abolitionists were up against conservatives of every kind, with their strong appeal to the sacred rights of property—which seemed more sacred still after the outbreak of the French Revolution. And then in 1793 Britain went to war. During the Second World War countries came to appreciate the difficulties of passing social legislation in wartime. even when it was not controversial in character. How much more difficult was it then to put through a measure that roused intense opposition, at a time when Britain was fighting for her very life against Napoleon. But it was done: in 1807 an Act of Parliament was passed, altogether prohibiting British subjects from engaging in the slave trade.

Slavery Abolished

But this Act, while it settled one great question, raised, by implication, two others. It prohibited the trade to British subjects. It could not extend to the subjects of other powers. Further, it necessarily called into question the institution of slavery itself. Before long, therefore, a new agitation started. In ten years this second campaign. too, had been brought to a successful conclusion: in 1833 Parliament abolished slavery throughout the British dominions, at a price of £20 million, paid by British taxpayers as compensation.

The other problem was more difficult, and forty years were required for its complete solution. Though some states were willing to follow Britain's lead—Denmark had even preceded her, outlawing her slave trade in 1792—those most deeply involved in the trade hung back. But by bribes of many kinds, by threats and persuasion Britain managed to induce the Portuguese, the Brazilians, the Spaniards, one by one. to abandon the trade; she shamed the French into the same course; the United States put an end to it immediately after the Civil War; and it was through British action that the East African slave trade to Egypt and the Persian Gulf was prohibited in the 1870s.

Effect on Trade

The abolition of the slave trade brought about a revolution in the economy of Africa. Considered simply in commercial terms, it meant cutting off the demand for the most valuable product the continent afforded. The humanitarians in England joined hands with the traders in promoting by every possible means a legitimate commerce that should take the place of the condemned trade and so remove the incentive to African chiefs to go on dabbling in it. This union of Christianity and commerce had its ludicrous side, which Dickens seized on in *Bleak House;* but it was a genuine alliance that deserves respect.

It seemed useless to try to resuscitate the West African gold trade: the fields had been overworked, the trade had shrunk to a trickle, and with the great discoveries of gold in other parts of the world from the fifties onwards, its importance declined still further. But there was one new commodity that West Africa had to offer— palm oil, which now began to be developed on a considerable scale in the Niger delta. It could be used in making candles; it provided a valuable lubricant for machinery; it furnished an important ingredient of margarine. The trade in West African palm-products has been subject, more than most, to fluctuations in price and demand; but in 1938 it accounted for more than a third of Nigeria's total exports.

Such efforts, however, though useful and important, did not achieve their object. The slave trade was not replaced, for a long time to come, by any other of equal value.

It is difficult to over-estimate the harm tropical Africa suffered from the trade. The whole business as it was seen by Europeans was bad enough but worse

SETTLEMENT OF MALACCA, 1795

Malacca, one of the Straits Settlements, was in 1511 captured by Albuquerque and became Portuguese. In 1641 it passed into possession of the Dutch and so remained until 1795, when it became a British possession. This engraving shows the settlement about that date.

things went on in the African interior, of which little or nothing is recorded. For the slaves were seized there by African or Arab middlemen, who systematically raided whole districts at a time, stirring up civil wars between neighbours so that they might buy the prisoners taken by the winning side. The slave trade blighted every region it touched and it killed every other trade in its way.

It was also a serious obstacle to the penetration of the interior of Africa, but humanitarians, traders and scientists alike were now anxious that the interior should be opened up to European influence. Their attention was first concentrated on the problem of the Niger. It had been rumoured for many centuries that there was a great river in West Africa, but nothing was known of its course—some geographers supposed that it was really the upper Nile. The problem was solved by a succession of British explorers, from Mungo Park to Richard Lander, who traced it down to the sea in 1830. Much of this work was financed, wholly or partly, by the British Government, which saw the opening of the interior as a valuable means of helping the campaign against the slave trade. It followed up Lander's success by promoting further investigation of the western Sudan and the Niger basin, notably by Heinrich Barth—a German in British service—in his great journey of 1849 and by W. B. Baikie (1854 and 1857).

A still more famous geographical conundrum was solved at this time. In 1858 J. H. Speke discovered Lake Victoria Nyanza. More important, he recognized it as the source of the White Nile, and on his second journey (1859-63) he was able to prove his case by following the river along almost its entire course from Victoria Nyanza to the Mediterranean.

These five men, though they differed widely from one another in temperament and character, must all be reckoned true explorers. They regarded their work as an object in itself. But the greatest of all African travellers, Livingstone, was not a pure explorer of this type: he began life as a missionary, and he remained one, in his own unique way, to the end. His journeys may almost be regarded as a series of campaigns against the slave trade. In the first and most important of them (1851-56), he traced the whole course of the River Zambesi, crossing Africa from one coast to the other. On the second (1858-64), he was a salaried official of the British Government, charged with the closer examination of the lower Zambesi and its tributaries. His third journey (1866-73) took him farther north, to the region of the great lakes. In the course of it he was relieved, as everybody knows, by H. M. Stanley. And when he died—worn out, travelling on through Africa to the end— Stanley took up his work, though in a wholly different spirit. By an extensive journey (1874-77), he settled some of the problems of East African geography that had baffled Livingstone and followed the great African river, the Congo, to the sea.

Now that the interior of the continent had been mapped in outline, Europeans sought to control it. Many causes lay behind the race for tropical Africa that now ensued (1879-1904). Economically, it was in part a by-product of the industrial development of Europe, a search for new sources of raw materials and wider markets for manufactured goods. Naturally it was furthered by some powerful sectional interests—shipping firms, for instance, like Woermann of Hamburg and the British India Steam Navigation Company. But it is to be seen, quite as much, in strictly political terms, as an extension of the diplomatic struggle of the European powers. African colonies might be worth having merely as coins for international bargaining. (It seems clear that Bismarck regarded them solely in this light.) Some

of them, too, had a real strategic value, affording naval bases, such as Diego Suarez in Madagascar. Then again, there is always in diplomacy the elusive factor of prestige. All the great European powers, except Russia, took part in the scramble. Some of their lesser neighbours, such as Italy and Spain, thought it beneath their dignity to stand aside—they too must have colonies of their own. Finally, it must be remembered that in some regions the race to gain territory in tropical Africa merely speeded up a process of expansion that had been going on for many years past: the French in West Africa, for example, continued to press methodically inland on lines laid down by Faidherbe in the fifties.

Under these impulses, and others besides, the European powers turned tropical Africa into a patchwork of their colonies and protectorates. At the end of twenty-five years' rivalry and hard bargaining, there were only two small states left that were not ruled by Europeans: Liberia, a Negro republic established in 1820 as a settlement for freed American slaves; and the venerable kingdom of Abyssinia, which successfully maintained its independence against the Italians in 1896, though it became their victim forty years later.

France and Britain remained the leading powers in West Africa; and they were

ANCIENT CAPITAL OF THE MALAGASY

Antananarivo, a town on the Ikopa River in Madagascar, was the capital in the days of King Andrianjaka. He had a huge stockade built, within which his house and those of his attendants were built, whilst his subjects lived outside. This illustration from Valentyne's Journal shows the town as it appeared in 1724.

joined by Germany, with her colonies of Togoland and the Cameroons (both dating from 1884), and by the Congo Free State, nominally independent, but in fact ruled as his personal domain by King Leopold II of the Belgians, until he made it over to his country in 1908. The Germans again established themselves farther south, between Angola, which remained in Portuguese hands, and the northern limits of the British Cape Colony.

In East Africa, Portuguese sovereignty was recognized from Delagoa Bay to Cape Delgado. North of that point, the coast was under the loose suzerainty of the Arab Sultan of Zanzibar, which was held to stretch inland also for an indefinite distance. But in 1884 the Germans broke into this region, and in due course the whole east coast was divided between Germany, Britain and Italy. France remained content with the great island of Madagascar and, in the north-east, a share of Somaliland, between British and Italian territory.

International Agreement

The boundaries between these colonies were arbitrarily drawn—often straight lines on inaccurate maps in London or Paris or Berlin—bisecting tribes and disregarding the economic structure of the continent. There can be no doubt that the development of Africa has suffered from its rapid and haphazard partition. The colonial policies of the seven powers involved have differed widely from one another on many important issues. International agreement has, however, been obtained on some points—the extinction of slavery, and the limitation of the traffic in firearms and liquor, for instance. And when, after Germany's defeat in 1918, her colonies became "mandates," held under the supervision of the League of Nations, international agreement on the fundamental principles and objectives of colonial government was brought a step nearer. International administration is another matter. None of the powers now holding African colonies seems prepared to make experiments in that direction.

These newly annexed territories did not become colonies in the full sense of the word. It is impossible for white men to make permanent homes in tropical Africa, except in a few small highland areas in the east. North Africa and South Africa, on the other hand, are temperate regions, whose modern history has been deeply affected by white settlement.

Algeria Founded

In the north, it begins with the French colonization of Algeria. The city of Algiers was for centuries the headquarters of a thriving community of pirates, who harassed the shipping of Western Europe and carried their Christian prisoners off into slavery. Many attempts were made by the maritime powers to suppress this ancient nuisance. The Americans took a hand in 1814; a British squadron bombarded Algiers in 1816, and another was sent in 1824. France determined to end the trouble for ever, and at the same time to display her revived naval and military strength, which had been eclipsed since 1815. She was also afraid of a possible British occupation of Algiers, and decided to get in first. A minor diplomatic dispute in 1827 was followed by the dispatch of a great expedition in 1830. In three weeks the campaign was over, and Algiers had become a French possession.

The new colony made a slow start. It was disapproved of by many Frenchmen at home as expensive and unnecessary; it was misgoverned; it was under constant attack from the unsubdued Arabs who surrounded it. But all the same, it made headway. The effective founders of Algeria were Clauzel and Bugeaud, who firmly laid down the lines its future development was to follow. The central region, round Algiers itself, became an agricultural colony of Europeans. The interior, which for a long time was barred to white men, was controlled by subordinate Arab chiefs. They were backed by a powerful military force, officered by Frenchmen, manned largely by native auxiliaries, the famous Zouaves. In ten years the number of European colonists had reached 30,000. When Bugeaud retired in 1847, there were 109,000. This was a remarkable achievement, due almost entirely to fresh immigration, for the death rate was exceedingly high. In the forties, for instance, it was reckoned at 1,416 per 1,000 births. This rate of development was not maintained. Under the Second Empire, Algeria was grossly mismanaged and a series of disasters fell upon its economy in the sixties. But after the Franco-Prussian War it went ahead very fast. In a little over thirty years the number of colonists doubled. By 1921 it was 791,000. Today it is close on a million, out of a total population for the whole country of about seven and a half millions.

Algeria has always been thought of as an extension of the home country—returning members, for instance, to the French parliament in just the same way as a department of France. It is the richest and most favoured part of the French empire.

The origin of the French protectorate in Tunisia (which was declared in 1881), was similar to that of Algeria. Again, France was anxious to reassert herself after the military defeat of 1870 and to forestall a possible rival—Italy, whose settlers in this region outnumbered the French. Disappointed in Tunis, the Italians fell back upon the less-fertile territory of Libya, which they took in 1912 from its former owners, the Turks, only to lose it again during the Second World War.

Suez Canal Opened

The French were also very anxious to secure control of Egypt: indeed they looked on it almost as theirs by right. They had always taken a close interest in the eastern Mediterranean; they had supported Mehemet Ali, the Pasha of Egypt, against Turkey and Britain in 1839 to 1841; it was a French engineer who planned the Suez Canal, and French investors subscribed more than half the capital with which it was built. In addition, Egypt was a vital link in the chain of British imperial strategy. Ever since 1837 the government mails to India had been carried through the Mediterranean and overland from Alexandria to Suez. The bulk of the shipping that used the canal, from its opening in 1869, was British, and in 1875 Britain

acquired seven-sixteenths of the shares in the canal company. Thus both Britain and France were deeply involved in Egypt. For a time they acted together, but when a rebellion broke out there in 1881, the French refused to join in suppressing it. Britain went ahead alone, and Egypt was under her protection for forty years.

British Protectorate in Egypt

She did much to justify herself as Egypt's protector. From 1883 to 1907 the real ruler of the country was Sir Evelyn Baring (Lord Cromer). He re-formed the entire government, greatly improving its financial position, giving the country a modern system of administration, far superior in honesty and justice to any it had ever known before. It was under his direction, too, that the Sudan was brought under joint Anglo-Egyptian rule in 1898. The regime he initiated there has been one of the outstanding successes of modern colonial administration.

Cromer's government was, however, wholly paternal. It was efficient, just, notably humane; but still it was government by aliens. Egyptian nationalists had always hated the European Powers' intervention, and when Cromer had gone their protests grew louder and more effective. In 1922 Britain agreed to bring her protectorate of Egypt to an end, retaining only a measure of control over her foreign relations and the right to station troops in the country to defend British and Egyptian interests. This settlement was again modified in Egypt's favour in 1936, and ten years later Britain began to withdraw from the last remnants of her privileged position. In 1954 a treaty was signed between the two powers, providing for the evacuation of Egypt by British forces. This was followed in 1956 by the Egyptian government's nationalisation of the Suez Canal.

The future of the joint sovereignty in the Sudan was another difficult issue. The British and Egyptian governments had both come to recognize that the Sudanese must have the right of self-determination, and in 1953 they arrived at an agreement, providing for early elections to a Sudanese parliament and for the establishment of a

SLAVE-DEALING ON THE GOLD COAST
Canoes laden with Negro slaves ply out to the waiting ships. This traffic was prohibited by Britain only in 1807, owing largely to the efforts of William Wilberforce.

totally independent Sudan, if that appeared to be the will of a substantial majority of the electorate. The elections of 1953 put the Nationalist Unity party firmly into power, which at first favoured a close connexion with Egypt but later swung over to advocating complete independence of Egypt and Britain alike.

The Cape of Good Hope was captured by Britain from Holland during the Napoleonic wars and was retained as a British possession in 1814. Since then, South Africa has seen little of the international rivalry that has raged over the rest of the continent. Its history has been dominated instead by two other problems: the relation between the two main European communities, Dutch and British; and the relation between the Europeans and the Africans (who outnumber the white men in the Union of South Africa by nearly four to one).

These two problems have always been closely intertwined. For it was on matters of native policy that the Dutch and British first fell out. The Dutch South African farmers were old-fashioned, conservative, Calvinist folk. They lived solitary lives, out of the world, untouched by new ideas of racial equality, whether they sprang from English humanitarianism or the French Revolution. They had always regarded the Africans as an inferior race, appointed to be slaves for ever. On the whole they treated them kindly, but quite despotically: against white men Africans had no rights, only duties to perform. When a new government was established in Capetown,

with liberal ideas on the treatment of primitive peoples, inevitably it found itself in conflict with the Dutch colonists. They were dismayed and angered by the new policy—above all the emancipation of the slaves in 1833. They took to the old remedy they had always resorted to when the control of their government annoyed them. In 1835 they began to trek off in large numbers into the unknown country to the north of the colony.

Three new settlements ultimately resulted from this Great Trek. The first of them, Natal, was on the coast; and with strategic considerations in mind the British Government stretched out a long arm and annexed it in 1843. The second settlement, round Winburg, was the nucleus of the Orange Free State. This one also passed under British rule for six years, but in 1854 it regained its independence. And lastly there were the scattered groups of trekkers who crossed the Vaal River—the most remote and intransigent of all. Though they described themselves as the South African Republic (the Transvaal) from 1853, they developed scarcely any political cohesion between themselves until the sixties.

The South African colonies, then, were divided into two pairs. To the north were the two Dutch colonies, on the coast the two directly ruled by Britain: Cape Colony, with a mixed population of British and Dutch; Natal, in which the British were soon in an overwhelming majority. In between these four small territories, and everywhere to the north of them, the

Flags shown are the
National Flags in 1914

AFRICA SHOWING
ITS PARTITION
AMONGST THE
EUROPEAN POWERS
1914

MILES
0   500   1000

BRITISH   FRENCH   PORTUGUESE

GERMAN   SPANISH   ITALIAN

BELGIAN   INDEPENDANT
            STATES

ATLANTIC OCEAN

INDIAN OCEAN

MOROCCO
ALGERIA
TUNIS
Tangier Ceuta
Algiers Bizerta
Tripoli
LIBYA
Alexandria
Suez
EGYPT
Cape
Bojador
RIO DE ORO
SENEGAL
FRENCH WEST AFRICA
ANGLO-EGYPTIAN SUDAN
ERITREA
GAMBIA
PORTUGUESE GUINEA
SIERRA LEONE
LIBERIA
IVORY COAST
GOLD COAST
TOGOLAND
NIGERIA
SPANISH GUINEA
CAMEROONS
FRENCH EQUATORIAL AFRICA
BELGIAN CONGO
ABYSSINIA
B. SOMALI
UGANDA
E. AFRICA
PROTECTORATE
ITALIAN SO
GERMAN E. AFRICA
ZANZIBAR
Cape Delgado
Loanda
ANGOLA
RHODESIA
Nyasaland
MOZAMBIQUE
MADAGASCAR
GERMAN S.W. AFRICA
BECHUANALAND
Delagoa
Bay
UNION OF SOUTH AFRICA
Durban
Cape Town
Port Elizabeth

N

Africans kept a measure of independence. Some of them—the Basuto and the Zulus for instance—were redoubtable fighters, not lightly to be interfered with. If the Europeans were to maintain their ascendancy, it was clearly desirable that they should unite, at least in some form of federation, for the purposes of defence. Two attempts were made to bring this about, by Sir George Grey in 1858 and by Lord Carnarvon in 1875-77. Both failed, partly through tactless management, but much more because of a conflict of interest and sentiment between the two pairs of colonies.

The Gold Rush

In the seventies a new economic factor appeared. Diamonds were found, in territory to which the Orange Free State had a good claim; but the diamond fields were annexed by the British Government. Still more important, in 1884 came the beginning of the gold discoveries in the Transvaal. The Rand gold rush and foundation of Johannesburg date from 1886.

The Transvaal Government took the opportunity to make what it could by taxing the prospectors who poured into the country. But the strangers—Outlanders, as they were called—were deeply unpopular. The majority of them, for one thing, were British; and they stood for a conception of life wholly different from that of the Afrikanders. They seemed to belong to almost another world, these bustling, efficient, money-making men, who turned the Rand into a huge new industrial region almost overnight. The Transvaalers did not wish to be drawn into the stream of modern economic life—fifty years before, their grandfathers had deliberately chosen to turn their backs on it. It was no argument to say that the gold discoveries would make them rich: all they wanted was to be left alone. They regarded the Outlanders as spies or intruders inside the country, who might in time demand the re-establishment of British rule, and they made the mistake of treating them as political serfs, hoping to keep them under by denying them the franchise and other civil rights.

They were also alarmed at the expansion of British influence in the country adjoining

the Transvaal to the north through the activity of the British South Africa Company, which secured its charter in 1889 and within a year had begun to take possession of Mashonaland (the central region of what is now called Southern Rhodesia). The Company was under the direction of Cecil Rhodes, who was also Prime Minister of Cape Colony from 1890 to 1896. Its establishment seemed to be part of a sinister design to encircle the Transvaal.

The worst fears of the republic were confirmed by the Jameson Raid in 1895. This was a hare-brained attempt at armed intervention on behalf of the Outlanders, made by a handful of British irresponsibles from the Company's territory. It had no military significance, but it made the political situation a great deal worse, strengthening the Transvaal Government, dividing Afrikanders from British, discrediting the British Government—for it soon appeared that Rhodes knew of the raid beforehand, and it was widely suspected that Chamberlain, the Colonial Secretary in London, knew something about it too.

War could now hardly be avoided. The Transvaal Government refused to modify its repressive measures against the Outlanders—indeed it stiffened them; and it was supported by the Orange Free State. In spite of long negotiations, conducted with conspicuous patience by the British High Commissioner, Milner, the two Dutch republics declared war in 1899.

Boer War

The fighting went badly for Britain until February, 1900, when the main Free State army surrendered at Paardeberg and Ladysmith was relieved. Thenceforward it was a matter of slow guerrilla warfare, which dragged on till 1902.

The peace settlement that followed the war is one of the triumphs of British Liberalism. For three years a cautious policy of reconstruction was pursued by the Conservative government. Then in 1906 the Liberals returned to power. Many of them—including the new Prime Minister, Campbell-Bannerman—had been bitterly opposed to the war while it was being fought. They were now able to show that their "pro-Boer" sentiments were genuine. They quickly announced that responsible government would be given to the Transvaal and the Orange Free State, and this was done in December, 1906, and June, 1907.

Now at last it seemed that the old project of uniting the four colonies under one government might be realized, and a National Congress met at Durban with this purpose in 1908. From its work there emerged the Union of South Africa, in which the four colonies joined together in 1910 to form one self-governing Dominion. There are few examples in history of an equally generous treatment of a defeated people.

Since the Union, though the old antagonism between British and Afrikanders has certainly not died, it has become merged in two other great problems: the treatment of the South African native population, and South African foreign policy. The first of these is, as we have seen, an old question, but it did not become conspicuous so long as the four colonies were separate, each of them free to pursue what native policy it pleased. The Union, however, brought it to the forefront. Since then the general tendency has been to depart from the more liberal British policy, expressed, for instance, in the Cape franchise law, which gave Africans the vote, subject to a literacy and property test. Instead, a policy of segregation has been pursued, designed to keep the lives of white and black South Africans rigidly apart.

Participation in Second World War

The strongest advocates of this policy—they would like to see it pressed much further still—have been the Afrikander Nationalists. They are inveterately hostile to the British connexion, and they have constantly urged that the Union should secede from the Commonwealth. They opposed participation in the First World War, and especially the campaigns for the reduction of the German colonies of South-west and East Africa, in which troops from the Union played an important part. Their sympathies were, all along, with Germany, not only in that war but again in the 1930s

—the extreme Nationalists formed a party on Nazi lines; and in 1939 they did all they could, once more, to keep their country neutral. But the bold and astute political leadership of General Smuts defeated them. It was his greatest achievement to have kept together a United Party, made up of British and moderate Afrikanders, which defeated the National Government in Parliament on the issue of participation in the Second World War in 1939.

British Rule in Ceylon

From 1814 to 1941 the history of the British and Dutch colonies in South-east Asia is quiet and peaceful, compared with the feverish rivalries of Africa. Britain consolidated her hold on Ceylon and extended her influence over the whole Malay peninsula; the Dutch carried further the administrative reforms initiated under the Batavian Republic; the region remained untouched by any great war.

When Britain took over Ceylon in 1795, she found Dutch rule effective only in the coastal plain: the king of Kandy still controlled the interior. After considerable provocation, the British Government determined to end this division of the country by bringing the whole of it under their control, and in 1815 the kingdom was annexed. The Kandyan nobles assisted the British to overthrow the king, who was tyrannical and unpopular; but when they saw what British administration meant—and particularly British justice, which denied them the right to extract arbitrary taxes from their tenants—they repented. For the next thirty years they were restless, giving constant trouble to the government; and it was under their leadership that a rebellion broke out in 1848. Though it was a small affair, suppressed in five days, it pointed to some remediable defects in the administration: in particular, it was clear that the civil service, owing to an unwise policy of economy laid down in the previous decade, was incompetent and out of touch with the people.

Reforms had already been introduced, however, before the rebellion broke out. They were now quickened and soon became effective. There was no further serious

VILLAGE HOUSE IN SUMATRA

Native houses in Sumatra today are similar to that reproduced here from Marsden's " History of Sumatra," published in 1810. Built of roughly trimmed logs, they have wide thatched roofs pinned down by long bamboo poles. On one side the thatch projects over a raised platform, where a woman is seen sewing. In front are two women pounding rice in the hollow of a flat stone, while farther off is a well with a bucket and a long pole by which the water was raised. Within the stockade are to be seen plantain trees and coconut palms, under the shade of which many of the villages are built. Sumatra is the second largest and the westernmost of the great Sunda Islands and is separated from the Malay Peninsula by the Malacca Strait. The island is one of the Dutch East Indies for which a system of government embodying a greater measure of local autonomy in a confederation under the Dutch Crown is being worked out.

INTERIOR OF A COMMUNAL HOUSE, NEW GUINEA

Surrounded by a strange assortment of household goods, this Papuan family is in residence in one of the large communal houses designed to accommodate several families. Such houses were often raised on piles to prevent attack by animals and danger from floods.

discontent in the island. It grew prosperous, especially after 1856, when the government began to restore the ancient irrigation system of the country, which had fallen into disuse centuries earlier. New crops were introduced, above all tea and rubber, which together accounted for about seven-eighths of the total exports of Ceylon in 1940.

But though Ceylon was wealthy and well administered, it could not remain untouched by the rise of nationalism in the East. In 1919 the Ceylon National Congress was founded, on the Indian model, to press for self-government, and this at once fomented inter-communal feeling. Constitutional reforms were introduced in 1924 and 1931, but they were not sufficient to satisfy the Ceylon nationalists. In 1945 a commission recommended a further extension of self-governing powers. In Ceylon, as in India, the safeguarding of minority

interests was the most difficult problem confronting the makers of the new constitution which came into effect in 1948.

Raffles's acquisition of Singapore was greatly disliked by the Dutch, and for a few years they pressed the British Government to abandon it. But in 1824, these attempts having failed, they agreed to accept the British position there, to cede Malacca and to withdraw for ever from the Malay peninsula: the British, on their part, handed over Bencoolen to the Dutch and withdrew altogether from Sumatra. This clear-cut demarcation of spheres of interest put Anglo-Dutch colonial relations in the East on a permanently satisfactory basis and determined the future government of Malaya: had it not been for the treaty of 1824, it is probable that part of the Malay peninsula would today be a Dutch colony.

The three small British colonies in Malaya were now grouped together to form the Straits Settlements. Until 1858 they remained under the rule of the East India Company, which had founded them. Then, with the dissolution of the Company, they were transferred to the India Office; and finally in 1867 they became a Crown Colony. Singapore grew steadily, in the fifties very fast: its trade almost doubled in a decade. Its merchants—the Chinese in particular—complained of the anarchy in the rest of the peninsula, urging the government to take action to end it. After resisting these requests for a long time the British Government at last changed its policy in 1873. The result was that within a year three of the western states—Perak, Selangor and Negri Sembilan—had agreed to accept British Residents. In 1887, Pahang made a similar agreement and in 1895 the four states were federated together. The sultans continued under British advice, to exercise substantial powers. The other five Malayan states came under British control in the twentieth century—Kedah, Perlis, Kelantan and Trengganu in 1909 by a treaty with Siam, their former suzerain; Johore in 1914, in agreement with its sultan.

The outstanding features of the history of British Malaya have been the development of Singapore and of rubber and tin production. Singapore is now a city of half a million people, one of the first ten ports of the world, and has been described as "the exchange mart as well as the gate of the Far East." Rubber-growing dates only from 1877, when seedlings were sent out from Kew for experiment: by 1940 Malaya was producing more than a third of the world's supply, and she produced the same proportion of the total output of tin.

All this means that Malaya is a rich country—immeasurably richer, for instance, than any colony in tropical Africa. Its government has therefore been able to provide social services on an unusually generous scale; and it can afford to discourage effectively the smoking of opium, even though an opium tax has long been one of the principal items of its revenue. In 1946-48 new constitutional arrangements were adopted. A political division was then made between a new Federation of Malaya (containing the nine States and the British Settlements of Malacca and Penang) and Singapore, which became a separate Crown Colony. Political progress in the Federation was impeded by the highly-organized campaign of the Communist terrorists, which reached its greatest intensity in 1950-51 and was then gradually mastered by the government, with the assistance of British troops. New constitutions were introduced, both in the Federation and in Singapore, in 1955. The elections held in the Federation resulted in a spectacular victory for a single coalition of parties, pledged to obtain political independence as fast as possible. A similar development was to be seen in Singapore. The two territories were now firmly set on the way to autonomy, separately or in combination, inside the British Commonwealth or outside it.

Reforms in Administration

When the Dutch recovered their eastern empire in 1816, they did not at once press ahead with the reforming policy that had followed the abolition of their East India Company. The government at home was reactionary and disliked the ideas of the republic; it was in constant difficulties through the uncomfortable union of Holland with Belgium, which lasted till 1833; it was also short of money, and that made it look on the East Indies primarily as a source of revenue. A new company, indeed, was established for their exploitation. True, it was closely controlled by the state; but it was a sinister omen. A fresh rebellion broke out in Java in 1825, and was not suppressed for five years. There was similar trouble in the Moluccas.

Effective and radical reform in the administration was not taken in hand until 1854. In the sixties a new factor appeared: the growth of a colonial opposition at home. One of the fruits of its persistent criticism was the abolition of the government monopoly of cultivation in spices, tea and tobacco, another step away from the old Company tradition. By the seventies private enterprise had come into its own, and state production was declining.

This was an example of the new spirit

that was beginning to inspire the government. In the course of the next seventy years the Dutch built up an admirable system of native administration, both in Java and in the other East Indian islands. In some respects, indeed—in the provision of medical services, for example, and the training of native doctors—it was notably ahead of its time. It is fair to say that in this period Dutch rule lived down its past mistakes and became in many important respects a pattern for the rest of the world.

It was also proposed in the seventies that a start should be made with institutions of popular local government, but after three inquiries the Dutch finally decided that the people were too immature for it to be effective, and the project was shelved until 1903. By the Decentralization Law of that year the central government received power to delegate some of its authority to local councils. The first of them, set up in 1905, covered three towns: two years later a council was established for each Residency in Java. The members were both natives and Europeans, but they were nominated by the government: the principle of election was conceded in 1917.

The modern political development of Java has been closely similar to that of British India. A nationalist movement appeared in 1908, demanding an immediate increase of self-government. It derided each constitutional concession made by the Dutch as inadequate. Thus, when in 1918 a *Volksraad*—an advisory parliament, whose membership was indirectly controlled by the government—was established, one of its first actions was to refuse to send a loyal address to the queen, and its members spent all their time in airing grievances. They behaved, in fact, as members of a representative assembly always behave when they are denied the responsibility of power—the history of the British Dominions and India provides many parallel cases. Dutch concession moved slowly. The *Volksraad* was reconstituted in 1927, with increased scope; but it was still indirectly very much under government influence, Batavia was over-represented on it, and it had no power to control the administration. By this time, however, nothing but sweeping reforms could satisfy the nationalists' demand. Their opportunity came with the Second World War, and after a fierce struggle the Dutch were obliged in 1949 (under pressure from the United Nations Organization) to concede complete independence to their East Indian colonies. The Republic of Indonesia was then established.

The recent history of the Dutch East Indies and Ceylon is highly significant. Faced with strong new nationalist movements all over the world, the European powers are at present withdrawing from many of their old colonial responsibilities, so that the twentieth century is witnessing the end of their world-wide domination, established in the nineteenth. Europe, however, still maintains one supremacy unchallenged. Nationalist movements in Africa and the East, though they differ very much in themselves, are all based upon European doctrines—Liberal, Socialist, Marxist. The political and economic supremacy of Europe may perhaps be declining; but European ideas still dominate the world.

Test Yourself

1. What part did the Portuguese play in the exploration of Africa?
2. Examine the stages by which the African slave trade was suppressed.
3. What is the importance of the career of Sir Stamford Raffles in the history of the Far East?
4. How did Britain come to intervene in the government of Egypt?
5. What were the main causes of the South African War of 1899-1902?
6. Account for the rise of the nationalist movement in the Dutch East Indies.

Answers will be found at the end of the book.

CHAPTER XIV

THE FAR EAST

BEFORE the Christian era there was a great civilized empire in the West and another and perhaps a greater civilization in the Far East, but Rome and China never met. Silk from China found its way to Rome in great quantities by the long land route across the whole breadth of Asia. The Chinese heard of Rome and the Romans vaguely knew that on the other side of the world was the land of the Seres, a vast, well-ordered and populous country inhabited by men of mild and frugal temper and enjoying a high degree of civilization. During many centuries, travellers brought back to the Mediterranean accounts of "that spacious seat of ancient civilization which we call China," but except for a brief period in the thirteenth and fourteenth centuries, when the Mongol Empire extended from the confines of Asia to the heart of Europe, direct intercourse between East and West was prevented by the jealous policy of the kingdoms of Western Asia and by the Isthmus of Suez, the little neck of land which blocked egress from the eastern end of the Mediterranean. It was not until the great Portuguese navigators of the fifteenth century found the way round the Cape of Good Hope into the Indian Ocean, that direct intercourse between Europe and China became possible.

Trade With China

Bartolomeu Dias discovered the Cape of Good Hope in 1486. Some ten years later Vasco da Gama reached India with four ships, the largest of which could have passed through Teddington Lock, and regular trading voyages to the East then began. In 1511 the Portuguese seized Malacca, the great trading centre in the Spice Islands, and established friendly relations with the Chinese merchants from Canton. Portuguese vessels began trading with Canton a few years later, and the Portuguese merchants were allowed to have a settlement of their own on a tiny peninsula in the Canton estuary called Macao,

where they managed their own affairs under the control and jurisdiction of the Chinese officials.

From their settlement at Macao, the Portuguese monopolized the trade of Canton and succeeded in excluding the Dutch and all other European rivals. It was not until the end of the seventeenth century that the East India Company, which had been granted a monopoly of trade in the eastern seas, succeeded in securing a permanent footing at Canton.

Foreign Privileges in China

After 1757 the whole foreign trade of China was carried on at Canton where alone foreign merchants were allowed to reside. Difficulties arose because the Chinese Government regarded Europeans as unruly barbarians incapable of appreciating, or participating in, China's civilization and therefore to be kept in due subjection. The foreign merchants were segregated in a row of buildings known as factories. They submitted to many humiliations because the trade was very lucrative, but they were exposed to the constant risk that if a case of homicide occurred, the Chinese might demand, under the doctrine of responsibility, the surrender of an innocent man for execution. The factory system eventually broke down partly for this reason and partly because after 1800 China fell into a general decay, but chiefly because the Chinese Government, decadent though it was, refused to deal with other sovereign states on a footing of equality. Grievances could not be remedied by negotiation, and eventually war between England and China broke out in 1839.

In 1842 peace was restored by the Treaty of Nanking, which opened the way for America and the chief European Powers. By a series of treaties signed during the next few years, not only was China forced to recognize the equality of other sovereign states, but the scales were tipped against her. For the next hundred years, until the

MAN AND WOMAN PLAYING WITH A CAT; FROM A JAPANESE PRINT, A.D. 1755

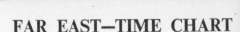

CHINESE DRAGON; 17th CENTURY A.D.

CHINESE BRONZE; A.D. 518

FAR EAST—TIME CHART

B.C.	
1122	Chou dynasty: real history begins.
551	Birth of Confucius.
136	Han dynasty institutes State Examinations.
121	Silk first introduced from China to Europe.

A.D.	
65	Introduction of Buddhism into China.
105	Paper invented in China by Ts'ai Lun.
552	Introduction of Buddhism into Japan.
645	Japan uses China as model to reform administration.
868	First book printed in China.
1231	Mongol Emperor Ghenghiz Khan begins invasion of China.
1271	Marco Polo travels to China.
1280	Khublai Khan establishes Yuan dynasty in China.
1294	First Catholic mission in China established by John of Montecorvino.
1368	Ming dynasty drives Mongols out of China.
1405	Chinese vessels sail to Africa.
1498	Vasco da Gama sails round the Cape.
1514	Trade with China commenced by Portuguese at Canton.
1549	Xavier, great Jesuit missionary, arrives in Japan.
1592	Japanese invade Korea: expelled by Chinese in 1597.
1597	Christians persecuted in Japan.
1637	Japan forbids intercourse with foreign countries.
1644	Ming dynasty overthrown by Manchus. Ch'ing dynasty reigns in Peking.
1661	Emperor K'ang Hsi issues famous Chinese dictionary.
1840–	Opium war. China cedes Hongkong and opens five "treaty ports" to foreign trade.
1842	
1850	Tai-ping rebellion rages for fifteen years.
1856–	Arrow war. Treaty of Tientsin and Conventions of Peking. China opens eight more treaty ports and allows missionaries to live in the interior and legations to be opened in Peking.
1860	
1891	Russia begins building Trans-Siberian Railway.
1894	Sino-Japanese war. Collapse of China starts "battle of the concessions."
1898	The "Hundred Days of Reform." Rise of National movement led by Sun Yat Sen.
1900	Boxer rising and siege of Legations in Peking.
1902	Anglo-Japanese alliance.
1904	Russo-Japanese war: collapse of Russia.
1910	Korea annexed by Japan.
1912	Manchu dynasty abdicates. China becomes a Republic.
1922	Washington Conference. Nine-Power Treaty.
1925	Death of Sun Yat Sen.
1928	National Government established at Nanking under Chiang Kai-Shek.
1931	Mukden incident. Japan takes possession of Manchuria.
1937	Japan starts campaign for conquest of China.
1941	Japan attacks America at Pearl Harbour.
1945	Second World War ends with surrender of Japan.
1949	National government disintegrates. People's Republic of China proclaimed in Peking.

PREPARING SILK; FROM A CHINESE PAINTING, A.D. 1100

abolition of extra-territoriality in 1943, foreigners enjoyed a specially privileged position. They were immune from the jurisdiction of Chinese law or Chinese courts, they had the right to reside in a number of specified towns called treaty ports and in some of these towns they maintained foreign municipal administrations, including control of the police, and levied taxation for municipal purposes. The taxes imposed on the foreign trade were also strictly limited by treaty. These unequal treaties became a bitter grievance but during the whole of the nineteenth century China was in such a state of disorder and her civilization in such a state of decay, that no attempt was made to reform her administration and to secure the abrogation of the unequal treaties until after her defeat by Japan in the first Sino-Japanese war of 1894-95.

Rise of Japan

Japan was discovered by the Portuguese in the middle of the sixteenth century, some thirty years after they first reached Canton. Japan was then approaching the end of a long period of civil war from which she at length emerged at the beginning of the seventeenth century. Peace was restored and a strong central administration set up mainly by the labours of three men who each in turn rose to supreme power—Nobunaga, Hideyoshi and Iyeyasu —the three great national heroes of Japan's century of greatness. Iyeyasu, the head of the Tokugawa clan, became Shogun in 1603. The title Shogun means commanding general. From a very early period the Emperor of Japan had carried out only the ceremonial and sacerdotal duties of his office, while the Shogun actually ruled the warlike clans and kept in subjection the feudal nobles among whom the land of Japan was divided. The Shogun thus usurped supreme power and the title became hereditary in one or other of the great feudal families. In 1603 Iyeyasu founded the Tokugawa Shogunate and established the system under which Japan was governed until 1868. The Emperor was kept in strict seclusion in his palace in Kyoto, closely guarded by the Shogun's

troops, while the Shogun kept court at Yedo, the modern Tokyo.

When the Portuguese first came to Japan the Japanese were eager for intercourse with Europeans, but after a time they became apprehensive of the disruptive effects of the activities of Portuguese and Spanish priests who carried to Japan the feuds which had turned large parts of Europe into a shambles in the name of religion. They also feared that the foreign religion might be the precursor of foreign armies. Eventually the Tokugawa Shoguns took the extreme step of banishing all foreigners with the exception of the Dutch who were shut up in a tiny little island off Nagasaki where their trade was limited to one ship a year. With the exception of this listening post every kind of intercourse with the outside world was forbidden. It was even forbidden to build ships capable of making an ocean voyage. The period of total seclusion lasted until 1853, when the United States, by a show of force, compelled Japan to open her ports and agree to commercial and diplomatic intercourse with foreign nations.

Many Japanese had already realized that the dangers of foreign aggression could not be averted by the ostrich-like policy of seclusion, and many also chafed under the arbitrary prohibitions which prevented Japan from taking an active part in the great movements going on in the world outside and so fulfilling what they believed to be her manifest destiny. The feeling rapidly gained ground that Japan must give up her medieval feudal system and transform herself into an industrial military state on the European model.

Restoration of Emperor's Authority

The method chosen for this change was the restoration of the Emperor to a position of authority which he had not occupied for nearly a thousand years. In 1868 the Shogun resigned his office and restored the administration to the Emperor. In the following year the heads of the four largest clans surrendered their fiefs to the Emperor and their example was soon followed by all the other clans. The Daimyo and the Samurai surrendered their privileges, territorial nobles became ministers in a central administration, the army and the navy were reorganized, bearing arms ceased to be an aristocratic privilege, and in less than ten years the whole administration was remodelled and every vestige of the feudal system removed.

The admiration felt in foreign countries for the patriotism and self-sacrifice which the Japanese people and their leaders displayed, diverted attention from the evil character of Japanese ambitions. The Emperor was assiduously built up as an object of religious veneration. Certain tribal myths regarding the divine origin of the islands of Japan and the descent of the Emperor in an unbroken line from divine ancestors were taught in the schools and universities as authentic history and the system of education was rigidly controlled with the object that every child should be indoctrinated with the belief in a divine land, a divine Emperor and the divine mission of the Yamato race to spread the rule of their Emperor over all neighbouring countries. A constitution was adopted with provisions that ensured that the General Staff, through the Ministers of War and the Navy, could, at any time, override the Prime Minister and the Cabinet and control the national policy.

Japan's War With China

The statesmen who brought about the Meiji Restoration were determined that Japan should fulfil her manifest destiny by conquering an empire on the mainland of Asia; and when they thought the time was ripe they made war on China with the object of detaching Korea from Chinese suzerainty. This act of aggression did not inspire alarm in either England or America. It seemed as if Korea, which was obviously incapable of standing alone, might fall under the domination of Russia and Japan's attack on China in 1894 was interpreted, therefore, as a measure of self-defence against Russia.

In the closing years of the sixteenth century, Russian Cossacks began crossing the Urals and in less than sixty years the first settlements were founded on the shores of the Pacific. Siberia was a vast empty country and the Russian explorers and settlers, following the line of least resistance, kept away from the more thickly populated regions in the south, owing allegiance to the Chinese Empire.

The Manchu Dynasty

The Manchu Dynasty began ruling China in 1644, and this led to a great resurgence of Chinese power under the two great Emperors K'ang Hsi and Ch'ien Lung, who each reigned for sixty years (1662 to 1723 and 1736 to 1796). By the Treaty of Nerchinsk, signed in 1689, the boundary between the two empires was fixed at the watershed running parallel to and a short distance north of the Amur River. Under Ch'ien Lung's successors in the nineteenth century, China fell into a lamentable state of disorder and decay and the advance guard of Russian empire builders began turning their attention to the vast territories south of the Amur River and the warm water ports that lay beyond. Count Muraviev was appointed governor-general of eastern Siberia in 1847 and soon afterwards sent exploring and even military expeditions down the Amur. During the Crimean War the need for quicker and easier communication with the Russian settlements on the Sea of Okhotsk became more urgent. China was in serious difficulties at this time with the Western Powers. Hostilities broke out in 1856, there was serious fighting at the mouth of the Peiho and elsewhere, and an Anglo-French force occupied Peking in 1860. Russia was no party to these disputes, but they presented her with the opportunity she needed. She obtained the cession in 1858 of the left bank of the Amur with rights of navigation and in 1860 the cession of the Maritime Province, also known as the Primorsk, which extends from the mouth of the Amur to the border of Korea. The city of Vladivostok was founded at the extreme southerly point of the Primorsk in 1861, and from that time on it was known that the Russians planned to build a trans-Siberian railway and hoped to gain access to warm water on the coast of Korea or in the Gulf of Pechili. These considerations lent urgency to Japan's programme of

EARLY NINETEENTH-CENTURY CHINESE COURT SCENE

A painting on glass (now in the Victoria and Albert Museum), by a Chinese artist illustrating the great formality which surrounded the Chinese court during the Manchu dynasty. The empress is seen seated upon the veranda of the palace, overlooking an ornamental lake. She is surrounded by high-born ladies of her court, one of whom is taking a cup of tea from an attendant, while others bring gifts. Two ladies-in-waiting stand ready to fan away the flies.

modernization in the nineteenth century.

Construction of the Siberian railway connecting Vladivostok with Russia began in 1891. In 1894, when the railway reached Lake Baikal, Japan made war on China with the object of forestalling Russia in Korea. She inflicted a crushing defeat on China, but by the very completeness of her victory she defeated her own ends. The European Powers, who were taken by surprise by the collapse of China, were not willing to allow Japan to reap the fruits of victory. They believed that China, like Africa, was ripe for carving up into colonies and spheres of influence, and Russia in particular objected to the proposed cession to Japan of the Liaotung Peninsula in South Manchuria, which conflicted with her own ambitions. The first move, which started what is known as the Battle of the Concessions, was the intervention of Russia, France and Germany which forced Japan to give up Liaotung in return for a money indemnity.

France and Russia had just drawn together in Europe in an entente which later became an alliance. They now acted in close accord in China and embarked on a scheme of imperialist penetration by means of state-owned railways. From a Russian sphere in the north and a French sphere in the south-west, railways, owned by Russia and France respectively, were to penetrate to the heart of China, meeting at Hankow on the Yangtse River and thus establish Franco-Russian domination of the wealthiest and most populous provinces of China.

China, however, believed that Russian intervention had saved her from Japanese domination. In 1896 she signed a secret Treaty of Alliance with Russia, granting her the right to carry the Siberian railway straight across Manchuria from Nerchinsk to Vladivostok instead of following the long northward bend of the Amur River. The section running through Manchuria was named the Chinese Eastern Railway. In 1898 Russia obtained the lease of the

Liaotung Peninsula, which Japan had been forced to return to China, together with the right to build a railway connecting the Chinese Eastern Railway with Dairen and Port Arthur, the port and naval base at the southern tip of the peninsula. The Battle of the Concessions reached its climax in 1898. China was forced to grant leases of Kiaochow to Germany, of Liaotung to Russia, of Kwangchouwan to France and of Weihaiwci and the Kowloon territory adjoining Hongkong to Great Britain. Russia obtained prior rights of exploitation in Manchuria, France in the south-west

provinces and Germany in Shantung.

These developments were a menace to the vast commercial interests built up by Great Britain during the previous two hundred years. They also infringed the principles of the open door and equal opportunity which were the only safeguard of China's integrity and which were supported by both Great Britain and America. America took no part in the Battle of the Concessions, and was unwilling to take positive action to defend the open-door principle. Great Britain, however, by the action she took in defence of her own

CULTIVATION OF TEA IN CHINA

One of a series of eighteenth-century Chinese water-colours in the Victoria and Albert Museum shows the cultivation of tea. The Chinese prided themselves upon their keen and refined taste in the art of brewing tea. Connoisseurs, such as the merchant here entertaining two Dutch guests, would drink only the infusion from carefully cultivated and selected leaf which had been brewed in spring water.

interests was able to make a substantial contribution towards preventing the dismemberment of China. She declared that concessions granted to French or Russian interests could not be regarded as industrial or commercial enterprises but as "a political movement against the British interests in the region of the Yangtse." She announced that she would oppose such concessions and that she would not allow foreign powers "to dot the coast of China with stations over which they have complete control." The British Government also obtained from China an exchange of notes in which the Chinese Government acknowledged "the great importance that has always been attached by Great Britain to the retention in Chinese possession of the Yangtse region, now entirely hers, as providing security for the free course and development of trade," and declared that it was "out of the question that territory in it should be mortgaged, leased or ceded to another power."

Russo-Japanese War

The humiliations inflicted upon China during the Battle of the Concessions provoked an anti-foreign movement which culminated in 1900 in the so-called Boxer Rebellion, the siege of the foreign legations in Peking and disorders in many parts of the country. The legations were relieved by an expeditionary force composed of European, American and Japanese troops. The court fled to Jehol and in the general breakdown of Chinese authority Russia, whose influence was already predominant in Korea, took military possession of the whole of Manchuria. The fear of Russian aggression in North China caused Great Britain to abandon one of her most deep-rooted traditions and enter into a military alliance with Japan. The treaty signed on January 30, 1902, safeguarded Japan against the danger of attack by a third power if she were at war with Russia. It was in effect a triumph for the war party in Japan for it made it certain that the questions at issue between Russia and Japan would be settled by war and not by negotiation and adjustment. War broke out in 1904 and again Japan surprised the

world by winning a sweeping victory over Russia. This greatly altered the balance of power in the Far East to the detriment of the countries chiefly concerned—China, Great Britain and America.

American Relations With Japan

During the last half of the nineteenth century, Americans were wholly absorbed in the domestic problems of the civil war and the conquest of the prairies. Towards the end of the century, when the prairies had been occupied and the last of the frontiers conquered, the more energetic spirits began to look outward across the sea again, and the United States began to take an active part in the international relations of the Pacific world. Captain Mahan's famous book, *The Influence of Sea Power upon History*, published 1891, stimulated the growth of imperialistic sentiment which favoured expansion overseas. Hawaii was annexed in 1898 and the Philippines in 1900. American opinion warmly favoured "gallant little Japan" in her struggle against the Russian colossus, and when war between Japan and Russia broke out, Theodore Roosevelt, President of the U.S.A., took action designed to prevent an attack upon Japan by any third power. In effect he made America an unsigned member of the Anglo-Japanese alliance; but no sooner was the war over than a dispute arose between America and Japan over the question of immigration into California. Americans then realized that in annexing the Philippines they had given a hostage to fortune and from then onward until 1941 the guiding principle of American Far Eastern policy was to be complaisant towards Japanese ambitions in Asia in order to give no excuse for a Japanese attack upon the Philippines.

Unfortunately Japanese ambitions rapidly assumed alarming proportions and were still further stimulated by the terms of the Anglo-Japanese alliance in which the British Government committed the extraordinary folly of invoking the assistance of Japan in defending India. Within a short time after the Russo-Japanese War it became the ultimate aim of Japanese policy to exclude British and American interests

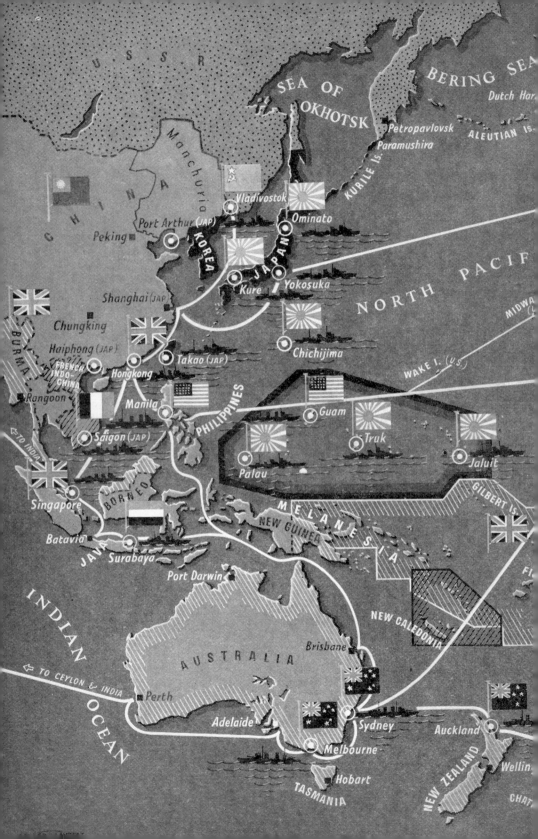

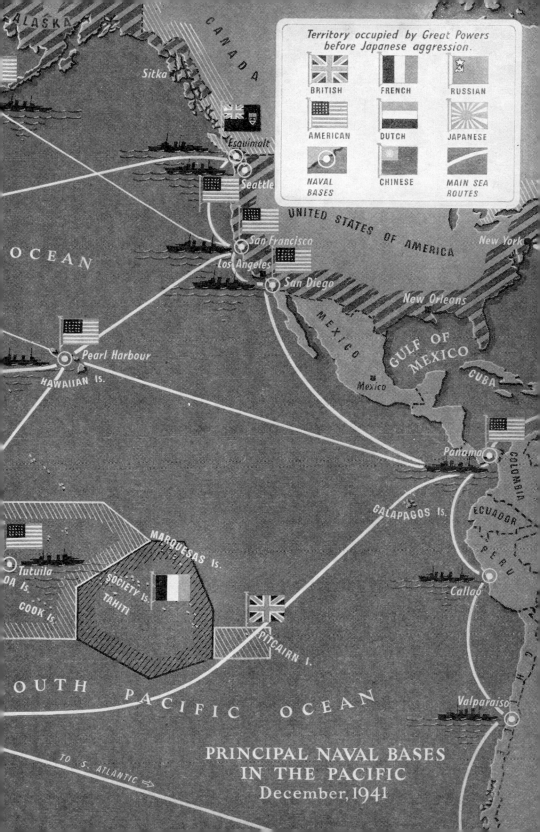

Territory occupied by Great Powers
before Japanese aggression.

BRITISH   FRENCH   RUSSIAN

AMERICAN   DUTCH   JAPANESE

NAVAL   CHINESE   MAIN SEA
BASES   ROUTES

PRINCIPAL NAVAL BASES
IN THE PACIFIC
December, 1941

PORTABLE STAGE IN CHINA

Travelling theatres such as this are even today by no means uncommon in China; the drama has given the masses of illiterates a knowledge of history, folklore and literary traditions. Stylistic in action, the plays are accompanied by traditional songs and, the stage being set up anywhere for the occasion, the actors frequently have to contend with the opposition of jugglers, contortionists and other side shows which provide considerable counter attractions. The painting is in the Victoria and Albert Museum.

from China and to drive the British out of India; but it was not till the First World War broke out in 1914 that the scope of Japanese ambitions became apparent. In the decade between the Russo-Japanese War and the First World War, Russia and Japan, stimulated thereto by the somewhat crude designs of American "big business" in relation to the railways in Manchuria, drew together and in a series of secret agreements (the last of which was signed in 1916) agreed to divide the outlying dependencies of China between them. Eastern Inner Mongolia, and South Manchuria with the South Manchuria Railway were allocated to Japan; Outer Mongolia and North Manchuria with the Chinese Eastern Railway to Russia. When the war broke out Japan sought to extend her sphere of control over China proper. Her first act was to take possession of Kiaochow and the railway built by the Germans connecting Kiaochow with Tsinan, the provincial capital of Shantung. She then, in January, 1915, presented a set of twenty-one demands to China. One of the objects of these demands was to strengthen the Japanese hold on South Manchuria and Eastern Inner Mongolia and to establish a similar stranglehold over Shantung; but there was another category of demands which related to China as a whole. These included demands that China should employ Japanese financial, political and military advisers, establish an arsenal under joint Japanese-Chinese control and obtain a fixed proportion of her arms requirements from Japan, and, in "important places," employ Japanese police officers and place the police under joint Japanese-Chinese control.

Japanese Interests in China

Bowing to the storm of criticism which these demands evoked, Japan abandoned those which contemplated a general control over the Chinese administration, but by means of an ultimatum succeeded in securing from the Chinese Government agreements which greatly strengthened her position in Shantung and in the region north of the Great Wall. As the war progressed Japan gradually laid claim to a general predominance in the affairs of east Asia. At the beginning of 1917 when the Allies needed the assistance of her navy she exacted from England, France and Italy secret promises that they would support her claims at the peace conference to succeed to the German special rights in Shantung. After much manœuvring China was brought into the war and power then fell into the hands of a corrupt group of militarists through whom Japan gained much of the substance of those of the twenty-one demands she had abandoned in 1915. Under the pretext that it was necessary to train and equip a Chinese army to fight on the Western Front a War Participation Bureau was set up and an "arms alliance" was concluded which gave Japan a considerable measure of control over Chinese military establishments and over the Chinese administration generally. Success also attended Japan's efforts to obtain from America recognition of her special position in China.

The war in Europe made security in the Pacific a matter of even greater importance for America than before. This was reflected in her attitude towards Japan. In 1915 when the text of the twenty-one demands became known, Mr. Bryan, the American Secretary of State, informed Japan that though the U.S. had grounds on which to object to the demands relative to Shantung, South Manchuria and Eastern Inner Mongolia, "nevertheless the U.S. frankly recognizes that territorial propinquity creates special relations between Japan and these districts." As the war progressed the U.S. took pains to assure Japan that America would do nothing contrary to Japanese interests in Manchuria, and in 1917 the U.S. Government readily responded to Japan's request for a formal confirmation of Secretary Bryan's assurances. Viscount Ishii was sent on a special mission to Washington to obtain this confirmation and his negotiations with Mr. Lansing, Secretary Bryan's successor, resulted in an exchange of notes dated November 3, 1917, in the following terms:

The Governments of Japan and the United States recognize that territorial propinquity creates special relations between countries, and consequently, the Government of the U.S. recognizes that Japan has special interests in China, particularly in the part to which her possessions are contiguous.

The territorial sovereignty of China, nevertheless, remains unimpaired, and the Government of the U.S. has every confidence in the repeated assurances of the Imperial Japanese Government that, while geographical position gives Japan such special interests, they have no desire to discriminate against the trade of other nations or to disregard the commercial rights heretofore granted by China in treaties with other powers.

While the Lansing-Ishii agreement was being negotiated in Washington revolution broke out in Petrograd (St. Petersburg) and the Russian Empire in Asia fell to pieces. This seemed to the Japanese a heaven-sent opportunity to build up an empire of their own out of the ruins of both China and Russia, and the corrupt puppet government in Peking showed itself to be a willing instrument for this purpose. It changed the name of the War Participation Army to Frontier Defence Army and made a new agreement for military collaboration which gave Japanese armies the right to march through Chinese territory. The allied intervention in Siberia, begun in July, 1918, at the invitation of the President of the United States, seemed to afford an opportunity for Japan to seize control of all eastern Siberia from the Pacific to Lake Baikal. While the other allies contributed about seven thousand men each Japan sent a force of seventy thousand men and endeavoured to gain control of Siberia by the accustomed method of bribing and supporting local leaders. A move was also made against Outer Mongolia which, with the support and encouragement of Russia, had shaken free from Chinese control at the time of the Chinese revolution in 1911. China had formally recognized the autonomy of Outer Mongolia, but in 1919 the Peking Government, acting as cover for Japan, sent an expeditionary force which forcibly reimposed Chinese control. At this moment, however, the tide which had been flowing in Japan's favour turned and ebbed the other way.

Japanese Setbacks

In 1919 the Red Army entered Siberia, advanced as far as Lake Baikal in July and then paused to await developments. Its arrival was the signal for risings throughout eastern Siberia. The White leaders whom Japan supported were little better than brigands, and the people had suffered severely from their cruelties and depredations. Before the end of the year they were all killed or driven out and Soviet administrations were set up in their place. These were subsequently united into the Far Eastern Republic which in turn was later incorporated in the U.S.S.R. In Outer Mongolia also, the Soviet troops appeared in the guise of deliverers and retired after Mongolian autonomy had been restored; and while all this was happening the puppet government kept in power in Peking by Japanese money was overthrown by a combination of rival war lords.

The chief reason for the rapid crumbling of the Japanese position was the onset of the post-war slump in 1920. Japan had made fantastic profits during the war, and while this lasted no one objected to money being wasted in various discreditable ways by those who claimed they were fulfilling

manifest destiny; but when the golden stream dried up the army fell out of favour and it was no longer possible to whip up support for further military adventures. There were thus some grounds for believing that Japan had taken to heart the lesson of Germany's downfall and would be willing to abandon her territorial ambitions in Asia. Both England and America hoped it might be possible to secure her collaboration in an arrangement designed to avert the possibility of future conflict in the Pacific. One of the chief causes of conflict was the competitive scramble for spheres of influence and exclusive privileges in China. Any such arrangement, therefore, would clearly have to be based upon a reaffirmation of the principles of the open door and equal opportunity, and its first objective would have to be the political and economic rehabilitation of China with the friendly co-operation of the powers chiefly concerned.

After preliminary consultation between England and America the delegates of nine countries assembled at Washington at the invitation of President Harding, in the autumn of 1921. The effect of the agreements reached at the Washington Conference was that, in return for a promise by Japan to collaborate with England and America and abandon aggression against China, measures of disarmament were adopted which made it physically impossible for any country to menace or commit aggression against Japan. The object of this collaboration, as expressed in Article 1 of the famous Nine Power Treaty, signed at Washington on February 8, 1922, was "to provide the fullest and most unembarrassed opportunity to China to develop and maintain for herself an effective and stable government." In pursuance of this aim it was agreed that spheres of influence should be abolished and that an attempt should be made to deal with those limitations upon her sovereignty which were China's ground of complaint against the "unequal treaties." The most serious of these were the provisions of the treaties which withdrew foreigners from Chinese jurisdiction and which deprived China of the right to fix

JAPANESE WRESTLERS

This engraving from Montavilla's "Travels in Japan" (1698), depicts a typical scene in a Japanese village. Groups of wrestlers are giving an exhibition in which all the scientific tricks of ju-jutsu are employed. Such bouts were very popular and drew large audiences, as may be gathered from the closely packed crowd against the barrier.

the rate of duties to be levied on her foreign trade. Commissions were therefore appointed to deal with the questions of extra-territoriality and the tariff.

The agreements reached at the Washington Conference were regarded at the time as a triumph of constructive statesmanship. In the inter-war period, the people of all countries desired above all else to be relieved of the burden of armaments and the fact that the limitation of armaments had actually been achieved, diverted attention from miscalculations which, now in the perspective of history, are not difficult to discern. The most serious of

these miscalculations related to the strength of the national movement in China and the essential aims of the traditional policy of Japan. Moreover, the absence of Russia wrecked the Washington Conference as surely as the absence of America wrecked the League of Nations.

The Nationalist movement in China was born in the closing years of the nineteenth century when Sun Yat-sen, the Father of the Chinese Republic, began his career as a revolutionary. It was a natural reaction against the humiliations suffered by China in the war with Japan, the Battle of the Concessions and the Boxer Rebellion, and when the first burst of anti-foreign fury was spent, it took the form of two parallel movements; one was a determination to drive out the Manchu Dynasty and the other was a serious effort to study foreign methods and acquire foreign learning. Both unfortunately led to frustration. The reformers persuaded themselves that the evils afflicting the political life of China would be cured by the expulsion of the Manchus, but when the Manchu Dynasty abdicated in 1912, they had nothing to put in its place except political forms and institutions borrowed from the parliamentary democracies of the West which were wholly unsuited to Chinese conditions.

Weakness of Chinese Republic

The transformation of the empire into a republic did not raise China's status among the nations. On the contrary, she suffered further encroachments upon her sovereign rights. The consular body in Shanghai obtained control of the Chinese courts that administered justice to the large Chinese population in the International Settlement; the collection of customs duties was taken out of Chinese hands and entrusted to foreigners and the diplomatic body in Peking assumed control of the disposition of the customs revenues. This latter encroachment, in particular, was more galling than any that China had suffered from the "unequal treaties" of the nineteenth century; but in the prolonged period of confusion and civil war that followed the revolution, most of China's well-wishers became convinced that her regeneration could only be effected under foreign tutelage. Accordingly, when the Washington Conference met in 1921, the purpose of the friendly collaboration proposed by England and America was to keep China in leading strings for her own good. No change was made in the foreign administered areas in the treaty ports or in the Chinese courts at Shanghai; the customs duties continued to be collected, and the revenue to be controlled by foreigners; China being deemed unfit to exercise the right of tariff autonomy, the conference agreed that the customs duties might be raised from five to seven and a

half per cent provided the additional revenue was spent under foreign control on such purposes as a commission appointed by the conference might decide. Similarly with regard to extra-territoriality another commission was appointed to consider what reforms were necessary before it would be safe to entrust Chinese courts with jurisdiction over foreigners. The Chinese delegates accepted these arrangements because they saw no way of obtaining a more complete measure of restoration of sovereign rights. China seemed to be faced with the bleak alternatives of submitting to Japanese domination or accepting the somewhat patronizing tutelage of England and America; but just about the time that the Washington Conference was meeting, the return of Russia to the Far East opened up a way of escape.

In 1919 the Soviet Deputy Commissar for Foreign Affairs, Karakhan, sent two communications to the Chinese Government stating the desire of the Soviet Government to abandon all Tsarist conquests, restore the Chinese Eastern Railway, return the Boxer indemnity and abolish extra-territoriality and similar privileges. A message was also published in the Press suggesting that the Red Army in Siberia might deliver the Chinese people from the oppression of foreign imperialists. These overtures were not taken seriously.

Relations With Russia

In 1920, however, local civil war resulted in a new combination of warlords replacing the Japanese-controlled puppet government in Peking and soon afterwards a Soviet emissary named Yourin arrived in Peking to negotiate a resumption of commercial relations between China and the Far Eastern Republic. His arrival synchronized with a Soviet inspired campaign against the "unequal treaties" and soon afterwards the new government in Peking cancelled the extra-territorial privileges of Russian subjects and withdrew recognition from the minister and consuls appointed by the Tsar. The nationals of two great European powers, Russia and Germany, had thus lost their rights of extra-territoriality, but China was unable to press her

JAPANESE AGGRESSION IN CHINA 1937-1945

INTERNATIONAL BOUNDARIES		LINE OF JAPANESE PENETRATION 1940	
RAILWAYS		LINE OF JAPANESE PENETRATION 1942	
LINE OF JAPANESE PENETRATION 1937-38		LINE OF JAPANESE PENETRATION 1944	
LINE OF JAPANESE PENETRATION 1938-39-40		ALLEGED AREAS OF CHINESE RESISTANCE BEHIND JAP LINES	

U · S · S · R

CHIFENGHSIEN

MUKDEN

MANCHURIA

KOREA

TARYK

1944 1937-38

PAOTOW KALGAN

TONGKOW

R. HWANG-HO

PEKING

DAIREN (JAP)

1938-39-40

KIACHOW TAIYUAN TIENTSIN

TSINGTAO

YELLOW

SEA

SIAN KAIFENG TSINAN

HAICHOW

SUCHOW

1944

1938-39

NANKING

1942

R YANG-TSE-KIANG

ICHANG

SHANGHAI

1940

HANKOW ANKING HANGCHOW

CHUNGKING

1938-39

HANKANG

BURMA ROAD

NANCHANG

CHANGSHA

1939

WENCHOW

EAST

KWEIYANG

1941

FOOCHOW CHINA

R. SIKIANG

SEA

1944

KWEILIN

1938

FORMOSA

AMOY

1939

CANTON 1938 SWATOW

1941

HONGKONG

FURTHEST EXTENT OF JAPANESE AGGRESSION

CHINA

KOREA

JAPAN

HAINAN

1939

advantage because she was still hopelessly divided against herself.

In 1917, the year when China under the ægis of Japan declared war against Germany, the southern radicals seceded and set up a so-called Constitutionalist government at Canton under Sun Yat-sen, who styled himself generalissimo. The leadership of Sun Yat-sen inspired great enthusiasm among the masses of the Chinese people and the Nationalist Party—the Kuomintang—which he had founded was generally regarded as embodying the one hope of China's regeneration. Unfortunately the Constitutionalist government in Canton was as unstable and as liable to disruption by civil war as the warlord government in Peking. In 1922, just after the Washington Conference had dispersed, Sun Yat-sen was obliged to leave Canton and take refuge in the French Concession at Shanghai. There he met a Soviet representative named Joffe. They agreed that conditions in China were not suited for Communism, but that the Comintern might assist the Chinese Nationalists to overcome both Chinese warlords and foreign imperialists. Sun Yat-sen believed that as the Communist Party had conducted the Russian revolution to a successful issue it might show the Kuomintang how to do the same in China. He was firmly convinced of the friendly and disinterested motives of the Comintern, though in fact the Comintern hardly made any secret of its intention to use the Kuomintang as a weapon to strike a blow at England and America. It hoped to capture control of the Kuomintang, swing the whole Nationalist movement over to Communism, start the world revolution in China, and drive England and America out of China and the British out of India.

Kuomintang Influence Spreads

In 1923, Borodin, an agent of the Comintern, appeared in Canton as adviser to Sun Yat-sen. The reorganization of the Kuomintang carried through on his advice proved extremely effective. Sun Yat-sen adopted the ideas of the single party state, the dictatorship of a single party which should establish and control the government, the committee system of administration for both party and government, intensive political training and the use of slogans, posters, plays and other methods of propaganda. The Kuomintang became the only political party with a definite set of principles and a well-organized administrative machine. Its influence spread rapidly throughout China and it won devoted adherents among the intellectual classes who are the natural leaders of the nation. In 1928, Kuomintang armies entered Peking with scarcely any fighting, the old warlord government disappeared and the new National Government of the Republic of China was established with its capital at Nanking on October 11, 1928.

Communist Interference

The Comintern spent enormous sums in the attempt to place Communists in control of the Kuomintang. The Chinese Communist Party was established by a few intellectuals in 1921, but their numbers increased rapidly after Borodin's arrival in Canton in 1923. Borodin persuaded Sun Yat-sen to allow Communists to become members of the Kuomintang, not as members of the Communist Party, but in their individual capacity, and for a time the Nationalist movement was swept into violent anti-foreign and anti-British courses. The British Government realized, however, that the Nationalist movement had found its feet and that the ideas of tutelage which had dominated the Washington Conference must be abandoned. In December, 1926, it communicated to China and the other signatories of the Nine Power Treaty a memorandum stating its views on this point and declaring its own determination to take immediate steps to meet the Nationalist demand for the abrogation of foreign privileges. Other countries including America came into line, and at about the same time the extremists were discredited by the discovery of documents which proved that the Comintern had been trying to use the Chinese revolution for its own ends and that the Chinese Communists had played an active part in the conspiracy to capture control of the Kuomintang. This enabled the moderate elements in the Kuomintang to gain control. The Communists were proscribed, relations with Soviet Russia were broken off and Borodin and the other agents of the Comintern were expelled in 1927. Friendly relations between the Nationalists and the Western Powers had thus been restored before the establishment of the Nanking Government in 1928.

Mukden Incident

The triumph of the Kuomintang, however, made a conflict with Japan inevitable. A resolution was adopted at the Washington Conference which purported to abolish spheres of interest, but so far as Japan was concerned, the abolition was illusory. She continued to enjoy all the special rights and privileges she had acquired in Manchuria. Her nationals had the right to own land and carry on farming, mining or any kind of business anywhere in the interior without being subject to Chinese jurisdiction. She governed the leased territory of Kwantung (the Liaotung Peninsula), including Dairen and Port Arthur, with practically full rights of sovereignty. She maintained the Kwantung Army in the leased territory, armed forces in many parts of Manchuria, railway guards in the railway areas and consular police throughout the districts. She owned the South Manchuria Railway and administered the railway areas, including several large towns and sections of populous cities and in these areas she controlled education, public utilities and the police and levied taxation for these purposes. Such a position made the exercise of China's sovereignty impossible. The Chinese, therefore, never lost an opportunity to obstruct the Japanese in the enjoyment of their rights or to undermine their position. In Japan, on the other hand, even the liberal elements, on whom England and America relied to carry out the policy agreed upon at Washington, never for a moment relaxed in their determination to maintain and even strengthen the Japanese hold over Manchuria, and when this was seriously threatened by the rising tide of nationalism after 1928, a situation arose which could only be resolved by force. Other causes contributed to the Japanese decision to break away from the Washington agreements. As the world economic crisis deepened, Japan found that she was expected to accept a collaborative role in a part of the world where she aspired to be the leader, while at the same time great injury was inflicted on her material interests and her national honour by restrictive immigration and tariff policies pursued by other powers in flagrant contradiction to the idealistic sentiments expressed in the Nine Power Treaty and the Covenant of the League of Nations. The oligarchs who determine national policy in Japan, therefore, decided that a favourable moment must be found for establishing Japanese control over Manchuria on a secure and permanent basis.

On September 18, 1931, the Japanese Army in Manchuria staged an "incident" on the railway line outside Mukden. Within twenty-four hours Japanese troops occupied all the chief towns in South Manchuria and in the course of the next twelve months the Japanese overran the whole of Manchuria, including the Russian zone in the north, and set up the puppet state of Manchukuo. The dispute was referred to the League of Nations but no effective steps were taken to restrain Japan.

Failure of the League

The collective security system supposed to have been established by the Covenant of the League of Nations was an illusion. In theory an aggressor would find overwhelming force arrayed against him and would therefore desist without any force being used. In fact, of the powers, apart from China, principally concerned — Russia, America and Great Britain—only Great Britain was a member of the League. Russia remained studiously aloof and America, equally isolationist, was determined to take no positive action either military or economic. Moreover, at the Washington Conference, England and America had both disarmed, had surrendered command of the sea in the Pacific, and had placed Japan in an impregnable position. Mr. Stimson, the American Secretary of State, was anxious to co-operate with the League. He believed that if the moral opinion of the world were mobilized it would prove an effective substitute for sanctions, but the result proved that he was mistaken.

Japan Withdraws From the League

The mere fact that Japan's actions were discussed by the League Powers at Geneva inflamed public opinion in Japan in support of the extremist policy of the army. In February, 1933, the Japanese Government gave notice of withdrawal from the League of Nations and Japan was then swept by a tempest of aggressive nationalism. The liberal elements retreated all along the line, assassination became a normal feature of political life and the government moved steadily towards complete totalitarianism. During the next four years preparations were openly made for renewed aggression on China. By various discreditable and violent means Japan endeavoured to penetrate into Inner Mongolia and to undermine Chinese authority in North China. They made no secret of their intention to detach the five northern provinces from China and on July 7, 1937, the army repeating the manoeuvre of 1931, staged an incident at the Marco Polo Bridge (Lukouchiao) near Peking. The Chinese Government rejected the Japanese proposal to localize the incident and this was the beginning of an eight-year war which was brought to a close only by the Japanese surrender in August, 1945.

China appealed again to the League of Nations, but the situation in Europe was much graver even than in 1931, and without America it was clear that nothing could be done. In order to ascertain beyond all doubt whether America was willing to take action the Council of the League referred the dispute to a conference of the parties to the Nine Power Treaty. The conference met in Brussels in November, 1937, and before it opened President Roosevelt tested public opinion in a speech at Chicago on October 5, in which he suggested that aggressor nations might be put in quarantine. The response, however, demonstrated that America had withdrawn deeper into isolationism than in 1931, and the powers

friendly to China could do no more than promise that they would individually give her such aid as was practicable.

The Chinese armies met with some successes in the earlier battles of the war, but superior skill and armaments prevailed, and the Chinese Government was forced to withdraw first to Hankow and then, in November, 1938, to Chungking, above the Yangtse gorges, which became the capital of Free China for the remainder of the war. The Chinese were encouraged to keep up their resistance to Japan by the hope that one day England and America would be drawn into the war. They did not realize how fatally England had weakened herself and strengthened Japan by her surrender of the command of the sea, and the rapid collapse of the British Empire in the Far East after the attack upon Pearl Harbour in December, 1941, was, therefore, a bitter disappointment. On the long view, however, though Pearl Harbour was a shattering blow, the decision of the Japanese High Command to attack both America and the British Empire ensured the ultimate defeat of Japan for it was only the direct attack by Japan that drew America out of isolationism and brought her into the war.

Communists and Manchuria

Though Japan has been defeated and cannot again become a menace for many years to come, after the Japanese surrender China was faced with fresh difficulties owing to the situation which developed during the war in regard to the Communists in north-west China. After Borodin's expulsion in 1927, Communist cells in various parts of South China maintained independent Soviet governments, and annual campaigns were waged by the Kuomintang armies under Chiang Kai-shek in order to suppress them. Eventually, in 1934, the Communists executed the famous Long March and settled down in the barren mountainous region where the boundaries of the three provinces, Shensi, Kansu and Ninghsia, meet. There they established the Shen-Kan-Ning Border Government which has continued to maintain close relations with the Comintern. The Press and radio in the Communist capital at Yenan copied the political line laid down in Moscow, but after 1927 the Chinese Communists received no aid from Russia or the Comintern.

The failure of the Comintern's policy in China was used as an argument by both sides in the conflict between Stalin and the Trotskyist opposition which was reaching its climax. Although the Comintern Congress of 1928 was dominated by Stalin, its general line was a revolutionary one. On the other hand, the reaction in China against both Communists and Russians was so strong that there was little opportunity for Comintern policy to be made effective. From 1931 onwards, Soviet policy in the Far East was increasingly affected by the growth of Japanese power after the occupation of Manchuria; Russian interests required that China should be able to resist Japan and this aim would be impeded by the encouragement of separatist Communist movements. Chinese Communism accordingly began to veer towards seeking a new period of national collaboration in order to resist the Japanese. A similar impulse was acted on by European Communist parties after the threat from Hitler became clear in 1933-34.

In 1935, after a lapse of seven years, the world congress of the Comintern met again suddenly in Moscow and passed resolutions instructing the Communist parties in all countries to adopt the policy of the popular front. They must no longer seek to overthrow the government and institutions of their country by violence, but must ally themselves with other parties of the left and seek to gain power by constitutional means. Special instructions were sent to the Communists in China to form a united front with the Kuomintang for the specific purpose of resisting Japanese aggression. The Yenan administration immediately made proposals in this sense which were decisively rejected by Chiang Kai-shek. Their suggestion was that the Communist Party and the Kuomintang should be equal allies in a coalition directed against Japan, but Chiang Kai-shek's view was that this would merely perpetuate the existing disunity, and that unless China were really unified she could not resist aggression.

On the outbreak of war in 1937 an accord was arranged between the National Government and Yenan, but this soon broke down in practice. Yenan continued to maintain its separate army and separate administration, there were clashes between Government and Communist forces and each side accused the other of being more concerned to extend its own areas of authority than to defeat the enemy. The Communists were confined mainly to rural and mountainous regions, and in the concluding stages of the war the chief anxiety of the Government was that they might take possession of cities evacuated by retreating Japanese. Fears were also expressed that if Russia entered the war against Japan she might seek to regain the rights and privileges which the Tsarist Government had obtained in Manchuria and that she might find the Communists a useful instrument for this purpose.

Defeat of Japan

During 1944 the Allies had to consider how best they could invade and subjugate Japan. If the invading army could be based on Manchuria this would clearly be a less difficult operation than an invasion carried out across the Pacific Ocean. Moreover, if the Allies were forced to adopt the latter alternative it was reported that the Japanese Government and army would retreat and carry on the conflict from Manchuria, which had been developed since 1930 as the industrial base of the Japanese Empire. It seemed imperative, therefore, that Russia should be persuaded to declare war on Japan. The subject was discussed at the Yalta Conference and on February 11, 1945, Stalin, Roosevelt and Churchill agreed that Russia should enter the war against Japan "in two or three months after Germany has surrendered" and that "the former rights of Russia violated by the treacherous attack of Japan in 1904 shall be restored." As regards Manchuria, this meant that Russia was to control the commercial port of Dairen and the naval base of Port Arthur and, as joint owner with China, control the operation of the two great trunk railways formerly known as the Chinese Eastern and the South Manchuria Railways. The agreement was kept secret and it was not until June 15 that its terms were communicated to Chiang Kai-shek. On August 9 Russia declared war on Japan and invaded Manchuria. On August 14 the Yalta stipulations were embodied in a treaty between China and Russia signed at Moscow. Atom bombs were dropped on Hiroshima and Nagasaki and the world war ended with the surrender of Japan on August 15, 1945.

Since 1941 the Kuomingtang had been sinking steadily deeper into corruption and incompetence and the general discontent was reflected in the growing power and prestige of the Communists. Mao Tse-Tung and Chou En-Lai, the leaders at Yenan, were men of high character and great ability. In the regions under communist control they had abolished graft, usury and land-lordism, the traditional abuses which had been the main cause of China's downfall, and by 1945 communists had been set up in fourteen areas reaching as far south as Canton. In these areas the communists had won the mass support of the peasants but they had never been faced with problems such as shipping, tariffs, currency and finance, which are dealt with at the national and international levels. Some form of co-operation between communists and Kuomintang might have provided the ideal solution for China's problems, but any chance there might have been of a settlement on these lines was finally wrecked by America's policy of intervention. The facts are set out in the White Book on China published by the American State Department in August, 1949.

By December, 1945, clashes between the armed forces of the nationalists and communists had become more frequent and General Marshall was sent on a mission to avert the large-scale civil war that seemed to be impending. Four years later, in October, 1949, General Marshall, giving evidence before a State Department conference in Washington, declared that Mao Tse-Tung and Chou En-Lai "undoubtedly were after a peaceful settlement on political lines." The Nationalists, on the other hand, as the White Book points out, "cherished the illusion that they could destroy the Communists by force of arms." General Marshall warned them that any such attempt "not only would fail but would plunge China into chaos and eventually destroy the National Government."

By 1949 inflation of the currency had got beyond control, the railways had ceased running and the people had been reduced to unprecedented depths of misery and despair. When the communists came down from the north "the nationalist armies did not have to be defeated, they disintegrated," and the People's Republic of China was proclaimed in Peking on October 1, 1949. The proclamation of the People's Republic marked the end of some forty years of confusion and almost incessant civil war. Remedies were very quickly found for the chaos and the evils of the Chiang Kai-shek regime and China has faced up to the tremendous task of transforming an agricultural civilization based on the family into an industrial civilization based on the individual.

Test Yourself

1. What were the "unequal treaties," and on what grounds did the Chinese consider them objectionable?
2. What was the Meiji Restoration? How was it effected and what were its results?
3. What was the Battle of the Concessions?
4. What were the Twenty-one Demands? To what extent were they acceded to and what changes did they effect?
5. When and with what objects was the Washington Conference convened and to what extent were those objects achieved?

Answers will be found at the end of the book.

CHAPTER XV

THE AGE OF PLANNING

THIS chapter is called *The Age of Planning* because one of the most significant features of the present century has been the increasing intervention of the State in economic life. Planning by governments has become almost universal and freedom of enterprise severely restricted. This development, however, has not been inspired everywhere by the same aims. Broadly speaking it may be said that two different, and often conflicting, ends have been put forward to justify it; one is that of national power, the other the promotion of human welfare. With the idea of planning for national power is associated that body of doctrines which may be called Fascism, and with that of planning for human welfare the ideas of social justice and Socialism. But planning, no matter what purpose it serves, dominates the history of our age.

Since 1900 the world has experienced war and peace, has seen states rise and fall, and has known prosperity and depression. But one influence has been constant—man's increasing control over the forces of Nature. We who live at the beginning of the Atomic Age scarcely need to be told that there is hardly any economic or political problem which is not, to a large degree, a result of the development of science. The revolutionary consequences of scientific change are a major cause of government planning. They have caused great increases in the production of goods but have also increased the instability of life. Hence they have provoked a demand for economic and social security which it seems possible to attain only through the imposition of state controls.

Reduction of Real Wages

The last half of the nineteenth century was one of rapid economic progress from which the working class in all industrial countries derived great benefits. But in the years between 1900 and 1914, it seemed as if this improvement was checked. Real wages, i.e. the value of wages judged by the quantity of goods they would buy, did not increase and, indeed, in some countries actually declined. This happened in spite of expanding world trade and improving profits. The cause of this apparent contradiction was a continuous rise in the prices of goods which, through making living more expensive, reduced the purchasing power of money. For example, prices rose in Britain between 1894 and 1914 by thirty per cent. An enormously increased output of gold from the mines of South Africa lay behind this change. Under the Gold Standard, the world monetary system then in operation, a bigger supply of gold meant more money, and this, through increasing the demand for goods, forced prices upwards.

Socialism in Germany

The consequence was labour discontent, particularly serious in France and Great Britain. Strikes and lock-outs affecting hundreds of thousands of workers a year took place. Tension and crisis in the international field was accompanied by tension and struggle in the relations between capital and labour.

During this period Socialism was largely confined to Europe for, elsewhere, the only countries in which it began to have an important influence were Australia and New Zealand. By the beginning of the century most European countries had organized socialist parties, which gained continually in strength. The most powerful was the German Social Democratic Party, which had been founded in 1869, and had already achieved considerable success in German elections. Its leader was a former factory worker, August Bebel, and its programme Marxist. According to this, the Erfurt Programme, adopted in 1889, the aim of the party was the substitution of social for capitalist ownership of the means of production. This alone, it asserted, could end the misery of the working class.

and it could be achieved only by a revolution carried out by the workers.

The Erfurt Programme had a great influence on the policies of socialist parties in other European countries. But it conflicted with another point of view which was more moderate, in that it argued that Socialism could be achieved by a series of reforms which would gradually eliminate Capitalism. Its principal advocates were Bernstein in Germany, Jaurès in France, and the Fabian Society in Britain.

Bernstein was the advocate of what was called Revisionism, for he rejected the revolutionary section of his party's programme and urged it to concentrate on the achievement of immediate and practical reforms. His influence was increased by set-backs experienced by the party at the General Elections of 1897 and 1907. The effect was to create something in the nature of a split consciousness in the German party. In theory it remained faithful to the Marxist doctrine of the Erfurt Programme, but in practice it became more and more moderate.

Socialism in France

Jaurès advocated what he described as penetration. He argued that the French Republic was not a class-state and not fundamentally hostile to the aspirations of the working class. "In municipalities, in parliament, in the central government," he asserted, "there has begun the penetration of socialistic and proletarian influence." Jaurès was opposed by the French Marxists under the leadership of Guesde, who believed that class-war, revolution and social ownership were the only possible elements of a socialist policy. A debate on the issues between Jaurès and the Marxists was the principal feature of an International Socialist Congress at Amsterdam in 1904, and Jaurès was defeated. As a result, the followers of Jaurès and Guesde united into a single party, which gained rapidly in political influence. Although Jaurès was defeated it cannot be said that his point of view lost its power. In practice the French Socialists followed a policy of penetration with some success, and, at the

price of expulsion from the party, three of their leaders Millerand, Briand, and Viviani, accepted ministerial posts.

In Britain, Marxism had very little effect. The Labour Party was founded in 1906 and, as it had developed from the Trade Union movement, was more interested in practical reforms than in the idea of revolutionary change. The most powerful socialist influence in Britain was the Fabian Society. Its policy was in many ways akin to that advanced by Jaurès. For the Fabians, as is shown in the voluminous and learned writings of Sidney and Beatrice Webb, the logic of capitalist development was not the class-war and revolution, but an increasing and peaceful transformation of the capitalist order through the extension of state and municipal activities.

The Second International

The socialist parties of Europe were associated in an international organization known as the Second International, because it followed the First International. This was founded by Karl Marx in 1864, and lasted only until 1876. Its members were mainly political exiles, like Marx himself, and its history largely a record of the struggle between Marx and the tempestuous and massive anarchist, Bakunin. The Second International began in 1889, and its concern with the question of gradualism has already been described. But another problem which occupied its attention was the question of working-class action in relation to war. This matter was discussed at the Congress held at Stuttgart in 1907, and a resolution adopted which defined the International's point of view. It was expressed in Marxist terms and stated that war was an evil of the capitalist system. "Wars between capitalist states are, as a rule, the consequence of their competitive struggle in the world market . . . they will not cease until the capitalist order has been abolished." The resolution went on to say that the International should work for the settlement of disputes by arbitration and concluded with a paragraph, for which Lenin was largely responsible, to assert that if war did break out the organized working-class movement should

SOLUTION OF A ROAD PROBLEM

By foresight and careful planning Stockholm has solved successfully the difficult problem of connecting the old town with the southern part of the city. The clover-leaf crossing avoids an otherwise inevitable bottleneck, and allows motor traffic, trams and pedestrians to move in comparative safety without delays and traffic jams.

exploit the situation to achieve a socialist revolution, and end hostilities. When war did break out in 1914, it broke the International, only Lenin and his followers and one or two other Socialist leaders, remaining faithful to its policy.

Another force which became important in working-class politics before 1914 was Syndicalism which, although its influence was not confined to France, was particularly powerful in that country. The Syndicalist point of view was that the workers had nothing to hope for from political parties or legislative reforms. Their task was to obtain control of the system of production through direct action in the form of the General Strike, and then to run industry through a number of syndicates, or workers' councils. Syndica-

list theory had an important influence in that Mussolini drew from it ideas which he later incorporated into the doctrine and organization of the Corporate State.

In all advanced countries in Europe substantial progress had been made by the beginning of the century towards the establishment of a system of social services to meet the needs of the new kind of society created by industrial development. In public health and education, in particular, a body of legislation existed which continued to grow. But the most significant innovations of this period took place in relation to what we should now call social security. This began with legislation introduced by Bismarck in Germany between 1883 and 1889, but spread rapidly to other countries, and became a factor of great economic and political importance.

In Germany, these social security measures took the form of a compulsory insurance system which covered sickness, accident and old age. It was continually extended and its administration made more efficient. There was no state provision to cover unemployment but a system of labour exchanges was created to assist unemployed workers in their search for jobs, and some of Germany's leading towns provided unemployment insurance schemes. Old-age pensions in Germany were based on insurance contributions, and it was Denmark which first introduced non-contributory pensions, that is, pensions received as a right, without any previous insurance payments. In France, in 1905, a system was created for the relief of the aged poor, the infirm, and the permanently disabled, out of funds supplied by the state and the local authorities. In 1905 a scheme to supplement trade union unemployment benefits from public money began, and in 1913 allowances for families containing more than three children were introduced. For Britain the significant year was 1911, when the Liberal Government, led by Asquith and Lloyd George, secured the passage of the National Insurance Act. Old age pensions on a non-contributory basis had been provided from 1908 and a system of labour exchanges brought into existence in 1909. This new body of legislation put Britain in the forefront in making provision against want. The adoption, under the Act of 1911, of state insurance against unemployment was, in particular, an important pioneering step, the first attempt in any part of the world to provide unemployment insurance on a national scale.

These developments were largely a result of the pressure which organized working-

MODERN TOWN PLANNING

This aerial view of Rossington, Yorkshire, shows how a rural site may be developed successfully. The centralization of industrial buildings, the provision of green belts, and the careful planning of broad roads for intercommunication—all prime factors in town planning—are seen to be related cleverly to existing topographical features.

class parties had begun to exert. Bismarck, the pioneer of this kind of legislation, said quite openly that he was introducing his own kind of socialism to counteract the growing power of socialist theories among the workers. In this respect the growth of the social services was certainly successful in Germany, and did much to cause the change from revolutionism to reformism in the Social Democratic Party. A similar effect was produced in other countries. The growth of the social services weakened the power of the Marxist argument that the state was an instrument used by the capitalists to exploit the working class. In this was to be found one important cause of the collapse of the Second International on the outbreak of war.

In the period from the outbreak of war in 1914 to the American financial and economic collapse in 1929, occurred the war, the peace treaties, the economic dislocation of the twenties, the Russian Revolution, the foundation of the Weimar Republic, and the achievement of power by the Fascists in Italy. It ended with the beginning of the world economic depression. An English historian has said that the American collapse created a new landscape. What was the character of the landscape destroyed? The answer is that it was one dominated by the uneasy but hopeful attempts of men to build a new world out of the disorder caused by war. While not a pleasant landscape, it was not nearly as gloomy as the one which lay ahead in the decade from 1929 to 1939.

Controls Caused by War

The First World War caused a great extension of state intervention. During it the principal belligerents, with the exception of the U.S.A., were forced to mobilize not only man-power but also their material resources. As the war proceeded it became more and more evident that victory would lie, not with the states with the bravest soldiers or the best generals, but with those able to bring the greatest weight of metal to bear against their enemies. Hence it was necessary to use every ounce of material and every square yard of factory space which could be spared from the production

of all except the barest civilian needs. Food was scarce and rationing had to be introduced, imports and exports had to be controlled. This meant the complete direction of economic life by the State. In Great Britain, for example, when hostilities ceased in 1918, the three government departments which dealt with ships, food and munitions controlled the greater part of the nation's supplies.

Difficulties of Reconstruction

Many of these controls were soon abolished after the armistice. But the war created a host of new problems which increased the need for state provision and, by reaction from the horror of events, stimulated the growth of the belief that the state should play a principal part in ensuring a good life for all. But the good life depended on something more than good intentions. The war had caused a world-wide shortage of goods of every conceivable kind needed for peaceful living. There was a scarcity of houses in every country. Capital had been destroyed on a big scale and concentration on war production had made replacement impossible.

Those countries which had been most badly affected by the war found it difficult to make a start on the reconstruction which was needed. By July, 1919, somewhere in the neighbourhood of fifty million people in Europe had become dependent on unemployment allowances, grave food deficiencies occurred, and diseases like tuberculosis and rickets took a heavy toll. The war and the revolutions which followed had shattered the financial structure of the continent and interfered with its normal channels of transport and trade. Inflation in a number of countries caused a fall in the value of savings and fixed incomes which impoverished many middle-class people who, as a consequence, supported extremist right-wing parties advocating an immoderate economic nationalism. A new European economy had to be built in which a number of nation states, each with the power to impose tariffs on imported goods, took the place of its former three empires. Communications with Russia, formerly an important source of foodstuffs and raw materials, had ceased as a result of revolution and civil war.

Those countries not so badly affected, Great Britain, the American states, and the neutrals, enjoyed a short-lived and frenzied trade boom. The acute shortage of goods caused a rapid rise in prices and business men made abnormal profits. Increases in wages were insufficient to clear the growing volume of goods and the boom came to an end in 1920. Stocks of goods were left on hand, unemployment reached previously unknown levels, and overseas markets collapsed. The year 1921 was one of the worst in the history of commerce.

Recovery was made difficult because of the determination to restore the Gold Standard. During the war the belligerents had printed large quantities of paper money, the Gold Standard had been suspended; the value of money had fallen. The new policy meant reduction of supplies of money to force up its value, and this caused falling prices and unemployment.

The restoration of the Gold Standard was not achieved internationally until 1928, when France fixed the value of the franc in terms of gold. And the Gold Standard of the twenties was not the same as before 1914. Then the United States had been in debt to the rest of the world, but it emerged from the war with the position reversed. The consequence was a continual flow of gold to the United States. To have preserved the Gold Standard, the United States should have used these additional supplies to increase its quantity of money. This would have caused American prices to rise and other countries would have been able to make bigger sales to American customers with the result that, after a time, the United States would have been forced to part with gold to pay for its excess of imports over exports. The Americans did not do this because they believed it would have caused them to suffer business depression and unemployment; instead they accumulated a huge stock of gold and other countries had to manage with a diminishing supply. To a lesser degree France also acquired large gold stocks and made the position worse. The scarcity of gold in all but two countries, as a result, made the

Gold Standard an ineffective instrument of international commerce. Until the American slump in 1929, the position was alleviated by extensive loans made by Americans to other countries, but when these came to an end the Gold Standard broke down.

Before 1914, one of the economic changes which provoked attention was the formation of larger business units, as a result of the amalgamation and combination of previously independent and competing firms. This would undoubtedly have continued if war had not occurred, but the war and its after-effects caused its more rapid development. These combinations took different forms, one was the trust, the establishment of central control over a number of undertakings, another was the cartel, a group of firms organized through a joint selling agency, and another the trade association, businesses in a particular trade combined to fix prices and allocate markets.

During the war, governments found that their control of industry was made more effective through the encouragement of combinations. In Britain, for example, the number of trade associations was considerably increased because the government found it easier to deal with them than with a multiplicity of individual firms. After the war, depression and falling prices caused capitalists to favour combination as a means of maintaining profits.

Capitalist combinations operated internationally as well as in particular countries. In a British Government report issued in 1927, it was estimated that one hundred and fourteen were in existence. An example was the European Steel Cartel, created in 1926 by the steelmakers of Germany, France, Luxemburg and Belgium, and later extended to cover other European countries. This fixed the total output of steel, allocated a proportion to each country, fined those firms which overproduced and compensated those which under-produced. Another was the International Match Corporation, which controlled one hundred and fifty factories in twenty-eight different countries. There were also links between the trusts of particular countries, for example, the British

MASS PRODUCTION

An important factor in recent industrial development is the perfection of mass production methods, resulting in greater efficiency and speed in production, lowering of costs, and standardization of equipment. Shown above is part of the assembly line in a motor works.

Imperial Chemical Industries was connected through Nobel, Ltd., with the German Dye Combine (I. G. Farben).

The significance of these combinations was that capitalists had discovered that planning, in the interest of profits, was desirable and unavoidable. Planning of this kind in some cases was harmful to the consumer in that it made him pay higher prices than were justified. But it also produced some benefits in the form of increased technical efficiency and reduced costs of production. Improvements in technical efficiency made it possible to say that, by 1925, the world was recovering from the effects of the war and was richer than in 1913. This was demonstrated by the Economic Section of the League of Nations which estimated that, between 1913 and 1925, the population of the world increased by five per cent, while the capacity of the world to produce goods increased by eighteen per cent. In fact, after the war had ended, the world moved into a new age, oil and electricity were replacing coal and steam as sources of power. The growth in the use of oil was rapid from about 1910, its effects were felt mainly in relation to overland and sea transport, but it was a powerful influence in industrial development as well. Electricity had little effect upon transport, but became increasingly the source of power on which industry depended. Its use made possible the establishment of industries in places which would have been impracticable in the age of coal and steam, for they no longer had to be near to coalfields.

Technical advance during this period also included the growth of mass-production. This may be said to have commenced in its modern form in 1913, when Henry Ford introduced the assembly line in his works at Detroit. The war, causing the standardization of industrial methods and the development of labour-saving machinery, brought about its extended adoption in all industrial countries. But improved methods were not confined to industry, they had great influence in agriculture as well. By 1928 the production of food was sixteen per cent greater than in 1913. This advance was not general in agricultural countries; in the peasant countries of

BRITISH COSTUME
of the
18th, 19th and 20th
CENTURIES

EARLY 18th. CENTURY: ELABORATE
FASHIONS IN QUEEN ANNE'S REIGN

MID 19th. CENTURY:
CRINOLINE FIRST SEEN
TOP HAT AT ITS ZENITH

LATE 19th. CENTURY
BOWLER HAT AND BUS

MID 18th. CENTURY;
HOOPED SKIRT AND
SLEEVED WAISTCOAT

EARLY 19th. CENTURY; HIGH WAISTED
EMPIRE STYLES ORIGINATING
IN FRANCE

EARLY 20th. CENTURY;
EDWARDIAN FASHIONS

1928; CLOCHE HAT AND SHORT
SKIRT FOR WOMEN, LOUNGE
SUIT FOR MEN

Eastern Europe, for example, the small farms made impossible the use of up-to-date machinery, and some observers have said that the disorders of the war and post-war period and the breaking-up of large estates actually caused a technical decline. But in other parts of the world technical advance caused over-production and it was in the middle twenties that schemes had to be introduced to maintain the prices of such commodities as wheat, rubber and coffee.

Origins of Fascism

By the time the world was showing these signs of recovery from the effects of the war there had appeared the political doctrine which is one of the original, if infamous, creations of the age of planning. This was Fascism, and its author was Benito Mussolini. Italy, the scene of its origin, was a country which had achieved national liberation in the nineteenth century, but had never managed to evolve a stable system of government. This was largely because, although a formal unity had been established, in fact, strong regional differences continued. The constitution provided for a limited monarchy similar to that of Great Britain, but in operation it was very different. Whereas Britain had disciplined political parties, these never existed in Italy. Instead, there were a number of ill-disciplined groups, none of which had followers all over the country. Universal suffrage was not introduced until 1913, and was neither appreciated nor used intelligently as a result of widespread illiteracy. Elections were corrupt, strikes and riots were common. The absence of parties capable of obtaining a parliamentary majority gave the king great power in the choice of governments, and prime ministers were usually men mainly distinguished by adroitness, their task being to keep together governments formed of political opponents.

Mussolini was originally a member of the Italian Socialist Party. When the First World War began, the party supported a policy of neutrality. Mussolini opposed this and resigned his membership, associating himself with an aggressive movement which had appeared to advocate Italy's entrance into the war. It was from this movement, and the personal conflict from which Mussolini suffered at this time —if his own story was true—that Fascism was born.

Italy suffered badly during the war, which it entered on the Allied side in 1915, and afterwards experienced serious dislocation and disorder. Demobilization was carried through inefficiently, strikes were widespread, and, in some cases, workers seized control of factories. The Italians were disappointed with the outcome of the war; they had ended as one of the victors but seemed unlikely to realize the territorial expansion for which they had hoped. Patriotic violence by the Fascists, whose numbers increased rapidly, became common, and, in the end, the threat of civil war in 1922 induced the king to ask Mussolini to form a government. Thus began what Fascist apologists called, in the grandiose language which Mussolini used and encouraged, the Fascist era.

Dictatorship

Mussolini had been much influenced by syndicalist political thought. It encouraged him to believe in violence and provided ideas about the organization of the state. He created workers' and employers' syndicates in Italy's industries to deal with questions of wage rates, hours of work, holidays, dismissals, and so on. But whereas the syndicalists had asked for the destruction of the centralized state, Mussolini increased centralization and used the syndicates as a means of ensuring economic discipline and unity between social classes. He repressed popular liberties and made himself dictator and Italy became a one-party, or totalitarian state. His intention was to bring the syndicates of workers and employers together in a series of corporations, and to supersede the Chamber of Deputies with a Chamber of Corporations. He had only got as far as this in 1939.

The real aim of Mussolini was to prepare the Italian people for war. This was not obvious in the early years of the Fascist regime, and many foreign observers excused his occasional belligerent speeches as the result of over-ebullience. They found reason to praise him because he made trains run to time, drained marshes, made new roads, stabilized hotel prices, experimented in the re-housing of slum dwellers, and built sanatoria for tubercular children. These achievements deserved some of the praise they obtained, but men must be judged not only by the good they do but by the evil they prepare. And apart from destroying political opposition and disciplining industry and finance, Mussolini used the educational system and the press to develop a warlike spirit in the Italian people, tried to create a well-equipped and well-trained army, and spent a great deal of money in increasing the size of his navy. Mussolini's plan, like that which Hitler executed with greater thoroughness later, was a plan for aggression from the beginning.

Germany, in the twenties, was anything but a menace to peace. The abdication of the Kaiser in 1918 had been followed by a revolution which made the Social Democrats the strongest party. Ebert, its leader, became first Chancellor and then President of the new republic. For this a constitution was devised in 1919 at Weimar. Through a system of proportional representation parties held seats in the Reichstag roughly according to the number of votes they obtained. This

POLITICAL SHOWMANSHIP

Hitler addressing a meeting in the huge Deutschlandhalle, Berlin. The Nazis employed mass meetings extensively as a means of winning support and spreading their propaganda.

helped to make effective democratic government difficult, for it encouraged the multiplication of parties, none of which could secure a working majority. The republic, therefore, had a sequence of coalition governments, and policy, instead of being determined in the Cabinet, was decided behind the scenes through bargaining between party leaders. The effectiveness of government was further weakened by the incapacity of German politicians to adjust themselves to the new situation. They had been accustomed to a position, under the Empire, in which the Kaiser and Chancellor decided policy and political parties protested or agreed. The idea of government resting upon the debates and votes of the Reichstag was something they could not assimilate. The stability of the State depended to a large degree upon the civil service and the army, in both of which the traditions of the Empire continued to exert a great influence.

Inflation in Germany

To make the life of the new state even more difficult, it was regarded by many Germans as part of Germany's humiliation in defeat. Further, the country suffered from grave economic disorder. Large scale unemployment became a permanent problem, Germany was expected to pay heavy reparations to the Allies, and many people were impoverished by the inflation of the currency between 1921 and 1923. Unemployment was partly a result of the postwar decline in world trade and, in so far as this caused Germany's problem, she was a fellow sufferer with Great Britain. The inflation was deliberately aggravated by the German Government to reduce the burden of its debt to the German people. Through the issue of unlimited quantities of paper money the value of debts was forced down until they became of negligible significance.

Reparations carried with them their own peculiar problem. It was that of obtaining sufficient foreign currency to make the required payments; this could be done only by the sale of goods abroad, which the Allies did not like and which they resisted because it deprived them of markets. In fact, after the currency was stabilized in 1923 and reparations scaled down under the Dawes plan of 1924, Germany borrowed so heavily from the United States, Britain and other countries, that she received far more than she paid out. As a result the country enjoyed a fictitious prosperity from 1925 to 1929, which encouraged foreign observers to think that the republic was proving a success. German industry was re-equipped and the social services extended out of the borrowed money and a new Germany, peaceful, progressive and unmilitaristic, seemed to have been born.

In other countries as well as Germany, socialist parties gained in strength after the First World War. In Austria the Social Democrats exercised a great influence, especially in Vienna, where their housing experiments proved of interest to the whole world. Britain had its first Labour Government in 1924, as the result of an inconclusive general election. But, on the whole, this period was one of defeat and retreat for socialist parties outside Russia. Counter revolutions had smashed attempts to establish Communist regimes in Finland and Hungary between 1917 and 1919, failure to obtain working majorities handicapped the parties of the West. The Second International was refounded in 1923, but proved to be only a shadow of its former self. What is more, it was bitterly assailed by the newly created Third International set up by the Communists in Moscow.

The Third International

The Third International, begun in 1919, was a result of both belief and expediency. Lenin, Trotsky, and their colleagues held, in accordance with the Marxist analysis of world development, that as capitalism was international in its effects, revolution against it in one place would spread elsewhere. The primary aim of the Third International, therefore, was the furtherance of world revolution. But, from the point of view of the immediate interests of the Soviet State, the International was expected to serve as a means of organizing foreign working-class opinion in its support. The new International soon adopted a policy of hostility towards the older socialist and labour movements of the West. At its second World Congress in 1920, it accepted the principle that the reformist and moderate elements in the leadership of labour should be attacked as betrayers of the true interests of the workers. National Communist Parties were instructed to struggle against the "Yellow" Second International, undermining its power and influence in every possible way.

Work of the I.L.O.

The members of labour organizations affiliated to the Second International, in fact, had been provided by the peace settlement with a new instrument through which it was possible to secure international reforms. This was the International Labour Organization. Article Eighteen of the League of Nations Covenant affirmed that "the members of the League will endeavour to secure and maintain fair and humane conditions of labour for men, women, and children." The International Labour Organization, or I.L.O. as it became known, was set up to implement this aim. Provision was made under its constitution for the separate representation of governments, workers, and employers at its General Conferences. Its first director, M. Albert Thomas, a French Socialist, was a man of energy and genius. Under his leadership the organization became responsible for many international conventions regulating wages, conditions of work, the treatment of the unemployed, pensions, and similar matters affecting the welfare of labour. The I.L.O., in fact, was one of the successes of the inter-war period and the war of 1939 did not bring an end to its beneficent influence.

The period from 1929 to 1939 will probably be regarded as one of the most miserable in the history of the world. There is little to ascribe to it but failure and disaster, for it began with one of the most severe economic depressions ever experienced, saw the commencement of Japan's aggression in the Far East, the rise of Hitler to power in Germany, Italy's attack on Abyssinia, the Spanish Civil

War, and the decline of the League of Nations. Planning became more important, the New Deal was introduced in the U.S.A., world opinion became more interested in communist planning in Russia, Germany and Italy tried to achieve self-sufficiency, the Popular Front Government in France attempted a far-reaching series of reforms.

During the twenties, the U.S.A. had enjoyed an almost unexampled prosperity, but in 1929 this showed signs of abatement. A building and constructional boom which had been in progress for three years was ending, the output of the motor industry was slowing up, so also was the production of steel. The building boom had caused an expenditure of thirty-eight billion dollars in four years, largely on the basis of borrowed money, and this had pushed up business profits. From 1927 to 1929, the American banking system had followed a policy of cheap money, i.e. lending at low rates of interest. These influences, and the belief of Americans that they had discovered the secret of perpetual prosperity, caused an orgy of speculative gambling in stocks and shares, again largely on the basis of borrowed money. In late October, 1929, a panic commenced on the stock market which, unlike others in the preceding eighteen months, could not be arrested. Within the course of three weeks, thirty billion dollars, or almost the equivalent of American expenditure in the First World War, was lost as a result of reductions in the price of stock. The United States had passed from prosperity to depression, thousands were ruined, and within a short time the unemployed numbered millions.

American Loans End

The effect of the American collapse was to bring to an end the flow of loans to foreign countries which had done so much to help recovery from the war. Some countries, especially Germany, had become so dependent upon borrowing from the United States that when the flow of dollars ceased they found it increasingly difficult to meet their obligations. As a consequence they had to economize in expenditure, wages were cut, and social service expan-

PRINCIPAL SOURCES O

| WHEAT | CANE SUGAR | BEET SUGAR | TEA | COFFEE | COCOA | RICE | CATTLE | SHEE |

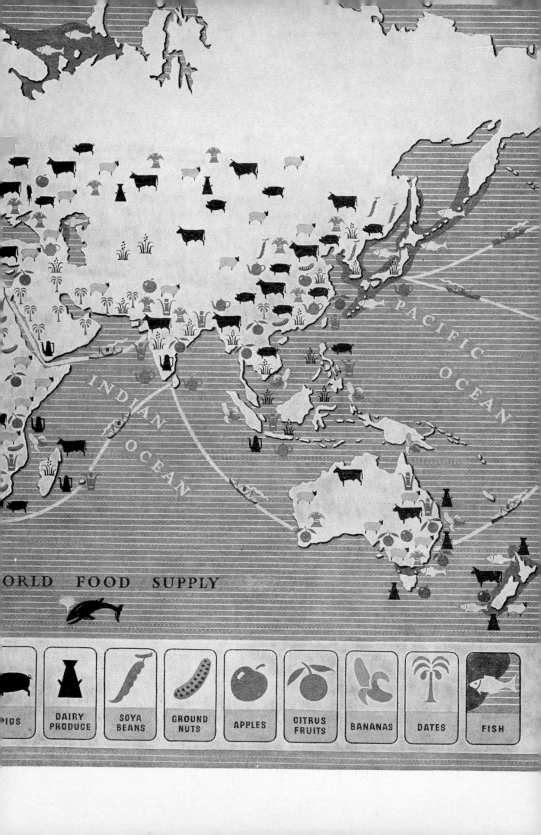

PACIFIC OCEAN

INDIAN OCEAN

ORLD FOOD SUPPLY

PIGS | DAIRY PRODUCE | SOYA BEANS | GROUND NUTS | APPLES | CITRUS FRUITS | BANANAS | DATES | FISH

sion halted. Prices fell and unemployment rose. Defaults on debt payments could not be avoided. Reparations were scaled down again under the Young Plan in 1929, suspended in 1931, and brought to an end in 1932. Within three years, world trade decreased by two-thirds and it was estimated by the League of Nations that the number of unemployed was thirty millions.

Results of "Over-production"

Bad as was the situation in the industrial countries, it was perhaps worse for producers of foodstuffs and raw materials. For these their principal markets were the great industrial countries which, because of depression and unemployment, reduced their purchases. By the end of 1933, the prices of raw materials had fallen by fifty per cent. The peasant countries of Eastern Europe were choked with surplus produce, a situation which made them heavily dependent on Germany when, under the Nazis, it began to offer a market. To try to maintain prices, schemes for the restriction of production and the destruction of crops became common. In this way occurred a paradox which perplexed the world, millions suffering want while goods were destroyed. In the recent economic history of the world nothing has made a more powerful impression on public opinion, unless it was the way in which unemployment disappeared and production increased later as a result of war.

The effects of the great depression in Germany have already been described. The shaky fabric of the Weimar Republic was incapable of standing the strain. The majority of Germans had never been convinced that democracy was a satisfactory system of government, it was opposed to the authoritarian tradition in which they had been reared. From its beginnings the republic had bitter enemies, who regarded its existence as proof of Germany's degradation. One of the parties which had appeared to express this point of view was that of the National Socialists, or Nazis, under the leadership of Hitler. It was founded in 1919 and its support originally came largely from the middle and lower-middle classes, who were terrified by the possibility of a communist revolution. Its electoral fortunes were best when economic conditions were worst.

The first breach in the democratic wall was made by Bruening, the Catholic Centre Chancellor, when, in 1930, to meet the economic situation, he began to legislate by decree under Article forty-eight of the constitution. This meant that government became independent of democratic control. In 1932, Bruening was succeeded by von Papen with a cabinet which, because of the large number of noblemen it included, was called "The Cabinet of the Barons," and the republic was almost extinct. The Nazis had been gaining greater strength at the general elections which followed each other in rapid succession and eventually Hindenburg, the President, after some hesitation, offered the Chancellorship to Hitler. Once the reins of power were in their hands the Nazis set to work to extinguish all opposition, and within a short time Germany became a totalitarian state.

Hitler in Power

Hitler's principal aim was the restoration of Germany's military power; in this respect his ambition knew no limits, he wished to make Germany the dominant state in the world. From his youth he had been an anti-Semite, and believed that the Jews were engaged in a conspiracy to achieve world domination. He hated Communism because Marx, its founder, was a Jew, and because the Communists preached the international solidarity of all workers, irrespective of nationality or colour.

Hitler's planning had two aims, the first to make Germany "racially pure," the second to make her invincible. To deal with the Jews in Germany was easy; they were killed, put into concentration camps, dispossessed of their property and positions and forced to live in ghettos. To make Germany fit for war one thing the Nazis did not overlook was the need to ensure full support on the home front, for one of their beliefs was that the First World War had been lost as a result of weak morale among German civilians. Hence the enormous attention they paid to propaganda. Broadcasting, the Press, education, films, the theatre and all other cultural institutions were used to break down any resistance to their ideas which individual Germans might cherish. Nazi totalitarianism was original, indeed, because of the intensity of its attack on the human mind. The Nazis believed that they could shape minds as they thought fit. Von Rauschning, a one-time associate of Hitler, has reported that scientists belonging to the Nazi technical organization envisaged a future in which they would produce whatever types of human beings were needed by the State.

The economic policy of the Nazis aimed at organizing Germany's resources in readiness for war. Orders for munitions and military equipment set the wheels of industry turning again and unemployment was eliminated. Germany's dependence on imported raw materials made it necessary to control foreign trade in order to give priority to essential military requirements among imports. Hitler and his advisers, however, saw even a limited dependence on imports as a source of weakness. The blockade of Germany had been one cause of her defeat in the First World War. Therefore Hitler proclaimed it his aim to make Germany independent of foreign supplies. Synthetic substitutes were used in place of a wide variety of imported raw materials and most of the small countries of eastern Europe were coerced through economic pressure into making trade agreements favourable to Germany's interests. In the foreign as well as in the domestic sphere economic policy thus became a means of preparing for aggression.

Hitler found an ally and imitator in Mussolini, who, between 1932 and 1936, lost his position as Fascist Dictator Number One in Europe. In 1933 and 1934 he resisted Hitler's intention to incorporate Austria in the German Reich. But in 1935 he decided that his long preparations to create a new Roman Empire were complete and attacked Abyssinia. This provoked the imposition of economic sanctions by the League of Nations against Italy. The League's action was enforced too timidly to succeed but Mussolini was convinced that Italy was vulnerable if she continued to depend on imports. Mussolini, therefore, proclaimed the need for Italian self-sufficiency. Italy began to manufacture synthetic substitutes for imported articles and materials, and her agriculture was reorganized to make her less dependent on foreign food.

Comintern Opposes Fascism

The course of events also caused Mussolini to decide he could no longer be on unfriendly terms with Hitler and in 1936 an alliance was formed between Germany, Italy and Japan. The instrument of their alliance was a pact directed against the spread of Communism, the Anti-Comintern Pact. Under the threats which Hitler made against Russia the Third International (Comintern) changed its policy. At its 1935 Congress it formed a policy which aimed at securing unity between all progressive forces in resistance to Fascism; instead of vilifying moderate labour leaders and despising liberals, communists were to find a basis for common action with them. This change was in line with the foreign policy pursued by Russia after her entrance into the League of Nations in 1934, the alliance of all "freedom-loving nations" against the Fascist International.

Popular Front Governments

As a result of the changed policy of the Third International, agreements were made between the left-wing parties not to oppose each other in some countries and Popular Front governments came into existence in France and Spain. The Popular Front Government in France, under the leadership of the socialist M. Léon Blum, produced a plan designed to provide a number of important social reforms. The French Government and the workers chose an ill-advised time to embark on a struggle for better living conditions. The reality that faced France was the growing might of Germany. M. Blum had to resign in 1937 but the Popular Front experiment lasted a few more months under Radical leadership before dissension brought it to an end. The other Popular Front Government, in Spain, was destroyed as a result of a civil war in which nationalist rebels led by General Franco, supported by Germany and Italy, revolted against the democratic republic.

After the fall of the second Labour Government in 1931, Great Britain had a National Government, first with Mr. MacDonald and then with Mr. Baldwin and Mr. Chamberlain as Prime Ministers. Recovery was good and steady, if unspectacular, progress was made in social legislation. The foreign policy of the government was to discourage the idea that there might be war as a result of ideological disagreement. Mr. Chamberlain thought he could persuade the dictators to see reason; he made a number of speeches in which he deplored the growing expenditure on armaments as harmful to the standard of life. He found it hard to believe that Hitler and Mussolini were the kind of men who preferred booty seized by conquest to prosperity.

In fact, the condition of Britain on the eve of war was not one likely to inspire belief in the democratic cause. Unemployment was still serious, whole regions had become practically derelict as a result of economic depression, agriculture was in a condition of semi-decay, unplanned building was ruining British towns and much of the countryside as well, and traffic congestion in the cities had become an almost insoluble problem. The situation seemed to many to require a bold policy of government planning to meet the future. But the planning which was actually done was that made necessary by war.

War and Cold War

The Second World War, like the first, caused a great extension of the powers of governments. At the height of his success Hitler produced a plan for Europe, the Nazi New Order, which aimed at creating a future in which Germans would be the masters and the other nations their servants. In spite of her early successes and the support of Italy and Japan, Germany was too weak to defeat the combined might of Britain, the Soviet Union and the United States. For four years these great combinations of powers were engaged in the

planning which total war demands. German air raids on Britain met eventually with massive retaliation from the R.A.F. and the American Air Force, a planned use of air power to destroy Germany's industrial centres which proved a turning point in the war. Another remarkable example of planning, this time in the use of scientific and industrial resources, was the development of the Atomic Bomb (used in the final weeks of the war against Japan) by Britain and the U.S.A.

Planning for reconstruction and security were the chief needs of the world after hostilities had ceased. In place of the defunct League of Nations a new international organization was brought into existence, the United Nations Organization. Its principal organs were the Security Council and the Assembly. A provision relating to the deliberations of the Security Council was that to be effective any decision, except those dealing with procedure, had to receive the support of the United States, the Soviet Union, the United Kingdom, France and China. A contrary vote from any of these vetoed the decision. Part of the plan for world security and world development represented by UNO involved the establishment of specialized agencies, of which the most important were for food and agriculture (F.A.O.), scientific and cultural co-operation (UNESCO) and the promotion of world health (W.H.O.). The I.L.O., still in existence, was taken over by UNO.

It soon became obvious that co-operation between the war-time allies, the Soviet Union on the one hand and the Western Powers on the other was likely to prove difficult. The main issues dividing these two groups were the future of Germany and the control of Atomic Energy. Agreement was reached at the Potsdam Conference in 1945 on a plan for the occupation of Germany, but from then onwards the story was one of almost continuous friction and disagreement. This led to the establishment of separate governments for the western and eastern halves of the country. In the western half a Federal Republic was brought into existence with the support of the Western powers, in the eastern half a

Communist régime was created by the Russians. Disagreement over the future of Germany reached its most dangerous point in 1948-49 when the Western Powers organized an Air Lift to counter a blockade of Berlin by the Russians. But the Air Lift, which involved over a quarter of a million flights into Berlin, was successful and the blockade was lifted just over twelve months after it had been introduced.

There was general recognition after the war that an international plan was needed to ensure that Atomic Energy would not again be used for destructive purposes and that its peaceful, constructive uses would be developed. The United Nations created an Atomic Energy Commission but the Soviet Union and the Western Powers failed to reach agreement on a system of control. Both disputing groups argued that the plans put forward by their opponents failed to provide security against the possibility of the use of atomic weapons in war. The United States and the powers associated with her regarded the growing stockpile of atomic bombs as the principal means available to deter the Soviet Union from using her massive armed forces for aggression. In 1949 it became certain that the Soviet Union had manufactured atomic bombs. Later the United Kingdom commenced atomic bomb tests and the United States and the Soviet Union acquired an even more terrible weapon, the hydrogen bomb.

The war proved to have enormously expanded Soviet power. She was able to draw most of the states of eastern and central Europe, Poland, Rumania, Hungary, Czechoslovakia, Bulgaria, Albania and Eastern Germany into a Communist bloc. The Communist parties of these states, together with that of Yugoslavia—expelled for its vigorous assertion of independence from Russian control in 1948—Italy and France were organized in the Cominform. This organization replaced the Comintern, dissolved during the war, and its purpose was to prosecute the Cold War with greater effectiveness. The Western Powers, on their side, introduced various plans to meet the Communist threat. The most important of these was a plan for defence, the North Atlantic Treaty Organization (NATO), which provided for the integration of the armed forces of its members. On French initiative a European Coal and Steel Community, designed to co-ordinate the development of heavy industry was established. To assist economic development an Organization for European Economic Co-operation and a European Payments Union were brought into existence. Finally a Council of Europe was established, but this provides little more than an opportunity for western politicians to discuss their common problems together.

Lastly we should note the economic and social changes which occurred in Britain after the war. The wartime Coalition Government under Mr. Churchill prepared various plans for improved social services and promised to maintain full employment. These plans were inherited and expanded by the Labour Government which was elected in 1945. They included educational reforms, national insurance, a national health service and children's allowances. The Labour Government also nationalized some leading industries, coal, electricity, gas, railways, road transport, and iron and steel. The last two have been de-nationalized by Conservative Governments since 1951 but the expanded social services maintained.

Test Yourself

1. What do you understand by gradualism? What was its significance in the development of socialism?
2. What were the chief causes of economic disorder after the First World War?
3. What are the chief causes of the growth of planning?
4. What were the political effects of the great economic depression?
5. Does history show that planning is a good or a bad thing?

Answers will be found at the end of the book.

CHAPTER XVI

WORLD POLITICS IN THE TWENTIETH CENTURY

THE first half of the twentieth century has proved to be a period of almost unrelieved crisis. Every year fresh problems in international affairs have caused the Great Powers to fear that war would provide the only solution. Fear, insecurity and rising armaments are the keynotes throughout. The years have been spent in waging two world-wide wars, and to make peace after the first took longer than the war itself. Indeed the settlement after the First World War, both in the West and in the Far East, seemed to raise more problems than it solved. Thus, excepting perhaps the few years between 1924 and 1929, it was a mockery to talk of peace amidst the economic chaos, undeclared wars, incidents, wars of nerves, and open banditry. The Second World War ended officially in 1945 but, all over the world, violence and disorder continue as they did after 1918. Agreement between the Great Powers, which alone can give confidence and order to the world at large, is still lacking. The picture of world politics is sombre and infinitely disordered, but certain elements can be disentangled.

Prestige of Britain

The great technical and industrial advances of the nineteenth century were based on coal, iron, steam and improved transport. In each one of these Great Britain was not only the first in the field of invention, but also materially well placed. Her early start, her material resources and the vigour of her people gave her advantages of which she made full use. With her population of forty-two millions in 1901, she held a position of world supremacy out of all proportion to her size. This prestige was due to the immense power developed by her highly organized industrial system and to the wealth accumulated from her commerce. Her wealth was invested in transport and business enterprises in her colonies and in foreign countries. These enterprises were similar to those on which her own power was based and by 1900 they were beginning seriously to compete against her in world markets.

Growth of U.S.A. and Germany

By 1900, both Germany and the United States of America were producing more iron and steel, and the latter more coal than Britain. Both countries had more modern machinery of greater efficiency, more extensive natural resources and larger populations. Both were in a position to challenge and to surpass Britain in her own field of industry and commerce. Nevertheless British power was still great and her prestige built up over the century since the Napoleonic wars, was greater still. But previously she had relied on an effortless superiority of power and it was around this that the whole international system had been constructed. In the twentieth century there is an element of competition and struggle. Britain was forced to give up her attitude of detachment in foreign affairs and to participate in the European alliance system.

World politics had to be adjusted to a new situation. Britain was no longer the possessor of an overwhelming superiority; she was now only one of the eight Great Powers, alongside the United States, Germany, France, Russia, Austria-Hungary, Italy and Japan. This had a profound effect on the European balance of power, for it had been Britain's influence outside the system of alliances, inclining first one way and then another, which had preserved the equilibrium between rival nations and so prevented large-scale war. Britain found little difficulty in adjusting herself to the new position in relation to America, but with Germany it was different. Germany had been forged into a Great Power with astonishing speed, and if hard work, highly organized industry and well-trained armies meant power and influence in the world, she could fairly claim an important place. But it was supremacy not partnership that Germany saw within her grasp, and supremacy, such as Britain had once held, was now for any nation impossible.

The change in Britain's relationship to the Great Powers all over the world was a basic cause of international instability as it necessitated readjustments everywhere. Britain proved herself powerful enough to survive the great strain on her organization imposed by two world wars, but in spite of victory and enhanced prestige she emerged shaken and impoverished. By 1918 it was clear that both America and Germany had bigger industrial resources than she; by 1945 Britain had become a borrowing instead of a lending Power. The change in Britain's position meant a shifting or sharing of the international responsibilities which she had shouldered so lightly before.

Influence of Nationalism

The powerful force of nationalism or self-determination had proved a stabilizing and unifying factor in Western Europe in the nineteenth century, although on the eastern fringes in the Balkans, in Russia and in Austria-Hungary it was creating serious problems before 1914. It had already spread abroad with remarkable rapidity when the First World War gave it added stimulus. Not only was it a ferment creating new states in Europe and Latin America, it was also affecting the East where Japan had demonstrated in the Russo-Japanese War of 1904, that an Eastern people could organize itself on Western lines and meet Western Powers on equal terms. After the First World War, self-determination slashed to ribbons the old-established frontiers of Europe and produced a pattern of jealous independent states, each protecting its frontiers with an army, and its struggling industries with tariff walls. These Succession States to the empires of Russia and Austria-Hungary proved intractable and awkward neighbours, often unwilling to accord their own subject minorities the fair treatment they themselves had once demanded. In the East, nationalism worked differently but with no less threatening effect. It has been extended and invigorated after each world war, and now the call for national independence re-echoes round South-east Asia, the eastern Mediterranean and North Africa. Nationalism and industrialism, once learned from the West, have become the weapons by which Western intrusion can be expelled.

Checks on International Trade

Nationalism, by dividing the world into increasingly numerous self-contained entities, cut at the root of that international trade on which so much of the prosperity of the Western Powers depended. That prosperity, and the rising standard of living which went with it, were due to the system of international trade which brought goods from every continent quickly and easily to the consumer. Britain claimed that the best results came from trading unhampered by government taxation in the form of protective tariffs. But nations beginning to compete in the world market later than Britain, found that free trade often strangled local industries in their early stages. Thus Germany, followed by almost every other state, adopted protection and nourished home production by taxing imports. Tariffs and still more the practice of dumping great quantities of goods economically manufactured under very large-scale production, with the object of underselling and thus driving locally produced articles off the market, were bringing the atmosphere of war into commerce before 1914.

The growth of the principle of nationality and the craving for absolute independence which went with it, resulted in self-sufficiency becoming a national aim. To achieve this, Great Powers competed for all parts of the earth's surface which were yet unclaimed. The First World War added more and smaller nations to those already trying to achieve economic self-sufficiency, in addition to dislocating the whole pre-war trading complex.

Great capitalists responsible for organizing industry and commerce irrespective

of their nationality, realized that the preservation of peace was essential to the
maintenance of the complicated web of
international exchange they had slowly
created. But their different views were
swamped by the doctrine of national self-
sufficiency, even when that entailed the
people suffering that their state might be
strong. This doctrine was seen in its
crudest form between the wars, and
exasperation at its hampering effect led
Germany, under Hitler, into the dangerous
system of regional autarky. Germany
might be able to produce substitutes for
rubber and other raw materials she could
not grow, but she could not exist without
foreign trade and at the same time maintain a good standard of living for her
people. Thus Hitler chose to build upon
the Continent a trading group dominated
by Germany and geared to German
economic needs. These needs, thus
narrowly interpreted, led to the political
dominance over, and eventual extinction of,
other nationalities. Yet there were sufficient raw materials for everyone if the
nations could have agreed on their distribution and exchange.

The idea of democracy was as characteristic of Western civilization as nationality.
In Europe and America, in the later nineteenth century the basis of political representation had been broadened; education
was being extended to include everyone and
more people were making their views
heard in public affairs. Governments
could not afford to neglect the opinions of
the newly enfranchised masses, but new
techniques of explanation were needed.
Mass opinion proved to be peculiarly
susceptible to propaganda and modern

SIXTY YEARS A QUEEN

*On June 22, 1897, Queen Victoria celebrated
her diamond jubilee. Of all the pageantry of
that day, the thanksgiving service at St.
Paul's Cathedral was the chief event. The
Queen is here shown immediately after the
ceremony, seated in her carriage with the
Prince of Wales and the Duke of Cambridge,
accompanied by the Princess of Wales and
Princess Christian—a remarkable example
of the success of early photography.*

EARLY MOTOR-DRIVEN AIRCRAFT

On December 17, 1903, at Kitty Hawk, America, Wilbur Wright carried out successful tests of his first motor-driven aircraft, attaining a speed of thirty miles an hour in a flight lasting fifty-nine seconds. Two years later the aeroplane became a practical proposition when Wilbur Wright flew for thirty-eight minutes, covering a distance of twenty-four miles.

industry has produced incomparable means of exercising such influence through the cheap newspaper, films and broadcasting.

Only after the First World War did mass opinion concern itself with foreign affairs which had till then been the domain of the professional diplomats. It was the alleged failure of these professionals to avert war, and fear of the secret diplomacy with which they were connected that increased public interest. John Citizen everywhere may have wished heartily enough to live his life unworried by wars, but it is clear that propaganda can turn him into a surprisingly dangerous character; Hitler, backed by a finely organized propaganda machine, could rouse the German nation to frenzied hatred of one country after another. There has proved to be more support of world organization for peace in theory, than there has been readiness to shoulder the responsibilities involved in practice.

Karl Marx had thought that "the worker has no country," and a general strike of all the workers involved, appeared a promising solution of the problem of international rivalry: government action would be paralysed and consequently war prevented. But the experience of 1914 in this respect was discouraging. The collapse of the well-

organized German Social Democratic Party showed how powerful was the appeal of national patriotism. War in 1939 appeared to have popular approval: there was no chance—as there had been in 1914 —of organized labour preventing it.

In spite of nationalism, self-sufficiency and economic rivalry, the twentieth century has seen the growth of strong forces favouring international organization. The importance of economic interdependence amongst nations in securing social betterment was perhaps more widely appreciated than the need for its political counterpart. But the dissolution of traditions, beliefs and institutions under the powerful solvent of two world wars has created a situation much more favourable for international endeavour in every field. Not a state in the world escaped the effects of the wars which ostensibly began in an Austro-Serbian and a German-Polish dispute. In 1929, the great trade slump beginning in America quickly spread over the world from China to Peru. The collapse of the New York Stock Market led through increased unemployment and decreased trade to a frenzied search for foreign markets and attempts to monopolize existing ones and thus played an indirect part in bringing about the Sino-Japanese War. The world was one, bound by invisible links, but it still had to be organized as one, just as the plain man everywhere had yet to realize how closely the common interest was linked with his own standards of life.

Communism provided one international idea inspiring zeal amidst disillusion and bewilderment. On this basis order had been brought into the multi-national Russian state after the total collapse of Tsarist autocracy, but it made little appeal to the Western World. Even in Russia itself, the idea of world revolution was modified by that of " Socialism in a single state " and thus linked Communism with the national policy of Russia.

But long before Russia's experiment in Communism, Europe had been feeling slowly towards another form of international organization. Services like the International Postal Union had worked successfully, and the Geneva Convention of 1864 was at least a good start towards international standards of conduct in war. Disarmament however, proposed at the Hague Conference of 1899, made no headway against international distrust: again in 1907 and time after time between the wars all efforts failed. But the method of arbitration had been found a satisfactory way of dealing with disputes. Even in the critical years before the First World War, nations were making treaties binding themselves to resort to this method in disputes not affecting their fundamental interest.

From these beginnings it was a big jump to the full scale international organization of the League of Nations in 1919, and the obvious failures to achieve disarmament or to remove distrust may easily be exaggerated. On the other hand much less spectacular work on public health, commissions of inquiry, the International Labour Office, and other bodies has proved both valuable and encouraging. It is significant that the United Nations Organization was formed as early as possible after the Second World War in spite of all the criticisms levelled against the League. U.N.O. begins its career on a basis of experience.

Europe before 1914 was Bismarck's Europe in dissolution. Under Bismarck's leadership Germany had arrived amongst the Great Powers and he was determined to make her position secure. He was successful in achieving a certain stability in Europe, but after his removal in 1890, Germany consciously pursued other objects by different means. Gradually there developed a whole series of stresses which eventually brought down the political structure in the chaotic ruin of the First World War. What were in brief the conflicting aims of the Great Powers before 1914?

Bismarck knew that Germany's seizure of Alsace-Lorraine would not go unchallenged. He proceeded to build up an alliance first with Austria-Hungary, the other German Power of Central Europe, and later with the newly united state of Italy. Thus was formed the Triple Alliance (1882)

SALOON CAR OF 1898

Compared with the modern compact and speedy saloon car, this four-h.p. Daimler of 1898 looks cumbersome and uncomfortable. One of the most important industrial developments of the twentieth century so far has been the perfection of the internal-combustion engine, which has made possible the extensive use of land and air transport.

in which the obvious flaw appeared to be the traditional enmity between Italy and Austria. But Bismarck, with the clear sight of a great statesman, realized—as others were to do when it was too late—that Austria was not quite the asset she seemed. By concluding a secret treaty with Russia in 1887, known as the Reinsurance Treaty, he hoped not only to secure Germany against any eventuality, but also to stabilize the uncertain policy of Austria.

Reversal of Bismarck's Policy

The accession of the young Emperor Wilhelm II in 1888 and Bismarck's dismissal two years later wrought a complete change in German policy. The treaty with Russia was dropped, and at the same time Germany, instead of seeking to stabilize Europe, began to adopt a challenging and provocative attitude. The challenge seemed especially directed against British naval and imperial supremacy, but it was felt by France and Russia, too, so that by 1907, Germany found herself faced by a Triple Entente, of these three Powers. Germany felt herself insecure and encircled by potential enemies. Austria was her only sure friend, and in consequence, German policy was linked more and more closely to that of her unstable companion. It was exactly what Bismarck had striven to avoid.

In the Dual Monarchy or Austro-Hungarian Empire, two racial minorities—the Germans and the Magyars—ruled over a Slav majority. The administrative problems resulting from this position were awkward and intractable, nor were they ever satisfactorily solved. The linguistic difficulties and the parliamentary obstruction practised by the subject Slav peoples, together with the problem of welding the different nationalities into a satisfactory army, were questions sufficient to necessitate the full attention of the government at home. In world politics, enmity with Russia was Austria's central theme, as the ambitions of the two countries came into conflict in the Balkans. Austria had wished to expand her empire down to the excellent port of Salonika on the Aegean Sea, while Russia had designs of long standing on Constantinople and the Straits. When in

1897, both countries agreed to forego their expansionist aims in the Balkans, there was peace for ten years. In 1908, however, Austria's Foreign Minister, Aehrenthal, obtained Turkish permission to construct a railway connecting Vienna with Salonika. A few months later, without even consulting his Allies, he declared the annexation to Austria of the Turkish province of Bosnia. Since Bosnia's population was Slav, this raised the whole question of Austria's relations with Serbia and Russia.

The small kingdom of Serbia had been recognized as independent by Turkey in 1878. She soon became ambitious to include within her frontiers the neighbouring territory inhabited by Slavs. The presence of an independent Slav state so near made Austria's internal Slav problem even more difficult. Austrian solutions were either to include the Slavs in a Trialist (instead of a Dual) Monarchy, or to crush the new state by means of a preventive war before it became too strong. In 1908 Aehrenthal saw a favourable opportunity for a preventive war, and in 1912 another. The danger was that Russia would stand by her Slav protégée and that all Europe would be involved. Relying on German aid, Austria was ready to take the risk. Germany tried to restrain her ally in the cause of European peace, but she could not let Austria go to war unsupported. If Germany's one ally were to be defeated, her own position would be desperate.

Austria Forces War

It was this that made Austro-Serbian jealousy so fatefully important to Europe from 1908-14. Once she felt confident of German support, Austria plunged into war with Serbia. Her action led straight to the world war of 1914. The Slavs of southeastern Europe constituted a problem requiring a skilful and considerate handling which Austria can hardly be said to have provided. Austria feared that any further Serbian expansion would bring about her own disintegration: Germany knew that this was probable and was determined at all costs to prevent it.

After agreeing with Austria to hold off the Balkans, Russia found an immense

TIME CHART
1801—1956

A.D.	
1801	First Parliament of Great Britain and Ireland meets.
	Danish fleet seized off Copenhagen by Nelson.
1803	Britain declares war on France.
	Robert Fulton experiments with steamboat.
1804	Bonaparte crowned Emperor of the French.
	Trevithick makes first steam locomotive.
1805	Nelson destroys Franco-Spanish fleet off Trafalgar.
	Napoleon defeats Austrians and Russians at Austerlitz.
1806	British occupy Cape of Good Hope.
	End of Holy Roman Empire.
1807	Sierra Leone and Gambia organized as Crown colonies.
	Abolition of the slave trade in British Empire.
1808	Peninsular War: Britain assists Portugal against France.
1810	Krupp works founded at Essen.
1812	Wellington enters Madrid.
	Napoleon retreats from Moscow.
1813	Trade monopoly of East India Company ended.
1814	Allies enter Paris: Napoleon banished to Isle of Elba.
	First Peace of Paris: Louis XVIII declared King of France.
	Congress of Vienna begins.
	First effective steam locomotive made by Stephenson.
1815	Napoleon lands in France: defeated at Waterloo.
	Napoleon exiled to St. Helena: Louis XVIII recalled. Second Peace of Paris.
	Congress of Vienna ends: organization of German Confederation.
1816	Restoration of Gold Standard in Britain.
1818	First steamship (the *Savannah*) crosses Atlantic.
1819	British found Singapore.
	McAdam invents new system of road making.
	Twelve-hour day for young workers established in England.
1824	Burmese War: British take Rangoon.
1825	Trade Unions legally recognized in England.
	First steam railway from Stockton to Darlington.
1827	Turkish and Egyptian fleets destroyed at Navarino by French and English.
	Autonomy of Greece secured.
1829	London police force remodelled by Sir Robert Peel.
1830	Charles X of France forced to abdicate.
1831	Faraday discovers electro-magnetism.
1832	First Reform Bill passed in Britain.
1833	Factory inspection introduced in England.
1841	Responsible government established in Canada.
1848	Revolutions in Austria, Germany, France and Italy.
	Republic declared in France—Louis Napoleon elected President.
	Chartists present petition to Parliament.
1851	First submarine cable laid from Dover to Calais.
1852	Louis Napoleon proclaimed emperor: new French constitution adopted.
1854	Crimean War.
1856	Peace concluded with Russia at Congress of Paris.
	Bessemer invents process for converting iron to steel.
1857	Indian Mutiny.
1859	Suez Canal begun—opened in 1869.
1860	Garibaldi proclaims Victor Emmanuel first King of Italy.
1862	Bismarck appointed Prussian Premier.
1866	Prussia defeats Austria in fight for supremacy in German Confederation.
1867	Dominion of Canada established.
1870	France declares war on Prussia.
1871	Franco-German Peace Treaty: William I proclaimed German Emperor at Versailles.
1876	Russo-Turkish War.
1877	Queen Victoria proclaimed Empress of India.
1878	Congress of Berlin: reorganization of Balkan States.
1879	Egypt placed under joint control of England and France.
1881	Panama Canal begun.
1882	British occupy Egypt and Sudan.
1889	Foundation of Second Socialist International.

A.D.	
1890	Fall of Bismarck.
1895	Marconi invents wireless telegraphy.
	Röntgen discovers X-rays.
1898	Zeppelin invents the airship.
	The Curies discover radium.
1899	Boer War between England and the Boers in South Africa.
1900	Foundation of British Labour Party.
1901	Commonwealth of Australia inaugurated.
1902	End of Boer War—Peace of Vereeniging.
1903	First flight by the Wright Brothers.
1904	*Entente Cordiale* between France and Britain.
1905	Norway declares herself independent of Sweden.
	Tangier incident.
1909	Blériot first crosses English Channel by air.
1910	Revolution in Portugal.
	Union of S. Africa becomes a dominion.
1911	Agadir Crisis.
	Parliament Act reduces power of House of Lords.
1914	Start of First World War.
	Suffragette riots in London.
	British protectorate over Egypt proclaimed.
1917	U.S.A. declares war on Germany.
	Revolution in Russia. Abdication of the Tsar.
1918	Russia makes separate peace at Brest-Litovsk.
	Revolution in Germany. End of First World War.
	British franchise extended to women.
1919	Treaty of Versailles signed: League of Nations formed.
	Foundation of National Socialist Party in Germany.
	Weimar Constitution adopted in Germany.
	Third International founded at Moscow.
1920	U.S.A. Senate refuses to ratify Versailles Treaty or join League of Nations.
1921	First Indian Parliament meets.
1922	Mussolini marches on Rome; forms his first government.
	Turks take Smyrna from Greeks.
	Independence of Egypt, under King Fuad, recognized.
	Irish Treaty establishes Irish Free State (Eire).
1923	Establishment of Union of Socialist Soviet Republics.
	French troops occupy Ruhr to enforce reparations payments.
1924	Britain's first Labour Government.
1925	Return of Britain to the Gold Standard.
	Locarno Conference and Treaty.
1926	Germany admitted to the League of Nations.
1929	Collapse of New York Stock Market. Beginning of world economic depression.
	Statute of Westminster defines status of British dominions.
1931	Britain abandons Gold Standard.
	Japan attacks Manchuria.
	Revolution in Spain. King flees abroad.
1933	Hitler becomes Chancellor of Germany.
	Germany and Japan leave the League of Nations.
1934	Russia admitted to the League of Nations.
	Italy attacks Abyssinia.
1935	Saar restored to Germany.
	Germany repudiates military clauses of Versailles Treaty.
1936	Germany occupies the Rhineland.
	Italy proclaims annexation of Abyssinia.
	Anti-Comintern Pact signed by Germany and Italy.
	Civil War in Spain begins.
1938	Germany annexes Austria. Munich agreement.
1939	Italy invades Albania. Germany attacks Poland: Second World War begins.
1942	Allied victories at Stalingrad and El Alamein.
1945	United Nations Organization founded. Germany and Japan defeated. End of Second World War.
	Labour Government in Britain.
1947	Formation of Dominions of India and Pakistan.
1949	North Atlantic Treaty Organization formed.
	Communists drive Chiang Kai-shek from China.
1950	Korean War begins: armistice 1953.
1953	Death of Stalin.
1956	Official denouncement of Stalin in U.S.S.R.

EASTERN EUROPE, 1914

Eastern European States showing their boundaries before the First World War. It is interesting to compare this map with that of the Ottoman Empire shown on page 248.

field for colonial expansion to the east and south-east of her empire. Her rapid progress brought her into difficulties with Japan in China and Manchuria, and with England in Afghanistan and Persia. She needed allies, and hastened to replace the German Reinsurance Alliance by one with France. French capital was thus secured to finance communications, urgently needed in the vast but backward Russian Empire. Defeat at the hands of Japan and the abortive revolution of 1905 both damaged Russian prestige abroad and demonstrated how far behind the other Powers in administrative and industrial development Russia was. Peace was an urgent necessity if the immense work of internal reorganization was to be undertaken successfully. On the other hand, Russian prestige must somehow be built up again, and her Foreign Minister Isvolsky hoped to achieve this by diplomatic successes in the Balkans. He had made a vague agreement with Aehrenthal by which Austria should annex Bosnia, and Russia obtain the opening of the Straits by joint diplomatic action against Turkey. Neither statesman seemed to worry about the position being governed by international treaty besides affecting Turkish sovereignty. Aehrenthal acted first and in 1908 annexed Bosnia, a Turkish province already administered by Austria but inhabited entirely by Slavs. Isvolsky felt cheated of his part of the bargain, and was eager to help the Serbs when they appealed to Russia to put a stop to Austrian annexation of Slav territory. It was only Germany's firm support of Austria that prevented war as Russia could not risk attack by the two countries at once. But though Russia withdrew, a dangerous situation had been created: her prestige could not afford another withdrawal.

Anglo-French Entente

Bismarck had succeeded in isolating France and in diverting her attention from Europe towards colonial enterprise in Africa. German refusal to renew the Reinsurance Treaty with Russia gave France her opportunity to re-enter the European alliance system. The union in 1891 between the Orthodox Christian despotism and the anti-clerical republic was extremely important to France at the time, though it did not prove very satisfactory to either party. France needed a nearer ally than the distant Russian autocrat, and her Foreign Minister, Delcassé, was anxious to come to terms with England. There were so many outstanding difficulties in all parts of the world between these two traditional enemies, that an alliance between them was considered by Germany as impossible. Nevertheless the Entente was brought about by patient negotiation. It was a diplomatic revolution. The settlement of Anglo-Russian differences in 1907 made possible a Triple Entente, a combination as powerful as the Triple Alliance.

Moroccan Incidents

One of the provisions of the Anglo-French agreement had been to leave Morocco as a French sphere of influence, and it was there that the solidarity of the new Entente was first tested. Twice, in 1905 and 1911, Germany made protests about French action in Morocco an excuse for attempts at winning diplomatic victories which would damage French prestige. On each occasion Franco-British solidarity surprised and thwarted German aims. These trivial Moroccan incidents very nearly plunged Europe into war, as Germany could not believe that Great Britain would ever go to war in a French quarrel. Each time Germany drew back, but in 1914 she put her belief to the test and proved disastrously wrong.

Great Britain had held herself aloof from European alliances until the clearly expressed hostility on the Continent during her Boer War (1899-1902) caused her to reconsider her position. She no longer held her long lead in industrial production and national wealth, and Germany seemed to be challenging her whole world position. It was the German decision to build a fleet on a large scale (1898-1912) that was most resented. Naval supremacy was the foundation stone of Britain's defence, her imperial communications and her commercial wealth. The revolution in naval design achieved by the *Dreadnought* in 1905 had rendered previous types obsolete,

OCCASION OF THE FIRST WORLD WAR

Assassination of the Archduke Franz Ferdinand of Austria and his wife on their way from the town hall at Sarajevo, on June 28, 1914, was the spark which set off the great conflagration of the First World War. The terrorist Princip is here seen held by the police a few moments after the assassination had taken place.

and the opportunity, thus presented of starting a naval building race on terms of equality was eagerly grasped by Germany. Great Britain hoped to come to terms on the naval, as on the colonial and other questions, but her advances were badly received in Germany (1898-1902). Japan was Britain's first ally (1902), followed by France in 1904 and by Russia in 1907.

No one in Europe was certain what Britain's attitude would be in the event of a European war: it was generally thought that she would not take part. All British naval and military plans, however, were co-ordinated with France on the assumption of an attack by Germany through Belgium. In 1912 it was arranged that the French Fleet should concentrate in the Mediterranean in the joint interest of the Entente, and that the British Navy should keep its main strength in the North Sea, defending the French Channel ports if

necessary. These strategic talks were secret even from many Cabinet ministers, and the country was more deeply committed to France than people in England or Europe realized. British opinion was not anti-German and it is doubtful if the policy of close strategic co-operation with the French would have commanded much popular support if it had been known. But when the test came in 1914, the crude German violation of the Belgian neutrality ranged the British behind their Government more wholeheartedly than even the ministers had expected. Throughout this period, however, Britain's interest was to preserve peace and in every crisis she was to be found, in the person of her Foreign Minister, Sir Edward Grey, urging her friends to be conciliatory and her enemies to be calm.

Such were the relations of the Great Powers, when, on June 28, 1914, a Serb nationalist killed Franz Ferdinand, the heir to the Austrian Empire, who was making a long-planned official visit to the Bosnian capital, Sarajevo. Why the Serb national day was chosen and why no special police protection was provided in this hostile town, remains a mystery. Whatever Austrian feelings about the murder may have been, it provided an excellent excuse for crushing an awkward neighbour. The Austrian ultimatum was designed to be unacceptable, but the Serbs were surprisingly compliant. If Austria had wished to keep peace, or even if she had not known that she could rely on German support, war could have been avoided. This time, however, she had decided on the extinction of Serbia, irrespective of the consequences. The First World War had begun.

Strategic Considerations

As crisis succeeded crisis in the years after 1905, the statesmen and strategists of Europe realized that war could not be avoided indefinitely. Europe was an armed camp with vast forces awaiting the word of their rulers to advance. Strategic considerations led many to think that the summer of 1914 would see the coming of war as thenceforth German military superiority would decline in relation to the reorganized Russian Army. The Allies had expected that any German invasion of France would take the route through Belgium, and would attempt a quick knock-out blow in the West: slower Russian mobilization would hinder Allied plans in the East. The excellence of the German military organization with its power and speed in attack had been foreseen, as had the predominance of the British Navy. Allied plans were built on their ability to hold the initial German attack and to prolong the war so that British blockade by sea would enforce the enemy's surrender by cutting off essential material and food. Lastly, in spite of all the secret diplomacy and understandings made in addition to public treaties, friends and enemies turned out to be exactly as had been expected. Germany and Austria were not supported by Italy, who had always shown leanings towards the rival group

and now remained neutral. Great Britain, France and Russia supported Serbia, and Japan joined them in the Pacific. Turkey, whose importance and strength had perhaps been underestimated by Allied diplomacy, joined Germany and cut off communication between Russia and her Western Allies.

German anticipations of a successful blitzkrieg seemed likely to be fulfilled when, in a single month, their forces swept through Belgium to the gates of Paris. But the French, in spite of enormous losses, kept their armies intact during the retreat and, with the help of a small British force won the Battle of the Marne in September, 1914. From this point the war in the West gradually bogged down into trench warfare in lines of continuous entrenchments stretching from the English Channel to Switzerland. The British Navy had quickly cleared the seas of enemy shipping and the blockade began.

In the East, Russian troops proved superior to the Austrians, but no match in arms or organization for the Germans. They had steadily to retreat from East Prussia and Poland until they stabilized a line from the Gulf of Riga on the Baltic to Rumania. The war thus tended to become static, a position neither side felt that it could afford. The blockade was seriously affecting Germany, but the Allies wanted a speedier means of ending the struggle.

Plans for Offensive Action

Allied soldiers and politicians differed radically as to how best to break the deadlock. Were there to be massed attacks on the trench system where the enemy was at his strongest, or expeditions—sideshows— against supposedly weak points, generally in Turkey? Winston Churchill in particular appreciated the great strategic possibilities of an attack on the Dardanelles, but the military prowess of the Turks and the difficulties of a combined operation from a distant base had been underestimated. The expedition (April-December, 1915), proved a failure, glorious but expensive; on the Turkish side it revealed a great leader of men in Mustapha Kemal. In the same year Italy was persuaded to join the

Allies by heavy bribes of Austrian and Turkish territory; but Bulgaria joined Germany and their combined attack completely destroyed Serbia. The Allies clung precariously to Salonika: their Balkan plans had collapsed.

The year 1916 was a turning point. The Allies launched large scale massed attacks in the West which seemed to make little progress. But the German staff took no encouragement from their result and now admitted that there was little chance of their victory on land. In the same year at Jutland, the first big sea battle of the war ended in the German fleet being pinned back in harbour; the prospects of a German victory at sea were regarded as negligible. Thus, Germany was forced to adopt new plans; she would turn the table of the blockade by unrestricted submarine warfare. It was calculated that Britain would be ruined after three months' ruthless campaign. When in the third month (April, 1917), nearly nine hundred thousand tons of merchant shipping were sunk the campaign appeared to be succeeding. But it involved the sinking of many American ships, and in the same month America joined the Allies.

Allied Counter-Attacks

American co-operation changed the whole aspect of the war at sea and strengthened Allied morale at a time when it was being seriously weakened by German successes. In November, 1917, the Eastern Front collapsed after the Russian Revolution and Russia made peace with Germany at Brest Litovsk (1918). The Germans now planned a double blow in the West by an attack in northern France connected with another in southern France launched from Italy. At Caporetto (October, 1917), the Italian Army was smashed, but difficulty in crossing the swollen rivers slowed the German advance. Reinforced from France, the Allies fought back on a line in front of Venice. In northern France von Ludendorff's attacks (March-July, 1918), were also at first an overwhelming success. But strong American forces were now reaching France and the Allies hung on desperately, conscious that these fresh and confident

troops would turn the scale. Such was Allied superiority in manpower that in July, 1918, they were able to launch the counter-attacks which brought victory.

Both sides had had to find means of breaking the deadlock of trench warfare. The Germans had tried the use of poison gas without great success and the British had developed the tank, but took time to appreciate its tactical use. The Allies placed more hope in attacks on Turkey, as that country had been on the verge of disintegration before the war. But it was not until 1918 that Turkey collapsed. Austria was another country the pre-war condition of which justified the expectation of internal revolution, but her resistance continued disconcertingly. Early in 1918 the new method of propaganda was brought to bear on the Austrian Army by the distribution of leaflets: its success was immediate in achieving disintegration.

Unified Command

During the war aircraft were developed from experimental scouting machines into an all-important tactical arm. Air attacks on cities by both sides had brought war into the homes of civilians, and necessitated elaborate defensive plans. Air superiority over the trenches was tactically invaluable and desperately contested until Allied supremacy in the new sphere was decisively established in 1918.

In the general direction of the war the outstanding problem was that of co-ordinating the efforts of the many countries which joined the Allies. In the economic field especially, planning on a vast scale was successfully undertaken. Politicians and soldiers often failed to agree on the conduct of the war, but the German victories in 1918 compelled the Allies to put aside their differences and to establish a unified command in the West. It fell to Marshal Foch to plan and achieve victory with all the resources of the French, British and American armies at his disposal. His success in the field was paralleled by that of Lloyd George as an inspiring leader of his country and organizer of the supplies on which victory depended.

It had been a war largely of manpower

FASCIST "MARCH" ON ROME

Benito Mussolini, hailed by the Italians as "The Man sent by God," is here seen leading his so-called "March" on Rome, October 28, 1922, accompanied by (left to right) Generals Balbo, de Bono, de Vecchi and Bianchi, all of whom held high positions in the Fascist State.

backed by artillery deployed on comparatively static fronts. Between twelve and fifteen million men are calculated to have lost their lives, and where the war had swayed backwards and forwards, unexampled devastation was left behind. At sea thirteen million tons of merchant shipping had been sunk. After such a mutilation it was hoped that this had been "the war to end war."

The staggering difficulty of making peace after an upheaval which had shaken the whole political and economic structure of the world, was not at once appreciated. Sudden relief from the anxiety and labour of war had left an atmosphere of easy-going confidence that the nightmare of the past was over; the politicians would ensure security in the future. It is difficult to regard the results of the politicians' work as anything but sterile. They were certainly too conscious of the past and too little appreciative of the great changes wrought in society by the war and the Russian Revolution of 1917. They had learnt much during the war about planning production

and supply on the Allied (and this was in effect an international) basis, but all this was thrown away for the sake of a return to nineteenth-century nationalism in the exaggerated form known as self-determination. The catchword had an emotional appeal which disguised the multiplication of exactly those economic evils which had helped to lead Europe to catastrophe in 1914.

The whole settlement took five years and was contained in the Treaties of Versailles with Germany, of St. Germain with Austria, of Neuilly with Bulgaria (1919), of Trianon with Hungary, of Sèvres (1920), and later of Lausanne (1923), with Turkey. Agreement on the policy to be pursued in the Far East was reached at the inter-Allied Washington Conference (1921-22). The whole treaty-complex, thus created, was so short-lived that some of the difficulties under which the peacemakers laboured must be recalled.

The enemy's collapse had been so sudden that when the Armistice with Germany was signed on November 11, 1918, the Allies were not in a position to present co-ordinated demands or plans for the general settlement. Even before the Armistice Europe was beginning to break up. Austria had split into its component parts. Poland had declared itself independent. In Germany revolution had brought new and untried men to the leadership of the Republic. The delegates at Versailles could not redraw the map of Europe on a clean sheet, even had they wished. In some areas people had taken the law into their own hands, in others the Allies had specific obligations to fulfil. The disregard of treaties by the Germans, the inhumanities of unrestricted submarine warfare and the devastation of northern France had roused everywhere bitter passions of hatred and revenge, which had been further inflamed by politicians electioneering on the slogan of "Make Germany Pay." In such an atmosphere a fair or lasting peace would have been a miracle. Working against time, with war and disorder still devastating Europe and amidst the fierce glare of publicity and the lobbying of more than thirty nations, let alone minorities hopeful of recognition, the peace delegations had no enviable task.

The armistice terms had been severe, but the Allies made President Wilson's Fourteen Points the basis of the treaty. These were too loosely drafted for a reference point. Broad idealistic aims, such as the abolition of secret treaties, disarmament, freedom of the seas, a League of Nations and the removal of trade barriers were found alongside provisions for restoring Alsace-Lorraine to France, and for creating the Polish State. To these had been added later the principle of self-determination. The application of these provisions involved intractable contradictions and grave differences amongst the delegations. Progress was slow until the effective treaty-making power was left to the Council of Four, composed of America,

SIGNING THE LOCARNO PACT

By the Treaty of Locarno, 1925, Germany, Belgium, France, Great Britain and Italy guaranteed the peace of Western Europe. As a result the Rhineland was evacuated and Germany became a member of the League of Nations. At the top of the table are the British representatives, Mr., later Lord, Baldwin, at that time Prime Minister; Sir Austen Chamberlain; Sir Cecil Hurst and Mr. Lampson. On the left of Mr. Lampson is the French Premier, M. Briand. With their backs to the camera are M. Berthelot, Dr. Benes and representatives of Poland and Belgium; facing the camera, reading from left to right, are Herr von Schubert; Herr Stresemann and Dr. Luther, then Premier of Germany; the Marquis de Medici, M. Pilatti and Signor Sciologa. Germany denounced the Pact in 1936.

France, Britain—the Big Three—and Italy.

President Wilson was the first President of the U.S.A. ever to leave his country during his term of office and his appearance in Europe raised wildly exaggerated hopes. He would be fair minded, untouched by the revengeful passions of Europe. Yet it was as much the narrow Democratic Party composition of the President's delegation as his own unyielding and inelastic mind that brought ruin on the settlement. His colleagues in responsibility were quicker, cleverer and more closely in touch with their peoples—Clemenceau, the cynical old journalist, with passionate memories of 1870, and Lloyd George, the volatile Welsh solicitor, who had carried his country to victory and then won an overwhelming vote of confidence.

Peace of Versailles

The first treaty, with Germany, was ready after three months' deliberations: incorporated in it was the Covenant of the League of Nations. Here lay the compromise fatal to its success. The ambitious and idealistic Covenant of the League of Nations, which was to herald a new era in international relations, lay next to a treaty full of penal clauses not always consistent with it. In circumstances of studied contempt the three hundred paged document was handed to the Germans without negotiation. They were allowed a fortnight to comment on its contents. It was thus a "dictated peace" with imperfections which, it was thought, negotiation might have avoided, and the League, from which Germany was excluded, was part of it. It was an unfortunate start for the League, but Wilson feared that his cherished scheme would never be agreed unless he could force Clemenceau's hand by including it in the treaty. France thought the guarantees of her own security and of German observance of the treaty, totally inadequate: only by America and Britain guaranteeing French frontiers was her agreement to the treaty obtained.

Reparations were not mentioned in the Fourteen Points. German war guilt was the Allies' justification for their demand. A clause in which German responsibility for the war was admitted, preceded the reparations provisions, but historians may question whether its authority is irreproachable. The reparations demands of the politicians reached astronomical figures compared with the economists' calculations of the enemy's capacity to pay. As no agreement was reached, the total sum was not mentioned in the treaty. While Germany consistently evaded her treaty obligations, the more precise definition of reparation payments was to bring dissension to the victors for ten years. Another indefinite suggestion that Germany's enforced disarmament would be followed by an all-round armament reduction, was to cause equal controversy. Unable to agree themselves, the Allies had eventually to recognize Germany's right to re-arm.

The territorial settlement was based on self-determination. Wilson subsequently admitted that he had not realized the racial and linguistic complexities involved in this simple phrase. In any event, it was expected that the necessarily rough and ready work of the boundary committees would be reviewed by the League as occasion arose. Although some attention was given to strategic requirements, economic considerations were neglected. The new frontiers hardly inspired confidence.

New Frontiers in Europe

In the West the return of Alsace-Lorraine to France and French occupation of the Saar coalfields for fifteen years were the only major changes, but in Eastern Europe new and unfamiliar names appeared as sovereign states in what had once been the empires of Russia and Austria-Hungary. Russia's Baltic provinces became the independent states of Finland, Estonia, Latvia and Lithuania. Poland was re-formed from Russian, Austrian and German territory: lacking natural frontiers everywhere, she had access to the sea near Danzig. Austria became a small republic with resources insufficient to sustain the old imperial capital of Vienna with its two million inhabitants. Imperial Austria's best industrial areas were given to Czechoslovakia, a straggling and strategically indefensible Slav state with dangerous minority problems. Serbia, enlarged by the addition of the southern Slav provinces of Austria, became Jugoslavia, "land of the southern Slavs." Rumania doubled her size at the expense of Hungary, Russia and Bulgaria. In flagrant disregard of self-determination Austria was not allowed to join Germany and surrendered to Italy the Trentino. Italy made further gains in Istria, but they fell far short of earlier Allied promises. Turkey voluntarily gave up her Arab provinces, but fought successfully under Kemal to retain her control of Asia Minor with a foothold in Europe at the Straits.

International Co-operation

These changes had revolutionized Europe and the Near East: their whole economic life had to be rebuilt. Less international disturbance was occasioned by the extinction of the German colonial empire as there had been little trade there. The empire was dispersed in the form of mandates from the League amongst Britain and her Dominions, with France and Japan also sharing. The mandatory Power reported annually to the League, but in effect became sovereign of the territory.

Great Britain had reason to be highly satisfied with the settlement which destroyed both the German colonial empire and her navy. But France had failed to achieve the security she desired against another German attack. The reasons for this grave disagreement between French and British viewpoints was insufficiently recognized. Russia and Germany were soon to be joined by America in being outside the League organization on which so much reliance had been placed for the adjustment of inequalities and injustices. To be successful, the treaty needed conscious effort besides goodwill. But the necessary propaganda was not undertaken. Once formed, the League was expected to lead the world. It should have been made clear that leadership must come from individual states working within the League.

The League was a great experiment in international co-operation, with limited aims. But goodwill and understanding were lacking to an extent unappreciated

even after the bitter controversies between Wilson and Clemenceau. Wilson provided the driving force behind the League. But even partnership with the vast resources and prestige of America only partially convinced European statesmen of its practicability. Thus the repudiation of both treaty and League by the American Senate was doubly disastrous. However, the organization, with a secretariat at Geneva, was already in existence. As a medium of world co-operation it never recovered from its bad start.

Member states covenanted not to go to war with other members until all opportunities of peaceful settlement had been exhausted. As any war or threat of war was to be a matter for the League's concern, its members could discuss and recommend as they thought fit. The League itself, without any funds or official representatives, could do nothing. It was no super-state but only a clearing house of opinion. Its prestige and power depended on its members' willingness to back their corporate decisions. Coercion against a member going to war in defiance of the Covenant was provided in the form of sanctions which were to be economic— these were obligatory on all members— and military. Military sanctions could only be recommended: it was hoped that economic action would prove effective enough to render them unnecessary. A permanent Court of International Justice at the Hague provided for arbitration in disputes referred to it by consent of both parties.

America Withdraws Support

In humanitarian work, the League formed a useful and successful medium for international action. In public health, repatriation of war prisoners, conditions of labour, the suppression of the trade in dangerous drugs and of traffic in women and children, excellent work was done by fact finding, comparison, argument and persuasion. But politically the League appeared too much an agent of the victorious powers to carry conviction. It was to have provided means of peaceful change, but it tended rigidly to defend the *status quo*. Tense situations do arise between

EUROPE AFTER VERSAILLES

This map shows the frontiers of Europe as decided by the Treaty of Versailles, 1919, and its subsidiary settlements, showing the rearrangement of the boundaries of Turkey in Europe, settled by the Treaty of Lausanne in 1923, which restored much territory to Turkey.

nations and, if no remedy exists, resort will be had to war. The fact of aggression, on which the League concentrated, does not necessarily indicate the merits of such a dispute. To the defeated and dissatisfied nations the League did not seem to provide an impartial court; it lacked co-ordinated war plans, and too many nations were absent.

Europe had hardly begun to put the

conditions and principles of Versailles to the test, when disastrous news from America overshadowed the experiment. In November, 1919, the Senate repudiated President Wilson's work at the conference. The keystone of the Versailles Treaty structure had been removed. America's reluctance to undertake the military and economic responsibilities of her position

as the world's most powerful state blighted
the League. Europe was uncertain whether
to attempt collective security or revert to
balance of power and alliances. The
resultant dualism of policy was to invali-
date every subsequent scheme that gave
promise of establishing international confidence. Britain as a satisfied Power wished
to see the League working well but, with
America no longer a party to it, collective
security had lost all reality. Distrusting its
efficacy, Britain gave luke-warm support.
This lack of clearly defined policy and
leadership on the part of Britain and the
unresolved differences with France that
resulted, contributed largely to the un-
settled state of Europe.

For France, the defection of America was

HITLER AND VON SEECKT
*The German Chancellor with General von
Seeckt seen at German army manœuvres
in September, 1936.*

shattering. Her one satisfactory guarantee
of security—the Anglo-American guarantee of her frontiers—had vanished. Militarily speaking France was for ten years
after the war the strongest Power in
Europe, but experience had shown that she
could not stand alone against Germany.
The lapse of the Anglo-American guarantee made it natural that France should
revert to her traditional policy of securing
allies in eastern Europe. In 1921 she made
a treaty with Poland and also entered into
close relations with the Little Entente of
Czechoslovakia, Jugoslavia and Rumania.

All of these states had made substantial
gains in 1918 and were keenly interested in
maintaining the Versailles settlement. Thus
was formed a bloc of states determined to
defend the *status quo*. Opposed to it was
the Revisionist bloc urging the revision of
Versailles to meet its grievances. In the
latter group were Germany, Hungary,
Bulgaria and Italy; for Italy had expected
a share of the German colonies. France
in seeking security for her own frontiers
was involving herself in the defence of the
status quo against any revisionism.

Franco-British differences were openly
admitted when Britain refused to co-
operate in the French occupation of the
Ruhr in 1923. Britain was not seriously
interested in the new frontiers of Eastern
Europe and for her own commercial
rehabilitation she wished to see German
industry prospering. Thus she fell an easy
victim to German propaganda against the
treaty and tended to regard France as being
unsporting to a beaten opponent. France,
on the other hand, dreaded the restoration
of German industry and war potential:
she considered that Britain was shirking her
responsibility for enforcing the treaty she
had signed. Undoubtedly Germany never
seriously attempted to carry out the terms
of Versailles. Stresemann and Hitler, with
military leaders like von Seeckt, were at one
in regarding Versailles as something which
had to be annihilated. Britain, in spite of
expert advice, would not recognize this.
France saw it clearly and as a defensive
measure sponsored an unsuccessful separatist movement in the Rhineland (1923-24).

The occupation of the Ruhr was another

result of French exasperation at German treaty evasions. In the face of much provocation and lying propaganda, the French attitude to Germans was stiff but correct. German propaganda blamed the iniquities of Versailles and the French for the chaos of internal violence and currency depreciation which the German Government could have stemmed, had it dared to stand up to the army or to impose taxation. But the Weimar Republic only existed because Germany had been defeated. Nationalism rallied round the "undefeated" army which had not signed the treaty as the Government had. Propaganda was hard at work for the army which was still the real authority, as it had been before the war. The Ruhr occupation redoubled the economic chaos in Germany when the floods of paper money printed by the Government washed away the savings of the middle and lower middle classes, leaving want and discontent behind. It was a fine recruiting ground for Hitler's confident nationalism.

Increasing Confidence

Although the Weimar Government had little backing at home, it provided a convenient screen behind which the Nationalists made ready to annihilate Versailles. Yet remarkable concessions were secured from the Allies owing to Franco-British dissension. In addition, at Rapallo in 1922, a Russo-German treaty of friendship was concluded, marking the first step of Russia towards more normal relationship with Europe. Outside Russia, the revolutionaries of the Third International, which had its headquarters at Moscow and aimed at undermining all capitalist governments, were gravely distrusted.

Italy was meanwhile providing an example of militant nationalism in action. Mussolini and his Fascists gained control in 1922 by overthrowing the discredited parliamentary government. Then, while the Powers were wrangling over the Ruhr, he made the murder of an Italian boundary commissioner on the Greco-Albanian frontier the occasion for occupying Corfu. This was an unjustifiable resort to war against a League member, but the Greek

appeal met with little response and Mussolini only withdrew after receiving an indemnity. That aggressive action paid good dividends was soon made clear on a larger scale.

New men came to the front both in Germany and France after the Ruhr occupation. Stresemann in Germany cleverly masked rearmament and nationalism behind an outward policy of fulfilment of Versailles. In France, Briand represented more liberal views. Between 1924 and 1929 these two, with Sir Austen Chamberlain, achieved a mutual understanding which brought increasing confidence and hope to Europe. France withdrew from the Ruhr; the Dawes plan (1924) put reparations on an agreed and better basis: at the Treaty of Locarno (1925) Britain and Italy joined with Belgium, France and Germany in a mutual guarantee of frontiers against aggression from either side. But Locarno only emphasized the failure to give similar guarantees for Eastern European frontiers, precisely at the time when the Allies were removing their last sanctions and controls from Germany. Outwardly, progress continued; Germany joined the League in 1926. Indeed the League began to assume an increasingly important role and in 1927, Russia, though not yet a member, sent representatives to co-operate on economic and disarmament problems.

New York Stock Market Collapse

It was hoped that another step forward had been taken in 1928, when the Briand-Kellogg pact, renouncing war as an instrument of policy, was signed by practically every country in the world. But the loose phraseology and the absence of sanctions to enforce it, rendered the pact a meaningless sham. Nevertheless improvement in confidence continued. Reparations were scaled down again in the Young Plan (1929), England and Russia came to an agreement and the Rhineland was evacuated (1930) five years before schedule.

The apparent lessening of political tension was brought to a rapid end by events in the economic field.

On October 29, 1929, nearly sixteen million shares changed hands on the New

York Stock Market. It was a crash of unprecedented scale, of which the effects were felt all over the world. American lending to Europe ceased and short-term loans were called in, setting up economic dislocation, social unrest and political instability. The volume of world trade within four years dwindled to under fifty per cent of its former total. Unemployment rose alarmingly, reaching thirteen millions in America. Country after country tried to stop the rot by higher protective tariffs and managed currencies, making it progressively harder to market goods abroad. Standards of living dropped as men and machines waited in idleness to prove their worth. There was one good result: reparations were swept away altogether.

Germany had completely modernized her industry, with much assistance from American loans. Her production had increased to a level exceeding the 1913 figure and unemployment was practically unknown. Within a year of the American slump the total of unemployed stood at six and a half millions (September, 1930), and it was from these disappointed and hopeless people that Hitler drew recruits. In 1932, Hitler's National Socialist Party obtained more than a third of the seats in the Reichstag. Stresemann had died in 1929, Austen Chamberlain resigned that year and Briand in 1932: Europe faced a grave situation under new leaders.

Japan Attacks China

At this critical time the League received a devastating blow from the Far East. The 1929 slump had halved Japanese export trade on which her whole economy was based. Military adventure was one solution to the agricultural and industrial depression at home, and in 1931 Japan, after long preparation took aggressive action against the Chinese province of Manchuria. The League condemned the obvious aggression but none of its members dared to take action. The nearest Powers—America and Russia—were not even members of the League and collective security was exposed as a fraud which failed to achieve either collective action or the security of members. In Britain neither leaders nor people had faced the implications that League membership might lead to a war in which the country might not otherwise have been involved: indecision was the result. Meanwhile Japan brushed aside futile efforts at appeasement and began plundering China, starting with Manchuria.

Hitler Becomes Chancellor

Hitler, representing a nationalism only cruder, more undignified and less concealed than that of Stresemann, became Chancellor in January, 1933. The League's long-postponed disarmament conference, then in session, could not have been less opportune. Germany was now openly revisionist. Europe turned from an illusory collective security to traditional alliances. Britain, however, still tried—as she did from 1919 to 1939—to avoid a division of Europe into two opposed alliances which, as 1914 had shown, made the localization of war impossible. Her attempt now stood in the way of clear-cut opposition to the aggression of Italian and German dictators. The value of this British policy really depended on vigorous support of the League. But timid leadership at home and Dominion objections to European commitments, combined to render that support half-hearted.

Russia had been Hitler's chief target in *Mein Kampf* and she now naturally drew closer to Western Europe. It was Hitler's aim—as it had been that of his predecessors in office—to prevent this *entente* becoming effective. Russia faced by enemies on two sides, Japan and Germany, began a period of active co-operation with the League which she joined in 1934. It was hoped that an eastern Locarno might now be agreed, but both Germany and her new ally Poland, with whom she had made a ten years' agreement, made difficulties. The project failed, but France took the opportunity to renew her alliance with Russia by a Mutual Assistance Pact (May, 1935).

In Italy, Mussolini had been quick to realize the importance of Hitler's success in Germany: he now urged France and Britain to revise the Versailles Treaty in a plan in which Germany should be invited to join. The scheme was not welcome or timely as Hitler had already launched a violent press and broadcasting campaign against Austria. Dollfuss, the Austrian Chancellor, led a clerical anti-socialist government, which relied on Mussolini's backing. In 1934, Dollfuss was murdered, but Italian mobilization on the frontier stopped any German attempt to exploit the Nazi-inspired crisis. Hitler was still too weak and too isolated to risk much. The next few months witnessed significant increases in German power. In January, 1935, a plebiscite, largely under British supervision, was held in the Saar, which for fifteen years had been governed by a League Commission. Rather than remain under the League, ninety per cent voted for return to Hitler's Germany, although the Catholics and Communists were politically the strongest parties. Hitler's aims were clear even when his method was cruel, and it was significant that he made an appeal stronger than that of the League.

Hitler proceeded to announce the reintroduction of conscription and the increase of his army to five hundred and fifty thousand men (May, 1935); in the same month Goering, his right-hand man, gave news that the German Air Force was in being, and a naval building programme begun. Pan-German nationalism, which meant the inclusion within Germany of areas inhabited predominantly by Germans, and the allegiance to Germany of all people of German descent even if domiciled abroad, was being openly advocated, but Europe still seemed united in resisting any expansion by Hitler. Two events of 1935 suddenly altered the situation. Britain made a pact with Germany recognizing the latter's right to naval rearmament up to thirty-five per cent of her own strength, and this gave colour to the view—strongly expressed in Russia—that Britain was not seriously opposed to German rearmament and expansion. Still more devastating to international confidence was Italy's decision to attack Abyssinia, a fellow member of the League, whose entry she had sponsored.

Italy's aggression had been planned many months before the attack but Britain had allowed the matter to drift. France was clear: fearing Germany, Foreign Minister Laval had made a pact with Italy and was not going to oppose her on a far-off colonial issue. The League declared Italy an aggressor and voted economic sanctions, but Laval did his utmost to prevent these being effective. As sanctions were not extended to cover oil, and as the Suez Canal was not closed, the action taken only exacerbated Italian opinion without achieving its object: the good faith of the Powers—particularly Britain and France—could not fail to be suspected. When the Hoare-Laval plan, giving Italy a large portion of Abyssinia was announced in December, 1935, these suspicions were confirmed, although the outcry of the British public forced the Government to withdraw the plan. It was too late to help Abyssinia, which was annexed by Italy in May, 1936. Sanctions were dropped two months later.

Rhineland Reoccupied

In March, 1936, Hitler took a big risk when he reoccupied the demilitarized zone of the Rhineland in violation of the freely negotiated Locarno Treaty. Neither France nor Britain was prepared to make any forceful protest and Hitler had thus shown that his enemies' determination to avoid war at almost any cost could be used to his advantage. Hitler realized too that the atmosphere of tension was useful to him both at home and abroad. As German power increased, France clung desperately to her Italian pact and Britain, too, thought it worth making considerable sacrifices to secure Italian friendship.

A military revolt against the Spanish Government began in July under General Franco with German and Italian help from the first. But although propaganda proclaimed the Spanish Civil War as a conflict of Fascist and Communist ideologies, France and Britain were determined to localize it by a scheme of non-intervention. All the interested Powers joined; but while legalities were being discussed, German and Italian troops and aircraft steadily reached the rebels and Russian supplies were sent to the aid of the Government. Non-intervention was a farce: yet the way France and Britain clung to it appeared to indicate a very strong reluctance to oppose aggression anywhere, provided they themselves were not attacked. Neville Chamberlain seemed determined to reach an agreement with Italy and in spite of Italian intervention in Spain and attacks on British shipping, a treaty was signed in April, 1938. Italian intervention, threats to Egypt and propaganda against French Mediterranean possessions all continued. Indeed Chamberlain's policy of appeasement looked very much like fear of war whatever the provocation. Mussolini's attack on Albania (April, 1939), and on France and Britain (June, 1940), showed the futility of the Italian Treaty.

The meaning of appeasement was not lost upon Hitler: his miscalculation was in the extent to which such a policy had the confidence of the British people. Neither France nor Britain was united on the intricate international issues, but it was clear that treaties with the dictators had lost all meaning. Lacking clear leadership from their governments and confused by the ideological claims of Fascism and Communism, the peoples of France and Britain appeared weak and supine to the world, before which the dictators boasted confidently of their power.

Austria, under the feeble dictatorship of Dollfuss's successor, Schuschnigg, was the first country in Europe to be extinguished. Mussolini, perhaps in return for German support over Abyssinia, no longer opposed German aggression. When German forces invaded Austria in March, 1938, there was no opposition. The German move had outflanked Czechoslovakia. This state became the target of German propaganda, harping on the alleged grievances of the German minority in the frontier region of Sudetenland. The Czechs tried to meet Hitler's demands, but they were not prepared to cede territory in which all their defences lay. France and Russia were pledged to defend her. France, however, decided to follow Neville Chamberlain's lead in attempting appeasement again. Chamberlain made himself personally responsible for the policy of forcing the cession of the Sudetenland on the unwilling Czechs as the only way of avoiding a

European war. Even when Hitler raised his terms at their second meeting, Chamberlain persisted in the policy of territorial surrenders which would leave the Czechs defenceless. At the final meeting at Munich (September, 1938), Chamberlain, Daladier (France), Hitler and Mussolini agreed on terms little different from the highest Hitler had asked: the Four Powers were to guarantee the new frontiers. Russia was unconsulted throughout.

Occupation of Czechoslovakia

Chamberlain had bought peace at the expense of the Czechs, but his appeasement had satisfied nobody. Hitler seems to have resented his interference, and in March, 1939, he violated his Munich promises by occupying the rest of Czechoslovakia. Britain and France had made no effort to enforce the guarantee of frontiers they had promised, and now they took no action. But Hitler's new aggression at least killed appeasement. Hitler realized that increasing British rearmament would soon become dangerous to him; he must act quickly to gain another success. German propaganda switched to Danzig and the Polish Corridor.

Poland was not prepared to yield and on March 31, 1939, an Anglo-French guarantee of her frontiers was given. Britain subsequently extended this guarantee to include Rumania, Turkey and Greece, thus suddenly undertaking commitments she had so long avoided. Stranger still, she undertook them on behalf of Poland, a state which had often defied the League, ill-used its minorities and, only a year before, helped in plundering Czechoslovakia. Hitler certainly doubted whether the Anglo-French guarantee could be genuine even when it was explicitly reiterated: would they fight for the Poles when they had helped him to score a bloodless victory over the Czechs?

The guarantees had been given before Russia had been consulted, as no difficulty in securing her co-operation was expected. Negotiations to this end were opened in April, 1939, but dragged on with the feeling on both sides that the other did not mean business. Anglo-French negotiators were hampered by Poland and the Baltic States fearing Russian aggression as much as German. In August the talks ended abruptly with the publication of the Soviet-German Pact of Non-Aggression. Hitler felt sure that without Russian help no one would attempt to aid Poland and war began September 1, 1939. Germany had miscalculated as France and Britain both declared war immediately. In the next three weeks the hopeless incapacity of the corrupt dictatorial Government of Poland was amply demonstrated by the German Army. But Russia had not reckoned on Germany's overwhelming superiority to France and Britain. She quickly gathered the fruits of her opportunist policy by overrunning part of Poland and the Baltic States; but her miscalculation of Anglo-French strength brought destruction on her own country in 1941, such as had never been known in her troubled history.

German Alliances

Hitler had been building up alliances for Germany, but his opportunist policy necessarily rendered them of doubtful value. In 1934 a ten-year pact had been made with Poland, and in 1936 an agreement with Italy which was later turned into a military alliance. At the same time Germany was obtaining adherents to the Anti-Comintern Pact in Japan (1936), Italy (1937), Spain and Hungary (1939). Now—a little surprisingly—Russia was linked up by a non-aggression pact; but the hard core of the German alliance system crystallized in November, 1937, when Germany, Italy and Japan signed a Mutual Assistance Pact in which the New Order, to be introduced into East and West alike, was recognized by all parties. Opposed to this so-called Berlin-Rome-Tokyo Axis were only France and Britain, for neutrals showed a distinct dislike for linking themselves with the two democratic allies. This neutral attitude, which was to prove fatal to the independence of one after another, was the effect as much of the timid indecision of Anglo-French policy between the wars as of Axis propaganda on the strength of its armaments.

Germany followed her lightning victory over Poland by a carefully planned destruc-

tion of Allied armies in the West. Denmark and Norway were overrun in April, 1940, and the big attack opened in the following month with the invasion of Belgium and Holland. A break-through near Sedan split the Allied armies into two and only by heroic efforts at sea was it possible to save anything. In the first days of June, 1940, nearly half a million men were withdrawn from the beaches of Dunkirk. The amazing achievement only camouflaged a catastrophic defeat. France surrendered in the same month. Winston Churchill, who had followed Chamberlain as Prime Minister in May, 1940, failed to save anything from the wreck of France, but he imbued the British people with a spirit of determined unity and hopeful resistance. Although the British Empire was now fighting alone, Churchill's leadership was an inspiration perhaps more effective than the weapons so grievously needed. Churchill's dour confidence was seen to be justified fully when in August-September, 1940, the Germans suffered defeats in their air attacks which were to be known as the Battle of Britain. Churchill and "the few" heroes of the air he immortalized, had turned back the tide of German success at last. Europe had won a breathing space by their efforts.

Germany Attacks Eastward

Turning to the East, Germany sent her armies in April, 1941, through Jugoslavia, Greece and Crete. Greece had been fighting Italy in Albania since October, 1940, but now she was overwhelmed. In May, the Germans captured Crete, without command of the sea, by using air superiority to effect parachute and airborne landings. Hitler had expected no resistance from the Balkans. The hitch there delayed his new project, finally decided upon in December, 1940, of an attack on Russia. This attack in June, 1941, overlooked the first principle of all German strategists, which was to avoid fighting on an eastern and western front simultaneously. Britain had not yet been disposed of and henceforth German efforts were to be divided. Russian forces were driven to within one hundred miles of Moscow. But by avoiding battle with the better equipped enemy wherever possible, they kept their strength intact for a counter offensive when German communications were long and vulnerable. The Second World War like its predecessor, was turning into a long war, instead of the blitzkrieg Germany had planned.

On December 7, 1941, the Japanese made a surprise raid on the American Navy at Pearl Harbour, and America at once joined the anti-Axis alliance. The Japanese swept almost without resistance through south-east Asia and the Pacific Islands, but their action at Pearl Harbour put the vast material resources of America at the Allies' disposal. American industrial organization was to prove one of the most powerful agencies of victory in the war. Franklin D. Roosevelt was also a great moral asset, for the American President had a wise foresight and human sympathy which caught the imagination. He immediately became

—with Churchill and Stalin—one of the Big Three responsible for Allied policy.

In 1942, the Allies were able to move forward from a precarious defensive to a vigorously offensive strategy. The year started badly. Hitler's control of Europe was more complete than that of Napoleon; and his aircraft and submarine bases could be so placed as to make the blockade of Britain more dangerous than in 1917. In July, sinkings of merchant shipping reached the highest point ever recorded. In the same month Rommel led the German and Italian forces to within sixty miles of Alexandria. In Russia, the Germans cleared the valuable Donetz and Don basins before pushing on to the Volga. It was the limit of Axis success. The winter 1942-43 saw the German Sixth Army surrounded at Stalingrad and slowly annihilated. Generals Alexander and Montgomery had already won a decisive

HITLER'S CONQUESTS

The map shows the extent to which the German Armies had overrun most of Europe and parts of North Africa by the summer of 1942.

GERMANY TODAY

This map of post-war Germany shows that a slice of Germany in the east is now part of Poland. This territory compensates Poland for the territory in the east lost to Russia.

victory at El Alamein (October 23, 1942), which freed Egypt, and in conjunction with the Anglo-American army landed in French North Africa, they wiped out the enemy forces on that continent.

By the summer of 1943, the attack on Sicily and Italy had begun. Germany herself was attacked from the air by day and night, with Anglo-American bomber forces often over one thousand aircraft strong, as German troops on the eastern front were steadily driven nearer their own frontiers by successive Russian attacks.

For three years Russia had borne by far the greatest burden of the fighting on land, but on June 6, 1944, General Eisenhower led the Anglo-American invasion of north-west Europe. Equal pressure could now be exerted from East and West. Supplied by an artificial harbour at Arromanches the Allies broke through the defences after a month's fighting, and by the beginning of 1945, Russian and Anglo-American armies were fighting towards each other in the heart of Germany. In May, unconditional surrender followed the news of Hitler's suicide. Mussolini had been killed by Italian partisans four days before.

Meanwhile the war was being carried closer to the homeland of Japan mainly by American land, sea and air attacks which led successively to the capture of the Philippines, Iwojima and Okinawa. In China an inconclusive struggle continued, but in Burma Allied forces fought doggedly while Imperial troops helped to clear Japanese defences in the islands of the South Pacific. All was ready for attacks on the Malayan Peninsula and the Japanese mainland when on August 6, 1945, the first atom bomb was dropped on Hiroshima. Japan capitulated within a few days and the Second World War was over.

Unparalleled material destruction, millions of homeless and displaced people, economic dislocation, famine and international lack of confidence remained. But even before the war had ended, the Allies had sponsored the formation of an international body—the United Nations Organization—in one more attempt to ensure that Western civilization used its great power in the peaceful solution of problems rather than in suicidal war.

The news from Hiroshima aroused feelings of wonder, guilt and apprehension which were soon to be magnified when facts about the vastly greater destructiveness of the hydrogen bomb became known.

The knowledge that atomic power developed for peaceful uses was lagging only a few years behind the spectacular mushrooms of devastation, failed to establish the morale of peoples who now knew that war might be a matter of danger to the whole human race. But even this fear could not engender trust between nations: rather it added to the existing tensions. As in the passing years some of the scars of war were obliterated, it was nevertheless easy to see that peace was as much a misnomer for the post-war period as it had been for the 1930s. "Cold War" was the phrase used for this world situation in which the U.S.A. and U.S.S.R. stood out from all others as powers of the first rank, but yet opposed each other everywhere. For the war-time alliance of the "Communist" U.S.S.R. with the "democratic" Western countries did not long survive the end of hostilities: indeed it had not worked easily before 1945. Much of the story of the post-war world can be grouped round this rivalry between U.S.A. and U.S.S.R., and the desire on each side of the "iron curtain" to exploit situations advantageously, even if shortsightedly.

In Asia the expulsion of Chiang Kai-shek from China signalled the arrival of a new Communist state of vast potentialities under the presidency of Mao Tse-tung. The new republic of India, too, in spite of internal difficulties, was able through its Prime Minister Mr. Nehru to project ideas of "neutralism" and peaceful victories into a world grown accustomed to think in terms of power and war. The under-developed countries of Asia especially in the south-east thus have strong and varied voices supporting their nationalist claims to independence.

Great Power rivalries seemed little assuaged by the presence of a United Nations Organization designed to eliminate such frictions peaceably. But when in 1950 North Korea invaded South Korea—an obvious reflection of U.S.S.R. v. U.S.A.—the United Nations were sufficiently strong to indict the aggressor and fight. The brunt of this war certainly fell on the U.S.A. whose national prestige was involved, but a multi-national force did campaign successfully against North Koreans and Chinese to the extent of restoring the independence of South Korea in 1953.

It may be significant that the dictatorship that had ruled Turkey for more than twenty-five years was peacefully overthrown in 1951 by the process of democratic elections. Two years later the death of Stalin, the dictator of the U.S.S.R., opened possibilities of change and of co-operation with non-Communist countries. The possibilities seemed enhanced when Stalin's régime was denounced as dictatorial and disastrous in the U.S.S.R. itself. Nevertheless, a decade after the war fear and tension rather than trust and settlement are the dominant international keynotes.

Test Yourself

1. Why was the Anglo-French Entente of 1904 a "diplomatic revolution"?
2. To what extent can it be said that Germany was responsible for
   (a) the First World War, or
   (b) the Second World War?
3. In what points does it now appear that the treaty makers at Versailles made mistakes? What reasons may be suggested as explanation?
4. What means of ensuring French security were suggested after 1918? What means are suggested now?
5. Where was appeasement tried and with what results? Would you agree with the judgment that "appeasement was never the right policy and in any case was too late"?
6. Why can 1942 be described as a turning point in the Second World War?

Answers will be found at the end of the book.

GUIDE TO MORE EXTENDED STUDY

EMERSON tells us that "Man is explicable by nothing less than all his history." It is also true to say that no one book, on such an extensive subject as the history of the world, however scholarly and comprehensive, can be expected to enter into all minute details, or to explore all the ramifications upon which its general conclusions are based. In a book such as this, therefore, every chapter must provide occasions when, if the author does not keep his inclinations well in hand, he may easily wander from the main theme and lose the student in by-ways of deep learning.

Every reader must have felt that there were many places where he himself would have liked to wander from the direct stream, to explore some tributary which promised to provide interest and enjoyment.

CHAPTER I

At the outset it should be noted that there are certain standard works which none, perhaps, would think of reading through from start to finish, yet which must be looked upon as indispensable for extensive reference. For such a purpose the most important are the Cambridge Histories, Ancient, Medieval and Modern. They are monuments of erudition and give comprehensive bibliographies. But most of the books to be mentioned here, besides being of quite recent date, are representative of the latest conclusions by the experts who have written them.

In conjunction with the first chapter the student will probably already have read *The Outline of History* by H. G. Wells. If not he should do so, for it is an original survey by an author of genius. The more advanced student might possibly follow up with A. J. Toynbee's *Study of History*, which compares the history of different civilizations. From the viewpoint of purely English History, the reader should make a point of studying that masterpiece of G. M. Trevelyan, *History of England,* and the *Oxford History of England,* a work being produced in many volumes, of which eight have so far been published.

CHAPTER II

The author of this chapter has himself pointed out that, up to a century ago, the sources for the study of the early history of the Eastern Mediterranean were confined to the Bible and the Greek and Roman classics. These, of course, should not be neglected in this connexion. Since any portion of the extensive field covered might well provide a lifetime's study, the inquirer may be lured into reading reports of archæological excavations. But before he can make good use of such data it is necessary to know something of the methods of the archæologist and the uses to which his discoveries can legitimately be put. So the student should read *How to Observe in Archæology*—an informative British Museum publication.

The entirety of this chapter can hardly be surveyed in one book. It must be grappled with by areas, cultures or periods. Some areas are well provided with literature; others not so well. But before attempting to master the whole picture the student would do well to peruse *New Light on the Most Ancient East* by G. V. Childe which covers the ground particularly well and fulfils its promise of dealing with the "Oriental Prelude to European History." H. R. Hall is another authority whose *Ancient History of the Near East* is not only dependable but (an equally important point) very readable.

To the history of Ur of the Chaldees there is no better introduction than C. J. Gadd's *History and Monuments of Ur,* authoritative and learned, well documented and well illustrated. For studying the third millennium general history P. Carleton's *Buried Empires,* and *History of Israel* by W. O. E. Oesterley and T. H. Robinson are suitable. Finally, Volume I of *A History of the Ancient World* by M. Rostovtzeff, which deals with the Orient and Greece, is very illuminating.

CHAPTER III

The discussion of the Classical World in this chapter should remind the reader that much information and first-hand account of the period may be had from works by ancient authors, most of which are available in translation. The works of Herodotus, Thucydides, Julius Cæsar, Livy, Tacitus and others may well be read in this connexion. The standard works covering the whole chapter are the *Cambridge Ancient History* (12 volumes) and Methuen's *History of the Greek and Roman World* (7 volumes). If these are not available the reader may depend upon M. I. Rostovtzeff's *A History of the Ancient World*; Volume I for Greece, Volume II for Rome. This is particularly valuable for its numerous and accurate illustrations.

Among the many helpful textbooks one should have at hand for reference are *A History of Greece* and *A History of Rome*, both by C. E. Robinson; as a reminder that there were other aspects of ancient life besides the political, *Life and Thought in the Greek and Roman World*, by M. Cary and T. J. Haarhoff, should be studied. Three other books, especially to do with Greece, which are particularly to be recommended, are the *Aegean Civilization*, by G. Glotz, *The Greek Commonwealth*, by A. E. Zimmern, and *The Economics of Ancient Greece*, by H. Michell. Turning to the Roman era, R. W. Moore's *The Roman Commonwealth* is a helpful introduction going beyond the ordinary historical data. To this should certainly be added *Trade Routes and Commerce of the Roman Empire*, by M. P. Charlesworth (Second Edition), for it is always of great interest to study the points and paths of contact with often quite distant lands. For the more advanced student, *An Economic History of Rome*, by Tenney Frank (Second Edition), will provide all he will need, and for the sociological aspect the *Social Life at Rome in the Age of Cicero*, by W. Warde Fowler, is recommended. This book, though forty years old, has never been superseded; but H. J. Haskell's *This Was Cicero*, develops the theory of "Modern Politics in a Roman Toga."

It is well known that the Roman Empire extended far afield. Therefore it is ad-visable to read one or two books dealing specifically with provincial Rome. One might well be *Roman Provincial Administration*, by G. H. Stevenson; another, *Roman Britain*, by R. G. Collingwood. These will serve to strengthen the understanding of the following chapter and the foundations of medieval Europe. The decay of classic Rome leads naturally to the Byzantine Empire, coeval with the declining Empire of the West. There are few books in English dealing with the Eastern Empire but an illuminating view of it may be obtained from *Byzantine Civilization*, by S. Runciman and *The Byzantine Empire*, by N. H. Baynes.

CHAPTER IV

Side by side with the Byzantine, the Western Empire leads to the threshold of medieval Europe. One of the best introductions to this era is *The Birth of the Middle Ages*, by H. St. L. B. Moss; and, since the period was essentially an age of faith, the important role which religion and the power of the papacy played in the destinies of states and peoples, should not be forgotten. *Five Centuries of Religion*, by G. G. Coulton, and *Church and State in the Middle Ages*, by A. L. Smith, may be relied upon to give this necessary background. But for those who wish to go still more deeply into the subject, much light may be obtained from Creighton's *History of the Papacy* and biographies of great ecclesiastics such as F. H. Dudden's *Gregory the Great* or *Pius II*, by C. M. Ady.

Since it is equally needful to learn as much as possible of social and civic life and of the growth of communal activities, M. V. Clarke's *The Medieval City-State* should be studied. For the parallel educational awakening H. Rashdall's *The Universities of Europe in the Middle Ages* (new edition) is recommended; and, as an admirable outline of a special period, *The Crusades*, by E. Barker.

With the ground thus fairly covered the picture may be amplified at will by more particular studies, such as T. Hodgkin's *Italy and Her Invaders*, C. H. Haskins's *The Normans in European History*, J. W. Thompson's *Feudal Germany*, and *Medieval*

France, edited by A. Tilley. Since the proper study of mankind is Man, biographies should be included. *Charlemagne*, by H. W. C. Davis; *Maid of France*, by A. Lang; *Henry V*, by C. L. Kingsford, and *Charles the Bold*, by J. F. Kirk, will be of great assistance.

CHAPTER V

This chapter deals mainly with the sixteenth and seventeenth centuries so that A. J. Grant's *History of Europe from 1494 to 1610* will be found to be a constant help in securing details. David Ogg's *Europe in the Seventeenth Century* provides a good account of the general tendencies of that period and an outline of the principal conflicts, with C. V. Wedgwood's *The Thirty Years War* as a useful volume to supplement the information on this particular aspect of the period. G. N. Clark's *The Seventeenth Century*, surveys the whole civilization of the age.

By no means should the reader omit Lord Acton's *Lectures on Modern History*, whilst R. H. Tawney's *Religion and the Rise of Capitalism* might also be studied with profit at this stage, and in order further to appreciate the influence of religious movements at this time P. Smith's *Life and Letters of Martin Luther* is to be recommended.

Very important sources of information are *Capital and Finance in the Age of the Renaissance*, by R. Ehrenberg; *The Civilization of the Renaissance in Italy*, by J. C. Burckhardt; G. J. Renier's *The Dutch Nation*, J. E. Neale's *The Age of Catherine de Medici*, and two works by P. Geyl—*The Revolt of the Netherlands* and *The Netherlands Divided*. If to these are added a few biographies—C. V. Wedgwood's *William the Silent*, R. B. Merriman's *Suleiman the Magnificent* and N. Ahnlund's *Gustavus Adolphus* (translated by M. Roberts), some of the most important events of this momentous period will have been covered.

CHAPTER VI

This chapter will probably prove to be one of the most fascinating, for from youth onwards the epic stories of the discovery and exploration of strange new lands by the early navigators have fired the imagination. For this reason little persuasion will be needed to urge the reader to pursue the subject more deeply. Nevertheless a few words of guidance may be offered.

To obtain a wide, general view of this age of expansion one might begin with *Travel and Travellers in the Middle Ages*, by A. P. Newton; or perhaps C. R. Beazley's *Prince Henry the Navigator*. From these two admirable accounts of early wanderings the reader is well launched upon adventure, able to decide whether to continue with volumes such as *Spain in America, 1450-1580*, by E. G. Bourne, *Latin America*, a brief survey by F. A. Kirkpatrick, and the *Spanish Conquistadores* by the same author; or attempt first to master the copious *Rise of the Spanish Empire in the Old World and the New*, four volumes by R. B. Merriman. W. H. Prescott's two pioneer works *History of the Conquest of Peru* and *History of the Conquest of Mexico* should not be neglected, although some present-day readers will prefer more recent authorities. Mention may be made of *Admiral of the Ocean Sea: A Life of Christopher Columbus*, by S. E. Morison, and *Hernan Cortes, Conqueror of Mexico*, by S. de Madariaga, two very different authors. R. G. B. Cunninghame-Graham, a vivid if inconsistent author, has written *The Conquest of New Granada; The Conquest of the River Plate; Pedro de Valdivia, Conqueror of Chile* and other good volumes. Add to these *The History of the Argentine Republic*, by F. A. Kirkpatrick, H. B. Parkes's *History of Mexico*, and the student will have covered the ground tolerably well.

CHAPTER VII

The period covered by this chapter, the second half of the seventeenth century, was dominated by one great figure—Louis XIV. In order to appreciate properly the background to this picturesque period it is suggested that the student should read *Louis XIV and the Greatness of France*, by Maurice Ashley. For a further study, D. Ogg's *Louis XIV* is recommended. But France was by no means the whole of the story. Both England and Holland shared the international stage, so that a good history of England and also of Holland should be selected, in which to read up the period. *The History of England, 1688-1815*, by G. M. Wrong, and the *History of Holland*, by G. Edmundson, will fulfil this purpose admirably. For the relationship between the two countries Edmundson is again the recommended author in his *Anglo-Dutch Rivalry, 1600-53;* and the very important *The Administration of John de Witt* and *William of Orange, 1651-88*, by J. Geddes are necessary concomitants. If more enlightenment be required, these may well be supplemented by two further volumes—both by G. J. Renier. These are *William of Orange* and *The Dutch Nation*. To these may be added an additional study—*The Netherlands Divided*, by P. Geyl. On the English side of the picture we shall find much to help us in H. Forneron's *Louise de Kérouaille, Duchess of Portsmouth*, translated by G. M. Crawford.

CHAPTER VIII

It seems probable that this chapter breaks new ground for many, if not most, readers. Most people are interested in modern Russia, but there is no doubt that in order to understand Russia of the twentieth century, its past history and the character of its peoples must be understood. For this purpose the reader is directed to Sir Bernard Pares's *History of Russia* and *A Survey of Russian History*, by B. H. Sumner. These are probably preferable to V. Kluchevsky's *History of Russia*, because, although the standard work by a pre-Revolutionary Russian historian, the latter is too voluminous for any but the specialist.

Further light on the history of the country —the more important since the Russia of the past was essentially religious—should be sought in W. H. Frere's *Some Links in the Chain of Russian Church History*. In the case of Russia, perhaps more than any other country, it is necessary to gain an insight into the character of the people. The student is therefore recommended to read two books by the well-known authority, Maurice Baring, *The Russian*

People and *Landmarks in Russian Literature*; and also H. W. Williams's *Russia of the Russians*. These provide clear and sympathetic interpretations of the social history of the people. Sir Donald M. Wallace's *Russia*, so startlingly revealing for the Russia of pre-Revolutionary times, will be found an indispensable work, whilst two other volumes that might well be studied are *Russia, A Social History*, by D. S. Mirsky, and *Outlines of Russian Culture*, by P. Miliukov, since it is always worth while to read such interpretations by native scholars. Pre-Revolutionary Russia is interpreted in *Russia in Flux*, by Sir John Maynard.

One aspect of the modern Russian State is dealt with in N. Berdyaev's *The Origins of Russian Communism*. A narrative history is W. H. Chamberlin's *The Russian Revolution*. For an uncritical exposition of the Soviet system, it will be difficult to better Sidney and Beatrice Webb's *Soviet Communism* or M. Dobb's *Soviet Planning and Labour in Peace and War*. Read also more informative and critical works such as *The Communist International*, by F. Borkenau, and *The Foreign Policy of Soviet Russia*, by Max Beloff.

CHAPTER IX

On the comparatively short period of recorded history of the American continent, a remarkably complete literature exists, but the student who wishes to pursue more deeply his studies of the New World, is recommended to get the bibliography by A. Nevins, published by the Historical Association. In a selection of general histories should be included *The Rise of American Civilization*, by C. and M. Beard (two volumes) and the *Epic of America*, by J. T. Adams. For the colonial period *The Roots of American Civilization*, by C. P. Nettels, is recommended.

For those specially interested in the coming of American independence there is J. C. Miller's *The Origins of the American Revolution*, while essential material is provided by *Speeches and Documents in American History*, edited by R. Birley. S. F. Bemis's *The Diplomatic History of the United States*, is very useful but not too easy.

Since the history of the United States is inseparable from the parallel progress of Canada, the above works should be supplemented by such books as D. Creighton's *Dominion of the North*, J. B. Brebner's *The North Atlantic Triangle* (historical with an economic bias), and *The Canadians: The Story of a People*, by G. M. Wrong. Another indispensable volume, for the understanding of Canadian history is *The Durham Report*, edited by R. Coupland.

As in other countries, the study of the public lives of great leaders will provide, in a particularly intimate way, sidelights upon contemporary events. The student of the United States might read, for instance, *The Life and Letters of Thomas Jefferson*, by F. W. Hirst; *The Age of Jackson*, by A. M. Schlesinger, jun.; *Abraham Lincoln*, by Lord Charnwood, and *Roosevelt*, by Gerald Johnson.

CHAPTER X

In this chapter the political happenings of the nineteenth century are discussed. There are two useful and readable textbooks bearing identical titles that should be kept in mind for this period—*Europe in the Nineteenth and Twentieth Centuries*. One, by A. J. Grant and H. Temperley covers 1789 to 1939; the other, by E. Lipson, covers 1815 to the Second World War. Both will be useful, too, with reference to Chapter XI. Having studied either or both of these books, the reader will, no doubt, wish to turn to more detailed works on the French Revolution. J. M. Thompson's *French Revolution*, Lord Acton's *Lectures on the French Revolution*, and H. A. L. Fisher's *Bonapartism*, can all be read with great confidence and benefit.

For the more advanced student there is that standard work by J. H. Clapham, *The Economic Development of France and Germany, 1815-1914*, which may be followed by A. J. P. Taylor's *The Course of German History*, D. Thompson's *Democracy in France*, and E. L. Woodward's *Three Studies in European Conservatism*. For the Italian aspect, G. M. Trevelyan's

classic works on the Risorgimento period, Mazzini's *Essays* (translated by J. Omey) and A. J. Whyte's *The Evolution of Modern Italy* are useful.

Finally read also *1848—The Revolution of the Intellectuals*, by L. B. Namier, *Karl Marx*, by E. H. Carr and the same author's *Michael Bakunin*, a close study of his rival, which are all scholarly and stimulating.

CHAPTER XI

A background to this chapter is provided by the works already introduced to supplement the last chapter, and volumes X and XI of the *Cambridge Modern History*. For further details of the period, W. Miller's *The Ottoman Empire and Its Successors, 1801-1927*, and J. A. R. Marriott's *The Eastern Question*, may also be studied.

For a particular and very significant period of international politics we should certainly read a small group of important studies bearing upon the momentous Congress of Vienna. Harold Nicolson has written an illuminating book with that title: and this can be well supplemented by such books as H. W. V. Temperley's *The Foreign Policy of Canning*, Algernon Cecil's *Metternich*, and A. Duff-Cooper's *Talleyrand*—the three greatest statesmen of the time.

Among the numerous books written to deal with the later political events of the Industrial Age, E. Brandenburg's *From Bismarck to the World War*, and the excellent study *Bismarck*, by C. G. Robertson, are particularly noteworthy. Two further stimulating studies, are *The Habsburg Monarchy, 1815-1918*, by A. J. P. Taylor, and B. H. Sumner's *Russia and the Balkans*.

CHAPTER XII

To deal adequately with the epic story of British expansion is obviously impossible in a single chapter, and the reader will find, therefore, that further reading is necessary to make the understanding of the subject more complete.

To begin with he will do well to keep in mind *The Cambridge History of the British Empire* (eight volumes), to which constant reference should be made. But more handy (though this runs into two volumes) is J. A. Williamson's *Short History of British Expansion*, which is quite full enough for all ordinary purposes. It would be as well, however, if before attempting to master this or other advanced works, the reader were to peruse W. K. Hancock's clear and popularly written *Argument of Empire*. This will give a tolerably good grounding and make the study of the same author's three-volume *Survey of British Commonwealth Affairs* easier.

Other books which will be found useful are P. Knaplund's *The British Empire, 1815-1939*, and A. P. Newton's *A Hundred Years of the British Empire*. But even without these it is possible to obtain ample information about the several members of the Commonwealth from authoritative books on each. Of such the following are recommended: R. Coupland's *India: A Restatement* (or, for more remote investigation, *The Advanced History of India*, by R. C. Majmudar, H. C. Raychandhuri and K. Dalta); G. E. Harvey's *British Rule in Burma*; two works by B. Fitzpatrick—*British Imperialism and Australia* and *The British Empire in Australia*; J. B. Condliffe's *New Zealand in the Making*; and, for South Africa, either a *History of South Africa*, by C. W. de Kiewiet, or E. A. Walker's volume of the same name. The two last mentioned may well serve to prepare the ground for the reader's study of the following chapter.

CHAPTER XIII

Having read one, or both, of the books on South Africa recommended above, the reader will be in a position to turn his attention to the remaining regions of this vast continent. In the search for further details of the history of what may be called "The Civilization of Africa," it would probably be as well first to read E. Prestage's *The Portuguese Pioneers*, Sir J. S. Keltie's excellent book on *The Partition of Africa* could then be read, to be followed by two authoritative books by Sir Reginald Coupland on East Africa. One is *East Africa and Its Invaders*; the other, *The Exploitation of East Africa, 1856-90*.

Choice of books to follow up with would probably include A. H. M. Jones and E. Monroe's *History of Abyssinia*, for the sources of the Nile, and *Modern Egypt*, by Lord Cromer. Keeping to the north *The Anglo-Egyptian Sudan*, by Sir Harold MacMichael, will strengthen our acquaintance with that country. An important role in the literature of African development is played by E. W. Bovill's book *Caravans of the Old Sahara*, an "Introduction to the History of the Western Sudan." Moving towards the west there are two very useful studies on *France Overseas*, by H. I. Priestley—one dealing with the old regime, the other with modern imperialism. For the Niger basin Sir Alan Burns's *History of Nigeria* should certainly be read. *The British Anti-Slavery Movement*, by Sir Reginald Coupland, is another essential book. For the tropical regions *Livingstone the Liberator*, by J. I. Macnair, and *The Financial and Economic History of the African Tropical Territories*, by Sir Alan Pim, will well repay reading.

This chapter extends beyond the African continent, and in places, supplements the story of British expansion as dealt with in Chapter XII. To extend study in this direction, it is worth while to read L. A. Mills's *Ceylon Under British Rule, 1795-1932*, Sir Frank Swettenham's *British Malaya* (Second Edition), L. A. Mills's *British Rule in Eastern Asia*, H. S. Furnivall's *Netherlands India*, and *Raffles of Singapore*, by Sir Reginald Coupland.

CHAPTER XIV

The survey shifts definitely to the Far East which was approached in the preceding chapter. The geographical setting in which the story is placed has an important bearing upon the subject. China's vastly complicated internal politics and Japan's claim for "living space" present together a jig-saw puzzle which has been to a great extent unravelled in this chapter. But the student of the Far Eastern question particularly has to depend upon those who have made the subject a matter of special research. To find the key to the problems of the Pacific, therefore, it may be as well to read first P. M. Roxby's *The Far*

Eastern Question in its Geographical Setting. If this is followed by *The Rulers of the Indian Ocean*, by G. A. Ballard, the student will find himself already introduced to the problem in its relation to Western politics. There are many other excellent books which will repay study, but before tackling these Japan's position, which so complicates the question, should be considered. Read, therefore, E. Satow's *Diplomat in Japan* and W. R. Crocker's *Japanese Population Problems*. For the student of its industrial and economic questions, G. C. Allen's *Japanese Industry* and J. E. and D. J. Orchard's *Japan's Economic Position* give ample information.

Having thus surveyed the two antagonistic forces in their Oriental aspect the reader should pursue the question of their relationship to the West by reading G. F. Hudson's *Far East in World Politics* and R. K. Douglas's *Europe and the Far East*. These may be followed by R. T. Pollard's *China's Foreign Relations*. Books dealing more particularly with British relations are many. The best are probably W. C. Costin's *Great Britain and China, 1833-60*, and J. B. Eames's *The English in China*.

For later developments one of the best and most concise is E. Teichman's *Affairs of China*, but G. E. Taylor's *Struggle for North China* and Gunther Stein's *The Challenge of Red China* may be considered as indispensable to obtain a full grasp of this complicated period. The reader may end this chapter's reading with *Japan in Defeat* (Chatham House) and Sir J. Pratt's *Expansion of Europe into the Far East*, and a new and enlarged form of *Japan in Defeat*—a second book sponsored by Chatham House.

CHAPTER XV

The reader will have noticed that, in these later chapters, the complexities of international relations have become exceedingly involved. The characteristics of modern history, if they are to be understood, depend for explanation more and more upon the specialist in the social, political and economic sciences, and it is preferable to select books showing a balanced judgment of the subject.

Perhaps one of the best to recommend for initial perusal with this chapter is E. Lipson's *A Planned Economy or Free Enterprise*—a sound attempt to discover the answer of history. This might be followed with *Capitalism, Socialism and Democracy*, by J. Schumpeter as an exposition of the three warring ideologies arising from modern social conditions. A conservative account of the development of Socialism and social services in the pre-1914 period may be gleaned from F. A. Ogg's *Economic Development of Modern Europe*, while quite another point of view is presented by Sidney Webb in *Towards Social Democracy*. The common aim of social service is well presented by many authors of varying views. Among them it is advisable to read C. W. Pipkin's *Social Politics in Modern Democracies* and E. Barker's *The Development of the Public Services in Western Europe, 1660-1930*—a short account of the progress made in Britain, France and Germany. If the student desires to tackle the effects of technical development really seriously there is L. Mumford's *Technics and Civilization* to help him in his deeper quest.

For study of Labour movements at home and abroad that first-hand account of the origin of the International Labour Office, *Yes, and Albert Thomas*, by E. J. Phelan, provides useful information. This may be followed by *The International Labour Movement*, by John Price, and *Workers Abroad*, by G. P. Jones, the latter a straightforward account of labour movements outside Britain.

For post-war tendencies one should consult J. M. Keynes's *The Economic Consequences of the Peace*, an attack on the Peace Settlement after the First World War and a recent criticism of this book under the title *The Carthaginian Peace*, by E. Mantoux. The advanced student may supplement this with A. L. Bowley's *Some Economic Consequences of the Great War*—full of statistics but simply presented.

There remain certain other factors of importance covered by the author upon which the reader may well wish to add to his knowledge. These include the growth of Germany towards Hitlerism, of Italy under Fascism, and of Communism. P. H. Asher's *National Self-Sufficiency*, an able examination of pre-war German and Italian economic policy, K. Heiden's *Der Führer*, and H. Finer's *Mussolini's Italy* are to be recommended under this heading.

CHAPTER XVI

For the last chapter, in which the author surveys the momentous period since the beginning of the present century, we might select first Viscount Grey's *Twenty-Five Years, 1892-1916*. In Winston Churchill's *The World Crisis, 1911-18*, of which there is an abridged and revised edition in one volume, the years leading up to the war of 1914 are surveyed and link up with the substance of the preceding chapter and pave the way for this one. Books of value to advanced students on this period are R. C. K. Ensor's *England, 1870-1914* and D. W. Brogan's *The Development of Modern France, 1870-1939*. For the inter-war years, so complex and comparatively recent, it is difficult to steer a course of balanced reading and sound opinion. However, E. H. Carr's remarkably clear account of *International Relations Between the Two World Wars, 1919-39*, can certainly be recommended, or, for the more advanced student, there is G. M. Gathorne-Hardy's *Short History of International Affairs*. Except for the advanced student, this may however be considered chiefly for reference, rather than for straight reading. There is also a new edition of Harold Nicolson's *Peacemaking, 1919*, which will well repay study. Much smaller, but equally worthy of attention are the pamphlets, issued under the auspices of the Historical Association, setting forth clearly *British Policy Since the War*, by G. P. Gooch, and *The Origins of the Second World War*, by W. N. Medlicott. The last-mentioned authority discusses the very complex political situation in his *British Foreign Policy Since Versailles, 1919-39*; while an indispensable and eminently readable book on Germany in defeat after 1918 is *The Assize of Arms* (only Volume I published), by General J. H. Morgan. The following books can

also be recommended with confidence; J. A. Spender's *Between Two Wars*, L. Fraser's *Germany Between Two Wars*, and W. M. Jordan's *Great Britain, France and the German Problem, 1919-39*.

The advanced student, wishing to go really deeply into the political currents and cross-currents of this momentous period, will find many books from which to choose. *Studies in Diplomacy and Statecraft*, by G. P. Gooch, is a remarkably fair-minded approach to its problems, or there is A. Zimmern's *The League of Nations and the Rule of Law, 1918-35*. But if these and others mentioned are difficult, they are all recommended for their reliability and the balanced manner of their presentation.

The following will also merit the reader's attention, E. L. Woodward's *Great Britain and the German Navy*, and J. Wheeler-Bennett's *Hindenburg* and *Brest-Litovsk : the Forgotten Peace*. To complete the study of the question from the German angle A. J. P. Taylor's *The Course of German History* is invaluable and for the antecedents of the Second World War, L. B. Namier's *Diplomatic Prelude, 1938-39*.

In these far-from-exhaustive suggestions for further reading, a period of some six thousand years of Man's history and achievements has been covered. If the reader should plan to read but a tithe of the books so airily recommended, he will indeed be well repaid for his trouble. On the other hand, should he find the foregoing list inadequate for his purpose, it is as well to point out that not only do most of the works here mentioned carry bibliographies of their own, but much useful information on the choice of books may be obtained from public libraries, technical institutes, university extra-mural departments and organizations specially formed to help students and advise on courses of reading —the study of history has literally no end. For Man is but half himself, the other half is his experience and, as Emerson signifies, if he is great enough, Man may mould his immediate environment and thus, to an extent, create the history of the future.

ANSWERS TO "TEST YOURSELF"

OF the questions propounded earlier in this volume many could well be the subjects of lengthy treatises. That the answers below are only outlines is due to two considerations: first, that history is a living subject which is developing from day to day and that the questions it raises will always be answered in different ways by different people; second, that the scope of this book does not permit answers of great length. The questions, and the outline answers given here, are intended to suggest profitable lines of inquiry. For more specific information, such as would be necessary to enable the bare outlines to be filled in in anything like detail, the student must turn to other and more specialized sources such as those mentioned in the preceding section.

CHAPTER II

1. The first millennium, B.C., for the following reasons: (i) Assyrian and later Babylonian domination cleared the routes of South-western Asia for trade and cultural contacts within the area; (ii) the beneficiaries of this political order were the coast folks with easiest access to Europe, the Phœnicians, who became the middlemen between East and West; (iii) the small states, weakened and kept down by Assyria and Babylonia, were an easy prey to Alexander's armies; (iv) the western armies, the Phœnician merchantmen, and the emigrant Jews were carriers of Semitic ideas and helped prepare the ground for the Christian "seed" soon after.

2. Political and cultural unity within an area is easier where physical barriers are few or easily overcome. Syria is built in five layers: the never-wide seacoast strips; hills in the west, the ravine in the centre, hills to the east, the fringe of the desert. The steep hills alone separate communities, isolate them, and give them distinctive characteristics according as they look westwards to the sea or eastwards to the desert. Syria politically and culturally is even now not a unity for the same reasons as B.C. Added to the natural physical barriers there were, B.C., also the accidental modifications of speech, population, ideas due to traders and armies present on the few main routes, but absent in the folds of the hills.

3. The sudden and final overthrow of Assyria was due mainly to exhaustion. From 1100 B.C., and more so since 740 B.C., Assyrian manpower was stretched out in campaigns of loot in all directions.

The native losses could not be made good by forcible deportation of captive peoples. After the time of Assurbanipal the rottenness of the nerve centre, Assyria proper, under the rule of apparently weak men, coincided with aggressive mood of men, well led, beyond the hill-curtain to the east, and the revitalized kingdom of Babylonia. A combined operation, probably accidental, was more than Assyria could withstand.

4. No satisfactory explanation is forthcoming. Writing was known in Canaan before Israel entered, and (see any Bible dictionary) some Hebrews knew how to write. But no evidence has been found, though Palestine is the most excavated country in South-western Asia. Maybe it is relevant to stress that, contrasted with neighbouring and larger kingdoms, Israel and Judah were economically less organized (cp. what is said of temple-state in Mesopotamia, in chapter), that, in consequence, the number of those able to write was small, and that, in fact, we have no more right to expect "libraries" there than in Moab or Edom.

5. Kind for kind was the rule till well towards our era. Cereals, silver, copper, according to weight rather than coinage. The Lydians under Crœsus, sixth century B.C., are reputed to have been the first to issue what we call money.

6. Meteoric iron was known to the ancients probably as early as 3000 B.C. The Hittites are said to have been the first to smelt iron, possibly about 1500 B.C. The development of the use of iron weapons and tools is the main characteristic of the first millennium B.C. Harder and more plentiful than bronze, iron gave

the conqueror a more efficient weapon and the settler a variety of tools.

CHAPTER III

1. The Greek population grew well beyond the economic resources of the valleys and mountains of the homeland, especially when a developing civilization demanded more than bare necessities. Trade and the need for emigration led to the founding of colonies, and Greek cities appeared along the Mediterranean coast.

2. "Democracy" meant quite literally "rule by the people." The city-states, which were independent political units, were small enough to permit the assembly of all free citizens for the government of their city. Such words as "policy" and "politics" come from the Greek word for city. The kings of early Athens were replaced by an aristocracy. Some steps towards reducing the arbitrary powers of the nobles were taken by Solon (c. 594 B.C.), but a dynasty of tyrants seized and held power for about forty years. When the last tyrant was expelled in 510 B.C., a democratic constitution, promulgated by Cleisthenes, came into being. The "Golden Age" of Athens followed the city's successful struggle against the Persians, and the constitution was given even more extreme democratic features, such as the election of nearly all officials by lot. The disastrous war with Sparta undermined the strength of Athens and the prestige of her constitution.

3. Originally Rome was essentially a military city-state, a hard, disciplined, thoroughly practical community. By training recruits from each conquered region and by employing these troops elsewhere under Roman officers, Rome increased the strength and number of her armies. Conquests were maintained by resident garrisons at fortified points interconnected by a system of first-class roads.

4. The profiteering exploitation of the opportunities afforded by long periods of war, the loss of land by soldiers unable on their return to repay money borrowed to work their farms in their absence, the inability of small farmers to compete with huge slave-run farms and growing destitu-tion and discontent, created a political situation which could hardly be neglected by ambitious generals and which the Senate was unable to control. When authority passed to such men the Republic had become an Empire.

5. At the centre of the structure of imperial Rome was the emperor, with his growing civil service of which the chief officials were drawn from the Equestrian Order, the second class in the state. The provinces were governed by propraetors, important military officers of senatorial rank, commanding any military forces stationed in their territory. They were assisted by equestrian procurators, who collected the taxes. Towns had their own municipal organization based on that of Rome, with their senates and local magistrates. Revenue came to the imperial treasury, the Fiscus, from taxes and from the vast imperial estates.

CHAPTER IV

1. Disunity within and increasing pressure from without summarize the main causes of the fall of the Roman Empire. Barbarian invasion had already become dangerous in the second half of the third century. Under Diocletian (284-303) the empire was divided into eastern and western sections and Rome was gradually superseded as capital. Renewed civil war during the next twenty-five years increased internal confusion and, with the foundation of Constantinople in 330, the western empire was left to look after itself. The armies increasingly depended on barbarian levies and, once the outer rim of the empire had been broken, its internal rottenness stood revealed.

2. The crowning of Charlemagne by Pope Leo III symbolized the birth of feudal Christendom, the division of the old imperial authority of Rome into the dual authority of emperor and pope. The alliance gave protection to the medieval Church and added dignity to the emperor and other secular monarchs. In 800 both the imperial crown and the papacy represented ideals of Christian unity; their clash paved the way for its abandonment.

3. In 1071 Jerusalem was captured by

the Seljuk Turks, who proved far less tolerant of traders and pilgrims than the Saracens whom they had conquered. Pope Urban II appealed to the chivalry of Europe to save the Holy City, and the Eastern Roman Emperor was also able to secure some help. Genuine Christian zeal, love of adventure, greed of conquest, hope for extension of trade, all combined to form the crusades. Attempts to establish feudal kingdoms in the east failed as did attempts permanently to hold Jerusalem. But the advance of the Turks was checked for two centuries; Venice enormously extended her commercial field; new interest in learning and the arts was awakened, and many new luxuries were introduced into European commerce.

4. Born in 1182 the son of Pietro Bernardone, a wealthy cloth merchant of Assisi, Francis spent an extravagant youth as the leader of a fashionable group of young and carefree companions. When he decided to obey the command "leave all and follow Me," four qualities remained with him from his youth: absolute honesty, unflinching courage, unfailing courtesy and inexhaustible kindness. His followers, the Grey Friars, encouraged by Pope Innocent III, soon numbered hundreds and, wandering barefooted begging their food, brought comfort and help to the sick and suffering.

5. In general, the first aim of a medieval town was to gain independence. In Germany where there was no sense of national unity, such independence meant that the overlord became a relatively independent sovereign and his city an independent sovereignty paying only nominal allegiance to the emperor. In countries where there was a strong central monarchy as in England and France, such independence meant only freedom from local feudal control; the town won independence but continued subject to the national government. In Italy, and to some extent in the Netherlands, real independence was easier to achieve. There were several types of city communities governed in general by wealthy families, merchant guilds and the like. In varying degree they made provision for their own defence and internal discipline.

6. The Renaissance was the climax of a long movement toward greater intellectual freedom leading to adventurous discovery in scientific, geographical, æsthetic and literary fields, and eventually towards nationalist and individual independence. The re-discovery of neglected elements of Greek and Roman culture—"humanism" —was an additional stimulus, especially in Italy which had greater leisure, luxury and learning than anywhere else in Europe.

CHAPTER V

1. The age of Luther saw the beginning of many of the changes which characterized the transition from medieval to modern times. The claim to interpret the Bible in one's own way expressed the movement towards intellectual freedom and "individualism"; the development of national Churches, and the translations of the Bible and of the Church services into mother tongues, expressed the transition from a conception of European unity to a Europe consisting of national and independent sovereignties. Changes in the economic structure paved the way for the replacement of the feudal by the mercantile outlook as the dominant one in the West.

2. During this period the focus of European politics moved from Italy and the Mediterranean to the western nations and the Atlantic. Northern Italy, wealthy, divided, unprotected, was a tempting region for possible conquest by the developing monarchies. The seventeen provinces of the Netherlands were inherited by Philip II of Spain. They rebelled against his tyranny and bigotry, and with some unofficial help from Elizabeth's Protestant England the northern provinces gained independence. The newly created "Holland" rapidly captured much of the world's maritime trade.

3. The emancipation of the commercial class from feudal control, particularly in England, the commercial development of Holland and discoveries in the New World, combined with the rapid development of urban life to make new demands on industry. The manufacture of silk and glass was introduced into France by Henry IV and Huguenot refugees founded

the glass industry in the English Midlands. Printing, the making of books, new methods of weaving and the manufacture of bricks and paper were encouraged in England, and more scientific methods of agriculture were first adopted in Holland. The term "revolution" is, perhaps, best justified by the developing specialization of industrial regions and the replacement of the guild system by private groups of industrial and commercial adventurers.

4. The Thirty Years War ended the long period of religious wars and the second phase of the struggle between France and the Habsburgs. It left Germany politically disintegrated and economically ruined, so that the western Powers were free to develop without interference. It left France the predominant Power in Europe for the next half-century, with Spain a pale shadow of its former greatness.

CHAPTER VI

1. It was prompted by the growth of an active nationalism, the desire to spread Christianity, the re-discovery of ancient geographical knowledge and speculation, the need for the products of the Far East, the partial closure of the old routes to the East by the advance of the Turks and their capture of Constantinople, the passing of the commercial centre of gravity from Venice and Genoa to the western nations, and the success of the early discoveries.

2. Spanish and Portuguese voyages of exploration were prompted by the same motive, that of finding a new route to the Far East. The Portuguese tried to establish a route round Africa; the Spaniards tried to find a route by sailing westwards round the world. Bartolomeu Dias rounded the Cape of Good Hope in 1488 and Vasco da Gama reached India in 1498. Albuquerque by 1515 had established Portuguese trading ascendency in the Indian Ocean. In 1492 Columbus had stumbled on the New World; Cortez conquered Mexico, Pizarro conquered Peru, and precious metals began to pour into Spain from South and Central America, Magellan sailed through the "Magellan" Strait, crossed the Pacific, discovered the "Philippine" Islands where he was killed, and left a remnant of his crew to complete the first voyage round the world.

3. These conquests were made on behalf of the Spanish Crown by adventurers financed by the monarchy and were in no sense national settlements. Consequently, viceroys and other officials were appointed by, and were responsible only to, the Crown. In theory, their policy was restricted to carrying out instructions sent out from Spain. The remoteness of the conquests made this hardly practicable and officials regarded their appointments as opportunities for enrichment. One important implication of this system was that it debarred American-born Spaniards (or Creoles) from important offices, to which the Crown was unlikely to appoint them.

4. While the colonists grew in numbers and in prosperity Spain and Portugal sank into relative powerlessness in Europe. Trading restrictions were increasingly irksome and the expulsion of the Jesuits by Charles III removed a compact body of loyalists; the success of the American revolution against Britain and Spain's help to the rebellious colonists, combined with the influence of the French Revolution, helped to stimulate revolutionary movements in Latin America. The further weakening of Spain and Portugal during the Napoleonic wars enabled their respective colonies to win independence.

5. The main similarities are their republican form of government, their traditional Spanish "quality" (except for Brazil), their rapid economic development and their close economic relationship with the U.S.A. Their differences are in their size, in the degree of white blood in their peoples, in the nature of their resources and in climate.

6. Portugal has turned to her empire in Africa for new sources of wealth and has begun a period of promising reconstruction. Spain, impeded by tradition, impoverished and divided, has not yet recovered from the Civil War of 1936-39.

CHAPTER VII

1. In theory the European monarchy was conceived as a benevolent and enlightened despotism, blessed with divine, and

therefore absolute, authority. Britain and the Netherlands were exceptions. In Britain monarchic will had been subordinated to the will of a parliament representative of the landed and merchant classes. In Holland, the seven provinces formed a republican federation with a central assembly known as the States General.

2. Mercantilism is that theory of national economy which subordinates the acquisition of individual wealth to the strength of the state. It aims at securing the maximum share of the world's trade for the country concerned, at fostering industry, at promoting self-sufficiency and at subordinating colonial economies to the trading interests of the mother country.

3. Holland achieved mercantile and maritime pre-eminence at a time when France and Britain were struggling to put their own houses in order. The loss of New Amsterdam to Britain ended Dutch expansion in the New World. Dutch enterprise was mainly restricted to the Spice Islands. Dutch resources were overstrained by their wars against Louis XIV. During the Napoleonic wars much of the Far Eastern trade passed to Britain, also the Cape of Good Hope and Ceylon, Holland's two important calling stations. Internal disunity further weakened Dutch resistance to the opposition of nations which industrialization was strengthening.

4. The struggle for colonies was essentially a struggle for commercial advantages, markets and sources for raw materials. To Britain the War of the Spanish Succession was an opportunity to extend her influence in the West Indies, Newfoundland and the Gulf of St. Lawrence, and to wrest trading privileges from Spain. In the War of the Austrian Succession (1740-48) and the Seven Years War (1756-63) Prussia and Austria fought for European territory, while Britain fought against France and Spain in India and North America. The French used the War of American Independence to turn the tables on the British. But Britain used the Napoleonic wars to consolidate the foundations of a new empire.

5. After the Thirty Years War which left Germany a chaos of distressed and mangled states, Brandenburg underwent a period of intensive reconstruction and economic development, acquired Prussian and Rhineland territories and emerged from the Spanish Succession war as the "Kingdom of Prussia." Its second king, Frederick William I, further strengthened the army and his son Frederick the Great was able to defy Austria and retain the wealthy province of Silesia.

6. The French Revolution affected international relations by declaring war on monarchic absolutism in the name of political liberty. The Napoleonic wars which continued the revolutionary war by their dimensions, their impoverishment of nations, their use of economic weapons, their wide mobilization of human and material resources and by Napoleon's bid for world power so changed the scope and conception of war as to affect permanently the relations of the Powers.

CHAPTER VIII

1. About 862 Varangians from the North Lands settled along the Dnieper Valley, established a Viking overlordship over the Slavonic peoples and set up royal authorities at Novgorod and Kiev. The consequent forging of unity and order was the origin of the Russian state. The Dnieper was the highway between the homes of the Northmen and Constantinople, so from the first Russia had Byzantine connexions. In 988 Vladimir was baptized and the conversion of Russia to the Eastern branch of the Christian Church began. From 1240 when the tide of Mongolian invasion from the East began to overwhelm Russia, to 1480 when Ivan the Great successfully defied Tartar authority, Asiatic influence predominated. The third stage was the gradual extension of the authority of the House of Moscow.

2. Russia by its connexion with the Byzantine Church was isolated from the influence which the papacy exerted on medieval Christendom in the West. After the Mongol conquest Russia was far more an Asiatic than a European state; its type of feudal society was different from the European. Moreover its vast forests, its

inhospitable plains and its extent, prevented the development of a central national administration which was a characteristic of Western Europe in the time of the Renaissance and Reformation, movements which left Russia unaffected.

3. Tsardom was a compound of Asiatic absolutism and Byzantine pomp. The absolute nature of oriental monarchy was far more intense than the European conception of sovereignty. In 1453 Constantinople was captured by Turks and the last symbol of imperial Cæsardom vanished from Europe. The Grand Duke of Moscow claimed that the mantle of the Eastern emperor had fallen on to his shoulders and in 1547 Ivan IV adopted the title of "Cæsar" or Tsar of All Russia. The blend of two types of absolute sovereignty made the Russian tsardom unique.

4. The isolation of Russian village communities in forest clearings, the tendency of peasant workers to wander to other places with the consequent loss to the lord of the labour on which he depended, made some system of stabilization inevitable. Serfdom had already begun to develop before it was officially established by a series of edicts from 1580 onwards. Serfdom became an increasing reality as more demands of service were made by tsars from lords, and as the villages were made the unit of taxation. The climax was probably reached in the reign of Catherine II. Serfdom was abolished by Alexander II in 1861.

5. Peter the Great's particular mission was to transform an Asiatic Russia centred round Moscow into a European Power having strong contacts with the West.

6. The fundamental purpose of Lenin was the forcible organization of Russia into a communist state as a nucleus of a world communist order. He thought of Communism as a system in which all human and material resources were regarded as belonging to the community as a whole and being available for distribution according to need. This was to be preceded by a period of "socialism" in which the state would own the major resources and divide products by the measure of work done. There was no widespread support for communist doctrines, and what desires the people had were restricted to greater personal security and comfort and, in the case of the peasants, for individual ownership of land. Of those who had definite ideas as to the nature of the necessary reforms of the Russian political, social, and economic structure many did not support the views of the Bolsheviks. Under Stalin the first part of Lenin's programme was completed and consolidated, but the new hierarchies which this created and the resistance of the rest of the world to the spread of Communism have so far prevented the full attainment of the communist ideal.

CHAPTER IX

1. When the British and French began to settle permanently in North America they went for a mixture of motives which in general meant the creation of new homes. Trading settlements, settlements of religious refugees or even the development of land granted by royal charter, implied private settlement and personal interest in the formation of a permanent and relatively independent colony.

2. The major part of the American population consists of the descendants of those who sought the New World to find wider opportunities for themselves and their children. Therefore independence and individual liberty have been persistent ideals, and their expression has been deeply coloured by the frontier pioneering environment. American democracy has been influenced by the belief that the responsibilities of government should be widely shared and not be in the hands of a particular class, and, by persistent efforts, to reconcile majority rule with respect for individualism, particularly in the economic field.

3. Canada, when the rebellious English colonies became the United States of America, was a recently acquired and essentially French fragment on the Lower St. Lawrence. A second province was founded by loyalists from the new American nation. Thus the division between Canada and the U.S.A. was at first very

distinct and was emphasized by the failure of the American attempt at conquest in the war of 1812. The granting of responsible self-government to Canada leading to virtual independence strengthened their loyalty, while the development of friendly and commercial relations with the United States by Canada and by Britain helped to maintain the developing nations as separate communities until their own economic growth and individual strength was sufficient to develop a co-operative partnership useful to both.

4. America's developing Pacific trade in the second half of the nineteenth century, the acquisition of Hawaii and of the Philippines, implied the active intrusion of the U.S.A. into the eastern Asiatic field where European nations and Japan were already developing rival claims. The First World War showed the importance for the United States, with its growing oversea interests, of having friendly powers on the opposite side of the Atlantic. A reaction to isolation caused the withdrawal of American support from the League of Nations but German and Japanese aggression and the subsequent threat of Communist expansion as well as the relative weakening of Britain recalled the U.S.A. to a leading role in the democratic world.

5. The economic confusion and the growing distress forced President Roosevelt in 1933 and the following years to increase central control over much of economic life. But many aspects of this intervention were temporary and none of them fundamentally infringed the traditional American reliance on private enterprise as the mainstay of economic life.

6. The "Founding Fathers" had hoped to see slavery disappear after the abolition of the slave trade in 1808. But the rise of cotton culture riveted it upon the southern states. Northern resistance to its spread and the effect on southern feeling of abolitionist agitation brought about the Civil War. The abolition of slavery after the war did not end the problem, for the Negroes were poor and still suffered from many forms of social, economic and political discrimination. In recent years large-scale migration of Negroes north-ward and increased economic opportunities for them, as well as more liberal attitudes, especially in the South, have mitigated these evils without solving the problem.

CHAPTER X

1. The French Revolution was essentially an attempt by a socially unrecognized, politically unrepresented, economically burdened middle-class, to end an obsolete and sterilizing feudal order with its privileged and ornamental aristocracy, and to set up a system of representative government. Its violence was in part due to the exploitation of the grievances of the urban poor by political groups and in part to fears of counter-revolutionary reprisals. A further characteristic was the expression by revolutionary writers of new conceptions of human rights, and of national sovereignty. Its result was to replace hereditary rule by popular sovereignty and to strengthen the state accordingly.

2. The settlement of 1815 attempted to "put back the clock," to restore overthrown monarchies, to maintain by joint intervention what was restored and to "chain the revolutionary monster." The revolutions of the early 1820s in Spain, Portugal, Naples and Piedmont were liberal movements against restored despotisms. The Greek revolt was a nationalist uprising by a subjected Christian people against their Turkish (Moslem) rulers. The Belgian rising of 1830 destroyed the ill-considered and unequal union of Holland and Belgium. The Poles attempted to end the partition and subjection of their country.

3. The political history of the century does reveal in France a persistent struggle between the ideas and parties which revealed themselves during the French Revolution and continued to divide the nation. The reigns of Louis XVIII and Charles X saw an attempt to restore absolutism and ecclesiastical privileges which ended with the July revolution of 1830. The reign of Louis Philippe was an unsatisfactory compromise between republican and monarchic aims and ended with the revolution of 1848 which after the failure of the socialist movement established

the short-lived Second Republic. This gave way to Napoleon III's Second Empire. Between the years 1871 and 1875 and after the defeat of France by Prussia and the defeat of the Paris Commune, the Third Republic was set up as the system which divided Frenchmen least.

4. The Revolution of 1848 illustrated the inability of European liberals to solve problems involving national questions by the application of the simple principle of representative government. The powerful divergences between reformist and socialist and nationalist movements were also revealed.

5. Nationalism became a confusing element in all cases where segregation by class was superimposed on distinctions of race, language or religion and where revolutionary energies could be captured for nationalist causes.

CHAPTER XI

1. The Congress system was in effect an attempt by the great Powers to maintain, by the threat of intervention, the monarchies which had fallen during the Revolutionary and Napoleonic wars and which the settlement of 1815 had restored. The divergent interests of the great Powers and the tendency of Great Britain to look with increasing favour on liberal and national movements prevented its further development.

2. British foreign policy in the first half of the nineteenth century feared Russian ambitions in the Mediterranean and, consequently, attempts to gain power and territory in the Balkans. Hence the support of Austrian strength as a check to Russian ambition and the maintenance of Turkish integrity were both objects of British policy. French ambitions in the eastern Mediterranean added another motive for Austrian friendship.

3. By (a) her new acquisitions of Rhenish territory in 1815 which made her the inevitable protector of western Germany against France; (b) her development of an economic system, the Zollverein, which excluded Austria and made Prussia the economic centre of the German states; (c) the deliberate creation of a strong

absolutist government with a powerful military machine capable, when the time arose, of defeating Austria in the Seven Weeks War and (d) the fact that Prussia was a fairly harmonious German state whereas Austria was a mixture of divided peoples.

4. The Industrial Revolution made Britain wealthy enough to be the deciding factor in the overthrow of Napoleon. It enabled her in the first half of the nineteenth century to create a world-wide trade and empire, to adopt a policy of free trade and international isolation and a rather dictatorial attitude to other nations. When, later in the century, other nations began to develop their own industrial resources, Britain had to face growing international rivalry in commercial fields, in areas of overseas expansion, and in naval building, with consequent changes in her attitude to other Powers. The relationship of continental Powers to one another was affected by the unequal rate of industrial development. This led to the replacement of France by Germany as the major continental Power.

5. National unity was achieved in Germany by one state's domination of the rest. Germany was Prussianized instead of Prussia being absorbed into the German nation. Bismarck, after creating a powerful and despotic Prussia, evicted Austria, the only possible competing state. The war brought the greater number of German states under Prussian domination. A deliberately engineered war against France brought the rest of the states under Prussian authority, and the German Empire, with the Prussian king as Emperor (Kaiser), was formed. Thus Bismarck was responsible for the creation of German unity which had been forged by the despotic will of a dominant and unscrupulously ambitious member of a group of sovereignties. His annexation of Alsace and Lorraine made permanent French hostility inevitable and foreshadowed the Franco-Russian alliance to check further German aggression.

6. The permanent and interlocking features of British foreign policy in the nineteenth century were (a) the maintenance of national security from external inter-

ference; (b) the maintenance of naval supremacy and of colonial and commercial outposts; (c) the preservation of the independence of the Low Countries and (d), though less consistently, the development of international co-operation and the upholding of liberal principles. Britain's relations with the Powers, particularly France, Germany and Russia were in turn affected by all these considerations.

CHAPTER XII

1. The American Revolution ended the mercantilist phase of empire and the attitude that colonies were simply convenient markets and sources of raw materials. In the nineteenth century, one group maintained that, in imperial expansion, there were opportunities for emigration, or they looked for commercial opportunities in the development of tropical regions, or in reciprocal trade with the growing colonies of settlement. The Free Traders, on the other hand, regarded ideas of imperial expansion as a menace to their ideal of a world trade with all nations co-operating harmoniously. The failure of this ideal led to a phase of more deliberate imperial expansion. Disraeli fostered pride in the idea of "The British Empire" and the Chamberlain school aimed at the creation of imperial economic self-sufficiency. Today more emphasis is laid on the development of self-governing institutions.

2. It had a general resemblance to the European revolutions in that it was a nationalist uprising against an unsympathetic and alien government and against a politically privileged minority, separate in religion and culture. By the eighteenth century the Protestant minority won independence for their privileged parliament and the removal of the commercial restrictions which they shared with other "colonies." The Union lost the Protestants their parliament, and left the Irish people proper the unprivileged, unrepresented and exploited peasantry they had always been since the first English occupation. When, later, quasi-independence was achieved the "six counties" of the north-east, Protestant and industrial in outlook, remained loyal to the British monarchy and parliament.

3. When discovered, Australia produced neither animal nor vegetable food suited to white people. The first settlers, confined by mountains to the south-east corner, planted crops and introduced sheep and cattle; but for some time they depended on food supplies from Britain. The discovery of new pastures beyond the mountains in 1813, the founding of new coastal settlements, the reclaiming of desert land and the breeding of merino sheep have combined to establish Australian economic independence. The discovery of gold led to rapid immigration and development. New Zealand took advantage of the forests and mineral wealth of North Island and of the rich pastures and arable land of South Island. The development of refrigeration enabled both countries to export meat and dairy produce.

4. During the early years of British occupation of Cape Colony there was little successful co-operation with the earlier Dutch settlers. The attempt in 1822 to make English the official language of the colony and the emancipation of slaves in 1833 drove out many of the Dutch to found new states. Increasing co-operation between the British and those who stayed was neutralized by growing friction in the new Dutch states, particularly after the settlement of the Outlanders in the Transvaal. After the Boer War and the creation of the Union a common South African national feeling showed signs of emerging but the national issue remained central in politics down to the Second World War.

5. The first criticism is that the sovereignty of a large part of India was for long left in the irresponsible hands of a commercial company. The system implied that British authority could be maintained and commercial advantages conserved only by force and this remained true, even after responsibility was assumed by the home government. Vast improvements, human and material, resulted from British occupation in India, but British soldiers and traders and the handful of administrators in the vast country of some four hundred million people formed an alien community which never became or wished to be integrated with the people at large.

6. The history of the West Indies since the emancipation of the slaves in the 1830s shows the difficulty of developing colonies where commodities, produced under an imperfectly developed system cannot, for price, compare favourably with similar goods produced in other countries, particularly America. It is clear, therefore, that to enable these islands to take their part usefully and economically in the British Commonwealth, support, both financial and managerial, and possibly some guarantee of markets for their products, must be freely given by Great Britain.

CHAPTER XIII

1. Portuguese exploration of Africa was mainly that of the western and south-eastern coastal regions, and was incidental to their successful attempt to find a route to India by way of the Cape. In 1434 Gil Eannes passed Cape Bojador; in 1443 Nuno Tristram reached Cape Verde; by 1460 the Guinea coast had been explored and slave traffic was already fifteen years old. Lagos, the first station, was opened in 1445. In 1482 Diego Cam reached the Congo mouth and explored fifteen hundred miles of coast. Dias reached the "Cape" in 1487, and Covilham, by way of the Red Sea, almost reached Madagascar. Vasco da Gama in 1492 reached and named Natal. Inland penetration by slave merchants was deepest round Angola.

2. Movements for the suppression of the slave trade developed in Britain in the eighteenth century. In 1787 a committee for total abolition was formed and Wilberforce voiced the appeal in parliament. There was considerable opposition, but slave trading was abolished by Great Britain in 1807 and by the United States in 1808 and slavery throughout the British Empire in 1833. Denmark had abandoned the traffic in 1792; Portugal, Brazil, Spain and France followed Britain. The East African slave trade to Egypt and the Persian Gulf was largely ended through British action in the 1870s.

3. Sir Stamford Raffles (1781-1826), when secretary to the Governor of Penang, was invalided to Malacca, which the East India Company was about to abandon.

A report by Raffles persuaded Lord Minto, Governor-General, to retain Malacca. Java was, for a time, a British possession through Raffles's intervention, but was returned to the Dutch, who determined to oust the British from the archipelago. Raffles set out to prevent this and founded Singapore as a defensive base in January, 1819.

4. The French had been interested in Egypt since Napoleon invaded it in 1797, and in the 1830s they supported Mehemet Ali's bid for independence, hoping for a measure of control if Egypt were freed from Turkish rule. It was a French engineer, de Lesseps, who planned the Suez Canal, and more than half the capital invested in it was French. Britain had opposed French attempts to control Egypt in 1797 and from 1833 to 1841 Britain had consistently supported the integrity of Turkish dominions and had an eye on overland routes to the East. After 1875 more than half of the shares of the Suez Canal were bought for Britain, and France and Britain began to regard Egypt as a joint responsibility. When France left Britain to suppress the rebellion of 1881, however, Britain undertook the responsibility herself, and Egypt remained a British protectorate until 1922.

5. After trouble between Dutch and British as to which people possessed the diamond mines of Kimberley, more serious trouble broke out in the Transvaal. Britain claimed it as a protectorate in 1877, and Gladstone returned it in 1881. The discovery of gold there brought throngs of adventurers known by the Boers as "Outlanders." They were given no civil or political rights even in their own town of Johannesburg. A small force stationed in Matabeleland to the north of the Transvaal, to protect the British company mining there, made an attempt under Jameson to help the Outlanders, with the connivance of Cecil Rhodes, the Cape Prime Minister. Both Rhodes and Jameson were disgraced, the British Government brought into disrepute, and the local quarrel fanned into a general struggle between British and Boers for the possession of South Africa, a struggle which

developed into the war of 1899-1902.

6. This was an expression of the general movement for colonial independence and the claim of the local educated classes for more share in the government and was stimulated by communist propaganda in the 1920s. It was encouraged, like similar movements in Asia, by Japanese victories over the western Powers in 1941-45.

CHAPTER XIV

1. The "unequal treaties" were those signed in the years after the Anglo-Chinese War (1839-42), by which the Chinese were compelled to open certain ports to foreign traders, and to admit foreign residents whose privileges included immunity from the jurisdiction of Chinese law, and the maintenance, in certain of the towns, of control of the police and municipal taxation. The Chinese objected in general to the presence of the foreigners, and, in particular, to their presence on such terms.

2. It restored the status and authority of the Emperor of Japan, with the implied overthrow of the feudal power which had long held that authority. The object was to utilize this central despotism for the conversion of Japan into a military state on the lines of the European Powers. It was effected by the compulsory surrendering of all feudal fiefs to the emperor, by the enforced abandonment of feudal privileges, and by the centralization of all executive offices. Its ultimate results were the hardening of Japan into a totalitarian military state, and the development of an ambition to free Asia from white intrusion and establish a Japanese empire.

3. Japan's attempt to carve out an exclusive domain led to intervention by European Powers interested in the Far East. Concessions demanded by Russia, France and Germany began to suggest that these Powers were contemplating the partition of China, a possibility which brought Britain and the United States into the field as Powers whose economic strength was sufficient for them to prefer an "open door" to all competition rather than exclusive spheres for some Powers.

4. In January, 1915, Japan, profiting by the outbreak of the First World War,

planned to extend her control over China, to which nation she presented the twenty-one demands, directed to the strengthening of Japan's hold over South Manchuria and Eastern Inner Mongolia, to the acquisition of Shantung and to the acquiring of a generally dominant position in the country. The result was to increase Chinese hostility to Japan, and at the Washington Conference of 1921 American pressure caused the temporary abandonment of Japan's more extreme demands.

5. The Washington Conference was convened in 1921. Its objects were to persuade Japan to change her territorial ambitions for a policy of international collaboration and, in particular, to regard China, not as potential prey, but as a nation to be helped to the achievement of efficient government, national stability and economic usefulness. In return, the western Powers adopted a scheme for the limitation of naval armaments which rendered Japan's position in the western Pacific unchallengeable.

CHAPTER XV

1. "Gradualism" is the moderate socialist doctrine which aims at the improvement of social conditions and the gradual elimination of the capitalist control of industry by the use of ordinary constitutional procedure. It tended to concentrate the attention of the workers on internal improvements in individual countries instead of on international revolutionary activity.

2. The First World War dislocated production and trade, producing a world shortage of goods and food, and causing vast unemployment. It changed the international distribution of bullion, destroyed the normal channels of world distribution, and made chaotic the international system of exchange. Internal inflation brought serious troubles, which, in some cases, a too-sudden deflation merely accentuated.

3. Planning, in the sense of a nationally controlled and directed economy, develops from three major causes:

(a) The desire to increase national power by the total control of all national resources for the creation of maximum military efficiency;

(b) The desire to attain a more equable distribution of available wealth for the general improvement of living conditions; and

(c) The desire to increase the nation's external purchasing power.

4. Internally the political results of the great economic depression were to weaken the faith in the capitalist and democratic system and, in consequence, to strengthen the political parties opposed to it. The growth of Communism evoked in some states a reactionary political hardening of authority. Externally the political response to the crisis was the development of international economic rivalry and the weakening of the international organization.

5. That which is "good" or effective for national power is not necessarily "good" for the general welfare of the nation's people, as a whole; nor is that which is good for general welfare within a nation necessarily good for human welfare as a whole. Whereas unplanned economies have led to the maladministration of wealth, the planned economies have failed to achieve a system by which the wealth of the nation is used to the best advantage for the whole community; such a system of itself necessitates a large measure of bureaucratic control.

CHAPTER XVI

1. The Anglo-French Entente of 1904 ended the centuries of rivalry and hatred which had persisted between the two nations since their national origins. England and France had fought against each other in every major war either nation had ever waged. Even at the time of the Entente, both nations had rival interests overseas, and Germany, to her own and everyone else's cost, refused to believe in the sincerity or permanence of the alliance.

2. (a) The fact that the history of Prussian expansion had been consistently based on calculated military aggression, together with the rapid growth of her industrial resources and the belief that wealthy nations would not willingly abandon their advantages to further the interests of other and less fortunate peoples, were influential

factors in persuading a new and vigorous Germany that her further development could be accomplished only by successful war; (b) In spite of German propaganda about the alleged hardships of the Versailles Treaty, and of the particularly severe impact upon her economy of the great depression, the responsibility of Germany for the Second World War can be directly established from the evidence of the Nuremberg trials.

3. The peace-makers at Versailles did their best to apply the principle of self-determination and to provide for the future by setting up the League of Nations. Their mistakes were due to an underestimate of the economic factor, to excluding the likelihood of the revival of Russia as a great Power and to their overestimate of the willingness of the western Powers to stand by the treaty they had made.

4. The main means of ensuring French security after 1918 was the League of Nations and the promised Anglo-American guarantee of her frontiers. The former's value largely disappeared with the withdrawal of America. The premature withdrawal from the Rhineland security zone enabled Hitler to refortify it and cut France off from her eastern allies.

5. "Appeasement" was tried by overlooking Germany's successive violations of treaties and her aggression against Spain, Czechoslovakia and Austria; Italy's violation of the Covenant and aggression in Spain; in the Pacific by condoning Japan's breach of the League Covenant. It was not the right policy because it was based on the view that the aggressors had "grievances" which could be remedied. Its justification could only be the time gained for British rearmament. We lack the facts to judge its effectiveness in this.

6. In 1942 the Allies moved from defensive warfare to offensive action; the reaching of the Donetz and Don basins by the Axis Powers was the turning point in their tide of success; the surrounding of the German Sixth Army at Stalingrad, the British victory at El Alamein, the allied landings in North Africa and the beginning of a serious bomber offensive against Germany were the beginning of the end.

INDEX

Numbers in italics indicate illustrations

ACKNOWLEDGEMENTS

The publishers wish to thank the following for permission to reproduce copyright material: the British Museum for illustrations appearing on pp. 56, 61, 76, 79, 82, 83, 86, 118, 195; the Victoria and Albert Museum for illustrations (Crown copyright reserved) on pp. 6, 14, 89, 100 (top), 101, 104, 111, 112, 143, 265, 267, 299, 300, 304, 313; the National Gallery for paintings on pp. 147, 150, 153, 217; the Bibliothèque Nationale, Paris, for the print on p. 158; the Brooklyn Museum, New York, for the painting on p. 200; the Bodleian Library, Oxford, for two prints from the Douce Collection on pp. 162 and 215; Trinity College, Cambridge, for the illustration on p. 71; Trinity College, Cambridge, the Friends of Canterbury Cathedral and Messrs. Percy Lund, Humphries and Co., Ltd., for two illustrations from the Canterbury Psalter on pp. 9 and 70; the Fitzwilliam Museum, Cambridge, for the illustration on p. 72; the Director of the Science Museum, South Kensington, for illustrations on pp. 46, 96, 241 (Crown copyright re-served); the National Maritime Museum for illustrations on pp. 127, 220, 225; the Visitors of the Ashmolean Museum, Oxford, for illustration on p. 25; Messrs. Kegan Paul, Trench, Trubner and Co., Ltd., for the illustration from *Israel* by Adolphe Lods on p. 23; The Society for Promoting Christian Knowledge for the drawing from *Digging Up Biblical History* by J. Garrow Duncan on p. 24; the John Rylands Library, Manchester, for the illustration on p. 22; Messrs. Putnam and Co., Ltd., for two photographs from *The Memoirs of Prince von Bülow* on pp. 250, 251; the Society for Cultural Relations with the U.S.S.R. for illustrations on pp. 183, the High Commissioner for Canada for pictures on pp. 196, 208, 209; the Australian News and Information Bureau for illustrations on pp. 254, 255; the High Commissioner for South Africa for the photograph on p. 261; the High Commissioner for India for the photograph on p. 268; Messrs. Aerofilms Ltd. for the photograph on p. 318.